www.wadsworth.com

www.wadsworth.com is the World Wide Web site for
Thomson Wadsworth and is your direct source to dozens
of online resources.

At www.*wadsworth.com* you can find out about
supplements, demonstration software, and student
resources. You can also send e-mail to many of our
authors and preview new publications and exciting new
technologies.

www.wadsworth.com
Changing the way the world learns®

THE NATURE OF ART

An Anthology

Second Edition

THOMAS E. WARTENBERG
Mount Holyoke College

THOMSON

WADSWORTH

Australia • Brazil • Canada • Mexico • Singapore • Spain • United Kingdom • United States

THOMSON

WADSWORTH

Publisher: *Holly J. Allen*

Philosophy Editor: *Steve Wainwright*

Assistant Editors: *Lee McCracken, Barbara Hillaker*

Editorial Assistant: *Gina Kessler*

Technology Project Manager: *Julie Aguilar*

Marketing Manager: *Worth Hawes*

Marketing Assistant: *Alexandra Tran*

Senior Marketing Communications Manager: *Stacey Purviance*

Creative Director: *Rob Hugel*

Executive Art Director: *Maria Epes*

Print Buyer: *Rebecca Cross*

Permissions Editor: *Joohee Lee*

Production Service: *Interactive Composition Corporation*

Cover Designer: Adrienne Aquino, Yvo Riezebos Design

Cover Image: Lincoln Seligman/Bridgeman Art Library/Getty Images

Compositor: *Interactive Composition Corporation*

Text and Cover Printer: Courier-Stoughton, Inc.

Library of Congress
Control Number: 2005933356

ISBN-13: 978-0-495-09355-8
ISBN-10: 0-495-09355-6

Thomson Higher Education
10 Davis Drive
Belmont, CA 94002-3098
USA

For more information about our products, contact us at:
Thomson Learning Academic Resource Center
1-800-423-0563

For permission to use material from this text or product, submit a request online at
http://www.thomsonrights.com.
Any additional questions about permissions can be submitted by e-mail to
thomsonrights@thomson.com.

CONTENTS

PREFACE TO THE SECOND EDITION

The question "What makes something a work of art?" has troubled philosophers throughout the history of aesthetics—the philosophical discipline that encompasses reflections on art and its nature. It has also been an issue that artistic practice itself has made prominent, for new artistic movements from the time of impressionism onward have always challenged traditional understandings of art in such a way that the status of their products as art has been questioned. Familiar to us all is the hostile reaction to new works, "My six-year-old daughter could have done that!" with its implicit challenge that the object in question does not deserve the label of "art."

This book assembles the major philosophical discussions of art's nature from the time of the ancient Greeks to the present day. In making my selections, my first concern has been to include all the central contributions to the ongoing philosophical discussion of art. In editing them for inclusion in this collection, I have attempted to make them easily comprehensible to students without sacrificing accuracy and comprehensiveness.

I have made a number of changes in this second edition in response to comments by users of this book, myself included. I have deleted a number of readings that didn't seem as useful as the others; I have revised some of the material to make the readings more comprehensible; and I have added some new readings that show additional aspects of the philosophical discussion of art's nature. In making these changes, I continue to keep an eye on presenting a comprehensive view of philosophical thinking about art and its nature. To help identify the various authors included, I have also added brief biographical information about each.

A major change in the second edition has been the deletion of all illustrations. In view of the availability of images on the Web, I do not think this will detract from the utility of this book. Instead, readers are encouraged to use the Web—with sites such as artchive.com—to find reproductions of the works mentioned, illustrations that are better than anything that could have been economically included here.

The idea for this anthology was the result of a course I taught for a number of years with Sam Mitchell, "Philosophy in Dialogue: Meaning, Time, and Beauty." Discovering that none of the standard aesthetics anthologies devoted enough attention to the question of what art is, I began to think about editing such an anthology myself. Although this text has evolved in a variety of ways, it owes its existence to that course and the students who have discussed this issue in it. My thanks to all of them and, especially, to Sam for supporting me in this endeavor.

This anthology has also benefited from the help of many other individuals. Alan Schiffmann once again gave me the benefit of his philosophic acumen and fine editorial eye. Without his efforts, my writing for this book would have been less clear, my positions less precisely formulated. As usual, I value the care he has expended in refining my words and ideas.

A number of people helped me decide what essays to include in this volume. Angela Curran, Noël Carroll, Stephen Davies, Cynthia Freeland, Paul Guyer, Patricia Mills, and John Varriano all made suggestions that have improved and expanded the scope of this volume. I would also like to thank Robert Wicks for some excellent advice on improving a number of the introductions to the selections. His knowledge saved me from some major errors. Careful and detailed comments on the manuscript by the following contributed significantly: Deane Curtin, Gustavus Adolphus College; Elmer Duncan, Baylor University; Tom Huhn, Wesleyan University; Mary Sirridge, Louisiana State University; and Kathleen J. Wininger, University of Southern Maine. Comments from the following reviewers improved the second edition: Richard Gale, University of Pittsburgh; Harold Lenfesty, West Texas A & M University; Gary Maciag, Siena College; James McGregor, Salem State College; Dale Murray, Virginia Commonwealth University; Douglas Oro, Harvard University; and Hugh Wilder, College of Charleston—as did the detailed comments by Angela Curran and Casey Haskins, both of whose experiences using the anthology helped me reshape it in positive ways.

The support of my two editors at Harcourt College Publishers, David Tatom and Michelle Vardeman, was crucial to the initial publication of this anthology. For their enthusiastic support in the development of the current edition, I want to thank my editors at Wadsworth Publishing, Steve Wainwright and Barbara Hillaker.

Finally, I dedicate this book to my son, Jake, whose intellectual curiosity and gracious modesty inspire me daily. Jake, I hope this dedication provides you with some indication of all you have meant to me.

Thomas E. Wartenberg
Lower Highland Lake
Goshen, Massachusetts

THE NATURE OF ART

An Anthology

Introduction: What Makes "Art" Such a Problematic Concept?

Suppose your best friend, proud of a very expensive painting he recently acquired, invites you over to admire it. Although you don't know quite what to expect, you are taken aback when your friend reveals his acquisition to you: It's just "a canvas about five foot by four: white. The background is white and if you screw up your eyes, you can make out some fine white diagonal lines."[1] "Is this simple, almost monochromatic canvas—hardly a painting at all— meant as a hoax?" you ask. Your friend protests angrily that he could make a tidy profit if he sold it back to the dealer. And, he goes on, the work is by an artist whose paintings hang in the Centre Pompidou, Paris's great museum of contemporary art. Do these facts affect your judgment of the painting? Should they? What about the opinion of a mutual friend that "It's a work of art, there's a system behind it. . . . It wasn't painted by accident, it's a work of art which stakes its claim as part of a trajectory" (*Art*, pp. 17–18)? Does evidence of deliberation establish this painting's status as a work of art? How important are your own, subjective reactions to the work? Finally, and most centrally, you puzzle, "What, if anything, makes something a work of art?"

The scenario just described is from *Art*, a very successful play by the French author Yasmina Reza. The questions it raises foreshadow much of the subject matter of this anthology. All the included selections contribute to the ongoing philosophic discussion about the nature of art. Some selections are drawn from the history of philosophy, going back over two thousand years; others are as recent as the "digital revolution." Some are written by philosophers working within the tradition of English-speaking or analytic philosophy; others stem from the European or Continental tradition. Some offer a crisp formula in answer to the question, What makes something a work of art? Others argue that no simple definition will do. And still others doubt that the whole enterprise makes sense. What unites them all, however, is their confrontation with this thorny philosophic issue.

---

[1] Yasmina Reza, *Art* (London: Faber and Faber, 1996), p. 1. Future references to this work are given parenthetically as *Art*.

SOME QUESTIONS FROM *Art* ABOUT ART

Before we think about the question, What is the nature of art? let's look more closely at the issues raised by the play. *Art* concerns Serge, an intelligent and cultured individual who buys an abstract painting, only to find himself caught up in a dispute with two of his best friends over its merits. Marc is a highly educated skeptic, who was once a mentor to Serge. Yvan, less self-assured, acts as a mediator between the two. The picture itself is an example of minimalism, a contemporary movement that banishes many traditional aspects of painting. For example, it rejects what was thought for centuries to be the premise of visual art, the faithful reproduction of the look of things in the natural world. The white square painting Serge is so proud of is what it is, a white painted square, representing nothing beyond itself. It harbors neither emotional content nor any of the other features familiarly associated with art. As such, its status is problematic, for it is difficult to see what about the work makes it a work of *art*, let alone one whose quality might justify its high price.

One cannot visit a museum exhibiting contemporary art without experiencing the same range of reactions. *Art* uses the dispute between the three friends to pose some hard questions about how, in our (post)modern world, we understand art.

Does the Artist's Intention Make It Art?

When Yvan defends his judgment that the white painting is a work of art, he refers to a system behind the painting, the fact that it is not the product of accident (*Art*, pp. 17–18). In philosophic terms, this assertion claims that the intention of the artist is a crucial element in determining that something is a work of art. Indeed, one of the philosophers represented in this volume, Monroe C. Beardsley (see Chapter 20), thinks it is *the* crucial element. The basic intuition—derived from common sense—behind the intentionality thesis is that art objects are created by artists who are consciously trying to make art. To characterize something as a work of art, then, is to presuppose or acknowledge that it is the product of an artist's intentional activity.

The role of the artist's intentions in the creation of art has been hotly debated. Those who argue for their relevance point out that art objects are a species of the broader class of artifacts, items produced by the skilled actions of human beings. Sunsets may be beautiful, they point out, but they are not works of art unless we attribute them to a Divine Artist. Surely what makes an object a work of art is that someone intended it to be one.

On the other side of this issue are those who deny intentions a necessary role in the creation of art objects. They point to the existence of cultures lacking a concept of art. Does this mean that none of the objects their artisans produce counts as art? Would this not be an unacceptable cultural egocentrism on our part? And because we deem them worthy of display in our museums and attend to them in the same ways we do to objects intentionally produced as art in our culture—think, for example, of the many African tribal objects such as divination masks that are to be found in many of our museums—don't we, in fact, already accept as *art* objects that may not have been intended as such?

A second problem with the intentionality thesis is that intentions by themselves seem inadequate to qualify something as a work of art. My intending that the doodles I draw on this napkin be a work of art is not sufficient to make them one. The recognition of others seems somehow required before something can qualify as art. To this, the intentionalist could rightly respond that not anyone can create a work of art, but only someone skilled enough to be considered an artist. But then we are faced with the question, What determines whether someone is an artist? If it is the ability to create genuine works of art, then we are back where we started.

These kinds of problems with the intentionality thesis have led some philosophers to include those who view, study, buy, and sell art in the consideration of what makes an artwork art.

Does the Fact That a Work Is Treated as Art by the Artworld Make It Art?

When Serge is pressed by Marc to defend his purchase, he appeals to authoritative opinion. For example, he says that, even though he paid 200,000 francs for the painting—the play takes place in Paris—he could sell it back to the gallery for substantially more. Later, he adds that the Centre Pompidou has three works by the same artist.

In both cases, Serge makes reference to the artworld to justify his claim that the white painting is a work of art. This term has been used by philosophers to characterize the social institution through which art is produced, exhibited, and sold. Although hard to specify precisely, the artworld is constituted by the practices of those social agents—presumably knowledgeable experts—who set prices and make decisions about which works to display in public, which books about art to publish, which artists and which works to include in college courses, and so forth. Museum directors, gallery owners, academics, critics—these are the functionaries of the artworld. And one very influential theory of art holds that it is they who determine whether something is a work of art (Chapter 19).

In the face of Marc's skepticism, Serge appeals to the authority of this world: to the price the white painting would fetch on the art market, and to the fact that other works by the same artist are in prestigious museum collections. If the painting is worth a lot of money, its creator is celebrated, and museums display this sort of work, doesn't that settle the question? Who is Marc to say otherwise?

The appeal of this institutional theory of art consists in part in its resolution of some of the problems we saw with the intentionality thesis. For example, works produced in other cultures will count as art so long as they reside in *our* museums, regardless of why they were produced. Such objects are art objects because key players in the artworld treat them as such.

Another advantage of this theory is that it doesn't subordinate art to some theorist's ideal. For centuries, the dominant view held in the West was that the goal of art was the faithful imitation of nature (see Chapters 1 and 2). If nothing else, the 20th century has treated this conception of art rudely, for relatively few of the most celebrated artworks of the last hundred years accurately represent the natural world. Art can no longer be limited to a single goal. The institutional theory is more inclusive than its rivals, precisely because it makes an object's status depend on how it is received and not on features intrinsic to it.

Still, does it make sense to accept certain opinions just because those who hold them are deemed experts? Even if we concede that the artworld plays a role in establishing what counts as art, on what criteria must its experts rely in making their judgments? What features are these experts trained to recognize when they determine that something is a work of art?

The idea here is that an object's being a work of art has something to do with its properties and not with the way in which people regard it. Only objects with these special characteristics should be accorded the status of art. If it does not seem right to allow the opinions of others, no matter how knowledgeable, to determine whether something qualifies as art, then what is the cognitive status of the judgments that any of us makes about works of art? Are they simply expressions of opinion, or do they make claims for which reasons can be given?

Are Judgments about Art Objective? Or Are They Simply Matters of Taste?

In his attempt to mediate the dispute between Marc and Serge, Yvan suggests that the root of their disagreement lies in their differing standards of taste. Thus, Marc's "taste is classical, he likes things classical, what do you expect..." (*Art*, p. 14). So no wonder he doesn't appreciate the white painting.

Yvan's effort at peacemaking invokes a perennial philosophic debate: Are judgments about works of art simply matters of taste, or are there objective standards to which appeal can be made? The disagreement between David Hume (Chapter 3) and Immanuel Kant (Chapter 4) is over precisely this issue. If there is no accounting for taste—Can I be mistaken in preferring vanilla to chocolate?—does the dispute between Marc and Serge, despite appearing to be factual, come down to no more than this?

One of the issues here is how far we can trust our untutored responses to works of art. For example, for many people the paintings of Claude Monet, one of the central figures in the impressionist movement, seem immediately accessible—beautifully rendered, capturing with vivid directness the experience of being in the natural world. How then to understand the derision that greeted the first showings of his work? What we now see as unquestioned masterpieces were regarded as clumsy travesties by most contemporaneous critics and viewers alike. Indeed, the impressionists had such difficulty entering the great annual salon exhibitions that they had to organize their own shows in order for their art to be seen.

The case of impressionism—as of all the great schools of painting since—suggests that judgments about art cannot be simply a matter of individual preference. Today we would disagree with a viewer in 1880 who claimed that a Monet landscape was too poorly executed to be a genuine work of art. But are viewers' reactions and responses irrelevant to deciding whether a painting by Monet is a work of art?

One way out of this quandary would be to suggest that some individuals are more qualified than others to make judgments about art.

Is One Artistic or Aesthetic Judgment as Good as Another?

At one point Serge, who is angered by Marc's deprecation of his painting, remarks, "I don't blame him for not responding to this painting, he hasn't the training, there's a whole apprenticeship you have to go through" (*Art*, p. 15). In other words, not all judgments about art are on an equal footing. Those who have had training in the appreciation of a given art form, such as painting or music, are more qualified to determine what are and are not instances of it. Once again, this theme is repeatedly sounded by philosophers. For example, both David Hume (Chapter 3) and Clive Bell (Chapter 10) assert the existence of a cultured elite, knowledgeable about the arts, and hence in a better position to pass judgment on such matters.

But if artworks are supposed to produce pleasure, what are we to say of an object most people find incomprehensible or even objectionable? Is it art because the experts say so? Isn't their training designed to induct a few into positions of cultural authority? And yet. . . .

And yet, haven't most of us found some artwork puzzling—Picasso's painting *Guernica,* or Eliot's poem *The Wasteland,* or a Coltrane jazz riff—then sought information about the work, and, having done so, come to better understand—and *appreciate*—it? Learning about the general cultural context, the artist's life, and the relevant history of that art form can help us see what the work is about and, thus, enrich the experience of viewing, reading, and listening. Does this mean that Serge, along with Hume and Bell, is right that only those with some training are equipped to judge that something is a work of art? If so, what does this training help us to identify in the work? What special *aesthetic* properties do artworks possess that distinguish them from all the other things we encounter in the world?

Does the Application of Aesthetic Concepts Make Something a Work of Art?

Consider Yvan's reaction when first shown the white painting:

Yvan: Oh, yes. Yes, yes.
Serge: Antrios.
Yvan: Yes, yes.
Serge: It's a seventies Antrios. Worth mentioning. He's going through a similar phase now, but this one's from the seventies.
Yvan: Yes, yes. Expensive?
Serge: In absolute terms, yes. In fact, no. You like it?
Yvan: Oh, yes, yes, yes.
Serge: Plain.

Yvan: Plain, yes . . . Yes . . . And at the same time . . .
Serge: Magnetic.
Yvan: Mm . . . yes . . .
Serge: You don't really get the resonance just at the moment.
Yvan: Well, a bit . . .
Serge: No, you don't. You have to come back in the middle of the day. That resonance you get from something monochromatic, it doesn't really happen under artificial light.(*Art*, pp. 12–13)

It seems that Serge's application of the adjectives "plain," "magnetic," and "resonant" justifies Yvan's appreciation of the painting as a work of art. Although these are normal English words, some philosophers believe that their use in this context goes beyond simple description. For example, it is true that the white painting is plain (that is, it does not appear to have much visual complexity), but given the aims of the minimalist movement, to describe Serge's canvas as plain is to ascribe to it an aesthetic virtue. It is the sort of thing one says of such works of art.

The term "aesthetics" has been used as a synonym for the "philosophy of art" since this field of philosophic inquiry came into being during the 18th century. Prior to this, "aesthetic"—derived from the Greek *aisthanesthai*, to perceive—was more or less synonymous with "sensory." But because philosophers saw our experience of beauty—both natural and artistic—as primarily a sensory matter, they began to use the term in its modern meaning. Thus, Immanuel Kant (see Chapter 4) used the term "aesthetic" to refer both to those general principles determining sensory knowledge and to the more specific principles for judging objects to be beautiful. As the earlier usage declined, the latter became the accepted characterization of the philosophic study of art.

The great idealist philosopher G. W. F. Hegel was the first to contest Kant's usage, rejecting both the limitation of the philosophy of art to questions of beauty and the consideration of natural beauty under the same rubric as the study of art (see Chapter 6). Many contemporary philosophers of art—myself included—agree with Hegel that the philosophy of art should be a separate discipline. We do not see ourselves as concerned with beauty in general, but only with art, and the latter as itself no longer focused solely on beauty.

I raise this issue now because it bears on the question of the types of properties artworks might be said to possess in distinction from other kinds of things. The traditional answer would be aesthetic properties, and *plain, magnetic*, and *resonant*, in our example, would then count as instances of such properties. Philosophers who deny that the philosophy of art is identical with aesthetics would characterize these as artistic properties, that is, properties that art objects have and that nonart objects lack.

A number of the philosophers represented in this anthology emphasize the role of artistic properties in determining whether something is a work of art. Martin Heidegger (Chapter 13), Nelson Goodman (Chapter 17), and Arthur Danto (Chapter 18) all agree that art objects have properties that other things lack—although they don't agree on what these properties are—and that it is possession of these properties that makes something a work of art.

Troubling questions arise for this view, too. Don't we have to know that something is a work of art before we attribute such artistic properties to it? Couldn't we attribute such properties to anything if we chose to view it as a work of art? Instead of just typing on the keys of my computer, I can sit back and savor the luminous quality of the light they reflect and the simplicity of their shape and placement together. Does my ability to admire the computer keyboard in this way make it a work of art?

Art has become a very different phenomenon in the 20th century from what it was in the 17th. Could our puzzlement about art be related to the fundamental changes in the meaning of art?

Is Contemporary Art Still Art?

In justifying his dismissal of the white painting, Marc explains how his reaction to it reflects a deeper discomfort with contemporary art: "I don't believe in the values which dominate contemporary art. The rule of novelty. The rule of surprise" (*Art*, p. 55). That Marc's hostility to recent art is widely shared is evident to anyone who reads the daily newspaper or watches the evening news, which frequently report controversies over public funding of art that appears aimed only at provocation. Robert Mapplethorpe's confrontational photography, Karen Finley's performance art, or Nigerian painter Chris Ofili's *Virgin Mary* seem to many to have lost touch with the values realized in earlier art.

In the selection from Martin Heidegger's *The Origin of the Work of Art* (Chapter 14), for example, we can sense an aspiration that art return to what Heidegger sees as its authentic mission: the revelation of the historical world that produced it. However, other philosophers, such as Arthur Danto (Chapter 18), Adrian Piper (Chapter 23), and Carolyn Korsmeyer (Chapter 25), see in contemporary art possibilities for novel expression. Whether contemporary art has lost sight of its mission as art—or even has a mission—are issues dividing critics, philosophers, and the art-consuming public.

THREE APPROACHES TO UNDERSTANDING ART

Our consideration of Reza's play, *Art*, has led us to explore a range of issues touching on questions about the nature of art. Although philosophers have written extensively about these issues, the play's success is evidence that a far wider public cares about them. Perhaps the obscure and difficult nature of so much contemporary work—"white paintings" have their analogues in music, dance, literature, film—lends a special urgency to this, the central question of the philosophy of art: What makes something a work of art?

Although this is posed as a question about the ontological status of the artwork in general, independent of its specific manner of instantiation—whether poem, symphony, or statue—there has been (*contra* Derrida [Chapter 24]) a general tendency among philosophers to treat visual art, especially painting, as paradigmatic. Although a number of the selections in this volume use literature as their point of reference, only Schopenhauer (Chapter 5) focuses primarily on music. The clear majority think painting is the quintessential art form.

As you become acquainted with the issues raised by these selections, bear in mind these questions: Does each of the accounts privilege, consciously or unconsciously, one or another art form? How does such a bias affect the general applicability of the theory of art put forward?

Defining Art

The readings in this volume represent three fundamentally different approaches to answering the question of art's nature. The first, and dominant, tendency proceeds by attempting a definition. Historically, this is the approach taken by the first philosopher of art, Plato, who defined art as imitation. Down through the centuries, the search for a definition continued, even among those who rejected Plato's thesis. By the early 20th century, with the advent of analytic philosophy—a style of thought captivated by advances in mathematical logic and its formal methods—this project had become one of attempting to specify necessary and sufficient conditions for the application of the concept "art": For the term to be meaningful, there must be criteria that allow one to tell whether something is, or is not, a work of art.

One of your tasks in reading this book is to assess the validity of such attempts to grasp art's nature. In doing so, it is important to keep in mind the distinction between what some philosophers have called the classificatory and evaluative senses of the term "art." For the most part, attempts to define art are intended in the former sense, that is, as distinguishing things that are art from things that are not. For example, the imitation theory proposes that only those things that are imitations of the "real world" are works of art. On these grounds, the white painting is excluded from the class of artworks, because it is not an imitation of anything.

But often, "art" is not used in this descriptive way, but in an evaluative manner—as when Marc protests that the white painting is not art because it isn't particularly good, at least not the sort of thing a knowledgeable art lover should take seriously. This, however, leaves no room for judging a work to be bad or inferior, but still art.

Take one purported definition—art communicates emotion between a creator and an audience. Any object—a painting, a poem, a symphony—would fail to be art if it failed to achieve such communication. But, just as philosophy can be done badly, so can art, and a definition of art needs to leave open this possibility. The communication theory, by conflating descriptive and evaluative meanings, precludes it.

Although there is a tendency to think about art objects in abstraction from anything else—a tendency typical of much recent analytic philosophy and exhibited here by my focus on the white painting—these objects are situated in a complex set of relationships. Other elements figuring in this matrix include, of course, the artist or creator of the work as well as the audience that experiences it, the conventions governing the art form and art as a whole, modes of artistic training, and so on.

Philosophers have differed on which elements are crucial. Thus, some philosophers fix on the artist (Collingwood, for example, in Chapter 11), even to the exclusion of the work. More counterintuitive still, the French literary theorist Roland Barthes (Chapter 22) thinks of the *audience* as the real site of artistic meaning. In contrast to these, some others (Martin Heidegger, for example, in Chapter 13) view the whole complex of relationships as crucial. So in seeking to define the nature of art, you must either decide which is the most important, i.e., the one needing definition, or you must conclude that the whole should be the object of the definition, rather than any of its aspects standing alone.

Skepticism toward Defining Art

The second approach to the central question of the philosophy of art—What makes something a work of art?—is skepticism about the possibility of definition. In a way, the skeptic argues, art is itself a phenomenon that by its nature defeats attempts to define it. Because, to Marc's chagrin, originality is a central value in at least contemporary art, painters, composers, and writers are continually striving to break the boundaries of what was previously considered art. The very examples theorists cite to justify the institutional theory—Marcel Duchamp's *Fountain*, for example—clearly did so. Duchamp took a mass-produced urinal, signed it with the name "R. Mutt," gave it the title *Fountain*, and submitted it for exhibition. If the mere act of naming, signing, and displaying a mass-produced urinal could result in a work of art, how could one possibly specify in advance what sorts of things can be so counted? Isn't art precisely the sort of phenomenon that breaks accepted conventions and challenges our prior convictions about what it is? And, if so, doesn't its very nature dictate the very impossibility of definition?

It was only in the latter half of the 20th century that philosophers raised skeptical doubts such as these. Within the analytic tradition, Morris Weitz (Chapter 16) best exemplifies this approach; within the Continental tradition, Jacques Derrida (Chapter 24) is today's reigning skeptic. Although Weitz and Derrida operate with very different conceptions of philosophy, they agree that the tradition was seriously mistaken in assuming that the appropriate goal for the philosophy of art was defining art's nature. Each in his own way sees art as defying the theorist's ability to conceptualize it.

This approach to the project of defining art is an instance of the broader strategy of antiessentialism. A philosophic position reaching all the way back to Aristotle, essentialism proposes that a variety of different particulars can all be referred to by the same word—fall under the same concept—only if there is some common essence or nature that they all share. Thus, according to this view, the reason each of us can be called a *person* is that there is an essence to personhood that each of us possesses. Entities lacking this essence, such as sticks or stones, are not persons. Whether some entities (computers or dolphins, for example) qualify as persons might not always be clear, but generally it is possible to distinguish between things that do and things that do not possess this essence.

The will to define art's nature is an instance of essentialism, assuming, as it does, that art has an essence that can be specified theoretically. Finding this essence will allow us to determine whether any given object is or is not art.

In the 20th century, essentialism has come under fire from a number of quarters. At issue is the adequacy of this account of how our conceptual schemes—or our language—work. It is no longer so widely accepted that recourse to essences is necessary to explain our ability to refer to a class of objects by a common term. (See my introduction to Chapter 16 for an alternative explanation of how such reference is accomplished.) In addition, the biases of traditional accounts of essence have been pointed out—for example, the familiar Aristotelian adage that man is the *rational animal*, privileges rationality, a characteristic that has been historically associated with men but which, according to Aristotle himself, women conspicuously lack. The general point is that the search for essences may harbor unacknowledged political agendas, identifying certain characteristics as essential to a given type, and implicitly stigmatizing other characteristics as defects.

In the case of art, attempts at definition have been used both to legitimate certain types of art and to denigrate others. Clive Bell's candidate, "significant form" (Chapter 10), vindicated the postimpressionist painting he championed while excluding the naturalistic works he disdained. The question remains, however, whether instances like this invalidate the essentialist project and, if so, how we should understand the functioning of general terms such as "art" in the absence of a set of necessary and sufficient conditions justifying their application.

Contextual Approaches

The third approach to art exemplified by the essays in this volume has its roots in Hegelian thought. Although he treated art as a form of philosophical—ultimately, timeless—truth, Hegel also characterized it as a succession of stages of development realized in different historically and culturally specific contexts. Subsequent philosophers of art, less confident than Hegel in the ultimate progression of art toward Truth, nonetheless took from him the idea that the nature of art could be understood properly only as expressions of those contexts. Instead of trying to develop a single, abstract definition of art, these modern theorists—from the philosopher Walter Benjamin (Chapter 14) to the artist and educator Douglas Davis (Chapter 29)—have focused on art's changing social role. Instead of treating art as a unitary phenomenon—they do not openly dismiss the possibility of definition—they emphasize socially conditioned transformations in its nature.

Among the reasons these philosophers (many of whom were influenced by Karl Marx) seem uninterested in defining art is that they think any such definition will be too abstract, made at too high a level of generality. For them, it is more important to understand the actual or concrete functioning of art in particular historical and social contexts than it is to devise a definition that will apply to all contexts without exception.

Following Marx's claims about the nature of society, Marxist theorists tend to operate within a framework that treats economic or material issues as basic. For these philosophers, all of what is generally called "culture," including art, is part of the superstructure. Although there is a great deal of disagreement about the exact nature of the relationship between base and super-structure, Marxists generally think that developments in the material base are decisive in understanding cultural change. To understand art, then, it is impor-tant to take note of changes in the general material structure of society—for example, fundamental changes in the social organization of production and exchange associated with the rise of a new class, such as the bourgeoisie—as well as changes in the mode of artistic production. As Marx quips in the first volume of *Das Kapital* in illustration of this point, Don Quixote suffered for not realizing that knight errantry was incompatible with all economic struc-tures. This explains why photographically reproduced art and the development of computer-related graphics technology interest these philosophers. From their point of view, the nature of art is fundamentally altered by such material or technological developments.

With the development of technologies of reproduction—first the photo-graph and now the computer—it seems that art objects—or, at least, replicas of them—can be endlessly disseminated. Instead of having to travel to Paris to see the *Mona Lisa,* I can now call up infinitely many images of the original while sitting at my terminal. For theorists operating within this third paradigm, their focus shifts to the question, "How do such developments in the mode of artis-tic production and dissemination affect art's very being?" If there is widespread agreement that these developments are decisive, there is no consensus on the nature of their effects.

A second fundamental issue for these theorists is the role that art plays in society. There is general agreement that the view, dating back to Kant (Chap-ter 4), that art requires our disinterested contemplation—that is, an awareness untainted by specific interests, desires, or concerns—is inadequate to under-standing the function of art. The question, then, is art's relation to social struc-tures, whether economic, gender, racial, or sexual. On the one hand, the arts are often seen as challenging prevailing social norms: The artist is a rebel who stands apart from society to condemn it. From this point of view, art celebrates the potential of the human species and castigates society for suppressing that potential. To borrow a phrase from the contemporary German philosopher Jürgen Habermas, art satisfies an emancipatory interest, the desire to be free of unnecessary and oppressive social constraints.

On the other hand, it is hard to ignore the role that some art, popular art especially, plays in the established order. Theodor Adorno's phrase, "the Cul-ture Industry" (see Chapter 15), indicates how art has been assimilated into the very same structures that dominate the production of material goods. Each of us can recall films that are less genuine works of art than cultural products that serve to strengthen or solidify faith in the status quo. War movies glorifying killing; romances suggesting that only heterosexual marriage offers the promise of true intimacy; comedies employing demeaning stereotypes, be they of African or Asian Americans, fat people, women, working class men—all these serve to normalize, hence to sustain, potentially oppressive social relationships.

Philosophers concerned with the social function of art will continue to ask whether the arts in our time function to challenge or support these relationships, and will continue to investigate how changes in the production and dissemination of artworks affect their meaning. Has art's cultural authority been undermined by technological and social developments? How does art function to prop up the dominant social order? Has the culture industry succeeded in taming and cashing in on gestures of artistic transgression? Or has art continued to play a socially and culturally subversive role? These are the sorts of issues raised by the third approach to the central question of the philosophy of art: What makes something a work of art?

ART IN THE CONTEMPORARY CONTEXT

Although philosophers have puzzled over art as long as philosophy has existed, developments in the arts of the 20th century, perhaps especially in painting, have deepened their puzzlement. Once, it had seemed evident that art generally strove to accurately represent what it depicted. But the development, in the late 19th and early 20th centuries, of schools of painting that eschewed accuracy of representation left the imitation theory behind. I am thinking here of such postimpressionist painters as Vincent Van Gogh and Edvard Munch, whose paintings often seem more concerned with conveying the artist's anguish. With the advent of abstract and conceptual art, all that remained for many traditional approaches to understanding art was a dignified burial.

These developments explain why the 20th century has provided such rich discussions in the philosophy of art. Prior to the 18th century, there was not even a concept of art resembling our own. As R. G. Collingwood points out (Chapter 11), art as we understand it was not distinguished from its earlier meaning—one that we still retain in such phrases as "the art of picture framing"—of an activity requiring specialized skill. Thus, not until the 19th century did the philosophy of art come into its own as a distinct philosophic discipline. However, 19th-century reflections on art do not reveal the intensity of puzzlement that clearly marks 20th-century discussions.

The artwork displayed in museums of contemporary art may bear only the faintest resemblance to the works in museums dedicated to the art of earlier ages. In the play *Art* with which I began this introduction, the three protagonists almost dissolve their friendship because of their deep disagreement over what constitutes a work of art. Although most of us may not be as ready to jettison our closest friends for the sake of our artistic allegiances, we share the same deep perplexities about contemporary works of art. Walking through museums, you can hear derisive comments reflecting deep suspicion of contemporary visual art; attending concerts of contemporary orchestral music, you can see audiences squirm at sounds reminiscent of a traffic jam; after sitting through films whose plots seem nonexistent, you may join viewers heading to the manager to request a refund. For those who wish the arts to address contemporary concerns, such developments are a source of deep anxiety. The selections in this volume will probably not put this anxiety to rest, but they may help the reader understand why for some the arts are such a troubling presence in our (post)modern world.

I

Art as Imitation: Plato

Plato (428–347 B.C.), the supreme philosophic stylist, was deeply suspicious of the arts because, in his view, they appeal to the emotions rather than to the intellect. In this selection, drawn from his great dialogue, *The Republic,* Plato's philosopher-hero Socrates explains to his young follower Glaucon why artists should be excluded from the ideal state the two of them are imagining. His reasons for this have to do both with the nature of art itself and with the effects works of art have on their audiences.

On metaphysical grounds, poetry and painting—the arts that most concern Socrates—will find no place in the perfect society. For Plato, the things of this world, such as tables and chairs, are not ultimately real. Because they come into being and pass away, because they admit of change, and because they are not perfect instances of their kind, such things lack the complete reality that the Forms, timeless and unchanging, enjoy. Familiar, everyday things have being only to the extent that they partake of, or participate in, the Forms, but they stand at one remove from that which most fully is, the eternal and immutable.

Plato's theory of art—that it is an imitation of an imitation—depends on his theory of Forms. (Plato does not think that music imitates anything, but elsewhere argues that the ideal state should include only music that does not stir emotions in undesirable ways.) In our selection, Socrates claims that artistic creations—paintings and poems—stand triply removed from the real; that is, there are two realms of existence more real than art objects, the Forms themselves, and the things of daily life. The basis for this view is the assumption that the goal of art is the imitation of mundane reality. Thus, the artist is even less attuned to reality than the craftsperson, for the latter at least seeks to copy the Form, whereas the former takes the everyday as his or her model—in effect copying the copy.

Using this theory as his premise, then, Socrates worries not just that art objects represent appearances of appearances but also that they play to the emotions and thus do not promote a proper understanding of the world. Thinking especially of literature—he uses the term "poetry" to characterize it—he is critical of its appeal to people's baser, more irrational side. In this sense, art constitutes a challenge to philosophy, which also seeks to influence people, but by rational argument rather than emotional appeal. The arts are to be banished so that the attitudes and actions of the citizens will not be tainted by inappropriate influences.

Thus, Plato's critique of art as imitation is linked to a negative appraisal of its social utility: Art is dangerous, for its appeal to the irrational distracts us from the legitimate claims of reason.

STUDY QUESTIONS ON THE READING

1.   Plato claims that artists are imitators. How does he justify this claim?

2.   Why does Plato think artists inferior to craftspeople?

3.   Homer, the author of the *Iliad* and the *Odyssey,* was revered by the Greeks as their great teacher, yet Socrates argues that Homer misunderstands virtue. What is the significance of this claim, and how does Socrates justify it?

4.   Why does Plato have Socrates banish artists from his ideal city? Do you see analogies between his position and those of contemporary politicians? What objections, if any, do you have to Plato's view?

5.   Can you offer counterexamples to Plato's theory of art as imitation of everyday reality? Think about developments in modern art and whether they fit this conception. Are there ways Plato's theory could be modified to handle any of these counterexamples? Explain.

6.   Plato clearly advocates restricting people's access to artistic creations. Are there ever situations in which some such restrictions are legitimate? What about works that contain violence? Sex? Explain.

❖

PLATO: THE REPUBLIC

Indeed, Socrates said, our city has many features that assure me that we were entirely right in founding it as we did, and, when I say this, I'm especially thinking of poetry.

What about it in particular? Glaucon said.

That we didn't admit any that is imitative. Now that we have distinguished the separate parts of the soul, it is even clearer, I think, that such poetry should be altogether excluded.

From *Republic* by Plato, translated by G. M. A. Grube. Reprinted with permission by Hackett Publishing Company.

What do you mean?

Between ourselves—for you won't denounce me to the tragic poets or any of the other imitative ones—all such poetry is likely to distort the thought of anyone who hears it, unless he has the knowledge of what it is really like, as a drug to counteract it.

What exactly do you have in mind in saying this?

I'll tell you, even though the love and respect I've had for Homer since I was a child make me hesitate to speak, for he seems to have been the first teacher and leader of all these fine tragedians. All the same, no one is to be honored or valued more than the truth. So, as I say, it must be told.

That's right.

Listen then, or, rather, answer.

Ask and I will.

Could you tell me what imitation in general is? I don't entirely understand what sort of thing imitations are trying to be.

Is it likely, then, that I'll understand?

That wouldn't be so strange, for people with bad eyesight often see things before those whose eyesight is keener.

That's so, but even if something occurred to me, I wouldn't be eager to talk about it in front of you. So I'd rather that you did the looking.

Do you want us to begin our examination, then, by adopting our usual procedure? As you know, we customarily hypothesize a single form in connection with each of the many things to which we apply the same name. Or don't you understand?

I do.

Then let's now take any of the manys you like. For example, there are many beds and tables.

Of course.

But there are only two forms of such furniture, one of the bed and one of the table.

Yes.

And don't we also customarily say that their makers look towards the appropriate form in making the beds or tables we use, and similarly in the other cases? Surely no craftsman makes the form itself. How could he?

There's no way he could.

Well, then, see what you'd call this craftsman?

Which one?

The one who makes all the things that all the other kinds of craftsmen severally make.

That's a clever and wonderful fellow you're talking about.

Wait a minute, and you'll have even more reason to say that, for this same craftsman is able to make, not only all kinds of furniture, but all plants that grow from the earth, all animals (including himself), the earth itself, the heavens, the gods, all the things in the heavens and in Hades beneath the earth.

He'd be amazingly clever!

You don't believe me? Tell me, do you think that there's no way any craftsman could make all these things, or that in one way he could and in another he couldn't? Don't you see that there is a way in which you yourself could make all of them?

What way is that?

It isn't hard: You could do it quickly and in lots of places, especially if you were willing to carry a mirror with you, for that's the quickest way of all. With it you can quickly make the sun, the things in the heavens, the earth, yourself, the other animals, manufactured items, plants, and everything else mentioned just now.

Yes, I could make them appear, but I couldn't make the things themselves as they truly are.

Well put! You've extracted the point that's crucial to the argument. I suppose that the painter too belongs to this class of makers, doesn't he?

Of course.

But I suppose you'll say that he doesn't truly make the things he makes. Yet, in a certain way, the painter does make a bed, doesn't he?

Yes, he makes the appearance of one.

What about the carpenter? Didn't you just say that he doesn't make the form—which is our term for the being of a bed—but only a bed?

Yes, I did say that.

Now, if he doesn't make the being of a bed, he isn't making that which is, but something which is like that which is, but is not it. So, if someone were to say that the work of a carpenter or any other craftsman is completely that which is, wouldn't he risk saying what isn't true?

That, at least, would be the opinion of those who busy themselves with arguments of this sort.

Then let's not be surprised if the carpenter's bed, too, turns out to be a somewhat dark affair in comparison to the true one.

All right.

Then, do you want us to try to discover what an imitator is by reference to these same examples?

I do, if you do.

We get, then, these three kinds of beds. The first is in nature a bed, and I suppose we'd say that a god makes it, or does someone else make it?

No one else, I suppose.

The second is the work of a carpenter.

Yes.

And the third is the one the painter makes. Isn't that so?

It is.

Then the painter, carpenter, and god correspond to three kinds of bed?

Yes, three.

Now, the god, either because he didn't want to or because it was necessary for him not to do so, didn't make more than one bed in nature, but only one, the very one that is the being of a bed. Two or more of these have not been made by the god and never will be.

Why is that?

Because, if he made only two, then again one would come to light whose form they in turn would both possess, and that would be the one that is the being of a bed and not the other two.

That's right.

The god knew this, I think, and wishing to be the real maker of the truly real bed and not just a maker of a bed, he made it to be one in nature.

Probably so.

Do you want us to call him its natural maker or something like that?

It would be right to do so, at any rate, since he is by nature the maker of this and everything else.

What about a carpenter? Isn't he the maker of a bed?

Yes.

And is a painter also a craftsman and maker of such things?

Not at all.

Then what do you think he does do to a bed?

He imitates it. He is an imitator of what the others make. That, in my view, is the most reasonable thing to call him.

All right. Then wouldn't you call someone whose product is third from the natural one an imitator?

I most certainly would.

Then this will also be true of a tragedian, if indeed he is an imitator. He is by nature third from the king and the truth, as are all other imitators.

It looks that way.

We're agreed about imitators, then. Now, tell me this about a painter. Do you think he tries in each case to imitate the thing itself in nature or the works of craftsmen?

The works of craftsmen.

As they are or as they appear? You must be clear about that.

How do you mean?

Like this. If you look at a bed from the side or the front or from anywhere else is it a different bed each time? Or does it only appear different, without being at all different? And is that also the case with other things?

That's the way it is—it appears different without being so.

Then consider this very point: What does painting do in each case? Does it imitate that which is as it is, or does it imitate that which appears as it appears? Is it an imitation of appearances or of truth?

Of appearances.

Then imitation is far removed from the truth, for it touches only a small part of each thing and a part that is itself only an image. And that, it seems, is why it can produce everything. For example, we say that a painter can paint a cobbler, a carpenter, or any other craftsman, even though he knows nothing about these crafts. Nevertheless, if he is a good painter and displays his painting of a carpenter at a distance, he can deceive children and foolish people into thinking that it is truly a carpenter.

Of course.

Then this, I suppose, is what we must bear in mind in all these cases. Hence, whenever someone tells us that he has met a person who knows all the crafts as well as all the other things that anyone else knows and that his knowledge of any subject is more exact than any of theirs is, we must assume that we're talking to a simple-minded fellow who has apparently encountered some sort of magician or imitator and been deceived into thinking him omniscient and that the reason he has been deceived is that he himself can't distinguish between knowledge, ignorance, and imitation.

That's absolutely true.

Then, we must consider tragedy and its leader, Homer. The reason is this: We hear some people say that poets know all crafts, all human affairs concerned with virtue and vice, and all about the gods as well. They say that if a good poet produces fine poetry, he must have knowledge of the things he writes about, or else he wouldn't be able to produce it at all. Hence, we have to look to see whether those who tell us this have encountered these imitators and have been so deceived by them that they don't realize that their works are at the third remove from that which is and are easily produced without knowledge of the truth (since they are only images, not things that are), or whether there is something in what these people say, and good poets really do have knowledge of the things most people think they write so well about.

We certainly must look into it.

Do you think that someone who could make both the thing imitated and its image would allow himself to be serious about making images and put this at the forefront of his life as the best thing to do?

No, I don't.

I suppose that, if he truly had knowledge of the things he imitates, he'd be much more serious about actions than about imitations of them, would try to leave behind many fine deeds as memorials to himself, and would be more eager to be the subject of a eulogy than the author of one.

I suppose so, for these things certainly aren't equally valuable or equally beneficial either. . . .

Then shall we conclude that all poetic imitators, beginning with Homer, imitate images of virtue and all the other things they write about and have no grasp of the truth? As we were saying just now, a painter, though he knows nothing about cobblery, can make what seems to be a cobbler to those who know as little about it as he does and who judge things by their colors and shapes.

That's right.

And in the same way, I suppose we'll say that a poetic imitator uses words and phrases to paint colored pictures of each of the crafts. He himself knows nothing about them, but he imitates them in such a way that others, as ignorant as he, who judge by words, will think he speaks extremely well about cobblery or generalship or anything else whatever, provided—so great is the natural charm of these things—that he speaks with meter, rhythm, and harmony, for if you strip a poet's works of their musical colorings and take them by themselves, I think you know what they look like. You've surely seen them.

I certainly have.

Don't they resemble the faces of young boys who are neither fine nor beautiful after the bloom of youth has left them?

Absolutely.

Now, consider this. We say that a maker of an image—an imitator—knows nothing about that which is but only about its appearance. Isn't that so?

Yes.

Then let's not leave the discussion of this point halfway, but examine it fully.

Go ahead.

Don't we say that a painter paints reins and a mouth-bit?

Yes.

And that a cobbler and a metal-worker makes them?

Of course.

Then, does a painter know how the reins and mouth-bit have to be? Or is it the case that even a cobbler and metal-worker who make them don't know this, but only someone who knows how to use them, namely, a horseman?

That's absolutely true.

And won't we say that the same holds for everything?

What?

That for each thing there are these three crafts, one that uses it, one that makes it, and one that imitates it?

Yes.

Then aren't the virtue or excellence, the beauty and correctness of each manufactured item, living creature, and action related to nothing but the use for which each is made or naturally adapted?

They are.

It's wholly necessary, therefore, that a user of each thing has most experience of it and that he tell a maker which of his products performs well or badly in actual use. A flute-player, for example, tells a flute-maker about the flutes that respond well in actual playing and prescribes what kind of flutes he is to make, while the maker follows his instructions.

Of course.

Then doesn't the one who knows give instructions about good and bad flutes, and doesn't the other rely on him in making them?

Yes.

Therefore, a maker—through associating with and having to listen to the one who knows—has right opinion about whether something he makes is fine or bad, but the one who knows is the user.

That's right.

Does an imitator have knowledge of whether the things he makes are fine or right through having made use of them, or does he have right opinion about them through having to consort with the one who knows and being told how he is to paint them?

Neither.

Therefore an imitator has neither knowledge nor right opinion about whether the things he makes are fine or bad.

Apparently not.

Then a poetic imitator is an accomplished fellow when it comes to wisdom about the subjects of his poetry!

Hardly.

Nonetheless, he'll go on imitating, even though he doesn't know the good or bad qualities of anything, but what he'll imitate, it seems, is what appears fine or beautiful to the majority of people who know nothing.

Of course.

It seems, then, that we're fairly well agreed that an imitator has no worthwhile knowledge of the things he imitates, that imitation is a kind of game and not something to be taken seriously, and that all the tragic poets, whether they write in iambics or hexameters, are as imitative as they could possibly be.

That's right.

Then is this kind of imitation concerned with something that is third from the truth, or what?

Yes, it is.

And on which of a person's parts does it exert its power?

What do you mean?

This: Something looked at from close at hand doesn't seem to be the same size as it does when it is looked at from a distance.

No, it doesn't.

And something looks crooked when seen in water and straight when seen out of it, while something else looks both concave and convex because our eyes are deceived by its colors, and every other similar sort of confusion is clearly present in our soul. And it is because they exploit this weakness in our nature that trompe l'oeil painting, conjuring, and other forms of trickery have powers that are little short of magical.

That's true.

And don't measuring, counting, and weighing give us most welcome assistance in these cases, so that we aren't ruled by something's looking bigger, smaller, more numerous, or heavier, but by calculation, measurement, or weighing?

Of course.

And calculating, measuring, and weighing are the work of the rational part of the soul.

They are.

But when this part has measured and has indicated that some things are larger or smaller or the same size as others, the opposite appears to it at the same time.

Yes.

And didn't we say that it is impossible for the same thing to believe opposites about the same thing at the same time?

We did, and we were right to say it.

Then the part of the soul that forms a belief contrary to the measurements couldn't be the same as the part that believes in accord with them.

No, it couldn't.

Now, the part that puts its trust in measurement and calculation is the best part of the soul.

Of course.

Therefore, the part that opposes it is one of the inferior parts in us.

Necessarily.

This, then, is what I wanted to get agreement about when I said that painting and imitation as a whole produce work that is far from the truth, namely, that imitation really consorts with a part of us that is far from reason, and the result of their being friends and companions is neither sound nor true.

That's absolutely right.

Then imitation is an inferior thing that consorts with another inferior thing to produce an inferior offspring.

So it seems.

Does this apply only to the imitations we see, or does it also apply to the ones we hear—the ones we call poetry?

It probably applies to poetry as well.

However, we mustn't rely solely on a mere probability based on the analogy with painting; instead, we must go directly to the part of our thought with which poetic imitations consort and see whether it is inferior or something to be taken seriously.

Yes, we must.

Then let's set about it as follows. We say that imitative poetry imitates human beings acting voluntarily or under compulsion, who believe that, as a result of these actions, they are doing either well or badly and who experience either pleasure or pain in all this. Does it imitate anything apart from this?

Nothing.

Then is a person of one mind in all these circumstances? Or, just as he was at war with himself in matters of sight and held opposite beliefs about the same thing at the same time, does he also fight with himself and engage in civil war with himself in matters of action? But there is really no need for us to reach agreement on this question now, for I remember that we already came to an adequate conclusion about all these things in our earlier arguments, when we said that our soul is full of a myriad of such oppositions at the same time.

And rightly so.

It *was* right, but I think we omitted some things then that we must now discuss.

What are they?

We also mentioned somewhere before that, if a decent man happens to lose his son or some other prized possession, he'll bear it more easily than the other sorts of people.

Certainly.

But now let's consider this. Will he not grieve at all, or, if that's impossible, will he be somehow measured in his response to pain?

The latter is closer to the truth.

Now, tell me this about him: Will he fight his pain and put up more resistance to it when his equals can see him or when he's alone by himself in solitude?

He'll fight it far more when he's being seen.

But when he's alone I suppose he'll venture to say and do lots of things that he'd be ashamed to be heard saying or seen doing.

That's right.

And isn't it reason and law that tells him to resist his pain, while his experience of it tells him to give in?

True.

And when there are two opposite inclinations in a person in relation to the same thing at the same time, we say that he must also have two parts.

Of course.

Isn't one part ready to obey the law wherever it leads him?

How so?

The law says, doesn't it, that it is best to keep as quiet as possible in misfortunes and not get excited about them? First, it isn't clear whether such things will turn out to be good or bad in the end; second, it doesn't make the future any better to take them hard; third, human affairs aren't worth taking very seriously; and, finally, grief prevents the very thing we most need in such circumstances from coming into play as quickly as possible.

What are you referring to?

Deliberation. We must accept what has happened as we would the fall of the dice, and then arrange our affairs in whatever way reason determines to be best. We mustn't hug the hurt part and spend our time weeping and wailing like children when they trip. Instead, we should always accustom our souls to turn as quickly as possible to healing the disease and putting the disaster right, replacing lamentation with cure.

That would be the best way to deal with misfortune, at any rate.

Accordingly, we say that it is the best part of us that is willing to follow this rational calculation.

Clearly.

Then won't we also say that the part that leads us to dwell on our misfortunes and to lamentation, and that can never get enough of these things, is irrational, idle, and a friend of cowardice?

We certainly will.

Now, this excitable character admits of many multicolored imitations. But a rational and quiet character, which always remains pretty well the same, is neither easy to imitate nor easy to understand when imitated, especially not by a crowd consisting of all sorts of people gathered together at a theater festival, for the experience being imitated is alien to them.

Absolutely.

Clearly, then, an imitative poet isn't by nature related to the part of the soul that rules in such a character, and, if he's to attain a good reputation with the majority of people, his cleverness isn't directed to pleasing it. Instead, he's related to the excitable and multicolored character, since it is easy to imitate.

Clearly.

Therefore, we'd be right to take him and put him beside a painter as his counterpart. Like a painter, he produces work that is inferior with respect to truth and that appeals to a part of the soul that is similarly inferior rather than to the best part. So we were right not to admit him into a city that is to be well governed, for he arouses, nourishes, and strengthens this part of the soul and so destroys the rational one, in just the way that someone destroys the better sort of citizens when he strengthens the vicious ones and surrenders the city to them. Similarly, we'll say that an imitative poet puts a bad constitution in the soul of each individual by making images that are far removed from the truth and by gratifying the irrational part, which cannot distinguish the large and the small but believes that the same things are large at one time and small at another.

That's right.

However, we haven't yet brought the most serious charge against imitation, namely, that with a few rare exceptions it is able to corrupt even decent people, for that's surely an altogether terrible thing.

It certainly is, if indeed it can do that.

Listen, then, and consider whether it can or not. When even the best of us hear Homer or some other tragedian imitating one of the heroes sorrowing and making a long lamenting speech or singing and beating his breast, you know that we enjoy it, give ourselves up to following it, sympathize with the hero, take his sufferings seriously, and praise as a good poet the one who affects us most in this way.

Of course we do.

But when one of us suffers a private loss, you realize that the opposite happens. We pride ourselves if we are able to keep quiet and master our grief, for we think that this is the manly thing to do and that the behavior we praised before is womanish.

I do realize that.

Then are we right to praise it? Is it right to look at someone behaving in a way that we would consider unworthy and shameful and to enjoy and praise it rather than being disgusted by it?

No, by god, that doesn't seem reasonable.

No, at least not if you look at it in the following way.

How?

If you reflect, first, that the part of the soul that is forcibly controlled in our private misfortunes and that hungers for the satisfaction of weeping and wailing, because it desires these things by nature, is the very part that receives satisfaction and enjoyment from poets, and, second, that the part of ourselves that is best by nature, since it hasn't been adequately educated either by reason or habit, relaxes its guard over the lamenting part when it is watching the sufferings of somebody else. The reason it does so is this: It thinks that there is no shame involved for it in praising and pitying another man who, in spite of his claim to goodness, grieves excessively. Indeed, it thinks that there is a definite gain involved in doing so, namely, pleasure. And it wouldn't want to be deprived of that by despising the whole poem. I suppose that only a few are able to figure out that enjoyment of other people's sufferings is necessarily transferred to our own and that the pitying part, if it is nourished and strengthened on the sufferings of others, won't be easily held in check when we ourselves suffer.

That's very true.

And doesn't the same argument apply to what provokes laughter? If there are any jokes that you yourself would be ashamed to tell but that you very much enjoy hearing and don't detest as something evil in comic plays or in private, aren't you doing the same thing as in the case of what provokes pity? The part of you that wanted to tell the jokes and that was held back by your reason, for fear of being thought a buffoon, you then release, not realizing that, by making it strong in this way, you will be led into becoming a figure of fun where your own affairs are concerned.

Yes, indeed.

And in the case of sex, anger, and all the desires, pleasures, and pains that we say accompany all our actions, poetic imitation has the very same effect on us. It nurtures and waters them and establishes them as rulers in us when they ought to wither and be ruled, for that way we'll become better and happier rather than worse and more wretched.

I can't disagree with you.

And so, Glaucon, when you happen to meet those who praise Homer and say that he's the poet who educated Greece, that it's worth taking up his works in order to learn how to manage and educate people, and that one should arrange one's whole life in accordance with his teachings, you should welcome these people and treat them as friends, since they're as good as they're capable of being, and you should agree that Homer is the most poetic of the tragedians and the first among them. But you should also know that hymns to the gods and eulogies to good people are the only poetry we can admit into our city. If you admit the pleasure-giving Muse, whether in lyric or epic poetry, pleasure and pain will be kings in your city instead of law or the thing that everyone has always believed to be best, namely, reason.

That's absolutely true.

Then let this be our defense—now that we've returned to the topic of poetry—that, in view of its nature, we had reason to banish it from the city earlier, for our argument compelled us to do so. But in case we are charged with a certain harshness and lack of sophistication, let's also tell poetry that there is an ancient quarrel between it and philosophy, which is evidenced by such expressions as "the dog yelping and shrieking at its master," "great in the empty eloquence of fools," "the mob of wise men that has mastered Zeus," and "the subtle thinkers, beggars all." Nonetheless, if the poetry that aims at pleasure and imitation has any argument to bring forward that proves it ought to have a place in a well-governed city, we at least would be glad to admit it, for we are well aware of the charm it exercises. But, be that as it may, to betray what one believes to be the truth is impious. What about you, Glaucon, don't you feel the charm of the pleasure-giving Muse, especially when you study her through the eyes of Homer?

Very much so.

Therefore, isn't it just that such poetry should return from exile when it has successfully defended itself, whether in lyric or any other meter?

Certainly.

Then we'll allow its defenders, who aren't poets themselves but lovers of poetry, to speak in prose on its behalf and to show that it not only gives pleasure but is beneficial both to constitutions and to human life. Indeed, we'll listen to them graciously, for we'd certainly profit if poetry were shown to be not only pleasant but also beneficial.

How could we fail to profit?

However, if such a defense isn't made, we'll behave like people who have fallen in love with someone but who force themselves to stay away from him, because they realize that their passion isn't beneficial. In the same way, because the love of this sort of poetry has been implanted in us by the upbringing we have received under our fine constitutions, we are well disposed to any proof that it is the best and truest thing. But if it isn't able to produce such a defense, then, whenever we listen to it, we'll repeat the argument we have just now put forward like an incantation so as to preserve ourselves from slipping back into that childish passion for poetry which the majority of people have. And we'll go on chanting that such poetry is not to be taken seriously or treated as a serious undertaking with some kind of hold on the truth, but that anyone who is anxious about the constitution within him must be careful when he hears it and must continue to believe what we have said about it.

I completely agree. . . .

2

ART AS COGNITION: ARISTOTLE

Aristotle (384–322 B.C.) shares with his teacher Plato a conception of art as imitation or, to employ the term used in this translation, *representation*. Unlike Plato, however, Aristotle is well disposed toward the arts in general and toward tragic drama in particular: Rather than competing with philosophy in the business of truth telling, art works in tandem with it. For Aristotle, a well-constructed tragedy is as suited to convey truths about human nature as is a philosophic treatise.

Despite his respect for art, Aristotle's writings lack Plato's mastery of literary form. Those of his works we still have often appear to be incomplete texts derived from notebooks and lecture notes. This accounts, in part, for their difficulty. Nonetheless, the ideas these texts contain—as well as the enormous influence they have exerted—justify the effort to unpack their concentrated content.

In his *Poetics,* from which this reading is excerpted, Aristotle describes the nature of poetry, which for him, as for Plato, means literary representation in general. The bulk of the text is an examination of tragic drama, one of ancient Greece's most highly developed art forms.

Aristotle sees all art, including music, dance, literature, painting, and sculpture, as representational. What poetry represents, however, is not the actual world, as Plato had contended, but things as they might or could be. This emphasis on the *possible* as the domain of art marks an important characteristic of Aristotle's theory and one that contributes to his positive assessment of the value of art.

Aristotle also claims that we find art pleasurable in virtue of its representational character. Because we learn from artistic representation, we can enjoy an artwork whose content would disgust us if it were real. Think, for example, of Oedipus returning to the stage after gouging out his eyes.

Although we would be repulsed by such a sight were it real, when we experience it in Sophocles' masterpiece we learn from the dramatic presentation of Oedipus's fate and take pleasure in it. Aristotle's emphasis on art's ability to teach makes his a cognitive theory of art.

The tendency, evident everywhere in Aristotle's philosophy, to classify related phenomena as species of a single genus reflects his training as a biologist. In the *Poetics,* this accounts for his stress on how the arts differ according to their media, objects, and manner of representation. These differentiae distinguish the types of art from one another.

Tragic drama is the art form analyzed in greatest detail. For Aristotle, tragedy represents serious action in dramatic form. Its purpose is to bring about a catharsis, a purging of the emotions, through the experience of fear and pity. Each element of this definition calls for explanation, and Aristotle duly expands on them. Important for our purposes is Aristotle's view that his definition allows him to rank certain types of tragedy above others because they more fully instantiate tragedy's essence. So, for example, he argues that it is better for a tragedy to concern someone with whom we can identify, thus neither markedly better nor markedly worse than most of us, who makes a mistake and suffers for it. Although Aristotle does not himself defend this claim, other than to say such tragedies best realize the art form's function or essence, the clear implication is that a protagonist of this kind is more likely to induce emotional catharsis.

The form of philosophic argument Aristotle uses here is known as teleological. *Telos* is the Greek word for goal or purpose. A philosophic account is teleological if it posits some goal or purpose and then shows how the relevant phenomena achieve it. Thus, Aristotle's conception of tragedy is teleological because he derives various claims about what tragedies should be like from his understanding of the art's goal or purpose. In fact, most of the discussion of tragedy in the *Poetics* is a teleological assessment of classic Greek drama.

STUDY QUESTIONS ON THE READING

1. How convincing do you find Aristotle's attempt to provide an account of our interest in art? Is our pleasure in art always cognitive? Why or why not?

2. Explain Aristotle's definition of tragedy. What element(s) does he see as central to tragedy, and why?

3. Aristotle claims that "poetry is a more serious and philosophical thing than history." What does he mean by this claim? Do you agree? Is it important for a tragedy to be more serious and philosophical than, say, history? Why or why not?

4. Aristotle says one type of tragic plot is the best. What is it, and why does he think it best?

5. Aristotle distinguishes between spectacle and the structure of incidents in a tragedy. How would you explain this distinction? Do you think it applies to contemporary works as well? Do you agree with Aristotle's contention that spectacle is less significant than the structure of incident? How would this apply to films you enjoy?

6. Does it make sense to say that tragedy has an essence and that tragedies can be ranked by how well they realize this essence? Explain.

7. Plato and Aristotle have very different views of how art affects its viewers. Whose view do you find more convincing, and why?

❖

ARISTOTLE: THE POETICS

CH. I

To discuss the art of poetry in general, as well as the potential of each of its types; to explain the unity of plot required for successful poetic composition; also to analyse the number and nature of the component parts of poetry; and to deal similarly with the other questions which belong to this same method of enquiry—these are my proposed topics, beginning in the natural way from first principles.

Now, epic and tragic poetry, as well as comedy and dithyramb (and most music for the pipe or lyre), are all, taken as a whole, kinds of mimesis [representation or imitation]. But they differ from one another in three respects: namely, in the *media* or the *objects* or the *mode* of mimesis. For just as there are people who produce mimetic images of many things in the media of colours and shapes (some relying on a skilled art, some on practice), and others who use the medium of the voice, so in the case of all the arts mentioned above mimesis is effected in the media of rhythm, language and melody.

But these can be employed separately or in combination, as follows:

(a) the arts of the pipe and lyre (and any other arts with a similar potential, such as that of the pan-pipes) use melody and rhythm alone;

(b) the art of dancing presents mimesis in the medium of rhythm without melody (for dancers, through the rhythms which shape their movements, engage in the mimesis of character, emotions and actions);

(c) the art which employs language alone, or language in metrical form (whether in a combination of metres or just one kind), is still without a name. For we have no common name for the mimes of Sophron and Xenarchus and Socratic dialogues, nor for any mimetic work which might be written in iambic trimeters or elegiac couplets or something else of this kind. . . . Homer and Empedocles have nothing in common except their metre; and so, while one must call the former a poet, the latter should be called a natural philosopher rather than a poet. A corollary is that even if someone should produce a mimesis in a mixture of all the metres (as Chairemon did in his mixed rhapsody, *Centaur*), he too must be called a poet. So let distinctions of these kinds be drawn in these matters.

(d) Finally, there are some poetic arts which employ all the stated media (that is, rhythm, melody and metre), such as dithyramb, nome, tragedy and comedy: they differ, though, in that some use all throughout, some only in parts. These, then, are the distinctions between the arts as regards the media of their mimesis.

CH. 2

Since mimetic artists portray people in action, and since these people must be either good or bad (for men's characters practically always conform to these categories alone), they can portray people better than ourselves, worse than ourselves, or on the same level. The same is true in painting: Polygnotus portrayed men who are superior, Pauson worse, and Dionysius on the same level. And it is evident that each of the stated types of mimesis will exhibit these differences, and will thus be distinguishable according to the variations in the objects which it represents. For such differences are possible in dancing, and in music for the pipe and lyre, as well as in the arts which use language alone or language in metre: for instance, Homer represented superior men, Cleophon men like us, Hegemon of Thasos (the first writer of parodies) and Nicochares (author of the *Deiliad*) inferior men. . . . This very distinction also separates tragedy from comedy: the latter tends to represent men worse than present humanity, the former better.

CH. 3

Beside the two already cited, there is a third distinction: namely, the mode in which the various objects are represented. For it is possible to use the same media to offer a mimesis of the same objects in any one of three ways: first, by alternation between narrative and dramatic impersonation (as in Homeric poetry); second, by employing the voice of narrative without variation; third, by a wholly dramatic presentation of the agents.

So then, as indicated at the outset, mimesis can be distinguished in these three respects: by its *media,* its *objects,* and its *modes.* Consequently, in one respect Sophocles uses the same mimesis as Homer, for in both cases the objects are good men; while in another respect, Sophocles and Aristophanes are parallel, since both use the mimetic mode of dramatic enactment.

It is because of this that some people derive the term *drama* itself from the enactive mimesis of agents. . . .

CH. 4

Poetry in general can be seen to owe its existence to two causes, and these are rooted in nature. First, there is man's natural propensity, from childhood onwards, to engage in mimetic activity (and this distinguishes man from other creatures, that he is thoroughly mimetic and through mimesis takes his first steps in understanding). Second, there is the pleasure which all men take in mimetic objects.

An indication of the latter can be observed in practice: for we take pleasure in contemplating the most precise images of things whose sight in itself causes us pain—such as the appearance of the basest animals, or of corpses. Here too the explanation lies in the fact that great pleasure is derived from exercising the understanding, not just for philosophers but in the same way for all men, though their capacity for it may be limited. It is for this reason that men enjoy looking at images, because what happens is that, as they contemplate them, they apply their understanding and reasoning to each element (identifying this as an image of such-and-such a man, for instance). Since, if it happens that one has no previous familiarity with the sight, then the object will not give pleasure *qua* mimetic object but because of its craftmanship, or colour, or for some other such reason.

Given, then, that mimetic activity comes naturally to us—together with melody and rhythm (for it is evident that metres are species of rhythm)—it was originally those with a special natural capacity who, through a slow and gradual process, brought poetry into being by their improvisations. And poetry was split into two types according to the poets' own characters: the more dignified made noble actions and noble agents the object of their mimesis; while lighter poets took the actions of base men and began by composing invectives, just as the other group produced hymns and encomia. . . .

To consider whether tragedy is by now sufficiently developed in its types—judging it both in itself and in relation to audiences—is a separate matter. At any rate, having come into being from an improvisational origin (which is true of both tragedy and comedy, the first starting from the leaders of the dithyramb, the second from the leaders of the phallic songs which are still customary in many cities), tragedy was gradually enhanced as poets made progress with the potential which they could see in the genre. And when it had gone through many changes, tragedy ceased to evolve, since it had attained its natural fulfilment.

It was Aeschylus who first increased the number of actors from one to two, reduced the choral parts, and gave speech the leading role; the third actor and scene-painting came with Sophocles. A further aspect of change concerns scale: after a period of slight plots and humorous diction, it was only at a late stage that tragedy attained dignity by departing from the style of satyr-plays, and that the iambic metre replaced the trochaic tetrameter. To begin with, poets used the tetrameter because the poetry had more of the tone of a satyr-play and of dance; and it was only when speech was brought in that the nature of the genre found its appropriate metre (the iambic is the most colloquial of metres, as we see from the fact that we frequently produce the rhythm of iambic lines in our conversation, while we rarely produce hexameters and only by departing from the register of ordinary speech).

There were further developments concerning the number of episodes, and we shall take as read the other particular elaborations which are said to have been effected, since it would be a large task to give a thorough account of every detail.

CH. 5

Comedy, as I earlier said, is a mimesis of men who are inferior, but not in a way which involves complete evil: the comic is one species of the shameful. For the comic is constituted by a fault and a mark of shame, but lacking in pain or destruction: to take an obvious example, the comic mask is ugly and misshapen, but does not express pain. Now, while the stages of tragedy's development, and those responsible for them, have been preserved, comedy's have not been, because it was not originally given serious attention. . . .

Epic conforms with tragedy insofar as it is a mimesis, in spoken metre, of ethically serious subjects; but it differs by virtue of using *only* spoken verse and of being in the narrative mode. There is also a difference of scale: whereas tragedy strives as far as possible to limit itself to a single day, epic is distinctive by its lack of a temporal limit, although in the early days poets of tragedy were as free in this respect as those of epic. The parts of epic are all common to tragedy, but the latter has some peculiar to itself. Consequently, whoever knows the difference between a good and a bad tragedy knows the same for epic too; for epic's attributes all belong to tragedy as well, though not all of tragedy's are shared by epic.

CH. 6

I shall discuss epic mimesis and comedy later. But let us deal with tragedy by taking up the definition of its essential nature which arises out of what has so far been said.

Tragedy, then, is a representation of an action which is serious, complete, and of a certain magnitude—in language which is garnished in various forms in its different parts—in the mode of dramatic enactment, not narrative—and through the arousal of pity and fear effecting the *katharsis* of such emotions.

By "garnished" language I mean with rhythm and melody; and by the 'various forms' I mean that some parts use spoken metre, and others use lyric song. Since the mimesis is enacted by agents, we can deduce that one element of tragedy must be the adornment of visual spectacle, while others are lyric poetry and verbal style, for it is in these that the mimesis is presented. By 'style' I mean the composition of the spoken metres; the meaning of 'lyric poetry' is entirely evident.

Since tragedy is a representation of an action, and is enacted by agents, who must be characterised in both their character and their thought (for it is through these that we can also judge the qualities of their actions, and it is in their actions that all men either succeed or fail), we have the plot-structure as the mimesis of the action (for by this term 'plot-structure' I mean the organisation of the events) while characterisation is what allows us to judge the nature of the agents, and 'thought' represents the parts in which by their speech they put forward arguments or make statements.

So then, tragedy as a whole must have six elements which make it what it is: they are plot-structure, character, style, thought, spectacle, lyric poetry. Two of these are the media, one the mode, and three the objects, of the mimesis—and that embraces everything. . . .

The most important of these elements is the structure of events, because tragedy is a representation not of people as such but of actions and life, and both happiness and unhappiness rest on action. The goal is a certain activity, not a qualitative state; and while men do have certain qualities by virtue of their character, it is in their actions that they achieve, or fail to achieve, happiness.

It is not, therefore, the function of the agents' actions to allow the portrayal of their characters; it is, rather, for the sake of their actions that characterisation is included. So, the events and the plot-structure are the goal of tragedy, and the goal is what matters most of all.

Besides, without action you would not have a tragedy, but one without character would be feasible, for the tragedies of most recent poets are lacking in characterisation, and in general there are many such poets. Compare, among painters, the difference between Zeuxis and Polygnotus: while Polygnotus is a fine portrayer of character, Zeuxis' art has no characterisation. Furthermore, if a poet strings together speeches to illustrate character, even allowing he composes them well in style and thought, he will not achieve the stated aim of tragedy. Much more effective will be a play with a plot and structure of events, even if it is deficient in style and thought.

In addition to these considerations, tragedy's greatest means of emotional power are components of the plot-structure: namely, reversals and recognitions. Moreover, it is symptomatic that poetic novices can achieve precision in style and characterisation before they acquire it in plot-construction—as was the case with virtually all the early poets. And so, the plot-structure is the first principle and, so to speak, the soul of tragedy, while characterisation is the element of second importance. (An analogous point holds for painting: a random distribution of the most attractive colours would never yield as much pleasure as a definite image without colour.) Tragedy is a mimesis of action, and only for the sake of this is it mimesis of the agents themselves.

Third in importance is thought: this is the capacity to produce pertinent and appropriate arguments, which is the task in prose speeches of the arts of politics and rhetoric. The older poets used to make their characters speak in a political vein, whereas modern poets do so in a rhetorical vein. Character is the element which reveals the nature of a moral choice, in cases where it is not anyway clear what a person is choosing or avoiding (and so speeches in which the speaker chooses or avoids nothing at all do not possess character); while thought arises in passages where people show that something is or is not the case, or present some universal proposition.

The fourth element is style: as previously said, I mean by this term the verbal expression achieved through the choice of words, which has the same force whether in verse or in prose. Of the remaining elements, lyric poetry is the most important of garnishings, while spectacle is emotionally powerful but is the least integral of all to the poet's art: for the potential of tragedy does not depend upon public performance and actors; and, besides, the art of the maskmaker carries more weight than the poet's as regards the elaboration of visual effects.

CH. 7

Given these definitions, my next topic is to prescribe the form which the structure of events ought to take, since this is the first and foremost component of tragedy. We have already laid down that tragedy is a representation of an action which is complete, whole and of a certain magnitude (for something can be whole but of no magnitude).

By 'whole' I mean possessing a beginning, middle and end. By 'beginning' I mean that which does not have a necessary connection with a preceding event, but which can itself give rise naturally to some further fact or occurrence. An "end," by contrast, is something which naturally occurs after a preceding event, whether by necessity or as a general rule, but need not be followed by anything else. The 'middle' involves causal connections with both what precedes and what ensues. Consequently, well designed plot-structures ought not to begin or finish at arbitrary points, but to follow the principles indicated.

Moreover, any beautiful object, whether a living creature or any other structure of parts, must possess not only ordered arrangement but also an appropriate scale (for beauty is grounded in both size and order). A creature could not be beautiful if it is either too small—for perception of it is practically instantaneous and so cannot be experienced—or too great, for contemplation of it cannot be a single experience, and it is not possible to derive a sense of unity and wholeness from our perception of it (imagine an animal a thousand miles long). Just, therefore, as a beautiful body or creature must have some size, but one which allows it to be perceived all together, so plot-structures should be of a length which can be easily held in the memory.

An artistic definition of length cannot be related to dramatic competitions and the spectators' concentration. For if a hundred tragedies had to compete, they would measure them by the water-clock (as people say they once did). The limit which accords with the true nature of the matter is this: beauty of size favours as large a structure as possible, provided that coherence is maintained. A concise definition is to say that the sufficient limit of a poem's scale is the scope required for a probable or necessary succession of events which produce a transformation either from affliction to prosperity, or the reverse.

CH. 8

A plot-structure does not possess unity (as some believe) by virtue of centring on an individual. For just as a particular thing may have many random properties, some of which do not combine to make a single entity, so a particular character may perform many actions which do not yield a single 'action,' Consequently, all those poets who have written a *Heracleid* or *Theseid,* or the like, are evidently at fault: they believe that because Heracles was a single individual, a plot-structure about him ought thereby to have unity. As in other respects, Homer is exceptional by the fineness of his insight into this point, whether we regard this as an acquired ability or a natural endowment of his: although composing an *Odyssey,* he did not include everything that happened to the hero (such as his wounding on Parnassus or his pretence of madness at the levy—events which involved no necessary or probable connection with one another). Instead, he constructed the *Odyssey* around a single action of the kind I mean, and likewise with the *Iliad.*

So then, just as in the other mimetic arts a unitary mimesis is a representation of a unitary object, so the plot-structure, as the mimesis of action, should be a representation of a unitary and complete action; and its parts, consisting of the events, should be so constructed that the displacement or removal of any one of them will disturb and disjoint the work's wholeness. For anything whose presence or absence has no clear effect cannot be counted an integral part of the whole.

CH. 9

It is a further clear implication of what has been said that the poet's task is to speak not of events which have occurred, but of the kind of events which *could* occur, and are possible by the standards of probability or necessity. For it is not the use or absence of metre which distinguishes poet and historian (one could put Herodotus' work into verse, but it would be no less a sort of history with it than without it): the difference lies in the fact that the one speaks of events which have occurred, the other of the sort of events which could occur.

It is for this reason that poetry is both more philosophical and more serious than history, since poetry speaks more of universals, history of particulars. A 'universal' comprises the *kind* of speech or action which belongs by probability or necessity to a certain *kind* of character—something which poetry aims at *despite* its addition of particular names. A 'particular,' by contrast, is (for example) what Alcibiades did or experienced.

This point has become clear in the case of comedy, where it is only after constructing a plot in terms of probable events that they give the characters ordinary names, so diverging from the iambic poets' practice of writing about individuals. In tragedy, on the other hand, the poets hold to the actual names. (The reason for this is that people are ready to believe in what is possible; and while we may not yet believe in the possibility of things that have not already happened, actual events are evidently possible, otherwise they would not have occurred.) Even so, there are some tragedies in which one or two of the familiar names are kept, while others are due to the poet; and some plays in which all are new, as in Agathon's *Antheus:* for in this play both the events and the names are equally the poet's work, yet the pleasure it gives is just as great. So, fidelity to the traditional plots which are the subject of tragedies is not to be sought at all costs. Indeed, to do this is absurd, since even familiar material is familiar only to a minority, but it can still afford pleasure to all.

It is clear, then, from what has been said that the poet should be a maker of plot-structures rather than of verses, in so far as his status as poet depends on mimesis, and the object of his mimesis is actions. And he is just as much a poet even if the material of his poetry comprises actual events, since there is no reason why *some* historical events should not be in conformity with probability, and it is with respect to probability that the poet can make his poetry from them. . . .

CH. 10

Plot-structures can be divided into the simple and the complex, for the actions which they represent consist naturally of these types. By a 'simple' action I mean one which is, as earlier defined, continuous and unitary, but whose transformation occurs without reversal or recognition. A 'complex' action is one whose transformation involves recognition or reversal, or both. Reversal and recognition should arise from the intrinsic structure of the plot, so that what results follows by either necessity or probability from the preceding events: for it makes a great difference whether things happen because of one another, or only *after* one another.

CH. 11

Reversal, as indicated, is a complete swing in the direction of the action; but this, as we insist, must conform to probability or necessity. Take, for example, Sophocles' *Oedipus Tyrannus*, where the person comes to bring Oedipus happiness, and intends to free him from his fear about his mother; but he produces the opposite effect, by revealing Oedipus' identity. And in *Lynceus* the one person is led off to die, while Danaus follows to kill him; yet it comes about that the latter's death and the former's rescue result from the chain of events.

Recognition, as the very name shows, is a change from ignorance to knowledge, bringing the characters into either a close bond, or enmity, with one another, and concerning matters which bear on their prosperity or affliction. The finest recognition occurs in direct conjunction with reversal—as with the one in the *Oedipus*. There are, of course, other kinds of recognition, for recognition can relate to inanimate or fortuitous objects, or reveal that someone has, or has not, committed a deed. But the type I have mentioned is the one which is most integral to the plot-structure and its action: for such a combination of recognition and reversal will produce pity or fear (and it is events of this kind that tragedy, on our definition, is a mimesis of), since both affliction and prosperity will hinge on such circumstances. . . .

Well then, reversal and recognition form two components of the plot-structure; the third is suffering. To the definitions of reversal and recognition already given we can add that of suffering: a destructive or painful action, such as visible deaths, torments, woundings, and other things of the same kind. . . .

CH. 13

It follows on from my earlier argument that I should define what ought to be aimed at and avoided in plot-construction, as well as the source of tragedy's effect. Since, then, the structure of the finest tragedy should be complex, not simple, and, moreover, should portray fearful and pitiful events (for this is the distinctive feature of this type of mimesis), it is to begin with clear that:

- (a) good men should not be shown passing from prosperity to affliction, for this is neither fearful nor pitiful but repulsive;
- (b) wicked men should not be shown passing from affliction to prosperity, for this is the most untragic of all possible cases and is entirely defective (it is neither moving nor pitiful nor fearful);
- (c) the extremely evil man should not fall from prosperity to affliction, for such a plot-structure might move us, but would not arouse pity or fear, since pity is felt towards one whose affliction is undeserved, fear towards one who is like ourselves (so what happens in such a case will be neither pitiful nor fearful).

We are left, then, with the figure who falls between these types. Such a man is one who is not preeminent in virtue and justice, and one who falls into affliction not because of evil and wickedness, but because of a certain fallibility (*hamartia*). He will belong to the class of those who enjoy great esteem and prosperity, such as Oedipus, Thyestes, and outstanding men from such families . . .

The second-best pattern (which some hold to be the best) is the kind which involves a double structure (like the *Odyssey*) and contrasting outcomes for good and bad characters. It is the weakness of audiences which produces the view of this type's superiority; poets are led to give the spectators what they want. But this is not the proper pleasure to be derived from tragedy—more like that of comedy: for in that genre people who are outright foes in the plot (say, Orestes and Aegisthus) go off as friends at the end, and nobody is killed.

CH. 14

The effect of fear and pity can arise from theatrical spectacle, but it can also arise from the intrinsic structure of events, and it is this which matters more and is the task of a superior poet. For the plot-structure ought to be so composed that, even without seeing a performance, anyone who hears the events which occur will experience terror and pity as a result of the outcome; this is what someone would feel while hearing the plot of the *Oedipus*. To produce this effect through spectacle is not part of the poet's art, and calls for material resources; while those who use spectacle to produce an effect not of the fearful but only of the sensational fall quite outside the sphere of tragedy: for it is not every pleasure, but the appropriate one, which should be sought from tragedy. And since the poet ought to provide the pleasure which derives from pity and fear by means of mimesis, it is evident that this ought to be embodied in the events of the plot.

Let us, then, take up the question of what sort of circumstances make an impression of terror or pity. These are the only possibilities: such actions must involve dealings between those who are bonded by kinship or friendship; or between enemies; or between those who are neither. Well, if enemy faces enemy, neither the deed nor the prospect of it will be pitiful (except for the intrinsic potential of visible suffering); and the same is true of those whose relations are neutral. What must be sought are cases where suffering befalls bonded relations—when brother kills brother (or is about to, or to do something similar), son kills father, mother kills son, or son kills mother. Now, one cannot alter traditional plots (I mean, Clytemnestra's death at Orestes' hands, or Eriphyle's at Alcmaeon's) but the individual poet should find ways of handling even these to good effect.

I should explain more clearly what I mean by 'to good effect.' It is possible

(a) for the deed to be done with full knowledge and understanding, as the old poets used to arrange it, and in the way that Euripides too made Medea kill her children;
(b) for the deed to be done, but by agents who do not know the terrible thing they are doing, and who then later recognise their bond-relationship to the other, as with Sophocles' *Oedipus* (that is an instance where the deed occurs outside the drama, but Astydamas' *Alcmaeon*, and Telegonus in *Odysseus Wounded*, supply examples within the play itself);
(c) alternatively, for one who is on the point of committing an incurable deed in ignorance to come to a recognition before he has done it.

These are the only possibilities, for either the deed is done or it is not, and the agents must either know the facts or be ignorant of them. Of these cases, the worst is where the agent, in full knowledge, is on the point of acting, yet fails to do so: for this is repulsive and untragic (as it lacks suffering). Consequently, poets only rarely do this (for instance, Haemon's intention against Creon in *Antigone*). Not much better is for the deed to be executed in such a case. A superior arrangement is where the agent acts in ignorance, and discovers the truth after acting: for here there is nothing repulsive, and the recognition produces a powerful effect. But the best case is the last I have listed—for example, where Merope is about to kill her son in the *Cresphontes*, but does not do so because she recognises him; likewise with sister and brother in *Iphigeneia*, and in the *Helle*, where the son, on the point of handing her over, recognises his mother. Hence, as said before, tragedies concentrate on a few families. Luck not art led poets to find how to achieve such an effect in their plots; so they have to turn to the families in which such sufferings have occurred.

Enough, then, about the structure of events and the required qualities of plots. . . .

CH. 25

On the subject of problems and their solutions, a clear idea of the number and types of issue can be gained from the following considerations. Since the poet, like the painter or any other image-maker, is a mimetic artist, he must in any particular instance use mimesis to portray one of three objects: the sort of things which were or are the case; the sort of things men say and think to be the case; the sort of things that should be the case. This material is presented in language which has foreign terms, metaphors, and many special elements; for we allow these to poets.

Furthermore, correct standards in poetry are not identical with those in politics or in any other particular art. Two kinds of failure are possible in poetry—one intrinsic, and the other contingent. If a poet lacks the capacity to achieve what he sets out to portray, the failure is one of poetic art. But this is not so if the poet *intends* to portray something which is erroneous, such as a horse with its two right legs simultaneously forward, or something which is a technical mistake in medicine or any other field. So, it is from these premises that the solutions to the charges contained in problems must be found.

Firstly, points concerning poetic art itself. Suppose the poet has produced impossibilities, then granted he has erred. But poetic standards will be satisfied, provided he achieves the goal of the art (which has been earlier discussed): that is, if by these means he increases the emotional impact either of the particular part or of some other part of the work. (An example is the pursuit of Hector.) If, however, the goal could be achieved better, or just as successfully, without the particular technical error, then the mistake is not acceptable: for, if possible, poetry should be altogether free of mistakes.

One must also ask whether the error concerns the poetic art or something extrinsic to it. For if, out of ignorance, a painter portrays a female deer *with* horns, this has less significance than attaches to a failure in mimesis.

Next, if the charge is one of falsehood, a possible defence is that things are being portrayed as they *should* be, just as Sophocles said that his poetic characters were as they should be, while Euripides' reflected ordinary reality. If neither category applies, then a solution may appeal to what people say, for instance in matters concerning the gods: as, while it may satisfy neither morality nor truth to say such things (and Xenophanes' criticisms may be justified), nevertheless people *do* say them.

Another possible defence is that something may be imperfect but does represent how things once were. Take the example concerning weapons ('Their spears stood upright on the butt-end'): this used to be the practice at the time, as it still is with the Illyrians. When asking whether someone has spoken or acted morally or otherwise, one should look to see not just if the deed or utterance is good or evil, but also to the identity of the agent or speaker, to the person with whom he deals, and to the occasion, means and purpose of what is done (e.g. whether the aim is to effect a greater good, or prevent a greater evil).

Other points must be resolved by consideration of style, for example by reference to a foreign term [. . .]. A passage may involve metaphor: for instance, 'All gods and men slept through the night,' while in the same passage Homer says 'whenever Agamemnon gazed across to the Trojan plane and the din of flutes and pipes.' 'All' stands by metaphor for 'many,' since all is a species of many [. . .]. Accentuation may be relevant, as with the solutions proposed by Hippias of Thasos [. . .] or punctuation [. . .] or double meaning [. . .] or verbal usage [. . .].

Whenever a word appears to entail a contradiction, one should consider how many meanings are possible in the linguistic context [. . .]. One should adopt the opposite procedure to the one which Glaucon describes by saying that some people make an unreasonable assumption and proceed to base their argument on acceptance of it; then, if something contradicts their own preconception, they criticise the poet as though *he* had made the initial assumption. This has happened in the case of Icarius: people presuppose that he was a Laconian, so they find it absurd that Telemachus did not meet him when he went to Sparta. But perhaps the Cephallenians' version is correct, for they claim that Odysseus married one of theirs, and that the father was called Icadius not Icarius. It is plausible that the problem is due to a mistake.

In general, cases of impossibility should be resolved by reference to the requirements of poetry, or to a conception of the superior, or to people's beliefs. Poetic requirements make a plausible impossibility preferable to an implausible possibility . . . not such as Zeuxis painted them, but better, for the artist should surpass his model. Irrationalities should be referred to 'what people say,' or shown not to be irrational (since it is likely that some things should occur contrary to likelihood). Contradictory utterances should be examined according to the same principles as verbal refutations, to see whether the sense is the same and has the same reference, and in the same way—if a poet is to be convicted of actually contradicting either himself or something which can be sensibly assumed. But it is correct to find fault with both illogicality and moral baseness, if there is no necessity for them and if the poet makes no use of the illogicality (as with Euripides and the case of Aegeus) or the baseness (as with Menelaus's in *Orestes*).

The charges brought against poets fall under five headings: impossibilities, irrationalities, morally harmful elements, contradictions, and offences against the true standards of the art. The solutions should be sought from the categories discussed above. . . .

3

ART AS OBJECT OF TASTE: DAVID HUME

David Hume (1711–1776), the eminent Scottish philosopher, is best known as an empiricist and a skeptic. In regard to art, Hume is less concerned with finding a definition of art than with exploring the question of whether there are objective standards for assessing the goodness of works of art.

Hume presents us with an antinomy—a pair of ideas, each with a claim on truth but seemingly mutually irreconcilable. On the one hand, most people believe it is possible to make critical judgments about the quality of works of art. When we think about comparing a great work of art, say the *Mona Lisa,* with a work that is merely pleasing, say a Norman Rockwell illustration, there is general agreement that the da Vinci painting is objectively better than the Rockwell. Consideration of such cases—Hume's examples are comparisons of the writers Ogilby and Milton, as well as Bunyan and Addison—forces one to acknowledge objective standards for critical judgments about art. The other pole of Hume's antinomy results from a consideration of what grounds such judgments. He asserts it can be nothing but taste, that is, whether a work of art actually affects the "sentiments," to use his terminology.

Relying on the idea of a "natural equality of taste"—that one's tastes are simply one's own and not subject to correction by others—Hume reasons that a critical judgment can be nothing more than the expression of an idiosyncratic reaction to a work. It follows, then, that there can be no objective standards of judgment, a view that contradicts the earlier conclusion that there must be such.

To resolve this dilemma, Hume asserts that, as a matter of brute empirical fact, our nature is so constituted that certain features of works of art just happen to please all human beings. Our universal susceptibility to certain qualities ensures that there will be universal agreement that some works of art are more beautiful than others, and therefore objectively better.

Despite his efforts to ground aesthetic judgments about the value of works of art in a uniform human nature, Hume acknowledges that there will inevitably be some aesthetic disagreement. But how can he account for them? Here, Hume is forced to invoke factors either in the psychological makeup of individuals, or in shared cultural preferences, that interfere with a person's otherwise natural ability to appreciate the beauty of a meritorious work of art. Only those with "strong sense, united to delicate sentiment, improved by practice, perfected by comparison, and cleared of all prejudice" are capable of discerning those qualities in the work that make it truly good. Thus, unable to locate objectivity in artworks themselves, Hume judges that only certain people are so well qualified that their responses really count.

Study Questions on the Reading

1. Hume asserts that beauty is not a quality of things themselves. What does he think instead?

2. Hume alludes to the saying "There is no disputing about taste." Does he agree with this statement? Why or why not?

3. Do you agree that certain people are simply in a better position than others to make value judgments about the quality of works of art? Why?

4. Hume asserts that certain works of art are universally admired. Do you agree with this? How important is this claim to his account?

5. Cultural variations play a role in Hume's claim that there will always be disagreement about art. Do you think he over- or underestimates the importance of cultural differences? Why?

David Hume: Of the Standard of Taste

THE great variety of Taste, as well as of opinion, which prevails in the world, is too obvious not to have fallen under every one's observation. Men of the most confined knowledge are able to remark a difference of taste in the narrow circle of their acquaintance, even where the persons have been educated under the same government, and have early imbibed the same prejudices. But those, who can enlarge their view to contemplate distant nations and remote ages, are still more surprized at the great inconsistence and contrariety. We are apt to call *barbarous* whatever departs widely from our own taste and apprehension: But soon find the epithet of reproach retorted on us. And the highest arrogance and self-conceit is at last startled, on observing an equal assurance on all sides, and scruples, amidst such a contest of sentiment, to pronounce positively in its own favour.

As this variety of taste is obvious to the most careless enquirer; so will it be found, on examination, to be still greater in reality than in appearance. The sentiments of men often differ with regard to beauty and deformity of all kinds, even while their general discourse is the same. There are certain terms in every language, which import blame, and others praise; and all men, who use the same tongue, must agree in their application of them. Every voice is united in applauding elegance, propriety, simplicity, spirit in writing; and in blaming fustian, affectation, coldness, and a false brilliancy: But when critics come to particulars, this seeming unanimity vanishes; and it is found, that they had affixed a very different meaning to their expressions. In all matters of opinion and science, the case is opposite: The difference among men is there oftener found to lie in generals than in particulars; and to be less in reality than in appearance. An explanation of the terms commonly ends the controversy; and the disputants are surprized to find, that they had been quarrelling, while at bottom they agreed in their judgment. . . .

It is natural for us to seek a *Standard of Taste*; a rule, by which the various sentiments of men may be reconciled; at least, a decision, afforded, confirming one sentiment, and condemning another.

There is a species of philosophy, which cuts off all hopes of success in such an attempt, and represents the impossibility of ever attaining any standard of taste. The difference, it is said, is very wide between judgment and sentiment. All sentiment is right; because sentiment has a reference to nothing beyond itself, and is always real, wherever a man is conscious of it. But all determinations of the understanding are not right; because they have a reference to something beyond themselves, to wit, real matter of fact; and are not always conformable to that standard. Among a thousand different opinions which different men may entertain of the same subject, there is one, and but one, that is just and true; and the only difficulty is to fix and ascertain it. On the contrary, a thousand different sentiments, excited by the same object, are all right: Because no sentiment represents what is really in the object. It only marks a certain conformity or relation between the object and the organs or faculties of the mind; and if that conformity did not really exist, the sentiment could never possibly have being. Beauty is no quality in things themselves: It exists merely in the mind which contemplates them; and each mind perceives a different beauty. One person may even perceive deformity, where another is sensible of beauty; and every individual ought to acquiesce in his own sentiment, without pretending to regulate those of others. To seek the real beauty, or real deformity, is as fruitless an enquiry, as to pretend to ascertain the real sweet or real bitter. According to the disposition of the organs, the same object may be both sweet and bitter; and the proverb has justly determined it to be fruitless to dispute concerning tastes. It is very natural, and even quite necessary, to extend this axiom to mental, as well as bodily taste; and thus common sense, which is so often at variance with philosophy, especially with the sceptical kind, is found, in one instance at least, to agree in pronouncing the same decision.

But though this axiom, by passing into a proverb, seems to have attained the sanction of common sense; there is certainly a species of common sense which opposes it, at least serves to modify and restrain it. Whoever would assert an equality of genius and elegance between OGILBY and MILTON, or BUNYAN and ADDISON, would be thought to defend no less an extravagance, than if he had maintained a mole-hill to be as high as TENERIFFE, or a pond as extensive as the ocean. Though there may be found persons, who give the preference to the former authors; no one pays attention to such a taste; and we pronounce without scruple the sentiment of these pretended critics to be absurd and ridiculous. The principle of the natural equality of tastes is then totally forgot, and while we admit it on some occasions, where the objects seem near an equality, it appears an extravagant paradox, or rather a palpable absurdity, where objects so disproportioned are compared together.

It is evident that none of the rules of composition are fixed by reasonings *a priori*, or can be esteemed abstract conclusions of the understanding, from comparing those habitudes and relations of ideas, which are eternal and immutable. Their foundation is the same with that of all the practical sciences, experience; nor are they any thing but general observations, concerning what has been universally found to please in all countries and in all ages. Many of the beauties of poetry and even of eloquence are founded on falsehood and fiction, on hyperboles, metaphors, and an abuse or perversion of terms from their natural meaning. To check the sallies of the imagination, and to reduce every expression to geometrical truth and exactness, would be the most contrary to the laws of criticism; because it would produce a work, which, by universal experience, has been found the most insipid and disagreeable. But though poetry can never submit to exact truth, it must be confined by rules of art, discovered to the author either by genius or observation. If some negligent or irregular writers have pleased, they have not pleased by their transgressions of rule or order, but in spite of these transgressions: They have possessed other beauties, which were conformable to just criticism; and the force of these beauties has been able to overpower censure, and give the mind a satisfaction superior to the disgust arising from the blemishes. ARIOSTO pleases; but not by his monstrous and improbable fictions, by his bizarre mixture of the serious and comic styles, by the want of coherence in his stories, or by the continual interruptions of his narration. He charms by the force and clearness of his expression, by the readiness and variety of his inventions, and by his natural pictures of the passions, especially those of the gay and amorous kind: And however his faults may diminish our satisfaction, they are not able entirely to destroy it. Did our pleasure really arise from those parts of his poem, which we denominate faults, this would be no objection to criticism in general: It would only be an objection to those particular rules of criticism, which would establish such circumstances to be faults, and would represent them as universally blameable. If they are found to please, they cannot be faults; let the pleasure, which they produce, be ever so unexpected and unaccountable.

But though all the general rules of art are founded only on experience and on the observation of the common sentiments of human nature, we must not imagine, that, on every occasion, the feelings of men will be conformable to these rules. Those finer emotions of the mind are of a very tender and delicate nature, and require the concurrence of many favourable circumstances to make them play with facility and exactness, according to their general and established principles. The least exterior hindrance to such small springs, or the least internal disorder, disturbs their motion, and confounds the operation of the whole machine. When we would make an experiment of this nature, and would try the force of any beauty or deformity, we must choose with care a proper time and place, and bring the fancy to a suitable situation and disposition. A perfect serenity of mind, a recollection of thought, a due attention to the object; if any of these circumstances be wanting, our experiment will be fallacious, and we shall be unable to judge of the catholic and universal beauty. The relation, which nature has placed between the form and the sentiment, will at least be more obscure; and it will require greater accuracy to trace and discern it. We shall be able to ascertain its influence not so much from the operation of each particular beauty, as from the durable admiration, which attends those works, that have survived all the caprices of mode and fashion, all the mistakes of ignorance and envy.

The same HOMER, who pleased at ATHENS and ROME two thousand years ago, is still admired at PARIS and at LONDON. All the changes of climate, government, religion, and language, have not been able to obscure his glory. Authority or prejudice may give a temporary vogue to a bad poet or orator; but his reputation will never be durable or general. When his compositions are examined by posterity or by foreigners, the enchantment is dissipated, and his faults appear in their true colours. On the contrary, a real genius, the longer his works endure, and the more wide they are spread, the more sincere is the admiration which he meets with. Envy and jealousy have too much place in a narrow circle; and even familiar acquaintance with his person may diminish the applause due to his performances: But when these obstructions are removed, the beauties, which are naturally fitted to excite agreeable sentiments, immediately display their energy; and while the world endures, they maintain their authority over the minds of men.

It appears then, that, amidst all the variety and caprice of taste, there are certain general principles of approbation or blame, whose influence a careful eye may trace in all operations of the mind. Some particular forms or qualities, from the original structure of the internal fabric, are calculated to please, and others to displease; and if they fail of their effect in any particular instance, it is from some apparent defect or imperfection in the organ. A man in a fever would not insist on his palate as able to decide concerning flavours; nor would one, affected with the jaundice, pretend to give a verdict with regard to colours. In each creature, there is a sound and a defective state; and the former alone can be supposed to afford us a true standard of taste and sentiment. If, in the sound state of the organ, there be an entire or a considerable uniformity of sentiment among men, we may thence derive an idea of the perfect beauty; in like manner as the appearance of objects in day-light, to the eye of a man in health, is denominated their true and real colour, even while colour is allowed to be merely a phantasm of the senses.

Many and frequent are the defects in the internal organs, which prevent or weaken the influence of those general principles, on which depends our sentiment of beauty or deformity. Though some objects, by the structure of the mind, be naturally calculated to give pleasure, it is not to be expected, that in every individual the pleasure will be equally felt. Particular incidents and situations occur, which either throw a false light on the objects, or hinder the true from conveying to the imagination the proper sentiment and perception.

One obvious cause, why many feel not the proper sentiment of beauty, is the want of that *delicacy* of imagination, which is requisite to convey a sensibility of those finer emotions. This delicacy every one pretends to: Every one talks of it; and would reduce every kind of taste or sentiment to its standard. But as our intention in this essay is to mingle some light of the understanding with the feelings of sentiment, it will be proper to give a more accurate definition of delicacy, than has hitherto been attempted. And not to draw our philosophy from too profound a source, we shall have recourse to a noted story in DON QUIXOTE.

It is with good reason, says SANCHO to the squire with the great nose, that I pretend to have a judgment in wine: This is a quality hereditary in our family. Two of my kinsmen were once called to give their opinion of a hogshead, which was supposed to be excellent, being old and of a good vintage. One of them tastes it; considers it; and after mature reflection pronounces the wine to be good, were it not for a small taste of leather, which he perceived in it. The other, after using the same precautions, gives also his verdict in favour of the wine; but with the reserve of a taste of iron, which he could easily distinguish. You cannot imagine how much they were both ridiculed for their judgment. But who laughed in the end? On emptying the hogshead, there was found at the bottom, an old key with a leathern thong tied to it.

The great resemblance between mental and bodily taste will easily teach us to apply this story. Though it be certain, that beauty and deformity, more than sweet and bitter, are not qualities in objects, but belong entirely to the sentiment, internal or external; it must be allowed, that there are certain qualities in objects, which are fitted by nature to produce those particular feelings. Now as these qualities may be found in a small degree, or may be mixed and confounded with each other, it often happens, that the taste is not affected with such minute qualities, or is not able to distinguish all the particular flavours, amidst the disorder, in which they are presented. Where the organs are so fine, as to allow nothing to escape them; and at the same time so exact as to perceive every ingredient in the composition: This we call delicacy of taste, whether we employ these terms in the literal or metaphorical sense. Here then the general rules of beauty are of use; being drawn from established models, and from the observation of what pleases or displeases, when presented singly and in a high degree: And if the same qualities, in a continued composition and in a smaller degree, affect not the organs with a sensible delight or uneasiness, we exclude the person from all pretensions to this delicacy. To produce these general rules or avowed patterns of composition is like finding the key with the leathern thong; which justified the verdict of SANCHO's kinsmen, and confounded those pretended judges who had condemned them. Though the hogshead had never been emptied, the taste of the one was still equally delicate, and that of the other equally dull and languid: But it would have been more difficult to have proved the superiority of the former, to the conviction of every by-stander. In like manner, though the beauties of writing had never been methodized, or reduced to general principles; though no excellent models had ever been acknowledged; the different degrees of taste would still have subsisted, and the judgment of one man been preferable to that of another; but it would not have been so easy to silence the bad critic, who might always insist upon his particular sentiment, and refuse to submit to his antagonist. But when we show him an avowed principle of art; when we illustrate this principle by examples, whose operation, from his own particular taste, he acknowledges to be conformable to the principle; when we prove, that the same principle may be applied to the present case, where he did not perceive or feel its influence: He must conclude, upon the whole, that the fault lies in himself, and that he wants the delicacy, which is requisite to make him sensible of every beauty and every blemish, in any composition or discourse. . . .

. . .[T]hough the principles of taste be universal, and nearly, if not entirely the same in all men; yet few are qualified to give judgment on any work of art, or establish their own sentiment as the standard of beauty. The organs of internal sensation are seldom so perfect as to allow the general principles their full play, and produce a feeling correspondent to those principles. They either labour under some defect, or are vitiated by some disorder; and by that means, excite a sentiment, which may be pronounced erroneous. When the critic has no delicacy, he judges without any distinction, and is only affected by the grosser and more palpable qualities of the object: The finer touches pass unnoticed and disregarded. Where he is not aided by practice, his verdict is attended with confusion and hesitation. Where no comparison has been employed, the most frivolous beauties, such as rather merit the name of defects, are the object of his admiration. Where he lies under the influence of prejudice, all his natural sentiments are perverted. Where good sense is wanting, he is not qualified to discern the beauties of design and reasoning, which are the highest and most excellent. Under some or other of these imperfections, the generality of men labour; and hence a true judge in the finer arts is observed, even during the most polished ages, to be so rare a character: Strong sense, united to delicate sentiment, improved by practice, perfected by comparison, and cleared of all prejudice, can alone entitle critics to this valuable character; and the joint verdict of such, wherever they are to be found, is the true standard of taste and beauty.

But where are such critics to be found? By what marks are they to be known? How distinguish them from pretenders? These questions are embarrassing; and seem to throw us back into the same uncertainty, from which, during the course of this essay, we have endeavoured to extricate ourselves.

But if we consider the matter aright, these are questions of fact, not of sentiment. Whether any particular person be endowed with good sense and a delicate imagination, free from prejudice, may often be the subject of dispute, and be liable to great discussion and enquiry: But that such a character is valuable and estimable will be agreed in by all mankind. Where these doubts occur, men can do no more than in other disputable questions, which are submitted to the understanding: They must produce the best arguments, that their invention suggests to them; they must acknowledge a true and decisive standard to exist somewhere, to wit, real existence and matter of fact; and they must have indulgence to such as differ from them in their appeals to this standard. It is sufficient for our present purpose, if we have proved, that the taste of all individuals is not upon an equal footing, and that some men in general, however difficult to be particularly pitched upon, will be acknowledged by universal sentiment to have a preference above others.

But in reality the difficulty of finding, even in particulars, the standard of taste, is not so great as it is represented. Though in speculation, we may readily avow a certain criterion in science and deny it in sentiment, the matter is found in practice to be much more hard to ascertain in the former case than in the latter. Theories of abstract philosophy, systems of profound theology, have prevailed during one age: In a successive period, these have been universally exploded: Their absurdity has been detected: Other theories and systems have supplied their place, which again gave place to their successors: And nothing has been experienced more liable to the revolutions of chance and fashion than these pretended decisions of science. The case is not the same with the beauties of eloquence and poetry. Just expressions of passion and nature are sure, after a little time, to gain public applause, which they maintain for ever. ARISTOTLE, and PLATO, and EPICURUS, and DESCARTES, may successively yield to each other: But TERENCE and VIRGIL maintain an universal, undisputed empire over the minds of men. The abstract philosophy of CICERO has lost its credit: The vehemence of his oratory is still the object of our admiration.

Though men of delicate taste be rare, they are easily to be distinguished in society, by the soundness of their understanding and the superiority of their faculties above the rest of mankind. The ascendant, which they acquire, gives a prevalence to that lively approbation, with which they receive any productions of genius, and renders it generally predominant. Many men, when left to themselves, have but a faint and dubious perception of beauty, who yet are capable of relishing any fine stroke, which is pointed out to them. Every convert to the admiration of the real poet or orator is the cause of some new conversion. And though prejudices may prevail for a time, they never unite in celebrating any rival to the true genius, but yield at last to the force of nature and just sentiment. Thus, though a civilized nation may easily be mistaken in the choice of their admired philosopher, they never have been found long to err, in their affection for a favorite epic or tragic author.

But notwithstanding all our endeavours to fix a standard of taste, and reconcile the discordant apprehensions of men, there still remain two sources of variation, which are not sufficient indeed to confound all the boundaries of beauty and deformity, but will often serve to produce a difference in the degrees of our approbation or blame. The one is the different humours of particular men; the other, the particular manners and opinions of our age and country. The general principles of taste are uniform in human nature: Where men vary in their judgments, some defect or perversion in the faculties may commonly be remarked; proceeding either from prejudice, from want of practice, or want of delicacy; and there is just reason for approving one taste, and condemning another. But where there is such a diversity in the internal frame or external situation as is entirely blameless on both sides, and leaves no room to give one the preference above the other; in that case a certain degree of diversity in judgment is unavoidable, and we seek in vain for a standard, by which we can reconcile the contrary sentiments.

A young man, whose passions are warm, will be more sensibly touched with amorous and tender images, than a man more advanced in years, who takes pleasure in wise, philosophical reflections concerning the conduct of life and moderation of the passions. At twenty, OVID may be the favourite author; HORACE at forty; and perhaps TACITUS at fifty. Vainly would we, in such cases, endeavour to enter into the sentiments of others, and divest ourselves of those propensities, which are natural to us. We choose our favourite author as we do our friend, from a conformity of humour and disposition. Mirth or passion, sentiment or reflection; whichever of these most predominates in our temper, it gives us a peculiar sympathy with the writer who resembles us.

One person is more pleased with the sublime; another with the tender; a third with raillery. One has a strong sensibility to blemishes, and is extremely studious of correctness: Another has a more lively feeling of beauties, and pardons twenty absurdities and defects for one elevated or pathetic stroke. The ear of this man is entirely turned towards conciseness and energy; that man is delighted with a copious, rich, and harmonious expression. Simplicity is affected by one; ornament by another. Comedy, tragedy, satire, odes, have each its partizans, who prefer that particular species of writing to all others. It is plainly an error in a critic, to confine his approbation to one species or style of writing, and condemn all the rest. But it is almost impossible not to feel a predilection for that which suits our particular turn and disposition. Such preferences are innocent and unavoidable, and can never reasonably be the object of dispute, because there is no standard, by which they can be decided.

For a like reason, we are more pleased, in the course of our reading, with pictures and characters, that resemble objects which are found in our own age or country, than with those which describe a different set of customs. It is not without some effort, that we reconcile ourselves to the simplicity of ancient manners, and behold princesses carrying water from the spring, and kings and heroes dressing their own victuals. We may allow in general, that the representation of such manners is no fault in the author, nor deformity in the piece; but we are not so sensibly touched with them. For this reason, comedy is not easily transferred from one age or nation to another. A FRENCHMAN or ENGLISHMAN is not pleased with the ANDRIA of TERENCE, or CLITIA of MACHIAVEL; where the fine lady, upon whom all the play turns, never once appears to the spectators, but is always kept behind the scenes, suitably to the reserved humour of the ancient GREEKS and modern ITALIANS. A man of learning and reflection can make allowance for these peculiarities of manners; but a common audience can never divest themselves so far of their usual ideas and sentiments, as to relish pictures which in no wise resemble them. . . .

4

ART AS COMMUNICABLE PLEASURE: IMMANUEL KANT

The theory of art Immanuel Kant (1724–1804) set out in his *Critique of Judgment*—the third of his famous three *Critiques*—has been enormously influential. Indeed, general acceptance of the term *aesthetics* as applied to the philosophy of art stems from Kant's discussion of art under what he takes to be the wider rubric of aesthetic judgment. Many of the more specific themes of Kant's philosophy of art—art's autonomy from specific interest, form as the object of aesthetic judgment, genius as the faculty of artistic creation—continue to be widely discussed as well.

Kant's theory of art is quite complex, for it attempts to solve a variety of puzzles. Foremost among these is Hume's antinomy: In what sense can judgments of artistic merit, which appear to be about our subjective feelings, be considered objective or factual? Because Kant bases his theory of art on his understanding of aesthetic judgment, which he takes to apply to nature in the first instance, one must begin there.

An aesthetic judgment concerning nature—that this sunset is beautiful, for example—is a peculiar sort of judgment for Kant. (He uses the term "judgment" to refer to all acts of mental cognition. Thus, whenever we are thinking, we are making judgments.) To conclude that something is beautiful does not in any way enhance our understanding of it, as does a mere empirical judgment—for example, that the setting sun has reddened the clouds; instead, we seem to be saying something about how our perception of it affects us. When I call the sunset beautiful, I refer to feelings the sunset produces in me, even though I express this in a judgment that attributes an apparently objective property—beauty—to it. The question for Kant, as for Hume, is how a judgment about our feelings can have objective validity—for, when I say that the sunset is beautiful, I seem to be saying more than that it appeals to me, claiming also in effect that the sunset's beauty is there for all to see.

Kant's solution to this problem improves on Hume's. Recall that the latter based the objectivity of judgments of taste on the presumed empirical truth that certain qualities of objects tend to produce pleasure in all human beings.

Kant sees this will not justify our belief that attributions of beauty to objects have normative force: When I say something is beautiful, I not only believe you *will* agree, but I think that, in some sense, you *should*.

Kant justifies the objective validity of aesthetic judgments by claiming that the feeling of pleasure conceptualized in such judgments is of a very specific sort. Unlike the feeling of pleasure produced by consuming an ice cream cone, the feeling of pleasure incident on the perception of a beautiful object does not arise from the satisfaction of a particular interest or desire. Rather, it is a disinterested pleasure derived from the mere contemplation of the object that induces it. The source of this pleasure, according to Kant, is in those features of the object uniquely suited to my perception. In Kantian terms, the form of a beautiful object causes the imagination (the mental faculty that allows me to apprehend any object) and the understanding (the faculty of conceptualization) to coincide in a special sort of harmony: It is as if the object were produced in order for it to be perceived by me. This free play of the faculties produces a pleasurable feeling of the sort that gives rise to the judgment that the object is beautiful. For this reason, we see beautiful objects as purposive, but without their fulfilling any actual purpose.

This account solves the problem of the objective validity of aesthetic judgments by claiming that the pleasure produced by beautiful things is such that any being equipped with the perceptual and cognitive faculties human beings possess *would* experience this pleasure. The attribution of beauty to an object is objectively valid in that it posits a subjective state that *all* human beings are capable of experiencing. Unlike Hume's solution, the universality of our susceptibility to aesthetic pleasure does not depend on an empirical generalization that admits of many exceptions; rather, it depends only on the most general structure of the human mind. Nonetheless, aesthetic judgments do not meet the rigorous standards for empirical knowledge Kant sets forth in his *Critique of Pure Reason*.

Many details of Kant's theory of natural beauty deserve further discussion. For example, the distinction between the beautiful and the sublime is important for his understanding of our aesthetic response to nature. But we need to remember that this account functions only as the first step in his theory of art. In moving to a consideration of art proper, Kant distinguishes it from various other branches of human activity—stressing, as he goes, that "art" always refers to human activity *freely* undertaken—but the relevant term he uses to characterize what we now call "art" is *fine art*. Fine art is a species of aesthetic art that attempts to produce pleasure through the form of its objects. So Kant defines "art" by reference to his theory of aesthetic judgment: Art objects are those created to produce aesthetic pleasure by virtue of their form.

In the following selection from the *Critique of Judgment*, Kant develops a number of different aspects of his theory of fine art. First, he argues that fine art must seem to us like a natural product. This is an important claim, for it grounds a naturalistic standard for judging works of art. Thus, according to Kant, noticing that a work of fine art was consciously produced to give us pleasure detracts from the work's ability to produce that pleasure. Only art objects that both reveal and yet conceal their nature as artifacts will produce in us a genuine aesthetic response.

This aspect of Kant's philosophy exhibits an interesting tension with his claim that art can express ideas, a claim that Schopenhauer will develop more fully in the next chapter. What Kant calls "ideas" are concepts that cannot be fully encountered in experience. Although there are perfectly valid examples of empirical concepts, such as "chair," within our experience, ideas such as beauty can never, according to Kant, be adequately instanced in the course of our daily lives. It is only art, with its ability to go beyond the quotidian, that provides us with sensory analogues of ideas.

Kant also develops a theory of genius to account for the production of art. The problem addressed by this account stems from the fact that, according to Kant, fine art has no rules: If it did, it would be knowledge. But if there are no rules, how can it be made? The genius simply has a natural ability to create objects that produce aesthetic pleasure in us. This account of genius was very influential in the 19th century, during the romantic movement especially.

Kant supplements his account of aesthetic judgment in his explanation of how we judge works of art. Defining an object's perfection as the harmony between its sensory features and its purpose, he claims that, in assessing art objects, we judge their perfection, not just their beauty. This allows him to hold, as had Aristotle, that we can judge as beautiful in art things we would find repellent in nature, such as war or disease. (Interestingly, for Kant the only emotion that cannot be redeemed in art is disgust!)

There are certainly elements of Kant's theory of art that seem problematic today, such as his endorsement of naturalism as the appropriate artistic style or his emphasis on form as the only aesthetically relevant feature of artworks. Nonetheless, his theory remains both insightful and influential. In the selections that follow, Kant's name is repeatedly invoked as a source of important insights.

STUDY QUESTIONS ON THE READING

1.   Why does Kant think that judging an object beautiful requires that we experience it as purposive? What does he mean by "purposive"?

2.   In what sense are aesthetic judgments universal for Kant? Must everyone agree to them? Is there disputing about taste?

3.   What is the distinction between the beautiful and the sublime for Kant? How does the sublime point beyond experience?

4.   Why does Kant think that there can be no science of the beautiful? Does this mean that artistic production requires no technical skills? Explain.

5.   Assess Kant's claim that art must be naturalistic. Why does he think this? Do you think this claim conflicts with our assessment of artworks? Are there examples of nonnaturalistic works you think beautiful? What would Kant say about them?

6.   Why is genius required to produce art, according to Kant? Do you agree with him? Why or why not?

7.   Can you think of an artwork whose content would cause disgust if it were a natural object? What might Kant say about this?

8.   Do you agree that Kant's theory of art improves on Hume's? If so, explain how Kant modifies Hume's claims. If not, what problem do you see in Kant's theory?

❖

IMMANUEL KANT: THE CRITIQUE OF JUDGEMENT

THE AESTHETIC REPRESENTATION OF THE FINALITY OF NATURE

THAT which is purely subjective in the representation of an Object, i.e. what constitutes its reference to the Subject, not to the object, is its aesthetic quality. On the other hand, that which in such a representation serves, or is available, for the determination of the object (for the purpose of knowledge), is its logical validity. In the cognition of an object of sense both sides are presented conjointly. In the sense-representation of external things the Quality of space in which we intuit them is the merely subjective side of my representation of them (by which what the things are in themselves as Objects is left quite open), and it is on account of that reference that the object in being intuited in space is also thought merely as a phenomenon. But despite its purely subjective Quality, space is still a constituent of the knowledge of things as phenomena. *Sensation* (here external) also agrees in expressing a merely subjective side of our representations of external things, but one which is properly their matter (through which we are given something with real existence), just as space is the mere *a priori* form of the possibility of their intuition; and so sensation is, none the less, also employed in the cognition of external Objects.

But that subjective side of a representation *which is incapable of becoming an element of cognition,* is the *pleasure* or *displeasure* connected with it; for through it I cognize nothing in the object of the representation, although it may easily be the result of the operation of some cognition or other. Now the finality of a thing, so far as represented in our perception of it, is in no way a quality of the object itself (for a quality of this kind is not one that can be perceived), although it may be inferred from a cognition of things. In the finality, therefore, which is prior to the cognition of an Object, and which, even apart from any desire to make use of the representation of it for the purpose of a cognition, is yet immediately connected with it, we have the subjective quality belonging to

From *The Critique of Judgment* by Immanuel Kant, translated with Analytical Indexes by James Creed Meredith. © 1928 Oxford University Press.

it that is incapable of becoming a constituent of knowledge. Hence we only apply the term "final" to the object on account of its representation being immediately coupled with the feeling of pleasure: and this representation itself is an aesthetic representation of the finality.—The only question is whether such a representation of finality exists at all.

If pleasure is connected with the mere apprehension (*apprehensio*) of the form of an object of intuition, apart from any reference it may have to a concept for the purpose of a definite cognition, this does not make the representation referable to the Object, but solely to the Subject. In such a case the pleasure can express nothing but the conformity of the Object to the cognitive faculties brought into play in the reflective judgement, and so far as they are in play, and hence merely a subjective formal finality of the Object. For that apprehension of forms in the imagination can never take place without the reflective judgement, even when it has no intention of so doing, comparing them at least with its faculty of referring intuitions to concepts. If, now, in this comparison, imagination (as the faculty of intuitions a priori) is undesignedly brought into accord with understanding (as the faculty of concepts) by means of a given representation, and a feeling of pleasure is thereby aroused, then the object must be regarded as final for the reflective judgement. A judgement of this kind is an aesthetic judgement upon the finality of the Object, which does not depend upon any present concept of the object, and does not provide one. When the form of an object (as opposed to the matter of its representation, as sensation) is, in the mere act of reflecting upon it, without regard to any concept to be obtained from it, estimated as the ground of a pleasure in the representation of such an Object, then this pleasure is also judged to be combined necessarily with the representation of it, and so not merely for the Subject apprehending this form, but for all in general who pass judgement. The object is then called beautiful; and the faculty of judging by means of such a pleasure (and so also with universal validity) is called taste. For since the ground of the pleasure is made to reside merely in the form of the object for reflection generally, consequently not in any sensation of the object, and without any reference, either, to any concept that might have something or other in view, it is with the conformity to law in the empirical employment of judgement generally (unity of imagination and understanding) in the Subject, and with this alone, that the representation of the Object in reflection, the conditions of which are universally valid *a priori,* accords. And, as this accordance of the object with the faculties of the Subject is contingent, it gives rise to a representation of a finality on the part of the object in respect of the cognitive faculties of the Subject. Here, now, is a pleasure which—as is the case with all pleasure or displeasure that is not brought about through the agency of the concept of freedom (i.e. through the antecedent determination of the higher faculty of desire by means of pure reason)—no concepts could ever enable us to regard as necessarily connected with the representation of an object. It must always be only through reflective perception that it is cognized as conjoined with this representation. As with all empirical judgements, it is, consequently, unable to announce objective necessity or lay claim to *a priori* validity. But, then, the judgement of taste in fact only lays claim, like every other empirical judgement, to be valid for every one, and, despite its inner contingency this is always possible. The only point that is strange or out of the way about it, is that it is not an empirical concept, but a feeling of pleasure (and so not a concept at all), that is yet exacted from every one by the judgement of taste, just as if it were a predicate united to the cognition of the Object, and that is meant to be conjoined with its representation.

A singular empirical judgement, as, for example, the judgement of one who perceives a movable drop of water in a rock-crystal, rightly looks to every one finding the fact as stated, since the judgement has been formed according to the universal conditions of the determinant judgement under the laws of a possible experience generally. In the same way one who feels pleasure in simple reflection on the form of an object, without having any concept in mind, rightly lays claim to the agreement of every one, although this judgement is empirical and a singular judgement. For the ground of this pleasure is found in the universal, though subjective, condition of reflective judgements, namely the final harmony of an object (be it a product of nature or of art) with the mutual relation of the faculties of cognition (imagination and understanding) which are requisite for every empirical cognition. The pleasure in judgements of taste is, therefore, dependent doubtless on an empirical representation, and cannot be united *a priori* to any concept (one cannot determine *a priori* what object will be in accordance with taste or not—one must find out the object that is so); but then it is only made the determining ground of this judgement by virtue of our consciousness of its resting simply upon reflection and the universal, though only subjective, conditions of the harmony of that reflection with the knowledge of objects generally, for which the form of the Object is final.

This is why judgements of taste are subjected to a Critique in respect of their possibility. For their possibility presupposes an *a priori* principle, although that principle is neither a cognitive principle for understanding nor a practical principle for the will, and is thus in no way determinant *a priori*.

Susceptibility to pleasure arising from reflection on the forms of things (whether of nature or of art) betokens, however, not only a finality on the part of Objects in their relation to the reflective judgement in the Subject, in accordance with the concept of nature, but also, conversely, a finality on the part of the Subject, answering to the concept of freedom, in respect of the form, or even formlessness, of objects. The result is that the aesthetic judgement refers not merely, as a judgement of taste, to the beautiful, but also, as springing from a higher intellectual feeling, to the *sublime*. Hence the above-mentioned Critique of Aesthetic Judgement must be divided on these lines into two main parts. . . .

GENERAL REMARK UPON THE EXPOSITION OF AESTHETIC REFLECTIVE JUDGEMENTS

In relation to the feeling of pleasure an object is to be counted either as *agreeable*, or *beautiful*, or *sublime*, or *good* (absolutely) (*iucundum, pulchrum, sublime, honestum*).

As the motive of desires the *agreeable* is invariably of one and the same kind, no matter what its source or how specifically different the representation (of sense and sensation objectively considered). Hence in estimating its influence upon the mind the multitude of its charms (simultaneous or successive) is alone relevant, and so only, as it were, the mass of the agreeable sensation, and it is only by its *Quantity,* therefore, that this can be made intelligible. Further, it in no way conduces to our culture, but belongs only to mere enjoyment.—The *beautiful,* on the other hand, requires the representation of a certain *Quality* of the Object, that permits also of being understood and reduced to concepts (although in the aesthetic judgement it is not so reduced) and it cultivates, as it instructs us to attend to finality in the feeling of pleasure.—The *sublime* consists merely in the *relation* exhibited by the estimate of the serviceability of the sensible in the representation of nature for a possible supersensible employment.—The *absolutely good,* estimated subjectively according to the feeling it inspires (the Object of the moral feeling) as the determinability of the powers of the Subject by means of the representation of an *absolutely necessitating* law, is principally distinguished by the *modality* of a necessity resting upon concepts *a priori,* and involving not a mere *claim,* but a *command* upon every one to assent, and belongs intrinsically not to the aesthetic, but to the pure intellectual judgement. Further, it is not ascribed to nature but to freedom, and that in a determinant and not a merely reflective judgement. But the *determinability of the Subject* by means of this idea, and, what is more, that of a Subject which can be sensible, in the way of a *modification of its state,* to *hindrances* on the part of sensibility, while, at the same time, it can by surmounting them feel superiority over them—a determinability, in other words, as moral feeling—is still so allied to aesthetic judgement and its *formal conditions* as to be capable of being pressed into the service of the aesthetic representation of the conformity to law of action from duty, i.e. of the representation of this as sublime, or even as beautiful, without forfeiting its purity—an impossible result were one to make it naturally bound up with the feeling of the agreeable.

The net result to be extracted from the exposition so far given of both kinds of aesthetic judgements may be summed up in the following brief definitions:

The *beautiful* is what pleases in the mere estimate formed of it (consequently not by intervention of any feeling of sense in accordance with a concept of the understanding). From this it follows at once that it must please apart from all interest.

The *sublime* is what pleases immediately by reason of its opposition to the interest of sense.

Both, as definitions of aesthetic universally valid estimates, have reference to subjective grounds. In the one case the reference is to grounds of sensibility, in so far as these are final on behalf of the contemplative understanding, in the other case in so far as, in their *opposition* to sensibility, they are, on the contrary, final in reference to the ends of practical reason. Both, however, as united in the same Subject, are final in reference to the moral feeling. The beautiful prepares us to love something, even nature, apart from any interest: the sublime to esteem something highly even in opposition to our (sensible) interest.

The sublime may be described in this way: It is an object (of nature) the *representation of which determines the mind to regard the elevation of nature beyond our reach as equivalent to a presentation of ideas.*

In a literal sense and according to their logical import, ideas cannot be presented. But if we enlarge our empirical faculty of representation (mathematical or dynamical) with a view to the intuition of nature, reason inevitably steps forward, as the faculty concerned with the independence of the absolute totality, and calls forth the effort of the mind, unavailing though it be, to make the representation of sense adequate to this totality. This effort, and the feeling of the unattainability of the idea by means of imagination, is itself a presentation of the subjective finality of our mind in the employment of the imagination in the interests of the mind's supersensible province, and compels us subjectively to *think* nature itself in its totality as a presentation of something supersensible, without our being able to effectuate this presentation *objectively.*

For we readily see that nature in space and time falls entirely short of the unconditioned, consequently also of the absolutely great, which still the commonest reason demands. And by this we are also reminded that we have only to do with nature as phenomenon, and that this itself must be regarded as the mere presentation of a nature-in-itself (which exists in the idea of reason). But this idea of the supersensible, which no doubt we cannot further determine—so that we cannot *cognize* nature as its presentation, but only *think* it as such—is awakened in us by an object the aesthetic estimating of which strains the imagination to its utmost, whether in respect of its extension (mathematical), or of its might over the mind (dynamical). For it is founded upon the feeling of a sphere of the mind which altogether exceeds the realm of nature (i.e. upon the moral feeling), with regard to which the representation of the object is estimated as subjectively final. . . .

§ 43   ART IN GENERAL.

(1.) *Art* is distinguished from *nature* as making (*facere*) is from acting or operating in general (*agere*), and the product or the result of the former is distinguished from that of the latter as *work* (*opus*) from operation (*effectus*).

By right it is only production through freedom, i.e. through an act of will that places reason at the basis of its action, that should be termed art. For, although we are pleased to call what bees produce (their regularly constructed cells) a work of art, we only do so on the strength of an analogy with art; that is to say, as soon as we call to mind that no rational deliberation forms the basis of their labour, we say at once that it is a product of their nature (of instinct), and it is only to their Creator that we ascribe it as art.

If, as sometimes happens, in a search through a bog, we light on a piece of hewn wood, we do not say it is a product of nature but of art. Its producing cause had an end in view to which the object owes its form. Apart from such cases, we recognize an art in everything formed in such a way that its actuality must have been preceded by a representation of the thing in its cause (as even in the case of the bees), although the effect could not have been *thought* by the cause. But where anything is called absolutely a work of art, to distinguish it from a natural product, then some work of man is always understood.

(2.) *Art,* as human skill, is distinguished also from *science* (as *ability* from *knowledge*), as a practical from a theoretical faculty, as technic from theory (as the art of surveying from geometry). For this reason, also, what one *can* do the moment one only *knows* what is to be done, hence without anything more than sufficient knowledge of the desired result, is not called art. To art that alone belongs for which the possession of the most complete knowledge does not involve one's having then and there the skill to do it. *Camper* describes very exactly how the best shoe must be made, but he, doubtless, was not able to turn one out himself.[1]

(3.) *Art* is further distinguished from *handicraft*. The first is called *free,* the other may be called *industrial art*. We look on the former as something which could only prove final (be a success) as play, i.e. an occupation which is agreeable on its own account; but on the second as labour, i.e. a business, which on its own account is disagreeable (drudgery), and is only attractive by means of what it results in (e.g. the pay), and which is consequently capable of being a compulsory imposition. Whether in the list of arts and crafts we are to rank watchmakers as artists, and smiths on the contrary as craftsmen, requires a standpoint different from that here adopted—one, that is to say, taking account of the proportion of the talents which the business undertaken in either case must necessarily involve. Whether, also, among the so-called seven free arts some may not have been included which should be reckoned as sciences, and many, too, that resemble handicraft, is a matter I will not discuss here. It is not amiss, however, to remind the reader of this: that in all free arts something of a compulsory character is still required, or, as it is called, a *mechanism,* without which the *soul,* which in art must be *free,* and which alone gives life to the work, would be bodyless and evanescent (e.g. in the poetic art there must be correctness and wealth of language, likewise prosody and metre). For not a few leaders of a newer school believe that the best way to promote a free art is to sweep away all restraint, and convert it from labour into mere play.

§ 44   FINE ART.

THERE is no science of the beautiful, but only a Critique. Nor, again, is there an elegant (*schöne*) science, but only a fine (*schöne*) art. For a science of the beautiful would have to determine scientifically, i.e. by means of proofs, whether a thing was to be considered beautiful or not; and the judgement upon beauty, consequently, would, if belonging to science, fail to be a judgement of taste. As for a beautiful science—a science which, as such, is to be beautiful, is

---

[1] In my part of the country, if you set a common man a problem like that of Columbus and his egg, he says, 'There is no art in that, it is only science': i.e. you *can* do it if you know *how*; and he says just the same of all the would-be arts of jugglers. To that of the tight-rope dancer, on the other hand, he has not the least compunction in giving the name of art.

a nonentity. For if, treating it as a science, we were to ask for reasons and proofs, we would be put off with elegant phrases (*bons mots*). What has given rise to the current expression *elegant sciences* is, doubtless, no more than this, that common observation has, quite accurately, noted the fact that for fine art, in the fulness of its perfection, a large store of science is required, as, for example, knowledge of ancient languages, acquaintance with classical authors, history, antiquarian learning, &c. Hence these historical sciences, owing to the fact that they form the necessary preparation and groundwork for fine art, and partly also owing to the fact that they are taken to comprise even the knowledge of the products of fine art (rhetoric and poetry), have by a confusion of words, actually got the name of elegant sciences.

Where art, merely seeking to actualize a possible object to the *cognition* of which it is adequate, does whatever acts are required for that purpose, then it is *mechanical*. But should the feeling of pleasure be what it has immediately in view it is then termed *aesthetic* art. As such it may be either *agreeable* or *fine* art. The description 'agreeable art' applies where the end of the art is that the pleasure should accompany the representations considered as mere *sensations,* the description 'fine art' where it is to accompany them considered as *modes of cognition.*

Agreeable arts are those which have mere enjoyment for their object. Such are all the charms that can gratify a dinner party: entertaining narrative, the art of starting the whole table in unrestrained and sprightly conversation, or with jest and laughter inducing a certain air of gaiety. Here, as the saying goes, there may be much loose talk over the glasses, without a person wishing to be brought to book for all he utters, because it is only given out for the entertainment of the moment, and not as a lasting matter to be made the subject of reflection or repetition. (Of the same sort is also the art of arranging the table for enjoyment, or, at large banquets, the music of the orchestra—a quaint idea intended to act on the mind merely as an agreeable noise fostering a genial spirit, which, without any one paying the smallest attention to the composition, promotes the free flow of conversation between guest and guest.) In addition must be included play of every kind which is attended with no further interest than that of making the time pass by unheeded.

Fine art, on the other hand, is a mode of representation which is intrinsically final, and which, although devoid of an end, has the effect of advancing the culture of the mental powers in the interests of social communication.

The universal communicability of a pleasure involves in its very concept that the pleasure is not one of enjoyment arising out of mere sensation, but must be one of reflection. Hence aesthetic art, as art which is beautiful, is one having for its standard the reflective judgement and not organic sensation.

§ 45   FINE ART IS AN ART, SO FAR AS IT HAS AT THE SAME TIME THE APPEARANCE OF BEING NATURE.

A PRODUCT of fine art must be recognized to be art and not nature. Nevertheless the finality in its form must appear just as free from the constraint of arbitrary rules as if it were a product of mere nature. Upon this feeling of freedom in the play of our cognitive faculties—which play has at the same time to be final—rests that pleasure which alone is universally communicable without being based on concepts. Nature proved beautiful when it wore the appearance of art; and art can only be termed beautiful, where we are conscious of its being art, while yet it has the appearance of nature.

For, whether we are dealing with beauty of nature or beauty of art, we may make the universal statement: *that is beautiful which pleases in the mere estimate of it* (not in sensation or by means of a concept). Now art has always got a definite intention of producing something. Were this "something," however, to be mere sensation (something merely subjective), intended to be accompanied with pleasure, then such product would, in our estimation of it, only please through the agency of the feeling of the senses. On the other hand, were the intention one directed to the production of a definite object, then, supposing this were attained by art, the object would only please by means of a concept. But in both cases the art would please, not in *the mere estimate of it,* i.e. not as fine art, but rather as mechanical art.

Hence the finality in the product of fine art, intentional though it be, must not have the appearance of being intentional; i.e. fine art must be clothed *with the aspect* of nature, although we recognize it to be art. But the way in which a product of art seems like nature, is by the presence of perfect *exactness* in the agreement with rules prescribing how alone the product can be what it is intended to be, but with an absence of *laboured effect* (without academic form betraying itself), i.e. without a trace appearing of the artist having always had the rule present to him and of its having fettered his mental powers.

§ 46   FINE ART IS THE ART OF GENIUS.

Genius is the talent (natural endowment) which gives the rule to art. Since talent, as an innate productive faculty of the artist, belongs itself to nature, we may put it this way: *Genius is the innate mental aptitude (ingenium) through which* nature gives the rule to art.

Whatever may be the merits of this definition, and whether it is merely arbitrary, or whether it is adequate or not to the concept usually associated with the word *genius* (a point which the following sections have to clear up), it may still be shown at the outset that, according to this acceptation of the word, fine arts must necessarily be regarded as arts of *genius*.

For every art presupposes rules which are laid down as the foundation which first enables a product, if it is to be called one of art, to be represented as possible. The concept of fine art, however, does not permit of the judgement upon the beauty of its product being derived from any rule that has a *concept* for its determining ground, and that depends, consequently, on a concept of the way in which the product is possible. Consequently fine art cannot of its own self excogitate the rule according to which it is to effectuate its product. But since, for all that, a product can never be called art unless there is a preceding rule, it follows that nature in the individual (and by virtue of the harmony of his faculties) must give the rule to art, i.e. fine art is only possible as a product of genius.

From this it may be seen that genius (1) is a *talent* for producing that for which no definite rule can be given: and not an aptitude in the way of cleverness for what can be learned according to some rule; and that consequently *originality* must be its primary property. (2) Since there may also be original nonsense, its products must at the same time be models, i.e. be *exemplary;* and, consequently, though not themselves derived from imitation, they must serve that purpose for others, i.e. as a standard or rule of estimating. (3) It cannot indicate scientifically how it brings about its product, but rather gives the rule as *nature.* Hence, where an author owes a product to his genius, he does not himself know how the *ideas* for it have entered into his head, nor has he it in his power to invent the like at pleasure, or methodically, and communicate the same to others in such precepts as would put them in a position to produce similar products. (Hence, presumably, our word *Genie* is derived from *genius,* as the peculiar guardian and guiding spirit given to a man at his birth, by the inspiration of which those original ideas were obtained.) (4) Nature prescribes the rule through genius not to science but to art, and this also only in so far as it is to be fine art. . . .

§ 48   THE RELATION OF GENIUS TO TASTE.

FOR *estimating* beautiful objects, as such, what is required is *taste;* but for fine art, i.e. the *production* of such objects, one needs *genius.*

If we consider genius as the talent for fine art (which the proper signification of the word imports), and if we would analyse it from this point of view into the faculties which must concur to constitute such a talent, it is imperative at the outset accurately to determine the difference between beauty of nature, which it only requires taste to estimate, and beauty of art, which requires genius for its possibility (a possibility to which regard must also be paid in estimating such an object).

A beauty of nature is a *beautiful thing;* beauty of art is a *beautiful representation* of a thing.

To enable me to estimate a beauty of nature, as such, I do not need to be previously possessed of a concept of what sort of a thing the object is intended to be, i.e. I am not obliged to know its material finality (the end), but, rather, in forming an estimate of it apart from any knowledge of the end, the mere form pleases on its own account. If, however, the object is presented as a product of art, and is as such to be declared beautiful, then, seeing that art always presupposes an end in the cause (and its causality), a concept of what the thing is intended to be must first of all be laid at its basis. And, since the agreement of the manifold in a thing with an inner character belonging to it as its end constitutes the perfection of the thing, it follows that in estimating beauty of art the perfection of the thing must be also taken into account—a matter which in estimating a beauty of nature, as beautiful, is quite irrelevant.—It is true that in forming an estimate, especially of animate objects of nature, e.g. of a man or a horse, objective finality is also commonly taken into account with a view to judgement upon their beauty; but then the judgement also ceases to be purely aesthetic, i.e. a mere judgement of taste. Nature is no longer estimated as it appears like art, but rather in so far as it actually *is* art, though superhuman art;

and the teleological judgement serves as basis and condition of the aesthetic, and one which the latter must regard. In such a case, where one says, for example, 'that is a beautiful woman,' what one in fact thinks is only this, that in her form nature excellently portrays the ends present in the female figure. For one has to extend one's view beyond the mere form to a concept, to enable the object to be thought in such manner by means of an aesthetic judgement logically conditioned.

Where fine art evidences its superiority is in the beautiful descriptions it gives of things that in nature would be ugly or displeasing. The Furies, diseases, devastations of war, and the like, can (as evils) be very beautifully described, nay even represented in pictures. One kind of ugliness alone is incapable of being represented conformably to nature without destroying all aesthetic delight, and consequently artistic beauty, namely, that which excites *disgust*. For, as in this strange sensation, which depends purely on the imagination, the object is represented as insisting, as it were, upon our enjoying it, while we still set our face against it, the artificial representation of the object is no longer distinguishable from the nature of the object itself in our sensation, and so it cannot possibly be regarded as beautiful. The art of sculpture, again, since in its products art is almost confused with nature, has excluded from its creations the direct representation of ugly objects, and, instead, only sanctions, for example, the representation of death (in a beautiful genius), or of the warlike spirit (in Mars), by means of an allegory, or attributes which wear a pleasant guise, and so only indirectly, through an interpretation on the part of reason, and not for the pure aesthetic judgement.

So much for the beautiful representation of an object, which is properly only the form of the presentation of a concept, and the means by which the latter is universally communicated. To give this form, however, to the product of fine art, taste merely is required. By this the artist, having practised and corrected his taste by a variety of examples from nature or art, controls his work and, after many, and often laborious, attempts to satisfy taste, finds the form which commends itself to him. Hence this form is not, as it were, a matter of inspiration, or of a free swing of the mental powers, but rather of a slow and even painful process of improvement, directed to making the form adequate to his thought without prejudice to the freedom in the play of those powers.

Taste is, however, merely a critical, not a productive faculty; and what conforms to it is not, merely on that account, a work of fine art. It may belong to useful and mechanical art, or even to science, as a product following definite rules which are capable of being learned and which must be closely followed. But the pleasing form imparted to the work is only the vehicle of communication and a mode, as it were, of execution, in respect of which one remains to a certain extent free, notwithstanding being otherwise tied down to a definite end. So we demand that table appointments, or even a moral dissertation, and, indeed, a sermon, must bear this form of fine art, yet without its appearing *studied*. But one would not call them on this account works of fine art. A poem, a musical composition, a picture-gallery, and so forth, would, however, be placed under this head; and so in a would-be work of fine art we may frequently recognize genius without taste, and in another taste without genius. . . .

§ 49   THE FACULTIES OF THE MIND WHICH CONSTITUTE GENIUS.

If, after this analysis, we cast a glance back upon the above definition of what is called *genius,* we find: *First,* that it is a talent for art—not one for science, in which clearly known rules must take the lead and determine the procedure. *Secondly,* being a talent in the line of art, it presupposes a definite concept of the product—as its end. Hence it presupposes understanding, but, in addition, a representation, indefinite though it be, of the material, i.e. of the intuition, required for the presentation of that concept, and so a relation of the imagination to the understanding. *Thirdly,* it displays itself, not so much in the working out of the projected end in the presentation of a definite *concept,* as rather in the portrayal, or expression of *aesthetic ideas* containing a wealth of material for effecting that intention. Consequently the imagination is represented by it in its freedom from all guidance of rules, but still as final for the presentation of the given concept. *Fourthly,* and lastly, the unsought and undesigned subjective finality in the free harmonizing of the imagination with the understanding's conformity to law presupposes a proportion and accord between these faculties such as cannot be brought about by any observance of rules, whether of science or mechanical imitation, but can only be produced by the nature of the individual.

Genius, according to these presuppositions, is the exemplary originality of the natural endowments of an individual in the *free* employment of his cognitive faculties. On this showing, the product of a genius (in respect of so much in this product as is attributable to genius, and not to possible learning or academic instruction) is an example, not for imitation (for that would mean the loss of the element of genius, and just the very soul of the work), but to be followed by another genius—one whom it arouses to a sense of his own originality in putting freedom from the constraint of rules so into force in his art, that for art itself a new rule is won—which is what shows a talent to be exemplary. Yet, since the genius is one of nature's elect—a type that must be regarded as but a rare phenomenon—for other clever minds his example gives rise to a school, that is to say a methodical instruction according to rules, collected, so far as the circumstances admit, from such products of genius and their peculiarities. And, to that extent, fine art is for such persons a matter of imitation, for which nature, through the medium of a genius, gave the rule.

But this imitation becomes *aping* when the pupil *copies* everything down to the deformities which the genius only of necessity suffered to remain, because they could hardly be removed without loss of force to the idea. This courage has merit only in the case of a genius. A certain *boldness* of expression, and, in general, many a deviation from the common rule becomes him well, but in no sense is it a thing worthy of imitation. On the contrary it remains all through intrinsically a blemish, which one is bound to try to remove, but for which the genius is, as it were, allowed to plead a privilege, on the ground that a scrupulous carefulness would spoil what is inimitable in the impetuous ardour of his soul. *Mannerism* is another kind of aping—an aping of *peculiarity* (originality) in general, for the sake of removing oneself as far as possible from imitators, while the talent requisite to enable one to be at the same time *exemplary* is absent.—There are, in fact, two modes (*modi*) in general of arranging one's thoughts for utterance. The one is called a *manner* (*modus aestheticus*), the other a *method* (*modus logicus*). The distinction between them is this: the former possesses no standard other than the *feeling* of unity in the presentation, whereas the latter here follows definite *principles*. As a consequence the former is alone admissible for fine art. It is only, however, where the manner of carrying the idea into execution in a product of art is *aimed at* singularity instead of being made appropriate to the idea, that *mannerism* is properly ascribed to such a product. The ostentatious (*précieux*), forced, and affected styles, intended to mark one out from the common herd (though soul is wanting), resemble the behaviour of a man who, as we say, hears himself talk, or who stands and moves about as if he were on a stage to be gaped at—action which invariably betrays a tyro.

§ 50   THE COMBINATION OF TASTE AND GENIUS IN PRODUCTS OF FINE ART.

To ask whether more stress should be laid in matters of fine art upon the presence of genius or upon that of taste, is equivalent to asking whether more turns upon imagination or upon judgement. Now, imagination rather entitles an art to be called an *inspired* (*geistreiche*) than a *fine* art. It is only in respect of judgement that the name of fine art is deserved. Hence it follows that judgement, being the indispensable condition (*conditio sine qua non*), is at least what one must look to as of capital importance in forming an estimate of art as fine art. So far as beauty is concerned, to be fertile and original in ideas is not such an imperative requirement as it is that the imagination in its freedom should be in accordance with the understanding's conformity to law. For in lawless freedom imagination, with all its wealth, produces nothing but nonsense; the power of judgement, on the other hand, is the faculty that makes it consonant with understanding.

Taste, like judgement in general, is the discipline (or corrective) of genius. It severely clips its wings, and makes it orderly or polished; but at the same time it gives it guidance, directing and controlling its flight, so that it may preserve its character of finality. It introduces a clearness and order into the plenitude of thought, and in so doing gives stability to the ideas, and qualifies them at once for permanent and universal approval, for being followed by others, and for a continually progressive culture. And so, where the interests of both these qualities clash in a product, and there has to be a sacrifice of something, then it should rather be on the side of genius; and judgement, which in matters of fine art bases its decision on its own proper principles, will more readily endure an abatement of the freedom and wealth of the imagination, than that the understanding should be compromised.

The requisites for fine art are, therefore, *imagination, understanding, soul,* and *taste. . . .*

5

ART AS REVELATION:
ARTHUR SCHOPENHAUER

Of all the philosophers we have read so far, Arthur Schopenhauer (1788–1860) endows art with greatest significance. For this gloomy thinker, art reveals the nature of reality and gives us access to metaphysical truths about existence.

Most of the elements of Schopenhauer's philosophy are found in Kant, but in their new home they receive very different connotations. Like his great predecessor, Schopenhauer distinguishes appearance from reality-in-itself: The world revealed to us in our everyday experience is a mere representation, governed by the principles of sufficient reason—that everything that happens does so for some reason—and of individuation (*principium individuationis*)— that each person or object is a being distinct from every other. The world revealed by science is simply a more abstract and systematic version of this world of experience. But where Kànt claimed that reality-in-itself is unknowable to beings like ourselves, Schopenhauer thinks that we have access to it through our own wills. The truth revealed by a contemplation of willing is that reality consists of nothing but endless striving, and the world as it appears is mere illusion. Life is a pointless game in which desire demands satisfaction, but in which satisfaction is fleeting. As for our precious individuality, that, too, is illusory, for beneath the appearance of distinctness the will unites all. Pessimism and resignation are the appropriate philosophic attitudes to take to this revelation.

In making these claims, Schopenhauer injects themes from Indian thought into Kant's philosophy. Indeed, Schopenhauer is the first Western philosopher to value non-Western philosophy as a source of important insight, the Kantian distinction between appearance and reality being for him just another version of the ancient Hindu doctrine that the world of the senses and of desire is mere illusion.

Given Schopenhauer's rather depressing view of things, it may be surprising that he waxes so lyrical about the power of art: Whereas science is necessarily limited to the realm of appearances, art can reveal metaphysical truth. Again like Kant, Schopenhauer places genius at the center of art, but now it is necessary not just for artistic creation, but also for appreciation. Through art the genius is able to rise above the stream of quotidian entanglements to disinterested contemplation of the world as it really is.

Just as the subject must be in a special state in order to appreciate art, the art object cannot represent things in their usual mode of existence. All art, with the exception of music, presents Ideas rather than things. Here, Schopenhauer, too, incorporates a Platonic element into his philosophy of art. Once again, the Forms resurface—Ideas in Schopenhauer's terminology—as archetypes of which empirical things merely partake. For Schopenhauer, art does not represent the merely empirical but rather the Ideas that lie behind it. A significant work of art, then, is not concerned with the particular, but rather with the universal Idea that stands behind it as its reality. Schopenhauer speaks here of the will as possessing different levels of objectivity—from the lowly plant to the higher animals—and of the Ideas representing these different levels to us.

Music, however, is different: Rather than simply representing Ideas (that is, levels of the will's objectification), music brings us into direct contact with the will itself. Music and the will are two intertranslatable languages in which everything said in one can be said in the other. This is why music is the "highest" form of art, permitting direct experience of the will both as the substance of ultimate reality and as insatiable.

If Schopenhauer thinks that the highest calling is in complete detachment, disinterested contemplation of the spectacle of universal striving, then the artist operates in the space between these realms, depicting the vanity of willing but not yet seized with the futility of all undertaking. As a result, the artist is, for Schopenhauer, a tragic figure, condemned to tell the truth about the world, yet doomed to fail.

STUDY QUESTIONS ON THE READING

1. How does Schopenhauer compare art and science? Does he see one as better than the other? Why?

2. Like Kant, Schopenhauer stresses the role of genius in art. What are the differences in their two views? Which do you find more appealing, and why?

3. How does Schopenhauer explain the distinction between the beautiful and the sublime? Why is the sublime especially important in his philosophy?

4. Again, like Kant, Schopenhauer thinks that art requires disinterested perception. What does he mean by "disinterested" and what makes his view different from Kant's?

5. Do you agree with Schopenhauer's contention that music is the most fundamental art form? What speaks in favor of his view? What speaks against it?

❖

ARTHUR SCHOPENHAUER: THE WORLD AS WILL AND REPRESENTATION

36

History follows the thread of events; it is pragmatic in so far as it deduces them according to the law of motivation, a law that determines the appearing will where that will is illuminated by knowledge. At the lower grades of its objectivity, where it still acts without knowledge, natural science as etiology considers the laws of the changes of its phenomena, and as morphology considers what is permanent in them. This almost endless theme is facilitated by the aid of concepts that comprehend the general, in order to deduce from it the particular. Finally, mathematics considers the mere forms, that is, time and space, in which the Ideas appear drawn apart into plurality for the knowledge of the subject as individual. All these, the common name of which is science, therefore follow the principle of sufficient reason in its different forms, and their theme remains the phenomenon, its laws, connexion, and the relations resulting from these. But now, what kind of knowledge is it that considers what continues to exist outside and independently of all relations, but which alone is really essential to the world, the true content of its phenomena, that which is subject to no change, and is therefore known with equal truth for all time, in a word, the *Ideas* that are the immediate and adequate objectivity of the thing-in-itself, of the will? It is *art*, the work of genius. It repeats the eternal Ideas apprehended through pure contemplation, the essential and abiding element in all the phenomena of the world. According to the material in which it repeats, it is sculpture, painting, poetry, or music. Its only source is knowledge of the Ideas; its sole aim is communication of this knowledge. Whilst science, following the restless and unstable stream of the fourfold forms of reasons or grounds and consequents, is with every end it attains again and again directed farther, and can never find an ultimate goal or complete satisfaction, any more than by running we can reach the point where the clouds touch the horizon; art, on the contrary, is everywhere at its goal. For it plucks the object of its contemplation from the stream of the world's course, and holds it isolated before it. This particular thing, which in that stream was an infinitesimal part, becomes for art a representative of the whole, an equivalent of the infinitely many in space and time. It therefore pauses at this particular thing; it stops the wheel of time; for it the relations vanish; its object is only the essential, the Idea. We can therefore define it accurately as *the way of considering things independently of the principle of sufficient reason,* in contrast to the way of considering them which proceeds in exact accordance with this principle, and is the way of science and experience. This latter method of consideration can be compared to an endless line running horizontally, and the former to a vertical line cutting the horizontal at any point. The method of consideration that follows the principle of sufficient reason is the rational method, and it alone is valid and useful in practical life and in science. The method of consideration that looks away from the content of this principle is the method of genius, which is valid and useful in art alone. The first is Aristotle's method; the second is, on the whole, Plato's. The first is like the mighty storm, rushing along without beginning or aim, bending, agitating, and carrying everything away with it; the second is like the silent sunbeam, cutting through the path of the storm, and quite unmoved by it. The first is like the innumerable violently agitated drops of the waterfall, constantly changing and never for a moment at rest; the second is like the rainbow silently resting on this raging torrent. Only through the pure contemplation described above, which becomes absorbed entirely in the object, are the Ideas comprehended; and the nature of *genius* consists precisely in the preeminent ability for such contemplation. Now as this demands a complete forgetting of our own person and of its relations and connexions, the *gift of genius* is nothing but the most complete *objectivity*, i.e., the objective tendency of the mind, as opposed to the subjective directed to our own person, i.e., to the will. Accordingly, genius is the capacity to remain in a state of pure perception, to lose oneself in perception, to remove from the service of the will the knowledge which originally existed only for this service. In other words, genius is the ability to leave entirely out of sight our own interest, our willing, and our aims, and consequently to discard entirely our own personality for a time, in order to remain *pure knowing subject,* the clear eye of the world; and this not merely for moments, but with the necessary continuity and conscious thought to enable us to repeat by deliberate art what has been apprehended, and "to fix in lasting thoughts the wavering images that float before the mind." . . .

37

Now according to our explanation, genius consists in the ability to know, independently of the principle of sufficient reason, not individual things which have their existence only in the relation, but the Ideas of such things, and in the ability to be, in face of these, the correlative of the Idea, and hence no longer individual, but pure subject of knowing. Yet this ability must be inherent in all men in a lesser and different degree, as otherwise they would be just as incapable of enjoying works of art as of producing them. Generally they would have no susceptibility at all to the beautiful and to the sublime; indeed, these words could have no meaning for them. We must therefore assume as existing in all men that power of recognizing in things their Ideas, of divesting themselves for a moment of their personality, unless indeed there are some who are not capable of any aesthetic pleasure at all. The man of genius excels them only in the far higher degree and more continuous duration of this kind of knowledge. These enable him to retain that thoughtful contemplation necessary for him to repeat what is thus known in a voluntary and intentional work, such repetition being the work of art. Through this he communicates to others the Idea he has grasped. Therefore this Idea remains unchanged and the same, and hence aesthetic pleasure is essentially one and the same, whether it be called forth by a work of art, or directly by the contemplation of nature and of life. The work of art is merely a means of facilitating that knowledge in which this pleasure consists. That the Idea comes to us more easily from the work of art than directly from nature and from reality, arises solely from the fact that the artist, who knew only the Idea and not reality, clearly repeated in his work only the Idea, separated it out from reality, and omitted all disturbing contingencies. The artist lets us peer into the world through his eyes. That he has these eyes, that he knows the essential in things which lies outside all relations, is the gift of genius and is inborn; but that he is able to lend us this gift, to let us see with his eyes, is acquired, and is the technical side of art. Therefore, after the account I have given in the foregoing remarks of the inner essence of the aesthetic way of knowing in its most general outline, the following more detailed philosophical consideration of the beautiful and the sublime will explain both simultaneously, in nature and in art, without separating them further. We shall first consider what takes place in a man when he is affected by the beautiful and the sublime. Whether he draws this emotion directly from nature, from life, or partakes of it only through the medium of art, makes no essential difference, but only an outward one. . . .

39

All these considerations are intended to stress the subjective part of aesthetic pleasure, namely, that pleasure in so far as it is delight in the mere knowledge of perception as such, in contrast to the will. Now directly connected with all this is the following explanation of that frame of mind which has been called the feeling of the *sublime*.

It has already been observed that transition into the state of pure perception occurs most easily when the objects accommodate themselves to it, in other words, when by their manifold and at the same time definite and distinct form they easily become representatives of their Ideas, in which beauty, in the objective sense, consists. Above all, natural beauty has this quality, and even the most stolid and apathetic person obtains therefrom at least a fleeting, aesthetic pleasure. Indeed, it is remarkable how the plant world in particular invites one to aesthetic contemplation, and, as it were, obtrudes itself thereon. It might be said that such accommodation was connected with the fact that these organic beings themselves, unlike animal bodies, are not immediate object of knowledge. They therefore need the foreign intelligent individual in order to come from the world of blind willing into the world of the representation. Thus they yearn for this entrance, so to speak, in order to attain at any rate indirectly what directly is denied to them. For the rest, I leave entirely undecided this bold and venturesome idea that perhaps borders on the visionary, for only a very intimate and devoted contemplation of nature can excite or justify it. Now so long as it is this accommodation of nature, the significance and distinctness of its forms, from which the Ideas individualized in them readily speak to us; so long as it is this which moves us from knowledge of mere relations serving the will into aesthetic contemplation, and thus raises us to the will-free subject of knowing, so long is it merely the *beautiful* that affects us, and the feeling of beauty that is excited. But these very objects, whose significant forms invite us to a pure contemplation of them, may have a hostile relation to the human will in general, as manifested in its objectivity, the human body. They may be opposed to it; they may threaten it by their might that eliminates all resistance, or their immeasurable greatness may reduce it to nought. Nevertheless, the beholder may not direct his attention to this relation to his will which is so pressing and hostile, but, although he perceives and acknowledges it, he may consciously turn away from it, forcibly tear himself from his will and its relations, and, giving himself up entirely to knowledge, may quietly contemplate, as pure, will-less subject of knowing, those very objects so terrible to the will. He may comprehend only their Idea that is foreign to all relation, gladly linger over its contemplation, and consequently be elevated precisely in this way above himself, his person, his willing, and all willing. In that case, he is then filled with the feeling of the *sublime;* he is in the state of exaltation, and therefore the object that causes such a state is called *sublime.* Thus what distinguishes the feeling of the sublime from that of the beautiful is that, with the beautiful, pure knowledge has gained the upper hand without a struggle, since the beauty of the object, in other words that quality of it which facilitates knowledge of its Idea, has removed from consciousness, without resistance and hence imperceptibly, the will and knowledge of relations that slavishly serve this will. What is then left is pure subject of knowing, and not even a recollection of the will remains. On the other hand, with the sublime, that state of pure knowing is obtained first of all by a conscious and violent tearing away from the relations of the same object to the will which are recognized as unfavourable, by a free exaltation, accompanied by consciousness, beyond the will and the knowledge related to it. This exaltation must not only be won with consciousness, but also be maintained, and it is therefore accompanied by a constant recollection of the will, yet not of a single individual willing, such as fear or desire, but of human willing in general, in so far as it is expressed universally through its objectivity, the human body. . . .

   . . . [W]hen we are abroad in the storm of tempestuous seas; mountainous waves rise and fall, are dashed violently against steep cliffs, and shoot their spray high into the air. The storm howls, the sea roars, the lightning flashes from black clouds, and thunder-claps drown the noise of storm and sea. Then in the unmoved beholder of this scene the twofold nature of his consciousness reaches the highest distinctness. Simultaneously, he feels himself as individual, as the feeble phenomenon of will, which the slightest touch of these forces can annihilate, helpless against powerful nature, dependent, abandoned to chance, a vanishing nothing in face of stupendous forces; and he also feels himself as the eternal, serene subject of knowing, who as the condition of every object is the supporter of this whole world, the fearful struggle of nature being only his mental picture or representation; he himself is free from, and foreign to, all willing and all needs, in the quiet comprehension of the Ideas. This is the full impression of the sublime. Here it is caused by the sight of a power beyond all comparison superior to the individual, and threatening him with annihilation. . . .

41

The course of our remarks has made it necessary to insert here a discussion of the sublime, when the treatment of the beautiful has been only half completed, merely from one side, the subjective. For it is only a special modification of this subjective side which distinguishes the sublime from the beautiful. The difference between the beautiful and the sublime depends on whether the state of pure, will-less knowing, presupposed and demanded by any aesthetic contemplation, appears of itself, without opposition, by the mere disappearance of the will from consciousness, since the object invites and attracts us to it; or whether this state is reached only by free, conscious exaltation above the will, to which the contemplated object itself has an unfavourable, hostile relation, a relation that would do away with contemplation if we gave ourselves up to it. This is the distinction between the beautiful and the sublime. In the object the two are not essentially different, for in every case the object of aesthetic contemplation is not the individual thing, but the Idea in it striving for revelation, in other words, the adequate objectivity of the will at a definite grade. Its necessary correlative, withdrawn like itself from the principle of sufficient reason, is the pure subject of knowing, just as the correlative of the particular thing is the knowing individual, both of which lie within the province of the principle of sufficient reason.

By calling an object *beautiful,* we thereby assert that it is an object of our aesthetic contemplation, and this implies two different things. On the one hand, the sight of the thing makes us *objective,* that is to say, in contemplating it we are no longer conscious of ourselves as individuals, but as pure, will-less subjects of knowing. On the other hand, we recognize in the object not the individual thing, but an Idea; and this can happen only in so far as our contemplation of the object is not given up to the principle of sufficient reason, does not follow the relation of the object to something outside it (which is ultimately always connected with relations to our own willing), but rests on the object itself. For the Idea and the pure subject of knowing always appear simultaneously in consciousness as necessary correlatives, and with this appearance all distinction of time at once vanishes, as both are wholly foreign to the principle of sufficient reason in all its forms. Both lie outside the relations laid down by this principle; they can be compared to the rainbow and the sun that take no part in the constant movement and succession of the falling drops. Therefore if, for example, I contemplate a tree aesthetically, i.e., with artistic eyes, and thus recognize not it but its Idea, it is immediately of no importance whether it is this tree or its ancestor that flourished a thousand years ago, and whether the contemplator is this individual, or any other living anywhere and at any time. The particular thing and the knowing individual are abolished with the principle of sufficient reason, and nothing remains but the Idea and the pure subject of knowing, which together constitute the adequate objectivity of the will at this grade. And the Idea is released not only from time but also from space; for the Idea is not really this spatial form which floats before me, but its expression, its pure significance, its innermost being, disclosing itself and appealing to me; and it can be wholly the same, in spite of great difference in the spatial relations of the form.

Now since, on the one hand, every existing thing can be observed purely objectively and outside all relation, and, on the other, the will appears in everything at some grade of its objectivity, and this thing is accordingly the expression of an Idea, everything is also *beautiful*. That even the most insignificant thing admits of purely objective and will-less contemplation and thus proves itself to be beautiful, is testified by the still life paintings of the Dutch. . . . But one thing is more beautiful than another because it facilitates this purely objective contemplation, goes out to meet it, and, so to speak, even compels it, and then we call the thing very beautiful. This is the case partly because, as individual thing, it expresses purely the Idea of its species through the very distinct, clearly defined, and thoroughly significant relation of its parts. It also completely reveals that Idea through the completeness, united in it, of all the manifestations possible to its species, so that it greatly facilitates for the beholder the transition from the individual thing to the Idea, and thus also the state of pure contemplation. Sometimes that eminent quality of special beauty in an object is to be found in the fact that the Idea itself, appealing to us from the object, is a high grade of the will's objectivity, and is therefore most significant and suggestive. For this reason, man is more beautiful than all other objects, and the revelation of his inner nature is the highest aim of art. Human form and human expression are the most important object of plastic art, just as human conduct is the most important object of poetry. Yet each thing has its own characteristic beauty, not only everything organic that manifests itself in the unity of an individuality, but also everything inorganic and formless, and even every manufactured article. For all these reveal the Ideas through which the will objectifies itself at the lowest grades; they sound, as it were, the deepest, lingering bass-notes of nature. . . .

52

The (Platonic) Ideas are the adequate objectification of the will. To stimulate the knowledge of these by depicting individual things (for works of art are themselves always such) is the aim of all the other arts (and is possible with a corresponding change in the knowing subject). Hence all of them objectify the will only indirectly, in other words, by means of the Ideas. As our world is nothing but the phenomenon or appearance of the Ideas in plurality through entrance into the *principium individuationis* [principle of individuation] (the form of knowledge possible to the individual as such), music, since it passes over the Ideas, is also quite independent of the phenomenal world, positively ignores it, and, to a certain extent, could still exist even if there were no world at all, which cannot be said of the other arts. Thus music is as *immediate* an objectification and copy of the whole *will* as the world itself is, indeed as the Ideas are, the multiplied phenomenon of which constitutes the world of individual things. Therefore music is by no means like the other arts, namely a copy of the Ideas, but a *copy of the will itself*, the objectivity of which are the Ideas. For this reason the effect of music is so very much more powerful and penetrating than is that of the other arts, for these others speak only of the

shadow, but music of the essence. However, as it is the same will that objectifies itself both in the Ideas and in music, though in quite a different way in
each, there must be, not indeed an absolutely direct likeness, but yet a parallel, an analogy, between music and the Ideas, the phenomenon of which in
plurality and in incompleteness is the visible world. . . .

The inexpressible depth of all music, by virtue of which it floats past us as
a paradise quite familiar and yet eternally remote, and is so easy to understand
and yet so inexplicable, is due to the fact that it reproduces all the emotions of
our innermost being, but entirely without reality and remote from its pain. In
the same way, the seriousness essential to it and wholly excluding the ludicrous
from its direct and peculiar province is to be explained from the fact that its
object is not the representation, in regard to which deception and ridiculousness alone are possible, but that this object is directly the will; and this is essentially the most serious of all things, as being that on which all depends.
How full of meaning and significance the language of music is we see from the
repetition signs, as well as from the *Da capo*[1] which would be intolerable in the
case of works composed in the language of words. In music, however, they are
very appropriate and beneficial; for to comprehend it fully, we must hear it
twice. . . .

The pleasure of everything beautiful, the consolation afforded by art, the
enthusiasm of the artist which enables him to forget the cares of life, this one
advantage of the genius over other men alone compensating him for the suffering that is heightened in proportion to the clearness of consciousness, and
for the desert loneliness among a different race of men, all this is due to the fact
that, as we shall see later on, the in-itself of life, the will, existence itself, is a
constant suffering, and is partly woeful, partly fearful. The same thing, on the
other hand, as representation alone, purely contemplated, or repeated through
art, free from pain, presents us with a significant spectacle. This purely know-
able side of the world and its repetition in any art is the element of the artist.
He is captivated by a consideration of the spectacle of the will's objectification.
He sticks to this, and does not get tired of contemplating it, and of repeating it
in his descriptions. Meanwhile, he himself bears the cost of producing that
play; in other words, he himself is the will objectifying itself and remaining in
constant suffering. That pure, true, and profound knowledge of the inner
nature of the world now becomes for him an end in itself; at it he stops. Therefore it does not become for him a quieter of the will, as we shall see in the following book in the case of the saint who has attained resignation; it does not
deliver him from life for ever, but only for a few moments. For him it is not the
way out of life, but only an occasional consolation in it, until his power, enhanced by this contemplation, finally becomes tired of the spectacle, and seizes
the serious side of things. The St. Cecilia of Raphael can be regarded as a symbol of this transition. . . .

---

[1] The letters *D.C.* (*Da Capo*) in a musical score indicate that the music should be repeated from
the top. [ed.]

6

ART AS THE IDEAL: G. W. F. HEGEL

If Schopenhauer's view of art depends on his general metaphysics, this is even more true for G. W. F. Hegel (1770–1831), for whom it is one of the forms of absolute spirit, one way in which *Geist* or spirit reveals itself as the essence of the world. Hegel believes the universe is a self-perpetuating, dynamic whole—spirit—whose articulation follows a rational plan that is revealed in art, religion, and philosophy, the three aspects of absolute spirit. What distinguishes art is that it remains tied to sensible form, that is, to the perceptible, particular work; religion and, even more so, philosophy have as *their* aim the articulation of truth in purely universal, that is to say, general terms. It is for this reason that art is the Ideal, for Hegel, a term that indicates the ineradicable presence of individuality and not the thorough-going universality of the Concept—his term for the fullest grasp of reality.

Our selection from Hegel's *Aesthetics*—another compilation from student transcriptions and the master's own lecture notes—begins with a general description of the nature of art. Hegel's philosophic methodology is to start with an abstract description of a certain idea or concept and then to show in more detail to what that idea or concept really amounts. Here, his first, very general claim is that art, as the Ideal, must be a totality. As in all aspects of Hegel's philosophy, this view is developed through the use of a number of philosophic concepts whose meaning is often hard to grasp. A totality, in Hegel's specific sense, is a particular type of whole, namely one in which each part reflects the nature of the whole. By analogy, in an organic whole such as the human body, the function of each part (for example, seeing for the eye) can only be comprehended with reference to the totality. In claiming that an art object is a totality, Hegel is asserting that each of its elements must reflect the content of the entire work, thereby conveying a sense of profound integration.

Hegel goes on to explore some of the implications of this view, asserting that "inner" and "outer" must be harmonized in a work of art. What this means becomes clearer when we realize that Hegel uses this claim to criticize those conceptions of art, dating back to Plato, that characterize it as imitative and its truth as mere correctness or accuracy of representation. He rejects so formal a conception of art—for him, art must have a *content* that is true. Once we recall that Hegel thinks art functions to reveal metaphysical truth, we can understand why he rejects formalism in favor of a more substantive conception of art's truth.

This claim gains more precision in Hegel's discussion of portraiture. There, he rejects the idea that a portrait should slavishly resemble its sitter's appearance; instead, it needs to display the subject's inner character through its depiction of external appearance. To do this requires that the painter *idealize* the sitter, ignoring many idiosyncrasies of appearance the better to reveal essential character. Hegel's examples of successful portraiture are the Madonnas of Raphael.

In the second section of our selection from his *Aesthetics,* Hegel differentiates three distinct species of art. This typology is characteristic of his general philosophy for, although it is developed as a set of logical distinctions within the concept of art itself, it simultaneously constitutes a sequence of historical types recapitulating art's progress toward its own essence.

The first type of art is symbolic, by which Hegel means art that has not yet embodied that harmony of form and content that he has just posited as its truth, for its content is too abstract. What he has in mind here are works from ancient Egypt—for example, the Sphinx—or India, and he criticizes these works for depicting only an eternal and unchanging realm and thereby failing to represent the dynamic nature of reality. Architecture is the art form that, for Hegel, remains locked in this perspective.

Hegel next discusses classical art, the art of ancient Greece, for him an advance over the symbolic, containing a higher degree of individuality. Although for Hegel sculpture typifies classic art, his paradigms of Greek art here are the tragedies, especially those of Sophocles. Two features of such works mark them as an advance in the development of art. The first is that the characters, although they remain types, have become individualized. The second is that their stories reveal tensions inherent in the greater drama that is human history. Although for Hegel these works are paradigms of art, in that their unity of form and content can never be equaled, they are not the complete realization of the concept of art.

Only romantic art fully realizes Hegel's conception of art as the Ideal, for it embodies a more complete conception of subjectivity than do the two earlier forms. As such, it is able to present, through its images, a sensory version of the metaphysical truth that all reality is spirit developing toward self-consciousness through human history. Shakespeare's plays, with their more self-conscious and reflective characters, such as Hamlet, are examples of this form of art. Because of its presentation of inwardness—characters who think self-consciously about themselves and their situation—this type of art cannot be realized in three dimensions, but only in painting, music, and literature.

Hegel's teleological conception of art as historical process, developing into its true nature as the beautiful Ideal, also gives rise to his famous thesis of the death of art. Although there is a great deal of scholarly disagreement over what exactly this amounts to, it is clear that Hegel thinks that, in his day, art has fulfilled its mission and should be replaced by philosophy. In our own day and against all expectation, Arthur Danto gives Hegel's improbable thesis new life in his contention that contemporary art has become philosophy (see Chapter 18).

STUDY QUESTIONS ON THE READING

1. Hegel argues that art cannot simply imitate nature. What reasons does he give for this claim? Do you agree with it? What might Plato say in response?

2. In his account of portraiture, Hegel claims that the portrait artist must idealize his subject. What does he mean by this? In your view, what should a portrait accomplish? Do you know of any works that contradict Hegel's claim?

3. Why does Hegel think that art must be serenely peaceful and blissful? How is this consistent with his high opinion of tragedy and romantic art? How could he respond to the objection that contemporary art is not like this?

4. Why does Hegel disparage irony?

5. Do you think that art could come to an end? In what sense, if any, might this be true?

6. Hegel's theory of art is antiformalist. Among the theories he objects to in this regard is Kant's. Which theory do you prefer, and why?

G. W. F. HEGEL: LECTURES ON FINE ARTS

THE BEAUTY OF ART OR THE IDEAL

In relation to the beauty of art we have three chief aspects to consider:

> *First*, the Ideal as such
> *Secondly*, the work of art as the determinateness of the Ideal
> *Thirdly*, the creative subjectivity of the artist.

A. THE IDEAL AS SUCH

1. BEAUTIFUL INDIVIDUALITY

The most general thing which can be said in a merely formal way about the ideal of art, on the lines of our previous considerations, comes to this, that, on the one hand, the true has existence and truth only as it unfolds into external

G. W. F. Hegel, *Hegel's Introduction to Aesthetics* by G. W. F. Hegel, translated by T. M. Knox, with an interpretive essay by Charles Karelis. Copyright © 1979. Reprinted with permission by Oxford University Press.

reality; but, on the other hand, the externally separated parts, into which it unfolds, it can so combine and retain in unity that now every part of its unfolding makes this soul, this totality, appear in each part. If we take the human form as the nearest illustration of this, it is, as we saw earlier, a totality of organs into which the Concept is dispersed, and it manifests in each member only some particular activity and partial emotion. But if we ask in which particular organ the whole soul appears as soul, we will at once name the eye; for in the eye the soul is concentrated and the soul does not merely see through it but is also seen in it. Now as the pulsating heart shows itself all over the surface of the human, in contrast to the animal, body, so in the same sense it is to be asserted of art that it has to convert every shape in all points of its visible surface into an eye, which is the seat of the soul and brings the spirit into appearance.—Or, as Plato cries out to the star in his familiar distich: 'When thou lookest on the stars, my star, oh! would I were the heavens and could see thee with a thousand eyes',[1] so, conversely, art makes every one of its productions into a thousand-eyed Argus, whereby the inner soul and spirit is seen at every point. And it is not only the bodily form, the look of the eyes, the countenance and posture, but also actions and events, speech and tones of voice, and the series of their course through all conditions of appearance that art has everywhere to make into an eye, in which the free soul is revealed in its inner infinity.

(*a*) With this demand for thoroughgoing possession of soul there arises at once the further question *what* this soul is, the eyes of which all points in the phenomenal world are to become. More precisely still, the question is what sort of soul it is that by its nature shows itself qualified to gain its true manifestation through art. . . .

The animation and life of *spirit* alone is free infinity; as such, the spirit in real existence is self-aware as something inner, because in its manifestation it reverts into itself and remains at home with itself. To spirit alone, therefore, is it given to impress the stamp of its own infinity and free return into itself upon its external manifestation, even though through this manifestation it is involved in restriction. Now spirit is only free and infinite when it actually comprehends its universality and raises to universality the ends it sets before itself; but, for this reason, it is capable by its own nature, if it has *not* grasped this freedom, of existing as restricted content, stunted character, and a mind crippled and superficial. In a content of such null worth the infinite manifestation of spirit again remains only formal, for in that case we have nothing but the abstract form of self-conscious spirit, and its content contradicts the infinity of spirit in its freedom. It is only by virtue of a genuine and inherently substantial content that restricted and mutable existence acquires independence and substantiality, so that then both determinacy and inherent solidity, content that is both substantial and restrictedly exclusive, are actual in one and the same thing; and hereby existence gains the possibility of being manifested in the restrictedness of its own content as at the same time universality and as the soul which is alone with itself.—In short, art has the function of grasping and

---

[1] Diogenes Laertius, *Plato*, 23 § 29.

displaying existence, in its appearance, as *true,* i.e. in its suitability to the content which is adequate to itself, the content which is both implicit and explicit. Thus the truth of art cannot be mere correctness, to which the so-called imitation of nature is restricted; on the contrary, the outer must harmonize with an inner which is harmonious in itself, and, just on that account, can reveal itself as itself in the outer.

(*b*) Now since art brings back into this harmony with its true Concept what is contaminated in other existents by chance and externality, it casts aside everything in appearance which does not correspond with the Concept and only by this purification does it produce the Ideal. This may be given out to be flattery by art, as, for example, it is said depreciatingly of portrait painters that they flatter. But even the portrait-painter, who has least of all to do with the Ideal of art, *must* flatter, in the sense that all the externals in shape and expression, in form, colour, features, the purely natural side of imperfect existence, little hairs, pores, little scars, warts, all these he must let go, and grasp and reproduce the subject in his universal character and enduring personality. It is one thing for the artist simply to imitate the face of the sitter, its surface and external form, confronting him in repose, and quite another to be able to portray the true features which express the inmost soul of the subject. For it is throughout necessary for the Ideal that the outer form should explicitly correspond with the soul. So, for example, in our own time what has become the fashion, namely what are called *tableaux vivants,*[2] imitate famous masterpieces deliberately and agreeably, and the accessories, costume, etc., they reproduce accurately; but often enough we see ordinary faces substituted for the spiritual expression of the subjects and this produces an inappropriate effect. Raphael's Madonnas, on the other hand, show us forms of expression, cheeks, eyes, nose, mouth, which, as forms, are appropriate to the radiance, joy, piety, and also the humility of a mother's love. Of course, someone might wish to maintain that all women are capable of this feeling, but not every cast of countenance affords a satisfactory and complete expression of this depth of soul.

(*c*) Now the nature of the artistic Ideal is to be sought in this reconveyance of external existence into the spiritual realm, so that the external appearance, by being adequate to the spirit, is the revelation thereof. Yet this is a reconveyance into the inner realm which at the same time does not proceed to the universal in its abstract form, i.e. to the *extreme* which *thinking* is, but remains in the *centre* where the purely external and the purely internal coincide. Accordingly, the Ideal is actuality, withdrawn from the profusion of details and accidents, in so far as the inner appears itself in this externality, lifted above and opposed to universality, as living individuality. For the individual subjective life which has a substantive content in itself and at the same time makes this content appear on itself externally, stands in this centre. In this centre the substantiality of the content cannot emerge explicitly in its universality in an abstract way; it remains still enclosed in individuality and therefore appears intertwined with a determinate existent, which now, for its part, freed from mere

---

[2] i.e. beautiful women set in a frame, to imitate some artist's picture.

finitude and its conditions, comes together with the inwardness of the soul into a free harmony. Schiller in his poem *Das Ideal und das Leben* [The Ideal and Life] contrasts actuality and its griefs and battles with the 'still shadow-land of beauty'. Such a realm of shadows is the Ideal; the *spirits* appearing in it are dead to immediate existence, cut off from the indigence of natural life, freed from the bonds of dependence on external influences and all the perversions and convulsions inseparable from the finitude of the phenomenal world. But all the same the Ideal treads into the sensuous and the natural form thereof, yet it still at the same time draws this, like the sphere of the external, back into itself, since art can bring back the apparatus,[3] required by external appearance for its self-preservation, to the limits within which the external can be the manifestation of spiritual freedom. Only by this process does the Ideal exist in externality, self-enclosed, free, self-reliant, as sensuously blessed in itself, enjoying and delighting in its own self. The ring of this bliss resounds throughout the entire appearance of the Ideal, for however far the external form may extend, the soul of the Ideal never loses itself in it. And precisely as a result of this alone is the Ideal genuinely beautiful, since the beautiful exists only as a total though subjective unity; wherefore too the subject who manifests the Ideal must appear collected together in himself again into a higher totality and independence out of the divisions in the life of other individuals and their aims and efforts.

(α) In this respect, amongst the fundamental characteristics of the Ideal we may put at the top this serene peace and bliss, this self-enjoyment in its own achievedness and satisfaction. The ideal work of art confronts us like a blessed god. For the blessed gods [of Greek art], that is to say, there is no final seriousness in distress, in anger, in the interests involved in finite spheres and aims, and this positive withdrawal into themselves, along with the negation of everything particular, gives them the characteristic of serenity and tranquillity. In this sense Schiller's phrase holds good: 'Life is serious, art cheerful.'[4]

Often enough, it is true, pedants have poked fun at this, on the ground that art in general, and especially Schiller's own poetry, is of a most serious kind; and after all in fact ideal art does not lack seriousness—but even in the seriousness cheerfulness or serenity remains its inherent and essential character. This force of individuality, this triumph of concrete freedom concentrated in itself, is what we recognize especially in the works of art of antiquity in the cheerful and serene peace of their shapes. And this results not at all from a mere satisfaction gained without struggle, but on the contrary, only when a deeper breach has rent the subject's inner life and his whole existence. For even if the heroes of tragedy for example, are so portrayed that they succumb to fate, still the heart of the hero recoils into simple unity with itself, when it says: 'It is so.' The subject in this case still always remains true to himself; he surrenders what he has been robbed of, yet the ends he pursues are not just taken from him; he renounces them and thereby does not lose *himself*. Man, the slave

---

[3] Hegel describes a "wide apparatus of geographical, historical, and even philosophical notes, facts, and knowledge" needed to enjoy art later in this section. [T.E.W.]

[4] The last line of Schiller's preface to *Wallenstein* (1799).

of destiny, may lose his life, but not his freedom. It is this self-reliance which even in grief enables him to preserve and manifest the cheerfulness and serenity of tranquillity.

(β) It is true that in romantic art the distraction and dissonance of the heart goes further and, in general, the oppositions displayed in it are deepened and their disunion may be maintained. So, for example, in portraying the Passion, painting sometimes persists in expressing the derision in the expressions of the military tormentors with the horrible grimaces and grins on their faces; and with this retention of disunion, especially in sketches of vice, sin, and evil, the serenity of the Ideal is then lost, for even if the distraction does not remain so fixedly as this, still something, if not ugly every time, at least not beautiful often comes into view. In another school of painting, the older Flemish one, there is displayed an inner reconciliation of the heart in its honesty and truthfulness to itself as well as in its faith and unshakeable confidence, but this firmness does not achieve the serenity and satisfaction of the Ideal. Even in romantic art, however, although suffering and grief affect the heart and subjective inner feeling more deeply there than is the case with the ancients, there do come into view a spiritual inwardness, a joy in submission, a bliss in grief and rapture in suffering, even a delight in agony. Even in the solemnly religious music of Italy this pleasure and transfiguration of grief resounds through the expression of lament. This expression in romantic art generally is 'smiling through tears'. Tears belong to grief, smiles to cheerfulness, and so smiling in weeping denotes this inherent tranquillity amidst agony and suffering. Of course smiling here ought not to be a mere sentimental emotion, a frivolous and self-conceited attitude of the man to misfortunes and his minor personal feelings; on the contrary, it must appear as the calmness and freedom of beauty despite all grief—as it is said of Chimena in the *Romances of the Cid:* 'How beautiful she was in tears.'[5] On the other hand, a man's lack of self-control is either ugly and repugnant, or else ludicrous. Children, e.g., burst into tears on the most trifling occasions, and this makes us smile. On the other hand, tears in the eyes of an austere man who keeps a stiff upper lip under the stress of deep feeling convey a totally different impression of emotion. . . .

(γ) In this fundamental principle the modern doctrine of irony too has its justification in a certain respect, except that irony, on the one hand, is often bare of any true seriousness and likes to delight especially in villains, and, on the other hand, ends in mere heartfelt longing instead of in acting and doing. Novalis,[6] for example, one of the nobler spirits who took up this position, was driven into a void with no specific interests, into this dread of reality, and was wound down as it were into a spiritual decline. This is a longing which will not let itself go in actual action and production, because it is frightened of being polluted by contact with finitude, although all the same it has a sense of the deficiency of this abstraction. True, irony implies the absolute negativity in which the subject is related to himself in the annihilation of everything specific and

---

[5] The quotation is from Herder's poetic version of the *Romances of the Cid*, I. 6.
[6] G. F. P. von Hardenberg, 1772–1801.

one-sided; but since this annihilation, as was indicated above in our consideration of this doctrine, affects not only, as in comedy, what is inherently null which manifests itself in its hollowness, but equally everything inherently excellent and solid, it follows that irony as this art of annihilating everything everywhere, like that heart-felt longing, acquires, at the same time, in comparison with the true Ideal, the aspect of inner inartistic lack of restraint. For the Ideal requires an inherently substantive content which, it is true, by displaying itself in the form and shape of the outer as well, comes to particularity and therefore to restrictedness, though it so contains the restrictedness in itself that everything *purely* external in it is extinguished and annihilated. Only on account of this negation of pure externality is the specific form and shape of the Ideal a manifestation of that substantive content in an appearance according with artistic vision and imagination. . . .

DEVELOPMENT OF THE IDEAL INTO THE PARTICULAR FORMS OF ART

What up to this point we have dealt with, in Part I, concerned the actuality of the Idea of the beautiful as the Ideal of art, but [no matter] under how many aspects we also developed the Concept of the ideal work of art, still all our distinctions bore only on the ideal work of art in *general*. But, like the Idea, the Idea of the beautiful is a totality of essential differences which must issue as such and be actualized. Their actualization we may call on the whole the *particular forms* of art, as the development of what is implicit in the Concept of the Ideal and comes into existence through art. Yet if we speak of these art forms as different species of the Ideal, we may not take 'species' in the ordinary sense of the word, as if here the particular forms came from without to the Idea as their universal genus and had become modifications of it: on the contrary, 'species' should mean nothing here but the distinctive and therefore more concrete determinations of the Idea of the beautiful and the Ideal of art itself. The general character of [artistic] representation, i.e., is here made determinate not from without but in itself through its own Concept, so that it is this Concept which is spread out into a totality of particular modes of artistic formation.

Now, in more detail, the forms of art, as the actualizing and unfolding of the beautiful, find their origin in the Idea itself, in the sense that through them the Idea presses on to representation and reality, and whenever it is explicit to itself either only in its abstract determinacy or else in its concrete totality, it also brings itself into appearance in another real formation. This is because the Idea as such is only truly Idea as developing itself explicitly by its own activity; and since as Ideal it is immediate appearance, and indeed with its appearance is the identical Idea of the beautiful, so also at every particular stage on which the Ideal treads the road of its unfolding there is immediately linked with every *inner* determinacy another *real* configuration. It is therefore all one whether we regard the advance in this development as an inner advance of the Idea in itself or of the shape in which it gives itself existence. Each of these two sides is immediately bound up with the other. The consummation of the Idea as content appears therefore simultaneously as also the consummation of form; and conversely the deficiencies of the artistic shape correspondingly prove to be a deficiency of the Idea which constitutes the inner meaning of the external appearance and in that appearance becomes real to itself. Thus if in this Part we encounter art-forms at first which are still inadequate in comparison with the true Ideal, this is not the sort of case in which people ordinarily speak of unsuccessful works of art which either express nothing or lack the capacity to achieve what they are supposed to represent; on the contrary, the specific shape which every content of the Idea gives to itself in the particular forms of art is always adequate to that content, and the deficiency or consummation lies only in the relatively untrue or true determinateness in which and as which the Idea is explicit to itself. This is because the content must be true and concrete in itself before it can find its truly beautiful shape.

. . .[W]e have three chief art-forms to consider:

(i) The *Symbolic*. In this the Idea still *seeks* its genuine expression in art, because in itself it is still abstract and indeterminate and therefore does not have its adequate manifestation on and in itself, but finds itself confronted by what is external to itself, external things in nature and human affairs. Now since it has only an immediate inkling of its own abstractions in this objective world or drives itself with its undetermined universals into a concrete existence, it corrupts and falsifies the shapes that it finds confronting it. This is because it can grasp them only arbitrarily, and therefore, instead of coming to a complete identification, it comes only to an accord, and even to a still abstract harmony, between meaning and shape; in this neither completed nor to be completed mutual formation, meaning and shape present, equally with their affinity, their mutual externality, foreignness, and incompatibility.

(ii) But, secondly, the Idea, in accordance with its essential nature, does not stop at the abstraction and indeterminacy of universal thoughts but is in itself free infinite subjectivity and apprehends this in its actuality as spirit. Now spirit, as free subject, is determined through and by itself, and in this self-determination, and also in its own nature, has that external shape, adequate to itself, with which it can close as with its absolutely due reality. On this entirely harmonious unity of content and form, the second art-form, the *classical*, is based. Yet if the consummation of this unity is to become actual, spirit, in so far as it is made a topic for art, must not yet be the purely absolute spirit which finds its adequate existence only in spirituality and inwardness, but the spirit which is still particular and therefore burdened with an abstraction. That is to say, the free subject, which classical art configurates outwardly, appears indeed as essentially universal and therefore freed from all the accident and mere particularity of the inner life and the outer world, but at the same time as filled solely with a universality particularized within itself. This is because the external shape is, as such, an external determinate particular shape, and for complete fusion [with a content] it can only present again in itself a specific and therefore restricted content, while too it is only the inwardly particular spirit which can appear perfectly in an external manifestation and be bound up with that in an inseparable unity.

Here art has reached its own essential nature by bringing the Idea, as spiritual individuality, directly into harmony with its bodily reality in such a perfect way that external existence now for the first time no longer preserves any independence in contrast with the meaning which it is to express, while conversely the inner [meaning], in its shape worked out for our vision, shows there only itself and in it is related to itself affirmatively.

(iii) But, thirdly, when the Idea of the beautiful is comprehended as absolute spirit, and therefore as the spirit which is free in its own eyes, it is no longer completely realized in the external world, since its true determinate being it has only in itself as spirit. It therefore dissolves that classical unification of inwardness and external manifestation and takes flight out of externality back into itself. This provides the fundamental typification of the *romantic* art-form; the content of this form, on account of its free spirituality, demands more than what representation in the external world and the bodily can supply; in romantic art the shape is externally more or less indifferent, and thus that art reintroduces, in an opposite way from the symbolic, the separation of content and form.

In this way, symbolic art *seeks* that perfect unity of inner meaning and external shape which classical art *finds* in the presentation of substantial individuality to sensuous contemplation, and which romantic art *transcends* in its superior spirituality. . . .

THE SYMBOLIC FORM OF ART

Now, with the development of the kinds of comedy we have reached the real end of our philosophical inquiry. We began with symbolic art where personality struggles to find itself as form and content and to become objective to itself. We proceeded to the plastic art of Greece where the Divine, now conscious of itself, is presented to us in living individuals. We ended with the romantic art of emotion and deep feeling where absolute subjective personality moves free in itself and in the spiritual world. Satisfied in itself, it no longer unites itself with anything objective and particularized and it brings the negative side of this dissolution into consciousness in the humour of comedy. Yet on this peak comedy leads at the same time to the dissolution of art altogether. All art aims at the identity, produced by the spirit, in which eternal things, God, and absolute truth are revealed in real appearance and shape to our contemplation, to our hearts and minds. But if comedy presents this unity only as its self-destruction because the Absolute, which wants to realize itself, sees its self-actualization destroyed by interests that have now become explicitly free in the real world and are directed only on what is accidental and subjective, then the presence and agency of the Absolute no longer appears positively unified with the characters and aims of the real world but asserts itself only in the negative form of cancelling everything not correspondent with it, and subjective personality alone shows itself self-confident and self-assured at the same time in this dissolution.

Now at the end we have arranged every essential category of the beautiful and every essential form of art into a philosophical garland, and weaving it is one of the worthiest tasks that philosophy is capable of completing. For in art we have to do, not with any agreeable or useful child's play, but with the liberation of the spirit from the content and forms of finitude, with the presence and reconciliation of the Absolute in what is apparent and visible, with an unfolding of the truth which is not exhausted in natural history but revealed in world-history. Art itself is the most beautiful side of that history and it is the best compensation for hard work in the world and the bitter labour for knowledge. For this reason my treatment of the subject could not consist in a mere criticism of works of art or an instruction for producing them. My one aim has been to seize in thought and to prove the fundamental nature of the beautiful and art, and to follow it through all the stages it has gone through in the course of its realization. . . .

7

ART AS REDEMPTION:
FRIEDRICH NIETZSCHE

Friedrich Nietzsche (1844–1900) is less concerned with the question "What is art?" than he is with the question "Why art?" That is, rather than trying to understand what distinguishes art from other aspects of human culture, such as science or craft, Nietzsche is primarily interested in why there is such a thing as art, what function it serves in human life.

Nietzsche's answer to "Why art?" is based on his view, derived from Schopenhauer, that life is inherently awful. To confront this truth directly would be fatal—we would simply perish of it. Thus, Nietzsche argues, art becomes a way to make life bearable, to go on in the face of the insight that it is not worth living.

But although all art is a response to the horrors of existence, Nietzsche holds that there are two fundamentally different types of art, the Apolline and the Dionysiac.[1] Here, he is heir to the distinction between the beautiful and the sublime elaborated in Kant and Schopenhauer. Apolline art, Nietzsche asserts, creates a dream world, an idealized realm that keeps at bay the terrors of existence. His example is Greek sculpture, which he sees as an idealization of human life, much as Hegel claims, although with a very different assessment of it.

Nietzsche connects the Apolline with the individuated world of appearances described by Kant and Schopenhauer, in which the individual is very much at home and in command. Dionysiac art, in contrast, is art that intoxicates, that dissolves individuality. To get a sense of what Nietzsche is referring to here, recall Schopenhauer's ecstatic description of the effects of sublime art (Chapter 5). Or, even better, think about what it feels like to be at a rock concert, literally taken over by the music, the audience moving as one. At such moments, Nietzsche holds, art redeems life by getting us to reject our

---

[1] The translation used here uses "Apolline" and "Dionysiac" in place of the more usual terms "Apollonian" and "Dionysian." I have followed that practice in my own introduction to the reading.

individuality and become one with the forces governing the universe as a whole.

Although Nietzsche treats these two artistic tendencies as distinct, he also argues that they are intimately related. Each exists in dynamic tension with the other. The achievements of Apolline art can only be understood as a conscious attempt to hold the Dionysiac at bay, and vice versa. Nietzsche's distinction between the Apolline and Dionysiac ultimately transcends its origin in his consideration of art and, specifically, Greek tragedy. For him, these two artistic tendencies come to denote larger cultural forces.

Thus, behind the Apolline he uncovers the more general tendency to deny life; the Dionysiac, by contrast, affirms life in all its terror. This dichotomy functions in Nietzsche's thought as the basis for a sweeping critique of European culture—not just of its art, but all its aspects, from science to morality. The only hope for the West, according to Nietzsche, is a rebirth of the Dionysiac.

Nietzsche's views about art, and culture more generally, have been widely influential in Continental thought. After a period in which he was more or less ignored, even dismissed as a protofascist, Nietzsche is now considered one of the seminal thinkers of the late 19th century.

STUDY QUESTIONS ON THE READING

1. Nietzsche associates Apolline art with dreams. What aspect of dreaming is important for him? In what sense are artworks of this type like dreams?

2. Dionysiac art is the art of intoxication, according to Nietzsche. Can you think of examples of such art? How does it differ from Apolline art?

3. What is the significance of Nietzsche's retelling of the Midas tale in section 3? How is tragedy related to this story?

4. Nietzsche claims that Greek tragedy involves a unification of the Dionysiac and the Apolline. Explain what he means by this claim. How can these two conflicting tendencies be united?

5. Aristotle also presented a theory of Greek tragedy (see Chapter 2). What are the differences between these two theories? Which do you think is more insightful, and why?

6. Why does Nietzsche see Euripides as the destroyer of Greek tragedy? How do his tragedies differ from the older ones, according to Nietzsche?

7. Why does Nietzsche align Euripides with Socrates? What is their common trait?

8. Do you agree with Nietzsche's assessment of art's cultural role? Why or why not?

❖

FRIEDRICH NIETZSCHE: THE BIRTH OF TRAGEDY

I

We shall have gained much for the science of aesthetics when we have come to realize, not just through logical insight but also with the certainty of something directly apprehended, that the continuous evolution of art is bound up with the duality of the *Apolline* and the *Dionysiac* in much the same way as reproduction depends on there being two sexes which co-exist in a state of perpetual conflict interrupted only occasionally by periods of reconciliation. We have borrowed these names from the Greeks who reveal the profound mysteries of their view of art to those with insight, not in concepts, admittedly, but through the penetratingly vivid figures of their gods. Their two deities of art, Apollo and Dionysos, provide the starting-point for our recognition that there exists in the world of the Greeks an enormous opposition, both in origin and goals, between the Apolline art of the image-maker or sculptor and the imageless art of music, which is that of Dionysos. These two very different drives exist side by side, mostly in open conflict, stimulating and provoking one another to give birth to ever-new, more vigorous offspring in whom they perpetuate the conflict inherent in the opposition between them, an opposition only apparently bridged by the common term 'art'—until eventually, by a metaphysical miracle of the Hellenic 'Will', they appear paired and, in this pairing, finally engender a work of art which is Dionysiac and Apolline in equal measure: Attic tragedy.

In order to gain a closer understanding of these two drives, let us think of them in the first place as the separate art-worlds of *dream* and *intoxication*. Between these two physiological phenomena an opposition can be observed which corresponds to that between the Apolline and the Dionysiac. . . .

The Greeks also expressed the joyous necessity of dream-experience in their Apollo: as the god of all image-making energies, Apollo is also the god of prophecy. According to the etymological root of his name, he is 'the luminous one', the god of light; as such, he also governs the lovely semblance produced by the inner world of fantasy. The higher truth, the perfection of these dream-states in contrast to the only partially intelligible reality of the daylight world, together with the profound consciousness of the helping and healing powers of nature in sleep and dream, is simultaneously the symbolic analogue of the ability to prophesy and indeed of all the arts through which life is made possible and worth living. But the image of Apollo must also contain that delicate line which the dream-image may not overstep if its effect is not to become pathological, so that, in the worst case, the semblance would deceive us as if it were

From "The Birth of Tragedy" from *Nietzsche: The Birth of Tragedy and Other Writings*, by Friedrich Nietzsche, ed. by Raymond Geuss and Ronald Speirs. © 1999 Cambridge University Press. Reprinted with permission.

crude reality; his image must include that measured limitation, that freedom from wilder impulses, that wise calm of the image-making god. In accordance with his origin, his eye must be 'sunlike'; even when its gaze is angry and shows displeasure, it exhibits the consecrated quality of lovely semblance. Thus, in an eccentric sense, one could apply to Apollo what Schopenhauer says about human beings trapped in the veil of maya:

> Just as the boatman sits in his small boat, trusting his frail craft in a stormy sea that is boundless in every direction, rising and falling with the howling, mountainous waves, so in the midst of a world full of suffering and misery the individual man calmly sits, supported by and trusting in the *principium individuationis*. (*World as Will and Representation*, 1, p. 416)

Indeed one could say that Apollo is the most sublime expression of imperturbable trust in this principle and of the calm sitting-there of the person trapped within it; one might even describe Apollo as the magnificent divine image of the *principium individuationis*, whose gestures and gaze speak to us of all the intense pleasure, wisdom and beauty of 'semblance'.

In the same passage Schopenhauer has described for us the enormous *horror* which seizes people when they suddenly become confused and lose faith in the cognitive forms of the phenomenal world because the principle of sufficient reason, in one or other of its modes, appears to sustain an exception. If we add to this horror the blissful ecstasy which arises from the innermost ground of man, indeed of nature itself, whenever this breakdown of the *principium individuationis* occurs, we catch a glimpse of the essence of the *Dionysiac*, which is best conveyed by the analogy of *intoxication*. These Dionysiac stirrings, which, as they grow in intensity, cause subjectivity to vanish to the point of complete self-forgetting, awaken either under the influence of narcotic drink, of which all human beings and peoples who are close to the origin of things speak in their hymns, or at the approach of spring when the whole of nature is pervaded by lust for life. In the German Middle Ages, too, ever-growing throngs roamed from place to place, impelled by the same Dionysiac power, singing and dancing as they went; in these St John's and St Vitus' dancers we recognize the Bacchic choruses of the Greeks, with their prehistory in Asia Minor, extending to Babylon and the orgiastic Sacaea. There are those who, whether from lack of experience or from dullness of spirit, turn away in scorn or pity from such phenomena, regarding them as 'popular diseases' while believing in their own good health; of course, these poor creatures have not the slightest inkling of how spectral and deathly pale their 'health' seems when the glowing life of Dionysiac enthusiasts storms past them.

Not only is the bond between human beings renewed by the magic of the Dionysiac, but nature, alienated, inimical, or subjugated, celebrates once more her festival of reconciliation with her lost son, humankind. Freely the earth offers up her gifts, and the beasts of prey from mountain and desert approach in peace. The chariot of Dionysos is laden with flowers and wreaths; beneath its yoke stride panther and tiger. If one were to transform Beethoven's jubilant 'Hymn to Joy' into a painting and place no constraints on one's imagination as the millions sink into the dust, shivering in awe, then one could begin to approach the Dionysiac. Now the slave is a freeman, now all the rigid, hostile barriers, which necessity, caprice, or 'impudent fashion' have established between human beings, break asunder. Now, hearing this gospel of universal harmony, each person feels himself to be not simply united, reconciled or merged with his neighbour, but quite literally one with him, as if the veil of maya had been torn apart, so that mere shreds of it flutter before the mysterious primordial unity. Singing and dancing, man expresses his sense of belonging to a higher community; he has forgotten how to walk and talk and is on the brink of flying and dancing, up and away into the air above. His gestures speak of his enchantment. Just as the animals now talk and the earth gives milk and honey, there now sounds out from within man something supernatural: he feels himself to be a god, he himself now moves in such ecstasy and sublimity as once he saw the gods move in his dreams. Man is no longer an artist, he has become a work of art: all nature's artistic power reveals itself here, amidst shivers of intoxication, to the highest, most blissful satisfaction of the primordial unity. Here man, the noblest clay, the most precious marble, is kneaded and carved and, to the accompaniment of the chisel-blows of the Dionysiac world-artist, the call of the Eleusinian Mysteries rings out: 'Fall ye to the ground, ye millions? Feelst thou thy Creator, world?'

2

So far we have considered the Apolline and its opposite, the Dionysiac, as artistic powers which erupt from nature itself, *without the mediation of any human artist,* and in which nature's artistic drives attain their first, immediate satisfaction: on the one hand as the image-world of dream, the perfection of which is not linked to an individual's intellectual level or artistic formation, and on the other hand as intoxicated reality, which has just as little regard for the individual, even seeking to annihilate, redeem, and release him by imparting a mystical sense of oneness. In relation to these unmediated artistic states in nature every artist is an 'imitator', and indeed either an Apolline dream artist or a Dionysiac artist of intoxication or finally—as, for example, in Greek tragedy—an artist of both dream and intoxication at once. This is how we must think of him as he sinks to the ground in Dionysiac drunkenness and mystical self-abandon, alone and apart from the enthusiastic choruses, at which point, under the Apolline influence of dream, his own condition, which is to say, his oneness with the innermost ground of the world, reveals itself to him *in a symbolic dream-image.*

Having set out these general assumptions and contrasts, let us now consider the *Greeks* in order to understand the degree and level to which those *artistic drives of nature* were developed in them. This will enable us to gain a deeper understanding and appreciation of the relationship between the Greek artist and his models, or, to use Aristotle's expression, 'the imitation of nature'. Despite all the dream literature of the Greeks and numerous dream anecdotes, we can speak only speculatively, but with a fair degree of certainty, about the

Greeks' *dreams*. Given the incredibly definite and assured ability of their eye to see things in a plastic way, together with their pure and honest delight in colour, one is bound to assume, to the shame of all those born after them, that their dreams, too, had that logical causality of line and outline, colour and grouping, and a sequence of scenes resembling their best bas-reliefs, so that the perfection of their dreams would certainly justify us, if comparison were possible, in describing the dreaming Greeks as Homers and Homer as a dreaming Greek—and in a more profound sense than if a modern dared to compare his dreaming with that of Shakespeare.

By contrast, there is no need for speculation when it comes to revealing the vast gulf which separated the *Dionysiac Greeks* from the Dionysiac Barbarians. From all corners of the ancient world (leaving aside the modern one in this instance), from Rome to Babylon, we can demonstrate the existence of Dionysiac festivals of a type which, at best, stands in the same relation to the Greek festivals as the bearded satyr, whose name and attributes were borrowed from the goat, stands to Dionysos himself. Almost everywhere an excess of sexual indiscipline, which flooded in waves over all family life and its venerable statutes, lay at the heart of such festivals. Here the very wildest of nature's beasts were unleashed, up to and including that repulsive mixture of sensuality and cruelty which has always struck me as the true 'witches' brew'. Although news of these festivals reached them by every sea- and land-route, the Greeks appear, for a time, to have been completely protected and insulated from their feverish stirrings by the figure of Apollo, who reared up in all his pride, there being no more dangerous power for him to confront with the Medusa's head than this crude, grotesque manifestation of the Dionysiac. Apollo's attitude of majestic rejection is eternalized in Doric art. Such resistance became more problematic and even impossible when, eventually, similar shoots sprang from the deepest root of the Hellenic character; now the work of the Delphic God was limited to taking the weapons of destruction out of the hands of his mighty opponent in a timely act of reconciliation. This reconciliation is the most important moment in the history of Greek religion; wherever one looks, one can see the revolutionary consequences of this event. It was the reconciliation of two opponents, with a precise delineation of the borders which each had now to respect and with the periodic exchange of honorific gifts; fundamentally the chasm had not been bridged. Yet if we now look at how the power of the Dionysiac manifested itself under pressure from that peace-treaty, we can see that, in contrast to the Babylonian Sacaea, where human beings regressed to the condition of tigers and monkeys, the significance of the Greeks' Dionysiac orgies was that of festivals of universal release and redemption and days of transfiguration. Here for the first time the jubilation of nature achieves expression as art, here for the first time the tearing-apart of the *principium individuationis* becomes an artistic phenomenon. That repulsive witches' brew of sensuality and cruelty was powerless here; the only reminder of it (in the way that medicines recall deadly poisons) is to be found in the strange mixture and duality in the affects of the Dionysiac enthusiasts, that phenomenon whereby pain awakens pleasure while rejoicing wrings cries of agony from the breast. From highest joy there comes a cry of horror or a yearning lament at some irredeemable loss. In those Greek festivals there erupts what one might call a sentimental tendency in nature, as if it had cause to sigh over its dismemberment into individuals. The singing and expressive gestures of such enthusiasts in their two-fold mood was something new and unheard-of in the Homeric-Greek world; Dionysiac *music* in particular elicited terror and horror from them. Although it seems that music was already familiar to the Greeks as an Apolline art, they only knew it, strictly speaking, in the form of a wave-like rhythm with an image-making power which they developed to represent Apolline states. The music of Apollo was Doric architectonics in sound, but only in the kind of hinted-at tones characteristic of the *cithara* [an ancient musical instrument]. It keeps at a distance, as something un-Apolline, the very element which defines the character of Dionysiac music (and thus of music generally): the power of its sound to shake us to our very foundations, the unified stream of melody and the quite incomparable world of harmony. In the Dionysiac dithyramb man is stimulated to the highest intensification of his symbolic powers; something that he has never felt before urgently demands to be expressed: the destruction of the veil of maya, oneness as the genius of humankind, indeed of nature itself. The essence of nature is bent on expressing itself; a new world of symbols is required, firstly the symbolism of the entire body, not just of the mouth, the face, the word, but the full gesture of dance with its rhythmical movement of every limb. Then there is a sudden, tempestuous growth in music's other symbolic powers, in rhythm, dynamics, and harmony. To comprehend this complete unchaining of all symbolic powers, a man must already have reached that height of self-abandonment which seeks symbolic expression in those powers: thus the dithyrambic servant of Dionysos can only be understood by his own kind! With what astonishment the Apolline Greeks must have regarded him! With an astonishment enlarged by the added horror of realizing that all this was not so foreign to them after all, indeed that their Apolline consciousness only hid this Dionysiac world from them like a veil.

3

In order to understand this, we need to dismantle the artful edifice of *Apolline culture* stone by stone, as it were, until we catch sight of the foundations on which it rests. The first things we observe here are the magnificent figures of the *Olympian* gods who stand on the gables of this building and whose deeds, represented in reliefs which can be seen gleaming from afar, adorn its friezes. If Apollo is also amongst their number, as just one god alongside others and without laying claim to the leading position, we should not allow this fact to confuse us. The very same drive which assumed sensuous form in Apollo gave birth to that entire Olympian world, and in this sense we are entitled to regard Apollo as its father. What, then, was the enormous need that gave rise to such a luminous company of Olympic beings?

Anyone who approaches these Olympians with another religion in his heart and proceeds to look for signs of moral loftiness in them, or indeed holiness, or incorporeal spirituality, or a loving gaze filled with compassion, will soon be forced to turn his back on them in dismay and disappointment. Nothing here reminds us of asceticism, of spirituality and duty; everything here speaks only of over-brimming, indeed triumphant existence, where everything that exists has been deified, regardless of whether it is good or evil. Thus the spectator may stand in some perplexity before this fantastic superabundance of life, asking himself what magic potion these people can have drunk which makes them see Helen, 'hovering in sweet sensuality', smiling at them wherever they look, the ideal image of their own existence. Yet we must call out to this spectator who has already turned away: 'Do not go away, but listen first to what popular Greek wisdom has to say about this inexplicably serene existence you see spread out before you here.' An ancient legend recounts how King Midas hunted long in the forest for the wise *Silenus,* companion of Dionysos, but failed to catch him. When Silenus has finally fallen into his hands, the King asks what is the best and most excellent thing for human beings. Stiff and unmoving, the daemon remains silent until, forced by the King to speak, he finally breaks out in shrill laughter and says: 'Wretched, ephemeral race, children of chance and tribulation, why do you force me to tell you the very thing which it would be most profitable for you *not* to hear? The very best thing is utterly beyond your reach: not to have been born, not to *be,* to be *nothing.* However, the second best thing for you is: to die soon.'

How does the world of the Olympian gods relate to this piece of popular wisdom? The relationship is that of the ecstatic vision of a tortured martyr to his torments.

The Olympian magic mountain now opens up, as it were, and shows us its roots. The Greeks knew and felt the terrors and horrors of existence; in order to live at all they had to place in front of these things the resplendent, dream-born figures of the Olympians. That enormous distrust of the Titanic forces of nature, that *moira* [fate] which throned, unpitying, above all knowledge, that vulture of man's great friend, Prometheus, that terrifying lot drawn by the wise Oedipus, that curse upon the family of Atreus which compels Orestes to kill his mother, in short that whole philosophy of the wood-god, together with its mythic examples, which destroyed the melancholy Etruscans—all this was constantly and repeatedly overcome by the Greeks, or at least veiled and withdrawn from view, by means of the artistic *middle world* of the Olympians. In order to be able to live, the Greeks were obliged, by the most profound compulsion, to create these gods. This process is probably to be imagined as taking place gradually, so that, under the influence of the Apolline instinct for beauty, the Olympian divine order of joy developed out of the original, Titanic divine order of terror in a series of slow transitions, in much the same way as roses burst forth from a thicket of thorns. How else could that people have borne existence, given their extreme sensitivity, their stormy desires, their unique gift for *suffering,* if that same existence had not been shown to them in their gods, suffused with a higher glory? The same drive which calls art into being to complete and perfect existence and thus to seduce us into continuing to live, also gave rise to the world of the Olympians in which the Hellenic 'Will' held up a transfiguring mirror to itself. Thus gods justify the life of men by living it themselves—the only satisfactory theodicy! Under the bright sunshine of such gods existence is felt to be worth attaining, and the real *pain* of Homeric man refers to his departure from this existence, particularly to imminent departure, so that one might say of them, reversing the wisdom of Silenus, that 'the very worst thing for them was to die soon, the second worst ever to die at all'. If a lament is ever heard, it sings of short-lived Achilles, of the generations of men changing and succeeding one another like leaves on the trees, of the demise of the heroic age. It is not unworthy of the greatest hero to long to go on living, even as a day-labourer. So stormily does the 'Will', on the level of the Apolline, demand this existence, so utterly at one with it does Homeric man feel himself to be, that even his lament turns into a song in praise of being.

At this point it must be said that this harmony, which modern men look on with such longing, this unity of man with nature, to which Schiller applied the now generally accepted art-word 'naive', is by no means such a simple, so-to-speak inevitable condition which emerges of its own accord and which we would be *bound* to encounter at the threshold of every culture, as a human paradise; people could only believe this at a time when they were bent on thinking of Rousseau's Emile as an artist, and entertained the illusion that in Homer they had found just such an artist as Emile, reared at the heart of nature. Wherever we encounter the 'naive' in art, we have to recognize that it is the supreme effect of Apolline culture; as such, it first had to overthrow the realm of the Titans and slay monsters, and, by employing powerful delusions and intensely pleasurable illusions, gain victory over a terrifyingly profound view of the world and the most acute sensitivity to suffering. But how rarely is that complete enthralment in the beauty of semblance which we call the naive actually achieved! And how ineffably sublime, for this very reason, is *Homer*, who, as an individual, stands in the same relation to that Apolline popular culture as the individual dream-artist does to the people's capacity for dreaming and indeed to that of nature in general. Homeric 'naïveté' can be understood only as the complete victory of Apolline illusion; it is an illusion of the kind so frequently employed by nature to achieve its aims. The true goal is obscured by a deluding image; we stretch out our hands towards the image, and nature achieves its goal by means of this deception. In the Greeks the 'Will' wanted to gaze on a vision of itself as transfigured by genius and the world of art; in order that the Will might glorify itself its creatures too had to feel themselves to be worthy of glorification; they had to recognize a reflection of themselves in a higher sphere without feeling that the perfected world of their vision was an imperative or a reproach. This is the sphere of beauty in which they saw their mirror images, the Olympians. With this reflection of beauty the Hellenic 'Will' fought against the talent for suffering and for the wisdom of suffering which is the correlative of artistic talent; as a monument to its victory, Homer stands before us, the naive artist.

4

The analogy with dream tells us something about this naive artist. If we imagine the dreamer calling out to himself in the midst of the illusory dream world, but without disturbing it, 'It is a dream, I will dream on', and if this compels us to conclude that he is deriving intense inward pleasure from looking at the dream, but if on the other hand the ability to dream with such inner pleasure in looking depends on us having entirely forgotten the day and its terrible importuning, then we may interpret all of these phenomena, under the guidance of Apollo, the diviner of dreams, roughly as follows. There is no doubt that, of the two halves of our lives, the waking and the dreaming half, the former strikes us as being the more privileged, important, dignified, and worthy of being lived, indeed the only half that truly is lived; nevertheless, although it may seem paradoxical, I wish to assert that the very opposite evaluation of dream holds true for that mysterious ground of our being of which we are an appearance. The more I become aware of those all-powerful artistic drives in nature, and of a fervent longing in them for semblance, for their redemption and release in semblance, the more I feel myself driven to the metaphysical assumption that that which truly exists, the eternally suffering and contradictory, primordial unity, simultaneously needs, for its constant release and redemption, the ecstatic vision, intensely pleasurable semblance. We, however, who consist of and are completely trapped in semblance, are compelled to feel this semblance to be that which truly is not, i.e. a continual Becoming in time, space, and causality—in other words, empirical reality. If we ignore for a moment our own 'reality' and if we take our empirical existence, and indeed that of the world in general, to be a representation generated at each moment by the primordial unity, we must now regard dream as the *semblance of the semblance* and thus as a yet higher satisfaction of the original desire for semblance. It is for this very reason that the innermost core of nature takes indescribable pleasure in the naive artist and the naive work of art which is also only the 'semblance of semblance'. *Raphael,* himself one of those immortal 'naive' artists, has depicted for us in a symbolic painting the reduction of semblance to semblance, the primal process of the naive artist and also of Apolline culture. In his *Transfiguration* the lower half of the picture, with the possessed boy, the despairing bearers, and the frightened, helpless disciples, shows us a reflection of the eternal, primal pain, the only ground of the world; here 'semblance' is a reflection of the eternal contradiction, the father of all things. From this semblance there now rises, like some ambrosian perfume, a vision-like new world of semblance, of which those who are trapped in the first semblance see nothing—a luminous hovering in purest bliss and in wide-eyed contemplation, free of all pain. Here, in the highest symbolism of art, we see before us that Apolline world of beauty and the ground on which it rests, that terrible wisdom of Silenus, and we grasp, intuitively, the reciprocal necessity of these two things. At the same time, however, we encounter Apollo as the deification of the *principium individuationis* in which alone the eternally attained goal of the primordial unity, its release and redemption through semblance, comes about; with sublime gestures he shows us that the whole world of agony is needed in order to compel the individual to generate the releasing and redemptive vision and then, lost in contemplation of that vision, to sit calmly in his rocking boat in the midst of the sea.

If one thinks of it as in any sense imperative and prescriptive, this deification of individuation knows just one law: the individual, which is to say, respect for the limits of the individual, *measure* in the Hellenic sense. As an ethical divinity Apollo demands measure from all who belong to him and, so that they may respect that measure, knowledge of themselves. Thus the aesthetic necessity of beauty is accompanied by the demands: 'Know thyself' and 'Not too much!', whereas getting above oneself and excess were regarded as the true hostile demons of the non-Apolline sphere, and thus as qualities of the pre-Apolline period, the age of the Titans, and of the extra-Apolline world, that of the barbarians. Prometheus had to be torn apart by vultures on account of his Titanic love for mankind; Oedipus had to be plunged into a confusing maelstrom of atrocities because his unmeasured wisdom solved the riddle of the Sphinx; these examples show how the Delphic god interpreted the Greek past.

The Apolline Greek, too, felt the effect aroused by the *Dionysiac* to be 'Titanic' and 'barbaric'; at the same time he could not conceal from himself the fact that he too was related inwardly to those overthrown Titans and heroes. Indeed he was bound to feel more than this: his entire existence, with all its beauty and moderation, rested on a hidden ground of suffering and knowledge which was exposed to his gaze once more by the Dionysiac. And behold! Apollo could not live without Dionysos. The 'Titanic' and 'barbaric' was ultimately just as much of a necessity as the Apolline! Let us now imagine how the ecstatic sounds of the Dionysiac festival, with its ever more seductive, magical melodies, entered this artificially dammed-up world founded on semblance and measure, how in these melodies all the unmeasurable excess in nature found expression in pleasure, suffering and knowledge, in a voice which rose in intensity to a penetrating shout; let us imagine how little the psalm-singing artist of Apollo and the ghostly sound of his harp could mean in comparison with this daemonic popular song! The Muses of the arts of 'semblance' grew pale and wan when faced with an art which, in its intoxication, spoke the truth; the wisdom of Silenus called out 'Woe, woe!' to the serene Olympians. The individual, with all his limits and measure, became submerged here in the self-oblivion of the Dionysiac condition and forgot the statutes of Apollo. *Excess* revealed itself as the truth; contradiction, bliss born of pain, spoke of itself from out of the heart of nature. Thus, wherever the Dionysiac broke through, the Apolline was suspended and annulled. But it is equally certain that, wherever the first onslaught was resisted, the reputation and majesty of the Delphic god was expressed in more rigid and menacing forms than ever before; for the only explanation I can find for the *Doric* state and Doric art is that it was a permanent military encampment of the Apolline: only in a state of unremitting resistance to the Titanic-barbaric nature of the Dionysiac could such a cruel and ruthless polity, such a war-like and austere form of education, such a defiantly aloof art, surrounded by battlements, exist for long. . . .

8

. . . Enchantment is the precondition of all dramatic art. In this enchanted state the Dionysiac enthusiast sees himself as a satyr, and *as a satyr he in turn sees the god*, i.e. in his transformed state he sees a new vision outside himself which is the Apolline perfection of his state. With this new vision the drama is complete.

This insight leads us to understand Greek tragedy as a Dionysian chorus which discharges itself over and over again in an Apolline world of images.

Thus the choral passages which are interwoven with the tragedy are, to a certain extent, the womb of the entire so-called dialogue, i.e. of the whole world on stage, the drama proper. This primal ground of tragedy radiates, in a succession of discharges, that vision of drama which is entirely a dream-appearance, and thus epic in nature; on the other hand, as the objectification of a Dionysiac state, the vision represents not Apolline release and redemption in semblance, but rather the breaking-asunder of the individual and its becoming one with the primal being itself. Thus drama is the Apolline embodiment of Dionysiac insights and effects, and is thereby separated by a vast gulf from the epic.

The *chorus* of Greek tragedy, the symbol of the entire mass of those affected by Dionysiac excitement, is fully explained by our understanding of the matter. Because we are accustomed to the position of the chorus, particularly the operatic chorus, on the modern stage, we were completely unable to understand how the tragic chorus of the Greeks was supposedly older, more original, indeed more important than the 'action' proper—although this is clearly what the historical evidence says; equally, we could not see how the high importance and originality traditionally attributed to the chorus was to be reconciled with the fact that it was said to be composed of lowly, serving creatures, indeed, initially, only of goat-like satyrs; the placing of the orchestra before the stage remained a constant puzzle to us; now, however, we have come to realize that the stage and the action were originally and fundamentally thought of as nothing other than a *vision* that the only 'reality' is precisely that of the chorus, which creates the vision from within itself and speaks of this vision with all the symbolism of dance, tone, and word. This chorus sees in its vision its lord and master Dionysos, and is therefore eternally the *serving* chorus; it sees how the god suffers and is glorified, and thus does not itself *act*. Despite its entirely subservient position in relation to the god, however, the chorus is nevertheless the highest, which is to say Dionysiac, expression of *nature,* and therefore speaks in its enthusiasm, as does nature herself, oracular and wise words; the chorus which *shares in suffering* is also the *wise* chorus which proclaims the truth from the heart of the world. This gives rise to that fantastical and seemingly distasteful figure of the wise and enthusiastic satyr who is at the same time 'the foolish man' in contrast to his god; a copy of nature and its strongest impulses, indeed a symbol of them, and at the same time the proclaimer of her wisdom and art; musician, poet, dancer, seer of spirits, all in one person.

According to this insight and according to the traditional evidence, *Dionysos,* the true hero of the stage and centre of the vision, is initially, in the earliest period of the tragedy, not truly present, but rather is imagined as being present; i.e. originally the tragedy is only 'chorus' and not 'drama'. Later the attempt is made to show the god as real and to present the visionary figure, together with the transfiguring framework, as visible to every eye; at this point 'drama' in the narrower sense begins. Now the dithyrambic chorus is given the task of infecting the mood of the spectators with Dionysiac excitement to such a pitch that, when the tragic hero appears on the stage, they see, not some grotesquely masked human being, but rather a visionary figure, born, as it were, of their own ecstasy. If we think of Admetus [a character in Euripides' *Alcestis.* TEW], lost in thought as he remembers his recently deceased wife Alcestis, and consuming himself entirely in mental contemplation of her—when, suddenly, the image of a woman, similar in form and with a similar walk, is led, veiled, towards him; if we think of his sudden, trembling restlessness, his stormy comparisons, his instinctive conviction—then we have an analogy for the feeling with which the spectator, in a state of Dionysiac excitement, saw approaching on the stage the god with whose suffering he has already become one. Involuntarily he transferred on to that masked figure the whole image of the god which he saw trembling magically before his soul, and he dissolved, so to speak, the reality of the figure into a ghostly unreality. This is the Apolline dream-state in which the day-world becomes shrouded, and a new, clearer, more comprehensible, more affecting world, but one which at the same time is more shadow-like, is born anew and presents itself, constantly changing, to our gaze. Accordingly, we recognize in tragedy a pervasive stylistic opposition: language, colour, mobility, dynamics, all of these diverge into distinct, entirely separated spheres of expression, into the Dionysiac lyric of the chorus on the one hand and the Apolline dream-world of the stage on the other. The Apolline appearances in which Dionysos objectifies himself are no longer an 'eternal sea, a changing weaving, a glowing life', as the music of the chorus is; they are no longer those energies which were only felt and not yet concentrated in an image, in which the enthusiastic servant of Dionysos senses the closeness of his god; now the clarity and firmness of the epic shaping speak to him from the stage, now Dionysos no longer speaks in the form of energies but rather as an epic hero, almost in the language of Homer.

9

Everything that rises to the surface in dialogue, the Apolline part of Greek tragedy, appears simple, transparent, beautiful. In this sense the dialogue is a copy of the Hellene, whose nature is expressed in dance, because in dance the greatest strength is still only potential, although it is betrayed by the suppleness and luxuriance of movement. Thus the language of Sophocles' heroes surprises us by its Apolline definiteness and clarity, so that we feel as if we are looking straight into the innermost ground of its being, and are somewhat astonished that the road to this ground is so short. But if we once divert our gaze from the character of the hero as it rises to the surface and becomes visible—fundamentally, it is no more than an image of light (*Lichtbild*) projected on to a dark wall, i.e. appearance (*Erscheinung*) through and through—if, rather, we penetrate to the myth which projects itself in these bright reflections, we suddenly experience a phenomenon which inverts a familiar optical one. When we turn away blinded after a strenuous attempt to look directly at the sun, we have dark, coloured patches before our eyes, as if their purpose were to heal them; conversely, those appearances of the Sophoclean hero in images of light, in other words, the Apolline quality of the mask, are the necessary result of gazing into the inner, terrible depths of nature—radiant patches, as it were, to heal a gaze seared by gruesome night. . . .

I shall now contrast the glory of passivity with the glory of activity which shines around the *Prometheus* of Aeschylus. What the thinker Aeschylus had to tell us here, but what his symbolic poetic image only hints at, has been revealed to us by the youthful Goethe in the reckless words of his Prometheus:

Here I sit, forming men
In my own image,
A race to be like me,
To suffer and to weep,
To know delight and joy
And heed you not,
Like me![1]

Raising himself to Titanic heights, man fights for and achieves his own culture, and he compels the gods to ally themselves with him because, in his very own wisdom, he holds existence and its limits in his hands. But the most wonderful thing in that poem about Prometheus (which, in terms of its basic thought, is the true hymn of impiety) is its profound, Aeschylean tendency to *justice*: the limitless suffering of the bold 'individual' on the one hand, and the extreme plight of the gods, indeed a premonition of the twilight of the gods, on the other; the power of both these worlds of suffering to enforce reconciliation, metaphysical oneness—all this recalls in the strongest possible way the centre and principal tenet of the Aeschylean view of the world, which sees *moira*, as eternal justice, throned above gods and men. If the boldness of Aeschylus in placing the world of the Olympians on his scales of justice seems astonishing, we must remember that the deep-thinking Greek had an unshakably firm foundation for metaphysical thought in his Mysteries, so that all attacks of scepticism could be discharged on the Olympians. The Greek artist in particular had an obscure feeling that he and these gods were mutually dependent, a feeling symbolized precisely in Aeschylus' Prometheus. The Titanic artist found within himself the defiant belief that he could create human beings and destroy the Olympian gods at least, and that his higher wisdom enabled him to do so, for which, admittedly, he was forced to do penance by suffering eternally. The magnificent 'ability' of the great genius, for which even eternal suffering is too small a price to pay, the bitter pride of the *artist*: this is the content and the soul of Aeschylus' play, whereas Sophocles, in his *Oedipus*, begins the prelude to the victory-hymn of the *saint*. But even Aeschylus' interpretation of the myth does not plumb its astonishing, terrible depths; rather, the artist's delight in Becoming, the serenity of artistic creation in defiance of all catastrophes, is merely a bright image of clouds and sky reflected in a dark sea of sadness. Originally, the legend of Prometheus belonged to the entire community of Aryan peoples and documented their talent for the profound and the tragic; indeed, it is not unlikely that this myth is as significant for the Aryan character as the myth of the Fall is for the Semitic character, and that the relationship between the two myths is like that between brother and sister. The myth of Prometheus presupposes the unbounded value which naive humanity placed *on fire* as the true palladium of every rising culture; but it struck those

---

[1] Goethe, *Prometheus*, lines 51 ff.

contemplative original men as a crime, a theft perpetrated on divine nature, to believe that man commanded fire freely, rather than receiving it as a gift from heaven, as a bolt of lightning which could start a blaze, or as the warming fire of the sun. Thus the very first philosophical problem presents a painful, irresolvable conflict between god and man, and pushes it like a mighty block of rock up against the threshold of every culture. Humanity achieves the best and highest of which it is capable by committing an offence and must in turn accept the consequences of this, namely the whole flood of suffering and tribulations which the offended heavenly powers *must* in turn visit upon the human race as it strives nobly towards higher things: a bitter thought, but one which, thanks to the *dignity* it accords to the offence, contrasts strangely with the Semitic myth of the Fall, where the origin of evil was seen to lie in curiosity, mendacious pretence, openness to seduction, lasciviousness, in short: in a whole series of predominantly feminine attributes. What distinguishes the Aryan conception is the sublime view that *active sin* is the true Promethean virtue; thereby we have also found the ethical foundation of pessimistic tragedy, its *justification* of the evil in human life, both in the sense of human guilt and in the sense of the suffering brought about by it. The curse in the nature of things, which the reflective Aryan is not inclined simply to explain away, the contradiction at the heart of the world, presents itself to him as a mixture of different worlds, e.g. a divine and a human one, each of which, taken individually, is in the right, but which, as one world existing alongside another, must suffer for the fact of its individuation. The heroic urge of the individual to reach out towards the general, the attempt to cross the fixed boundaries of individuation, and the desire to become the *one* world-being itself, all this leads him to suffer in his own person the primal contradiction hidden within the things of this world, i.e. he commits a great wrong and suffers. Thus great wrongdoing is understood as masculine by the Aryans, but as feminine by the Semites, just as the original wrong was committed by a man and the original sin by a woman. These, incidentally, are the words of the warlocks' chorus:

> *So what, if women on the whole*
> *Take many steps to reach the goal?*
> *Let them run as fast as they dare,*
> *With one good jump a man gets there.*[2]

Anyone who understands the innermost kernel of the legend of Prometheus—namely that wrongdoing is of necessity imposed on the titanically striving individual—is bound also to sense the un-Apolline quality of this pessimistic view of things, for it is the will of Apollo to bring rest and calm to individual beings precisely by drawing boundaries between them, and by reminding them constantly, with his demands for self-knowledge and measure, that these are the most sacred laws in the world. But lest this Apolline tendency should cause form to freeze into Egyptian stiffness and coldness, lest the

---

[2] Goethe, *Faust*, I, 398 ff.

attempt to prescribe the course and extent of each individual wave should cause the movement of the whole lake to die away, the flood-tide of the Dionysiac would destroy periodically all the small circles in which the one-sidedly Apolline will attempted to confine Hellenic life. That sudden swell of the Dionysiac tide then lifts the separate little waves of individuals on to its back, just as the Titan Atlas, brother of Prometheus, lifted up the earth. This Titanic urge to become, as it were, the Atlas of all single beings, and to carry them on a broad back higher and higher, further and further, is the common feature shared by the Promethean and the Dionysiac. In this respect the Prometheus of Aeschylus is a Dionysiac mask, whereas the aforementioned deep strain of justice in Aeschylus reveals to those with eyes to see his paternal descent from Apollo, the god of individuation and of the boundaries of justice. The double essence of Aeschylus' Prometheus, his simultaneously Apolline and Dionysiac nature, could therefore be expressed like this: 'All that exists is just and unjust and is equally justified in both respects.'

That is your world. That you call a world.[3]

I O

It is a matter of indisputable historical record that the only subject-matter of Greek tragedy, in its earliest form, was the sufferings of Dionysos, and that for a long time the only hero present on the stage was, accordingly, Dionysos. But one may also say with equal certainty that, right down to Euripides, Dionysos never ceased to be the tragic hero, and that all the famous figures of the Greek stage, Prometheus, Oedipus etc., are merely masks of that original hero, Dionysos. . . .

I I

Greek tragedy perished differently from all the other, older sister-arts: it died by suicide, as the result of an irresolvable conflict, which is to say tragically, while all the others died the most beautiful and peaceful deaths, fading away at a great age. . . .

It was *Euripides* who fought this death-struggle of tragedy; the later branch of art is known as the *New Attic Comedy,* in which tragedy lived on in degenerate form, as a monument to its own exceedingly laborious and violent demise. . . .

Essentially, the spectator now heard and saw his double on the Euripidean stage, and was delighted that the latter knew how to speak so well. This delight was not the end of it; the people themselves took lessons in oratory from Euripides, something of which he boasts in his contest with Aeschylus, where he claims that, thanks to him, the people have learned to observe, to negotiate,

---

[3] Goethe, *Faust,* I, 409.

and to draw conclusions artfully and with the most cunning sophistication. By radically changing public speech like this, it was he who made the New Comedy at all possible. For from now on it was no longer a secret how, and in which turns of phrase, everyday life could be represented on stage. Bourgeois mediocrity, on which Euripides built all his political hopes, now had its chance to speak, whereas previously the character of language had been determined by the demi-god in tragedy and by the drunken satyr or half-man in comedy. Thus Aristophanes' Euripides praises himself for the way he has represented general, familiar, everyday life and activity, things which everyone is capable of judging. If the broad mass now philosophizes, conducts trials, and administers land and property with unheard-of cleverness, then this was his achievement, the successful result of the wisdom he had injected into the people. . . .

I 2

Let us think of our own puzzlement about the *chorus* and the *tragic hero* of that tragedy, both of which we were unable to reconcile either with our habits or with the historical tradition—until, that is, we rediscovered this very same doubleness in the origin and essence of Greek tragedy, as the expression of two interwoven artistic drives, *the Apolline and the Dionysiac.*

What we now see revealed, indeed brilliantly illuminated, is the tendency of Euripides, which was to expel the original and all-powerful Dionysiac element from tragedy and to re-build tragedy in a new and pure form on the foundations of a non-Dionysiac art, morality, and view of the world. . . .

In a certain sense Euripides, too, was merely a mask; the deity who spoke out of him was not Dionysos, nor Apollo, but an altogether newborn daemon called *Socrates.* This is the new opposition: the Dionysiac versus the Socratic, and the work of art that once was Greek tragedy was destroyed by it. Although Euripides may try to comfort us with his recantation, he fails; the most glorious temple lies in ruins; what use to us is the lament of the destroyer or his confession that it was the most beautiful of temples? And even the fact that Euripides was punished by being transformed into a dragon by every judge of art throughout the ages—who could be satisfied with such a miserable compensation?

Let us now take a closer look at this *Socratic* tendency with which Euripides opposed and defeated Aeschylean tragedy. . . .

There is not a trace left here of that epic condition of losing oneself in semblance, of the dispassionate coolness of the true actor who, at the very height of his activity, is nothing but semblance and delight in semblance. Euripides is the actor with the pounding heart, with his hair standing on end; he draws up his plan as a Socratic thinker; he executes it as a passionate actor. Neither in the planning nor in the execution is he a pure artist. Thus Euripidean drama is simultaneously fiery and cool, equally capable of freezing and burning; it is impossible for it to achieve the Apolline effect of epic poetry, but on the other hand it has liberated itself as far as possible from the Dionysiac elements, and it now needs new means of stimulation to have any effect at all, means which are no longer part of the two artistic drives, the Apolline and the Dionysiac. These stimulants are cool, paradoxical *thoughts*—in place of Apolline visions—and fiery *affects*—in place of Dionysiac ecstasies—and, what is more, thoughts and affects most realistically imitated, not ones which have been dipped in the ether of art.

We have come to see that Euripides had no success at all in putting drama on to purely Apolline foundations, and that his non-Dionysiac tendency got lost in a naturalistic and un-artistic one. We can therefore now get closer to the nature of *aesthetic Socratism*, whose supreme law runs roughly like this: 'In order to be beautiful, everything must be reasonable'—a sentence formed in parallel to Socrates' dictum that 'Only he who knows is virtuous.' With this canon in his hand Euripides measured every single element—language, characters, dramatic construction, choral music—and rectified it in accordance with this principle. What we criticize so frequently as a poetic flaw and a step backwards in Euripides' work, as compared with Sophoclean tragedy, is mostly the product of that penetrating critical process, that bold application of reason. . . .

[I]n league with Socrates, Euripides dared to be the herald of a new kind of artistic creation. If this caused the older tragedy to perish, then aesthetic Socratism is the murderous principle; but insofar as the fight was directed against the Dionysiac nature of the older art, we may identify Socrates as the opponent of Dionysos, the new Orpheus who rises up against Dionysos and who, although fated to be torn apart by the maenads of the Athenian court of justice, nevertheless forces the great and mighty god himself to flee.

8

ART AS COMMUNICATION OF FEELING:
LEO N. TOLSTOY

The great Russian novelist Leo N. Tolstoy (1828–1910), author of *War and Peace* and *Anna Karenina*, developed his own original philosophy of art. Concerned to justify lavish expenditure on the production of works of art such as operas, in *What Is Art?* Tolstoy argues that art is important even amid extensive poverty and deprivation.

To defend art as a social enterprise, Tolstoy offers a definition: Through the use of such devices as color, sound, and movement, art communicates to its audience a feeling or emotion that the artist has previously experienced.

For Tolstoy, art is like language in general: a means of communication. He thinks of language as fundamentally a means for conveying one person's thoughts to another. Thus, when I say that I believe there are planets other than our own with intelligent life on them, I am communicating to you a thought that I have. I am transferring information. With art, the process of communication involves, instead, the transfer of emotions or feelings. When I listen to the first movement of Schubert's *String Quintet in C-major,* I experience for myself the composer's deep sense of yearning. In both cases, something is being communicated between two people, beliefs in one case, feelings in the other.

Tolstoy argues the superiority of this conception of art over those previously advanced by philosophers, but more important still is his brief for the social utility of art. No one can doubt the importance of speech, for it allows human beings to convey to one another their thoughts and experiences. In Tolstoy's view, art is no less central to human existence, for it makes accessible the feelings of other human beings. This is vital to human solidarity, because it allows one access to the felt experience of those in circumstances other than one's own. Moreover, by making the best feelings of one age accessible to the next, art furthers the spiritual evolution of humankind.

Tolstoy is particularly militant in his rejection of the idea that whatever is generally accepted as art should be so considered. In his view, an adequate theory of art will provide criteria for discriminating genuine from spurious works of art and will challenge received assessments of the quality of works.

STUDY QUESTIONS ON THE READING

1.   What are Tolstoy's criticisms of the view that art must be defined as the beautiful? Which theories that you have read would be subject to this critique? In your view, are his criticisms of these theories successful? Why or why not?

2.   Why does Tolstoy think that linking art with the production of the viewer's pleasure is an error? Do you think he is right in this assessment? Explain.

3.   Do you see any problems in Tolstoy's view of art as the communication of feelings between human beings? Are there ways of communicating feelings that are not artistic?

4.   Is Tolstoy's account of the social role of art valid? Why or why not?

5.   Should a definition of art accept as art all works commonly judged as such? Or could such a definition validly exclude works that do not meet its conditions? Explain.

LEO TOLSTOY: WHAT IS ART?

[A]ll the aesthetic definitions of beauty come down to two fundamental views: one, that beauty is something existing in itself, a manifestation of the absolutely perfect—idea, spirit, will, God; the other, that beauty is a certain pleasure we experience, which does not have personal advantage as its aim.

The first definition was adopted by Fichte, Schelling, Hegel, Schopenhauer, and by the philosophizing Frenchmen—Cousin, Jouffroy, Ravaisson *et al.*, not to mention the second-rate aesthetic philosophers. The same objective–mystical definition of beauty is held by the greater portion of educated people in our time. It is a widely spread understanding of beauty, especially among people of the older generation.

The second definition of beauty, as a certain pleasure we receive which has no personal advantage as its aim, is spread mostly among English aestheticians, and is shared by the other, mostly younger, portion of our society. . . .

On the one hand, beauty is understood as something mystical and very exalted, but unfortunately very indefinite and, therefore, inclusive of philosophy, religion, and life itself, as in Schelling, Hegel and their German and French followers; or, on the other hand, according to the definition of Kant and his

---

followers, beauty is only a particular kind of disinterested pleasure that we receive. In this case the concept of beauty, though seemingly very clear, is unfortunately also imprecise, because it expands in the other direction—meaning that it includes the pleasure derived from drinking, eating, touching soft skin, etc., as is admitted in Guyau, Kralik *et al.*

It is true that, in following the development of the teaching concerning beauty, one can observe that at first, from the time when aesthetics emerged as a science, the metaphysical definition of beauty prevailed, while the closer we come to our own time, the more there emerges a practical definition, recently acquiring a physiological character, so that one even comes upon aestheticians such as Véron and Sully, who attempt to do without the concept of beauty entirely. But such aestheticians have very little success, and the majority of the public, and of artists and scholars as well, firmly hold to the concept of beauty as defined in the majority of aesthetic systems—that is, either as something mystical or metaphysical, or as a particular kind of pleasure.

What essentially is this concept of beauty, to which people of our circle and day hold so stubbornly for the defining of art?

We call beauty in the subjective sense that which affords us a certain kind of pleasure. In the objective sense, we call beauty something absolutely perfect which exists outside us. But since we recognize the absolutely perfect which exists outside us and acknowledge it as such only because we receive a certain kind of pleasure from the manifestation of this absolutely perfect, it means that the objective definition is nothing but the subjective one differently expressed. In fact, both notions of beauty come down to a certain sort of pleasure that we receive, meaning that we recognize as beauty that which pleases us without awakening our lust. In such a situation, it would seem natural for the science of art not to content itself with a definition of art based on beauty—that is, on what is pleasing—and to seek a general definition, applicable to all works of art, on the basis of which it would be possible to resolve the question of what does or does not belong to art. But, . . . no such definition exists. All attempts to define absolute beauty in itself—as an imitation of nature, as purposefulness, as correspondence of parts, symmetry, harmony, unity in diversity and so on—either do not define anything, or define only certain features of certain works of art, and are far from embracing everything that all people have always regarded and still regard as art.

An objective definition of art does not exist; the existing definitions, metaphysical as well as practical, come down to one and the same subjective definition, which, strange as it is to say, is the view of art as the manifestation of beauty, and of beauty as that which pleases (without awakening lust). Many aestheticians have felt the inadequacy and instability of such a definition, and, in order to give it substance, have asked themselves what is pleasing and why, thus shifting the question of beauty to the question of taste, as did Hutcheson, Voltaire, Diderot *et al.* But (as the reader can see both from the history of aesthetics and from experience) no attempts to define taste can lead anywhere, and there is not and can never be any explanation of why something is pleasing to one man and not to another, or vice versa. Thus, existing aesthetics as a whole consists not in something such as might be expected of an intellectual activity calling itself a science—namely, in a definition of the properties and laws of art, or of the beautiful, if it is the content of art, or in a definition of the properties of taste, if it is taste that decides the question of art and its worth, and then, on the basis of these laws, the recognition as art of those works that fit them, and the rejection of those that do not fit them—but instead it consists in first recognizing a certain kind of work as good because it pleases us, and then in constructing such a theory of art as will include all works found pleasing by a certain circle of people. There exists an artistic canon according to which the favourite works of our circle are recognized as art (Phidias, Sophocles, Homer, Titian, Raphael, Bach, Beethoven, Dante, Shakespeare, Goethe *et al.*), and aesthetic judgements must be such as can embrace all these works. One has no difficulty finding in aesthetic literature judgements of the worth and significance of art based not on known laws, according to which we regard this or that object as good or bad, but on whether it conforms to the artistic canon we have established. . . .

All existing aesthetic systems are constructed on this plan. Instead of giving a definition of true art and then, depending on whether a work fits or does not fit this definition, judging what is and what is not art, a certain series of works found pleasing for some reason by people of a certain circle is recognized as art, and a definition of art such as will include all these works is then invented. . . . Whatever follies may be committed in art, once they are accepted among the upper classes of our society, a theory is at once elaborated to explain and legitimize these follies, as if there had ever been epochs in history when certain exceptional circles of people had not accepted and approved of false, ugly, meaningless art, which left no traces and was completely forgotten afterwards. And we can see by what is going on now in the art of our circle what degree of meaninglessness and ugliness art can attain to, especially when, as in our time, it knows it is regarded as infallible.

Thus the theory of art based on beauty, expounded by aesthetics and professed in vague outlines by the public, is nothing other than the recognition as good of what has been and is found pleasing by us—that is, by a certain circle of people.

In order to define any human activity, one must understand its meaning and significance. And in order to understand the meaning and significance of any human activity, it is necessary first of all to examine this activity in itself, as dependent on its own causes and effects, and not with regard to the pleasure we receive from it. But if we accept that the aim of any activity is merely our own pleasure, and define it merely by that pleasure, then this definition will obviously be false. That is what has happened with the definition of art. . . .

Just as people who think that the aim and purpose of food is pleasure cannot perceive the true meaning of eating, so people who think that the aim of art is pleasure cannot know its meaning and purpose, because they ascribe to an activity which has meaning in connection with other phenomena of life the false and exclusive aim of pleasure. People understand that the meaning of eating is the nourishment of the body only when they cease to consider pleasure the aim of this activity. So it is with art. People will understand the meaning of art only when they cease to regard beauty—that is, pleasure—as the aim of this activity. To recognize beauty, or the certain kind of pleasure to be derived from art, as the aim of art, not only does not contribute to defining what art is, but, on the contrary, by transferring the question to a realm quite alien to art—to metaphysical, psychological, physiological, and even historical discussions of why such-and-such a work is pleasing to some, and such-and-such is not pleasing, or is pleasing to others—makes that definition impossible. And just as discussing why one person likes pears and another meat in no way helps to define what the essence of nourishment is, so, too, the resolution of questions of taste in art (to which all discussions of art involuntarily come down) not only does not contribute to understanding what makes up that particular human activity which we call art, but makes that understanding completely impossible.

To the question, what is this art to which are offered in sacrifice the labours of millions of people, the very lives of people, and even morality, the existing aesthetic systems give answers all of which come down to saying that the aim of art is beauty, and that beauty is known by the pleasure it gives, and that the pleasure given by art is a good and important thing. That is, that pleasure is good because it is pleasure. So that what is considered the definition of art is not a definition of art at all, but is only a ruse to justify those sacrifices which are offered by people in the name of this supposed art, as well as the egoistic pleasure and immorality of existing art. And therefore, strange as it is to say, despite the mountains of books written on art, no precise definition of art has yet been made. The reason for this is that the concept of beauty has been placed at the foundation of the concept of art.

* * *

What then is art, if we discard the all-confusing concept of beauty? The latest and most comprehensible definitions of art, independent of the concept of beauty, would be the following: art is an activity already emerging in the animal kingdom out of sexuality and a propensity for play (Schiller, Darwin, Spencer), accompanied by a pleasant excitation of nervous energy (Grant Allen). This is the physiological-evolutionary definition. Or, art is an external manifestation, by means of lines, colours, gestures, sounds, or words, of emotions experienced by man (Véron). This is the practical definition. Or, according to Sully's most recent definition, art is 'the production of some permanent object or passing action, which is fitted not only to supply an active enjoyment to the producer, but to convey a pleasurable impression to a number of spectators or listeners, quite apart from any personal advantage to be derived from it.'

In spite of the superiority of these definitions over metaphysical definitions based on the concept of beauty, they are still far from precise. The first, physiological-evolutionary definition is imprecise because it speaks not of the activity that constitutes the essence of art, but of the origin of art. The definition by physiological impact upon man's organism is imprecise because many other activities of man can fit into it as well, as occurs in the new aesthetic theories which reckon as art the making of beautiful clothing and pleasant perfumes and even foods. The practical definition which supposes art to be the expression of emotions is imprecise because a man may express his emotions by means of lines, colours, sounds and words without affecting others by it, and the expression will then not be art.

The third definition, by Sully, is imprecise because under the production of objects that afford pleasure to the producer and a pleasant impression to the spectators or listeners, apart from any advantage to them, may be included the performance of magic tricks, gymnastic exercises and other activities which are not art, and, on the other hand, many objects that produce an unpleasant impression, as, for instance, a gloomy, cruel scene in a poetic description or in the theatre, are unquestionably works of art.

The imprecision of all these definitions proceeds from the fact that in all of them, just as in the metaphysical definitions, the aim of art is located in the pleasure we derive from it, and not in its purpose in the life of man and of mankind.

In order to define art precisely, one must first of all cease looking at it as a means of pleasure and consider it as one of the conditions of human life. Considering art in this way, we cannot fail to see that art is a means of communion among people.

Every work of art results in the one who receives it entering into a certain kind of communion with the one who produced or is producing the art, and with all those who, simultaneously with him, before him, or after him, have received or will receive the same artistic impression.

As the word which conveys men's thoughts and experiences serves to unite people, so art serves in exactly the same way. The peculiarity of this means of communion, which distinguishes it from communion by means of the word, is that through the word a man conveys his thoughts to another, while through art people convey their feelings to each other.

The activity of art is based on the fact that man, as he receives through hearing or sight the expressions of another man's feelings, is capable of experiencing the same feelings as the man who expresses them.

The simplest example: a man laughs, and another man feels merry; he weeps, and the man who hears this weeping feels sad; a man is excited, annoyed, and another looking at him gets into the same state. With his movements, the sounds of his voice, a man displays cheerfulness, determination, or, on the contrary, dejection, calm—and this mood is communicated to others. A man suffers, expressing his suffering in moans and convulsions—and this suffering is communicated to others; a man displays his feeling of admiration, awe, fear, respect for certain objects, persons, phenomena—and other people become infected, experience the same feelings of admiration, awe, fear, respect for the same objects, persons or phenomena.

On this capacity of people to be infected by the feelings of other people, the activity of art is based.

If a man infects another or others directly by his look or by the sounds he produces at the moment he experiences a feeling, if he makes someone yawn when he himself feels like yawning, or laugh, or cry, when he himself laughs or cries over something, or suffer when he himself suffers, this is not yet art.

Art begins when a man, with the purpose of communicating to other people a feeling he once experienced, calls it up again within himself and expresses it by certain external signs.

Thus, the simplest case: a boy who once experienced fear, let us say, on encountering a wolf, tells about this encounter and, to call up in others the feeling he experienced, describes himself, his state of mind before the encounter, the surroundings, the forest, his carelessness, and then the look of the wolf, its movements, the distance between the wolf and himself, and so on. All this—if as he tells the story the boy relives the feeling he experienced, infects his listeners, makes them relive all that the narrator lived through—is art. Even if the boy had not seen a wolf, but had often been afraid of seeing one, and, wishing to call up in others the feeling he experienced, invented the encounter with the wolf, telling it in such a way that through his narrative he called up in his listeners the same feeling he experienced in imagining the wolf—this, too, is art. In just the same way, it is art if a man, having experienced in reality or in imagination the horror of suffering or the delight of pleasure, expresses these feelings on canvas or in marble in such a way that others are infected by them. And in just the same way, it will be art if a man has experienced or imagined the feelings of merriment, joy, sadness, despair, cheerfulness, dejection, and the transitions between these feelings, and expresses them in sounds so that listeners are infected by them and experience them in the same way as he has experienced them.

Feelings, the most diverse, very strong and very weak, very significant and very worthless, very bad and very good, if only they infect the reader, the spectator, the listener, constitute the subject of art. The feeling of self-denial and submission to fate or God portrayed in a drama; the raptures of lovers described in a novel; a feeling of sensuousness depicted in a painting; the briskness conveyed by a triumphal march in music; the gaiety evoked by a dance; the comicality caused by a funny anecdote; the feeling of peace conveyed by an evening landscape or a lulling song—all this is art.

Once the spectators or listeners are infected by the same feeling the author has experienced, this is art.

To call up in oneself a feeling once experienced and, having called it up, to convey it by means of movements, lines, colours, sounds, images expressed in words, so that others experience the same feeling—in this consists the activity of art. Art is that human activity which consists in one man's consciously conveying to others, by certain external signs, the feelings he has experienced, and in others being infected by those feelings and also experiencing them.

Art is not, as the metaphysicians say, the manifestation of some mysterious idea, beauty, God; not, as the aesthetician-physiologists say, a form of play in which man releases a surplus of stored-up energy; not the manifestation of emotions through external signs; not the production of pleasing objects; not, above all, pleasure; but is a means of human communion, necessary for life and for the movement towards the good of the individual man and of mankind, uniting them in the same feelings.

Just as, owing to man's capacity for understanding thoughts expressed in words, any man can learn all that mankind has done for him in the realm of thought, can in the present, owing to the capacity for understanding other people's thoughts, participate in other people's activity, and can himself, owing to this capacity, convey the thoughts he has received from others, and his own as they have emerged in him, to his contemporaries and to posterity; so, owing to man's capacity for being infected by other people's feelings through art, he has access to all that mankind has experienced before him in the realm of feeling, he has access to the feelings experienced by his contemporaries, to feelings lived by other men thousands of years ago, and it is possible for him to convey his feelings to other people.

If people were incapable of receiving all the thoughts conveyed in words by people living before them, or of conveying their own thoughts to others, they would be like beasts or like Kaspar Hauser.

If men were not possessed of this other capacity—that of being infected by art—people would perhaps be still more savage and, above all, more divided and hostile.

And therefore the activity of art is a very important activity, as important as the activity of speech, and as widely spread.

As the word affects us not only in sermons, orations and books, but in all those speeches in which we convey our thoughts and experiences to each other, so, too, art in the broad sense of the word pervades our entire life, while, in the narrow sense of the word, we call art only certain of its manifestations.

We are accustomed to regard as art only what we read, hear, see in theatres, concerts and exhibitions, buildings, statues, poems, novels . . . But all this is only a small portion of the art by which we communicate with one another in life. The whole of human life is filled with works of art of various kinds, from lullabies, jokes, mimicry, home decoration, clothing, utensils, to church services and solemn processions. All this is the activity of art. Thus we call art, in the narrow sense of the word, not the entire human activity that conveys feelings, but only that which we for some reason single out from all this activity and to which we give special significance.

This special significance has always been given by all people to the part of this activity which conveys feelings coming from their religious consciousness, and it is this small part of the whole of art that has been called art in the full sense of the word.

This was the view of art among the men of antiquity—Socrates, Plato, Aristotle. The same view of art was shared by the Hebrew prophets and the early Christians; it is understood in the same way by the Muslims and by religious men of the people in our time.

Some teachers of mankind, such as Plato in his *Republic,* the first Christians, strict Muslims, and Buddhists, have often even rejected all art.

People holding this view of art, contrary to the modern view which considers all art good as long as it affords pleasure, thought and think that art, unlike the word, to which one need not listen, is so highly dangerous in its capacity for infecting people against their will, that mankind would lose far less if all art were banished than if every kind of art were tolerated.

Those people who rejected all art were obviously wrong, because they rejected what cannot be rejected—one of the most necessary means of communication, without which mankind cannot live. But no less wrong are the people of our civilized European society, circle and time, in tolerating all art as long as it serves beauty—that is, gives people pleasure.

Formerly, there was fear that among objects of art some corrupting objects might be found, and so all art was forbidden. Now, there is only fear lest they be deprived of some pleasure afforded by art, and so all art is patronized. And I think that the second error is much greater than the first and that its consequences are much more harmful.

9

ART AS SYMPTOM: SIGMUND FREUD

In his 1908 paper "The Relation of the Poet to Day-Dreaming," from which the present reading is selected, Sigmund Freud (1856–1939) presents a psychoanalytic conception of literature and, by extension, art in general. Psychoanalysis is a theory developed by Freud to explain the behavior of the psychologically disturbed people who came to him for relief. Its principles extend further than this, however, so that Freud and his followers often see psychoanalysis as a general theory of human behavior and even of culture.

Fantasies, dreams, and slips of the tongue are among the phenomena that Freud believes give us access to deep truths about human nature. They are revelatory because they expose the working of the unconscious, an aspect of our mental life to which Freud attributes immense importance. For him, conscious, waking life is like the tip of an iceberg, with the unconscious playing the role of the huge, submerged mass hidden from view. The goal of psychoanalysis is to bring that hidden mass to light.

For example, Freud claims that dreams need to be understood as camouflaged wishes. The reason for the camouflage is that the content of a dream—something that could be expressed as a thought, such as "I wish my brother were dead!"—is something that the person who had the dream would repudiate and deny when he or she was awake and conscious. In the dream, various techniques of distortion and disguise allow this pent-up thought to emerge, providing satisfaction for the dreamer. For Freud, most dreams express wishes of either a sexual or a self-aggrandizing nature.

What does this have to do with art? The artist's unconscious is less repressed or hidden than others', Freud argues. Feeling a deep need to express unconscious thoughts and emotions, artists create works that, like dreams, are really the fulfillment of concealed wishes.

Freud points to popular fiction—with its unflinching heroes and adoring heroines—as an example. Such works express the writer's fantasies of invulnerability and sexual potency. And the evident pleasure readers derive from these works attests that these fantasies are not peculiar to the writer.

A further important aspect of Freud's analysis of art is that works of art satisfy a specific type of wish on the part of the artist: Taking material from the present, the work re-presents a situation from childhood in reconfigured form.

Like dreams, works of art thus embody all three modes of temporality—past, present, and future—in a unique synthesis.

In this selection Freud gives a mainly theoretical overview of his conception of art, but other writings provide detailed psychoanalytic interpretations of specific artworks. For example, he uses psychoanalysis to explain the haunting smile on Leonardo da Vinci's famous masterpiece *Mona Lisa*. Although previous writers had claimed that the mysterious nature of Mona Lisa's smile was due to its ambiguity—the simultaneous manifestation of both tenderness and menace—none were able to explain why Leonardo had rendered his subject in this way. Freud admits that the smile must be a faithful representation of the model's face—but Leonardo used "the most elaborate artifices" to keep this smile on his model's face, Freud recounts for us—he asks why Leonardo should have been so fascinated by her smile that it became a recurring motif in his painting. Freud answers that it recalls Leonardo's mother's smile, thus activating the pleasure he felt in this most blissful period of his life. Freud confirms this interpretation by reference to a supposed memory Leonardo relates of being attacked by a vulture as a child, a memory that Freud judges to be a fantasy that shows Leonardo's attachment to his mother in the absence of his father.

One issue that Freud's analysis foregrounds is why audiences find works of art gratifying. If the work is simply the artist's disguised wish-fulfillment, why should a viewer find looking at it pleasurable too, rather than disgusting or embarrassing? Freud's answer is that the artist does two things: First, he disguises the egotistical nature of the work and, second, his aesthetic presentation provides a type of "fore-pleasure" for viewers. As a result, Freud suggests, the viewer of a work of art may be allowed to enjoy his own daydreams "without reproach or shame."

Psychoanalytic conceptions of art, then, are less concerned with distinguishing works of art from other products of human activity than they are with explaining why people are moved by them. This approach to art has been deeply influential, especially among theorists concerned with the appeal of popular culture.

STUDY QUESTIONS ON THE READINGS

1. How does a work of art embody the three different modes of time, according to Freud? Does it do so in exactly the same way as a fantasy? Explain.

2. How do dreams distort the wishes whose fulfillment they represent? What is the parallel in regard to works of art?

3. Does Freud's theory provide a plausible account of popular fiction? Can Freud's analysis of popular literature be extended to all literary works? If so, how? If not, what does this say about his theory?

4. Do you agree with Freud that the artist is a special sort of person, with a different relationship to her unconscious from that most people develop and maintain?

5.   Freud suggests that art has a special relationship to childhood play. Does this make sense to you? Why or why not?

6.   Nietzsche also spoke of dreams in his characterization of the Apolline. What similarities and differences do you see in his theory and Freud's?

❖

SIGMUND FREUD: THE RELATION OF THE POET TO DAY-DREAMING

We laymen have always wondered greatly—like the cardinal who put the question to Ariosto—how that strange being, the poet, comes by his material. What makes him able to carry us with him in such a way and to arouse emotions in us of which we thought ourselves perhaps not even capable? Our interest in the problem is only stimulated by the circumstance that if we ask poets themselves they give us no explanation of the matter, or at least no satisfactory explanation. The knowledge that not even the clearest insight into the factors conditioning the choice of imaginative material, or into the nature of the ability to fashion that material, will ever make writers of us does not in any way detract from our interest.

If we could only find some activity in ourselves, or in people like ourselves, which was in any way akin to the writing of imaginative works! If we could do so, then examination of it would give us a hope of obtaining some insight into the creative powers of imaginative writers. And indeed, there is some prospect of achieving this—writers themselves always try to lessen the distance between their kind and ordinary human beings; they so often assure us that every man is at heart a poet, and that the last poet will not die until the last human being does. . . .

Let us try to learn some of the characteristics of day-dreaming. We can begin by saying that happy people never make phantasies, only unsatisfied ones. Unsatisfied wishes are the driving power behind phantasies; every separate phantasy contains the fulfilment of a wish, and improves on unsatisfactory reality. The impelling wishes vary according to the sex, character and circumstances of the creator; they may be easily divided, however, into two principal groups. Either they are ambitious wishes, serving to exalt the person creating them, or they are erotic. In young women erotic wishes dominate the phantasies

From *The Collected Papers, Volume 4* by Sigmund Freud. Authorized translation under supervision of Joan Riviére. Published by Basic Books, Inc. by arrangement with The Hogarth Press, Ltd. and The Institute of Psycho-Analysis, London. Reprinted by permission of Basic Books, a member of Perseus Books, L.L.C.

almost exclusively, for their ambition is generally comprised in their erotic longings; in young men egoistic and ambitious wishes assert themselves plainly enough alongside their erotic desires. But we will not lay stress on the distinction between these two trends; we prefer to emphasize the fact that they are often united. In many altar-pieces the portrait of the donor is to be found in one corner of the picture; and in the greater number of ambitious day-dreams, too, we can discover a woman in some corner, for whom the dreamer performs all his heroic deeds and at whose feet all his triumphs are to be laid. Here you see we have strong enough motives for concealment; a well-brought-up woman is, indeed, credited with only a minimum of erotic desire, while a young man has to learn to suppress the overweening self-regard he acquires in the indulgent atmosphere surrounding his childhood, so that he may find his proper place in a society that is full of other persons making similar claims.

We must not imagine that the various products of this impulse towards phantasy, castles in the air or day-dreams, are stereotyped or unchangeable. On the contrary, they fit themselves into the changing impressions of life, alter with the vicissitudes of life; every deep new impression gives them what might be called a 'date-stamp'. The relation of phantasies to time is altogether of great importance. One may say that a phantasy at one and the same moment hovers between three periods of time—the three periods of our ideation. The activity of phantasy in the mind is linked up with some current impression, occasioned by some event in the present, which had the power to rouse an intense desire. From there it wanders back to the memory of an early experience, generally belonging to infancy, in which this wish was fulfilled. Then it creates for itself a situation which is to emerge in the future, representing the fulfilment of the wish—this is the day-dream or phantasy, which now carries in it traces both of the occasion which engendered it and of some past memory. So past, present and future are threaded, as it were, on the string of the wish that runs through them all.

A very ordinary example may serve to make my statement clearer. Take the case of a poor orphan lad, to whom you have given the address of some employer where he may perhaps get work. On the way there he falls into a day-dream suitable to the situation from which it springs. The content of the phantasy will be somewhat as follows: He is taken on and pleases his new employer, makes himself indispensable in the business, is taken into the family of the employer, and marries the charming daughter of the house. Then he comes to conduct the business, first as a partner, and then as successor to his father-in-law. In this way the dreamer regains what he had in his happy childhood, the protecting house, his loving parents and the first objects of his affection. You will see from such an example how the wish employs some event in the present to plan a future on the pattern of the past.

Much more could be said about phantasies, but I will only allude as briefly as possible to certain points. If phantasies become over-luxuriant and over-powerful, the necessary conditions for an outbreak of neurosis or psychosis are constituted; phantasies are also the first preliminary stage in the mind of the symptoms of illness of which our patients complain. A broad by-path here branches off into pathology.

I cannot pass over the relation of phantasies to dreams. Our nocturnal dreams are nothing but such phantasies, as we can make clear by interpreting them.[1] Language, in its unrivalled wisdom, long ago decided the question of the essential nature of dreams by giving the name of 'day-dreams' to the airy creations of phantasy. If the meaning of our dreams usually remains obscure in spite of this clue, it is because of the circumstance that at night wishes of which we are ashamed also become active in us, wishes which we have to hide from ourselves, which were consequently repressed and pushed back into the unconscious. Such repressed wishes and their derivatives can therefore achieve expression only when almost completely disguised. When scientific work had succeeded in elucidating the distortion in dreams, it was no longer difficult to recognize that nocturnal dreams are fulfilments of desires in exactly the same way as day-dreams are—those phantasies with which we are all so familiar.

So much for day-dreaming; now for the poet! Shall we dare really to compare an imaginative writer with 'one who dreams in broad daylight', and his creations with day-dreams? Here, surely, a first distinction is forced upon us; we must distinguish between poets who, like the bygone creators of epics and tragedies, take over their material ready-made, and those who seem to create their material spontaneously. Let us keep to the latter, and let us also not choose for our comparison those writers who are most highly esteemed by critics. We will choose the less pretentious writers of romances, novels and stories, who are read all the same by the widest circles of men and women. There is one very marked characteristic in the productions of these writers which must strike us all: they all have a hero who is the centre of interest, for whom the author tries to win our sympathy by every possible means, and whom he places under the protection of a special providence. If at the end of one chapter the hero is left unconscious and bleeding from severe wounds, I am sure to find him at the beginning of the next being carefully tended and on the way to recovery; if the first volume ends in the hero being shipwrecked in a storm at sea, I am certain to hear at the beginning of the next of his hairbreadth escape—otherwise, indeed, the story could not continue. The feeling of security with which I follow the hero through his dangerous adventures is the same as that with which a real hero throws himself into the water to save a drowning man, or exposes himself to the fire of the enemy while storming a battery. It is this very feeling of being a hero which one of our best authors has well expressed in the famous phrase, '*Es kann dir nix g'schehen!*'[2] It seems to me, however, that this significant mark of invulnerability very clearly betrays—His Majesty the Ego, the hero of all day-dreams and all novels.

The same relationship is hinted at in yet other characteristics of these ego-centric stories. When all the women in a novel invariably fall in love with the hero, this can hardly be looked upon as a description of reality, but it is easily understood as an essential constituent of a day-dream. The same thing holds good when the other people in the story are sharply divided into good and bad,

---

[1] Cf. Freud, *The Interpretation of Dreams*.

[2] Anzengruber. [The phrase means 'Nothing can happen to you!'—Trans.]

with complete disregard of the manifold variety in the traits of real human beings; the 'good' ones are those who help the ego in its character of hero, while the 'bad' are his enemies and rivals.

We do not in any way fail to recognize that many imaginative productions have travelled far from the original naïve day-dream, but I cannot suppress the surmise that even the most extreme variations could be brought into relationship with this model by an uninterrupted series of transitions. It has struck me in many so-called psychological novels, too, that only one person—once again the hero—is described from within; the author dwells in his soul and looks upon the other people from outside. The psychological novel in general probably owes its peculiarities to the tendency of modern writers to split up their ego by self-observation into many component-egos, and in this way to personify the conflicting trends in their own mental life in many heroes. There are certain novels, which might be called 'excentric', that seem to stand in marked contradiction to the typical day-dream; in these the person introduced as the hero plays the least active part of anyone, and seems instead to let the actions and sufferings of other people pass him by like a spectator. Many of the later novels of Zola belong to this class. But I must say that the psychological analysis of people who are not writers, and who deviate in many things from the so-called norm, has shown us analogous variations in their day-dreams in which the ego contents itself with the role of spectator.

If our comparison of the imaginative writer with the day-dreamer, and of poetic production with the day-dream, is to be of any value, it must show itself fruitful in some way or other. Let us try, for instance, to examine the works of writers in reference to the idea propounded above, the relation of the phantasy to the wish that runs through it and to the three periods of time; and with its help let us study the connection between the life of the writer and his productions. Hitherto it has not been known what preliminary ideas would constitute an approach to this problem; very often this relation has been regarded as much simpler than it is; but the insight gained from phantasies leads us to expect the following state of things. Some actual experience which made a strong impression on the writer had stirred up a memory of an earlier experience, generally belonging to childhood, which then arouses a wish that finds a fulfilment in the work in question, and in which elements of the recent event and the old memory should be discernible.

Do not be alarmed at the complexity of this formula; I myself expect that in reality it will prove itself to be too schematic, but that possibly it may contain a first means of approach to the true state of affairs. From some attempts I have made I think that this way of approaching works of the imagination might not be unfruitful. You will not forget that the stress laid on the writer's memories of his childhood, which perhaps seems so strange, is ultimately derived from the hypothesis that imaginative creation, like day-dreaming, is a continuation of and substitute for the play of childhood.

We will not neglect to refer also to that class of imaginative work which must be recognized not as spontaneous production, but as a re-fashioning of ready-made material. Here, too, the writer retains a certain amount of independence, which can express itself in the choice of material and in changes in the material chosen, which are often considerable. As far as it goes, this material is derived from the racial treasure-house of myths, legends and fairy-tales. The study of these creations of racial psychology is in no way complete, but it seems extremely probable that myths, for example, are distorted vestiges of the wish-phantasies of whole nations—the age-long dreams of young humanity.

You will say that, although writers came first in the title of this paper, I have told you far less about them than about phantasy. I am aware of that, and will try to excuse myself by pointing to the present state of our knowledge. I could only throw out suggestions and bring up interesting points which arise from the study of phantasies, and which pass beyond them to the problem of the choice of literary material. We have not touched on the other problem at all, *i.e.* what are the means which writers use to achieve those emotional reactions in us that are roused by their productions. But I would at least point out to you the path which leads from our discussion of day-dreams to the problems of the effect produced on us by imaginative works.

You will remember that we said the day-dreamer hid his phantasies carefully from other people because he had reason to be ashamed of them. I may now add that even if he were to communicate them to us, he would give us no pleasure by his disclosures. When we hear such phantasies they repel us, or at least leave us cold. But when a man of literary talent presents his plays, or relates what we take to be his personal day-dreams, we experience great pleasure arising probably from many sources. How the writer accomplishes this is his innermost secret; the essential *ars poetica* lies in the technique by which our feeling of repulsion is overcome, and this has certainly to do with those barriers erected between every individual being and all others. We can guess at two methods used in this technique. The writer softens the egotistical character of the day-dream by changes and disguises, and he bribes us by the offer of a purely formal, that is, aesthetic, pleasure in the presentation of his phantasies. The increment of pleasure which is offered us in order to release yet greater pleasure arising from deeper sources in the mind is called an 'incitement premium' or technically, 'fore-pleasure'. I am of opinion that all the aesthetic pleasure we gain from the works of imaginative writers is of the same type as this 'fore-pleasure', and that the true enjoyment of literature proceeds from the release of tensions in our minds. Perhaps much that brings about this result consists in the writer's putting us into a position in which we can enjoy our own day-dreams without reproach or shame. Here we reach a path leading into novel, interesting and complicated researches, but we also, at least for the present, arrive at the end of the present discussion.

10

ART AS SIGNIFICANT FORM: CLIVE BELL

Clive Bell (1881–1964), art critic as well as philosopher of art, was a member of the Bloomsbury Group, a circle of important artists and intellectuals that included, among others, Virginia Woolf and John Maynard Keynes. Quite taken by revolutionary developments in postimpressionist painting, Bell sought to develop a conception of art that would demonstrate that the advanced painting of his day was genuine and, indeed, significant art.

Although Bell's influential book, *Art*—from which this selection is taken— aims to legitimate a variety of forms of postimpressionist painting, it will be useful for us to consider the effect of cubism on Bell's thinking. Developed in the first two decades of the 20th century by Pablo Picasso and Georges Braque, cubist painting eschews the goal of accurate representation, its subjects appearing in distorted or simplified form. Along with Bell, many intellectuals of the time regarded cubism as the future of painting.

But cubism also presents a problem for the philosophy of art. If the cubist painter does not aim to reproduce reality faithfully—a conception of art's purpose that stretches back to Plato, as we have seen—then what is the essence of art? Bell's answer is that *significant form* is the quality distinguishing artworks from other things. A piece of abstract art is art, provokes a particular kind of feeling in the viewer—an aesthetic emotion—because, according to Bell, the placement and relationship of lines and colors on the canvas exhibits significant form. Representational works are judged in the same way: They qualify as art to the extent that their formal properties have significant form. But this means that their artistic value is independent of their representational content as well as their ability to express emotion.

Bell's attempt to produce a definition of art that encompasses the great works of the past as well as the latest advanced work is noteworthy—for not only does he offer a conception of art that moves beyond the idea of representation; he also insists that art criticism should be based upon a definition of art. Thus, he uses his own definition—which uncouples faithful representation from aesthetic merit— to criticize those artists who he thought failed to produce works of significance.

Bell endows the ecstatic quality of aesthetic experience with quasi-religious significance. The great value of art lies in its ability to shake us out of our everyday lives, to connect us with a deeper reality.

Study Questions on the Reading

1.   Bell claims that there is a kind of emotion—"aesthetic emotion"—that works of art produce in their viewers. What type of emotion is this? Have you ever experienced it? When? If something failed to stir you in this way, would that mean it was not art? Why or why not?

2.   According to Bell, the presence of "significant form" is what distinguishes works of art from other types of things. What does he mean by this term? Is there a noncircular way to characterize what significant form is? Explain.

3.   Bell is critical of works of art that aim at accuracy of representation. Do you agree that this is not a suitable goal for art? How does Bell's position on representation relate to his definition of art?

4.   Bell claims that most people do not experience art in an aesthetically appropriate way. How does he think that they do appreciate it? Do you agree with him? Why or why not?

5.   How important is the existence of photography for Bell's view? Explain.

6.   Do you think that Bell has produced a successful account of what constitutes art? What similarities do you see in his account with that of Kant?

❖

Clive Bell: Art

The starting-point for all systems of aesthetics must be the personal experience of a peculiar emotion. The objects that provoke this emotion we call works of art. All sensitive people agree that there is a peculiar emotion provoked by works of art. I do not mean, of course, that all works provoke the same emotion. On the contrary, every work produces a different emotion. But all these emotions are recognisably the same in kind; so far, at any rate, the best opinion is on my side. That there is a particular kind of emotion provoked by works of visual art, and that this emotion is provoked by every kind of visual art, by pictures, sculptures, buildings, pots, carvings, textiles, &c., &c., is not disputed, I think, by anyone capable of feeling it. This emotion is called the aesthetic emotion; and if we can discover some quality common and peculiar to all the objects that provoke it, we shall have solved what I take to be the central problem of aesthetics. We shall have discovered the essential quality in a work of art, the quality that distinguishes works of art from all other classes of objects.

For either all works of visual art have some common quality, or when we speak of "works of art" we gibber. Everyone speaks of "art," making a mental

---

From *Art* by Clive Bell. © 1927 Trafalgar Square. Originally published in 1914.

classification by which he distinguishes the class "works of art" from all other classes. What is the justification of this classification? What is the quality common and peculiar to all members of this class? Whatever it be, no doubt it is often found in company with other qualities; but they are adventitious—it is essential. There must be some one quality without which a work of art cannot exist; possessing which, in the least degree, no work is altogether worthless. What is this quality? What quality is shared by all objects that provoke our aesthetic emotions? What quality is common to Sta. Sophia and the windows at Chartres, Mexican sculpture, a Persian bowl, Chinese carpets, Giotto's frescoes at Padua, and the masterpieces of Poussin, Piero della Francesca, and Cézanne? Only one answer seems possible—significant form. In each, lines and colours combined in a particular way, certain forms and relations of forms, stir our aesthetic emotions. These relations and combinations of lines and colours, these aesthetically moving forms, I call "Significant Form"; and "Significant Form" is the one quality common to all works of visual art.

At this point it may be objected that I am making aesthetics a purely subjective business, since my only data are personal experiences of a particular emotion. It will be said that the objects that provoke this emotion vary with each individual, and that therefore a system of aesthetics can have no objective validity. It must be replied that any system of aesthetics which pretends to be based on some objective truth is so palpably ridiculous as not to be worth discussing. We have no other means of recognising a work of art than our feeling for it. The objects that provoke aesthetic emotion vary with each individual. Aesthetic judgments are, as the saying goes, matters of taste; and about tastes, as everyone is proud to admit, there is no disputing. A good critic may be able to make me see in a picture that had left me cold things that I had overlooked, till at last, receiving the aesthetic emotion, I recognise it as a work of art. To be continually pointing out those parts, the sum, or rather the combination, of which unite to produce significant form, is the function of criticism. But it is useless for a critic to tell me that something is a work of art; he must make me feel it for myself. This he can do only by making me see; he must get at my emotions through my eyes. Unless he can make me see something that moves me, he cannot force my emotions. I have no right to consider anything a work of art to which I cannot react emotionally; and I have no right to look for the essential quality in anything that I have not *felt* to be a work of art. The critic can affect my aesthetic theories only by affecting my aesthetic experience. All systems of aesthetics must be based on personal experience—that is to say, they must be subjective.

Yet, though all aesthetic theories must be based on aesthetic judgments, and ultimately all aesthetic judgments must be matters of personal taste, it would be rash to assert that no theory of aesthetics can have general validity. For, though A, B, C, D are the works that move me, and A, D, E, F the works that move you, it may well be that x is the only quality believed by either of us to be common to all the works in his list. We may all agree about aesthetics, and yet differ about particular works of art. We may differ as to the presence or absence of the quality x. My immediate object will be to show that significant form is the only quality common and peculiar to all the works of visual art that move me; and I will ask those whose aesthetic experience does not tally with mine to see whether this quality is not also, in their judgment, common to all works that move them, and whether they can discover any other quality of which the same can be said.

Also at this point a query arises, irrelevant indeed, but hardly to be suppressed: "Why are we so profoundly moved by forms related in a particular way?" The question is extremely interesting, but irrelevant to aesthetics. In pure aesthetics we have only to consider our emotion and its object: for the purposes of aesthetics we have no right, neither is there any necessity, to pry behind the object into the state of mind of him who made it. Later, I shall attempt to answer the question; for by so doing I may be able to develop my theory of the relation of art to life. I shall not, however, be under the delusion that I am rounding off my theory of aesthetics. For a discussion of aesthetics, it need be agreed only that forms arranged and combined according to certain unknown and mysterious laws do move us in a particular way, and that it is the business of an artist so to combine and arrange them that they shall move us. These moving combinations and arrangements I have called, for the sake of convenience and for a reason that will appear later, "Significant Form." A third interruption has to be met. "Are you forgetting about colour?" someone inquires. Certainly not; my term "significant form" included combinations of lines and of colours. The distinction between form and colour is an unreal one; you cannot conceive a colourless line or a colourless space; neither can you conceive a formless relation of colours. In a black and white drawing the spaces are all white and all are bounded by black lines; in most oil paintings the spaces are multi-coloured and so are the boundaries; you cannot imagine a boundary line without any content, or a content without a boundary line. Therefore, when I speak of significant form, I mean a combination of lines and colours (counting white and black as colours) that moves me aesthetically.

Some people may be surprised at my not having called this "beauty." Of course, to those who define beauty as "combinations of lines and colours that provoke aesthetic emotion," I willingly concede the right of substituting their word for mine. But most of us, however strict we may be, are apt to apply the epithet "beautiful" to objects that do not provoke that peculiar emotion produced by works of art. Everyone, I suspect, has called a butterfly or a flower beautiful. Does anyone feel the same kind of emotion for a butterfly or a flower that he feels for a cathedral or a picture? Surely, it is not what I call an aesthetic emotion that most of us feel, generally, for natural beauty. I shall suggest, later, that some people may, occasionally, see in nature what we see in art, and feel for her an aesthetic emotion; but I am satisfied that, as a rule, most people feel a very different kind of emotion for birds and flowers and the wings of butterflies from that which they feel for pictures, pots, temples and statues. Why these beautiful things do not move us as works of art move is another, and not an aesthetic, question. For our immediate purpose we have to discover only what quality is common to objects that do move us as works of art. . . .

Since we call a quality that does not raise the characteristic aesthetic emotion "Beauty," it would be misleading to call by the same name the quality that does. To make "beauty" the object of the aesthetic emotion, we must give to the word an over-strict and unfamiliar definition. . . . Clearly the word "beauty" is used to connote the objects of quite distinguishable emotions, and that is a reason for not employing a term which would land me inevitably in confusions and misunderstandings with my readers. . . .

The hypothesis that significant form is the essential quality in a work of art has at least one merit denied to many more famous and more striking—it does help to explain things. We are all familiar with pictures that interest us and excite our admiration, but do not move us as works of art. To this class belongs what I call "Descriptive Painting"—that is, painting in which forms are used not as objects of emotion, but as means of suggesting emotion or conveying information. Portraits of psychological and historical value, topographical works, pictures that tell stories and suggest situations, illustrations of all sorts, belong to this class. That we all recognise the distinction is clear, for who has not said that such and such a drawing was excellent as illustration, but as a work of art worthless? Of course many descriptive pictures possess, amongst other qualities, formal significance, and are therefore works of art: but many more do not. They interest us; they may move us too in a hundred different ways, but they do not move us aesthetically. According to my hypothesis they are not works of art. They leave untouched our aesthetic emotions because it is not their forms but the ideas or information suggested or conveyed by their forms that affect us. . . .

Most people who care much about art find that of the work that moves them most the greater part is what scholars call "Primitive." Of course there are bad primitives. For instance, I remember going, full of enthusiasm, to see one of the earliest Romanesque churches in Poitiers (Notre-Dame-la-Grande), and finding it as ill-proportioned, over-decorated, coarse, fat and heavy as any better class building by one of those highly civilised architects who flourished a thousand years earlier or eight hundred later. But such exceptions are rare. As a rule primitive art is good—and here again my hypothesis is helpful—for, as a rule, it is also free from descriptive qualities. In primitive art you will find no accurate representation; you will find only significant form. Yet no other art moves us so profoundly. Whether we consider Sumerian sculpture or pre-dynastic Egyptian art, or archaic Greek, or the Wei and T'ang masterpieces, or those early Japanese works of which I had the luck to see a few superb examples (especially two wooden Bodhisattvas) at the Shepherd's Bush Exhibition in 1910, or whether, coming nearer home, we consider the primitive Byzantine art of the sixth century and its primitive developments amongst the Western barbarians, or, turning far afield, we consider that mysterious and majestic art that flourished in Central and South America before the coming of the white men, in every case we observe three common characteristics—absence of representation, absence of technical swagger, sublimely impressive form. Nor is it hard to discover the connection between these three. Formal significance loses itself in preoccupation with exact representation and ostentatious cunning.[1] . . .

---

[1] This is not to say that exact representation is bad in itself. It is indifferent. A perfectly represented form may be significant, only it is fatal to sacrifice significance to representation. The quarrel between significance and illusion seems to be as old as art itself, and I have little doubt that what makes most palaeolithic art so bad is a preoccupation with exact representation. Evidently palaeolithic draughtsmen had no sense of the significance of form. Their art resembles that of the more capable and sincere Royal Academicians: it is a little higher than that of Sir Edward Poynter and a little lower than that of the late Lord Leighton. That this is no paradox let the cave-drawings of Altamira, or such works as the sketches of horses found at Bruniquel and now in the British Museum, bear witness. If the ivory head of a girl from the Grotte du Pape, Brassempouy (*Musée St. Germain*) and the ivory torso found at the same place (*Collection St. Cric*), be, indeed, palaeolithic, then there were good palaeolithic artists who created and did not imitate form. Neolithic art is, of course, a very different matter.

Let no one imagine that representation is bad in itself; a realistic form may be as significant, in its place as part of the design, as an abstract. But if a representative form has value, it is as form, not as representation. The representative element in a work of art may or may not be harmful; always it is irrelevant. For, to appreciate a work of art we need bring with us nothing from life, no knowledge of its ideas and affairs, no familiarity with its emotions. Art transports us from the world of man's activity to a world of aesthetic exaltation. For a moment we are shut off from human interests; our anticipations and memories are arrested; we are lifted above the stream of life. The pure mathematician rapt in his studies knows a state of mind which I take to be similar, if not identical. He feels an emotion for his speculations which arises from no perceived relation between them and the lives of men, but springs, inhuman or super-human, from the heart of an abstract science. I wonder, sometimes, whether the appreciators of art and of mathematical solutions are not even more closely allied. Before we feel an aesthetic emotion for a combination of forms, do we not perceive intellectually the rightness and necessity of the combination? If we do, it would explain the fact that passing rapidly through a room we recognise a picture to be good, although we cannot say that it has provoked much emotion. We seem to have recognised intellectually the rightness of its forms without staying to fix our attention, and collect, as it were, their emotional significance. If this were so, it would be permissible to inquire whether it was the forms themselves or our perception of their rightness and necessity that caused aesthetic emotion. But I do not think I need linger to discuss the matter here. I have been inquiring why certain combinations of forms move us; I should not have travelled by other roads had I enquired, instead, why certain combinations are perceived to be right and necessary, and why our perception of their rightness and necessity is moving. What I have to say is this: the rapt philosopher, and he who contemplates a work of art, inhabit a world with an intense and peculiar significance of its own; that significance is unrelated to the significance of life. In this world the emotions of life find no place. It is a world with emotions of its own.

To appreciate a work of art we need bring with us nothing but a sense of form and colour and a knowledge of three-dimensional space. That bit of knowledge, I admit, is essential to the appreciation of many great works, since many of the most moving forms ever created are in three dimensions. To see a cube or a rhomboid as a flat pattern is to lower its significance, and a sense of three-dimensional space is essential to the full appreciation of most architectural forms. Pictures which would be insignificant if we saw them as flat patterns are profoundly moving because, in fact, we see them as related planes. If the representation of three-dimensional space is to be called "representation," then I agree that there is one kind of representation which is not irrelevant. Also, I agree that along with our feeling for line and colour we must bring with us our knowledge of space if we are to make the most of every kind of form. Nevertheless, there are magnificent designs to an appreciation of which this knowledge is not necessary: so, though it is not irrelevant to the appreciation of some works of art it is not essential to the appreciation of all. What we must say is that the representation of three-dimensional space is neither irrelevant nor essential to all art, and that every other sort of representation is irrelevant.

That there is an irrelevant representative or descriptive element in many great works of art is not in the least surprising. . . . Representation is not of necessity baneful, and highly realistic forms may be extremely significant. Very often, however, representation is a sign of weakness in an artist. A painter too feeble to create forms that provoke more than a little aesthetic emotion will try to eke that little out by suggesting the emotions of life. To evoke the emotions of life he must use representation. Thus a man will paint an execution, and, fearing to miss with his first barrel of significant form, will try to hit with his second by raising an emotion of fear or pity. But if in the artist an inclination to play upon the emotions of life is often the sign of a flickering inspiration, in the spectator a tendency to seek, behind form, the emotions of life is a sign of defective sensibility always. It means that his aesthetic emotions are weak or, at any rate, imperfect. Before a work of art people who feel little or no emotion for pure form find themselves at a loss. They are deaf men at a concert. They know that they are in the presence of something great, but they lack the power of apprehending it. They know that they ought to feel for it a tremendous emotion, but it happens that the particular kind of emotion it can raise is one that they can feel hardly or not at all. And so they read into the forms of the work those facts and ideas for which they are capable of feeling emotion, and feel for them the emotions that they can feel—the ordinary emotions of life. When confronted by a picture, instinctively they refer back its forms to the world from which they came. They treat created form as though it were imitated form, a picture as though it were a photograph. Instead of going out on the stream of art into a new world of aesthetic experience, they turn a sharp corner and come straight home to the world of human interests. For them the significance of a work of art depends on what they bring to it; no new thing is added to their lives, only the old material is stirred. A good work of visual art carries a person who is capable of appreciating it out of life into ecstasy: to use art as a means to the emotions of life is to use a telescope for reading the news. You will notice that people who cannot feel pure aesthetic emotions remember pictures by their subjects; whereas people who can, as often as not, have no idea what the subject of a picture is. They have never noticed the representative element, and so when they discuss pictures they talk about the shapes of forms and the relations and quantities of colours. Often they can tell by the quality of a single line whether or no a man is a good artist. They are concerned only with lines and colours, their relations and quantities and qualities; but from these they win an emotion more profound and far more sublime than any that can be given by the description of facts and ideas. . . .

. . . Unfortunately, people are apt to be less modest about their powers of appreciating visual art. Everyone is inclined to believe that out of pictures, at any rate, he can get all that there is to be got; everyone is ready to cry "humbug" and "impostor" at those who say that more can be had. The good faith of people who feel pure aesthetic emotions is called in question by those who have never felt anything of the sort. It is the prevalence of the representative element, I suppose, that makes the man in the street so sure that he knows a good picture when he sees one. For I have noticed that in matters of architecture, pottery, textiles, &c., ignorance and ineptitude are more willing to defer to the opinions of those who have been blest with peculiar sensibility. It is a pity that cultivated and intelligent men and women cannot be induced to believe that a great gift of aesthetic appreciation is at least as rare in visual as in musical art. . . . For I am certain that most of those who visit galleries do feel very much what I feel at concerts. They have their moments of pure ecstasy; but the moments are short and unsure. Soon they fall back into the world of human interests and feel emotions, good no doubt, but inferior. I do not dream of saying that what they get from art is bad or nugatory; I say that they do not get the best that art can give. I do not say that they cannot understand art; rather I say that they cannot understand the state of mind of those who understand it best. I do not say that art means nothing or little to them; I say they miss its full significance. I do not suggest for one moment that their appreciation of art is a thing to be ashamed of; the majority of the charming and intelligent people with whom I am acquainted appreciate visual art impurely; and, by the way, the appreciation of almost all great writers has been impure. But provided that there be some fraction of pure aesthetic emotion, even a mixed and minor appreciation of art is, I am sure, one of the most valuable things in the world—so valuable, indeed, that in my giddier moments I have been tempted to believe that art might prove the world's salvation.

Yet, though the echoes and shadows of art enrich the life of the plains, her spirit dwells on the mountains. To him who woos, but woos impurely, she returns enriched what is brought. Like the sun, she warms the good seed in good soil and causes it to bring forth good fruit. But only to the perfect lover does she give a new strange gift—a gift beyond all price. Imperfect lovers bring to art and take away the ideas and emotions of their own age and civilisation. In twelfth-century Europe a man might have been greatly moved by a Romanesque church and found nothing in a T'ang picture. To a man of a later age, Greek sculpture meant much and Mexican nothing, for only to the former could he bring a crowd of associated ideas to be the objects of familiar emotions. But the perfect lover, he who can feel the profound significance of form, is raised above the accidents of time and place. To him the problems of archaeology, history, and hagiography are impertinent. If the forms of a work are significant its provenance is irrelevant. Before the grandeur of those Sumerian figures in the Louvre he is carried on the same flood of emotion to the same aesthetic ecstasy as, more than four thousand years ago, the Chaldean lover was carried. It is the mark of great art that its appeal is universal and eternal. Significant form stands charged with the power to provoke aesthetic emotion in anyone capable of feeling it. The ideas of men go buzz and die like gnats; men change their institutions and their customs as they change their coats; the intellectual triumphs of one age are the follies of another; only great art remains stable and unobscure. Great art remains stable and unobscure because the feelings that it awakens are independent of time and place, because its kingdom is not of this world. To those who have and hold a sense of the significance of form what does it matter whether the forms that move them were created in Paris the day before yesterday or in Babylon fifty centuries ago? The forms of art are inexhaustible; but all lead by the same road of aesthetic emotion to the same world of aesthetic ecstasy.

ART AS EXPRESSION: R. G. COLLINGWOOD

R. G. Collingwood's (1889–1943) theory of art makes two distinctive claims: That the work of art is a purely imaginary object, existing only and truly in the artist's mind, and that it is an expression of the artist's emotion.

The first claim, that art objects are imaginary entities, is surely paradoxical. After all, the world seems abundantly populated with works of art, from sculptures and paintings to songs and films. Why would one claim that these objects are not the real works of art?

To test the plausibility of this idea, consider a symphony. We might listen to it on the radio or a CD, but we would not say that the work is identical with the sounds we are hearing, for it transcends any and all specific performances it might be given. The same is true of a novel. I can read a copy of *War and Peace*, but that novel is not just my copy of it. How are we, then, to understand the being of works of art?

Collingwood's suggestion—that the work exists in the artist's mind—is one solution to this question. If the work is an imaginary object, then we can understand why it is not identical with any of its physical manifestations, these being the means the artist employs to get others to experience the work, that is, to have it present to *their* imaginations. Communication is incidental to, not a defining feature of, the artwork. In this respect, Collingwood's theory differs fundamentally from Tolstoy's (Chapter 8). For Collingwood, one reason why communication is incidental to the being of the artwork is that he views artistic creation as essentially a process of self-acknowledgment. Like the author of *War and Peace*, he sees emotion as crucially important in the creation of art. But Collingwood's account of the emotions is very different from Tolstoy's.

We often do not know, according to Collingwood, which emotion grips us. We are aware that we are feeling something, but we need to undergo a process, often linguistic, to allow us to understand which emotion it is. For example, if someone runs into my car, initially I might simply be conscious of being in a state of emotional turmoil. As I then express my emotion, swearing at the other driver, I become aware that I am angry. By means of this outburst, I discover what I feel.

Artists proceed in similar fashion—aware some emotion is affecting them, they give form to it through the works they create. The difference between my expression of anger (swearing) and the artist's (painting a picture) is that the artist explores the particularity of her emotion, taking great pains to understand it as the specific instance it is—for example, what makes *this* anger the very specific case of anger that it is. The artist is simply a person who is more interested than most in deciphering her emotions.

For this reason, Collingwood does not believe that the physical entities or events usually identified as works of art really are the works or, as he puts it, art proper. Of course, those physical manifestations play a crucial role in the *audience's* experience of art. But the goal of art is not communication; rather, making art, for Collingwood, is the process by means of which the artist expresses his own emotion *for himself*. Communicating that emotion to others is secondary.

Collingwood is also concerned to differentiate artistic creation proper from all other forms of making things. Again, it is the role of individuality that marks the difference: Whereas crafts aim at making things that fit a general description—a bed or a dress—the artist aims at creating an individual thing— this very poem and no other. Throughout, Collingwood insists on the unique character of the artwork, criticizing other theorists for failing to acknowledge its particularity.

STUDY QUESTIONS ON THE READING

1.   What relevance does Collingwood's discussion of the history of the concept "art" have for his theory of art?

2.   Why does Collingwood think that art consists in the expression of emotion rather than its arousal? Do you agree? Explain.

3.   Why does Collingwood say that someone who has not expressed an emotion does not know which emotion it is? Is his account of the process of expression adequate to explain how and why art is produced? Why or why not?

4.   Does Collingwood think there are specifically aesthetic emotions? Why or why not?

5.   What does Collingwood mean by claiming that art proper concerns imaginary objects? How could he defend his position against the obvious retort that this makes irrelevant the physical entities we normally refer to as art?

6.   Is Collingwood's view of art as imaginary more plausible for certain art forms than for others? What does this say, if anything, about the attempt to provide a single definition of art?

R. G. COLLINGWOOD: THE PRINCIPLES OF ART

The business of this book is to answer the question: What is art?

A question of this kind has to be answered in two stages. First, we must make sure that the key word (in this case 'art') is a word which we know how to apply where it ought to be applied and refuse where it ought to be refused. It would not be much use beginning to argue about the correct definition of a general term whose instances we could not recognize when we saw them. Our first business, then, is to bring ourselves into a position in which we can say with confidence 'this and this and this are art; that and that and that are not art'. . . .

Secondly, we must proceed to a definition of the term 'art'. This comes second, and not first, because no one can even try to define a term until he has settled in his own mind a definite usage of it: no one can define a term in common use until he has satisfied himself that his personal usage of it harmonizes with the common usage. Definition necessarily means defining one thing in terms of something else; therefore, in order to define any given thing, one must have in one's head not only a clear idea of the thing to be defined, but an equally clear idea of all the other things by reference to which one defines it. People often go wrong over this. They think that in order to construct a definition or (what is the same thing) a 'theory' of something, it is enough to have a clear idea of that one thing. That is absurd. Having a clear idea of the thing enables them to recognize it when they see it, just as having a clear idea of a certain house enables them to recognize it when they are there; but defining the thing is like explaining where the house is or pointing out its position on the map; you must know its relations to other things as well, and if your ideas of these other things are vague, your definition will be worthless. . . .

HISTORY OF THE WORD 'ART'

In order to clear up the ambiguities attaching to the word 'art', we must look to its history. The aesthetic sense of the word, the sense which here concerns us, is very recent in origin. *Ars* in ancient Latin, like τέχνη in Greek, means something quite different. It means a craft or specialized form of skill, like carpentry or smithying or surgery. The Greeks and Romans had no conception of what we call art as something different from craft; what we call art they regarded merely as a group of crafts, such as the craft of poetry (ποιητικη τέχνη, *ars poetica*), which they conceived, sometimes no doubt with misgivings, as in principle just like carpentry and the rest, and differing from any one of these only in the sort of way in which any one of them differs from any other.

It is difficult for us to realize this fact, and still more so to realize its implications. If people have no word for a certain kind of thing, it is because they are not aware of it as a distinct kind. Admiring as we do the art of the ancient Greeks, we naturally suppose that they admired it in the same kind of spirit as ourselves. But we admire it as a kind of art, where the word 'art' carries with it all the subtle and elaborate implications of the modern European aesthetic consciousness. We can be perfectly certain that the Greeks did not admire it in any such way. They approached it from a different point of view. What this was, we can perhaps discover by reading what people like Plato wrote about it; but not without great pains, because the first thing every modern reader does, when he reads what Plato has to say about poetry, is to assume that Plato is describing an aesthetic experience similar to our own. The second thing he does is to lose his temper because Plato describes it so badly. With most readers there is no third stage.

Ars in medieval Latin, like 'art' in the early modern English which borrowed both word and sense, meant any special form of book-learning, such as grammar or logic, magic or astrology. That is still its meaning in the time of Shakespeare: 'lie there, my art', says Prospero, putting off his magic gown. But the Renaissance, first in Italy and then elsewhere, re-established the old meaning; and the Renaissance artists, like those of the ancient world, did actually think of themselves as craftsmen. It was not until the seventeenth century that the problems and conceptions of aesthetic began to be disentangled from those of technic or the philosophy of craft. In the late eighteenth century the disentanglement had gone so far as to establish a distinction between the fine arts and the useful arts; where 'fine' arts meant, not delicate or highly skilled arts, but 'beautiful' arts (*les beaux arts, le belle arti, die schöne Kunst*). In the nineteenth century this phrase, abbreviated by leaving out the epithet and generalized by substituting the singular for the distributive plural, became 'art'. . . .

EXPRESSING EMOTION AND AROUSING EMOTION

Our first question is this. Since the artist proper has something to do with emotion, and what he does with it is not to arouse it, what is it that he does? It will be remembered that the kind of answer we expect to this question is an answer derived from what we all know and all habitually say; nothing original or recondite, but something entirely commonplace.

Nothing could be more entirely commonplace than to say he expresses them. The idea is familiar to every artist, and to every one else who has any acquaintance with the arts. To state it is not to state a philosophical theory or definition of art; it is to state a fact or supposed fact about which, when we have sufficiently identified it, we shall have later to theorize philosophically. For the present it does not matter whether the fact that is alleged, when it is said that the artist expresses emotion, is really a fact or only supposed to be one. Whichever it is, we have to identify it, that is, to decide what it is that people are saying when they use the phrase. Later on, we shall have to see whether it will fit into a coherent theory.

They are referring to a situation, real or supposed, of a definite kind. When a man is said to express emotion, what is being said about him comes to this. At first, he is conscious of having an emotion, but not conscious of what this emotion is. All he is conscious of is a perturbation or excitement, which he feels going on within him, but of whose nature he is ignorant. While in this state, all he can say about his emotion is: 'I feel . . . I don't know what I feel.' From this helpless and oppressed condition he extricates himself by doing something which we call expressing himself. This is an activity which has something to do with the thing we call language: he expresses himself by speaking. It has also something to do with consciousness: the emotion expressed is an emotion of whose nature the person who feels it is no longer unconscious. It has also something to do with the way in which he feels the emotion. As unexpressed, he feels it in what we have called a helpless and oppressed way; as expressed, he feels it in a way from which this sense of oppression has vanished. His mind is somehow lightened and eased.

This lightening of emotions which is somehow connected with the expression of them has a certain resemblance to the 'catharsis' by which emotions are earthed through being discharged into a make-believe situation; but the two things are not the same. Suppose the emotion is one of anger. If it is effectively earthed, for example by fancying oneself kicking some one down stairs, it is thereafter no longer present in the mind as anger at all: we have worked it off and are rid of it. If it is expressed, for example by putting it into hot and bitter words, it does not disappear from the mind; we remain angry; but instead of the sense of oppression which accompanies an emotion of anger not yet recognized as such, we have that sense of alleviation which comes when we are conscious of our own emotion as anger, instead of being conscious of it only as an unidentified perturbation. This is what we refer to when we say that it 'does us good' to express our emotions.

The expression of an emotion by speech may be addressed to some one; but if so it is not done with the intention of arousing a like emotion in him. If there is any effect which we wish to produce in the hearer, it is only the effect which we call making him understand how we feel. But, as we have already seen, this is just the effect which expressing our emotions has on ourselves. It makes us, as well as the people to whom we talk, understand how we feel. A person arousing emotion sets out to affect his audience in a way in which he himself is not necessarily affected. He and his audience stand in quite different relations to the act, very much as physician and patient stand in quite different relations towards a drug administered by the one and taken by the other. A person expressing emotion, on the contrary, is treating himself and his audience in the same kind of way; he is making his emotions clear to his audience, and that is what he is doing to himself.

It follows from this that the expression of emotion, simply as expression, is not addressed to any particular audience. It is addressed primarily to the speaker himself, and secondarily to any one who can understand. Here again, the speaker's attitude towards his audience is quite unlike that of a person desiring to arouse in his audience a certain emotion. If that is what he wishes to do, he must know the audience he is addressing. He must know what type of stimulus will produce the desired kind of reaction in people of that particular sort; and he must adapt his language to his audience in the sense of making sure that it contains stimuli appropriate to their peculiarities. If what he wishes to do is to express his emotions intelligibly, he has to express them in such a way as to be intelligible to himself; his audience is then in the position of persons who overhear him doing this. Thus the stimulus-and-reaction terminology has no applicability to the situation.

The means-and-end, or technique, terminology too is inapplicable. Until a man has expressed his emotion, he does not yet know what emotion it is. The act of expressing it is therefore an exploration of his own emotions. He is trying to find out what these emotions are. There is certainly here a directed process: an effort, that is, directed upon a certain end; but the end is not something foreseen and preconceived, to which appropriate means can be thought out in the light of our knowledge of its special character. Expression is an activity of which there can be no technique.

EXPRESSION AND INDIVIDUALIZATION

Expressing an emotion is not the same thing as describing it. To say 'I am angry' is to describe one's emotion, not to express it. The words in which it is expressed need not contain any reference to anger as such at all. Indeed, so far as they simply and solely express it, they cannot contain any such reference. . . .

The reason why description, so far from helping expression, actually damages it, is that description generalizes. To describe a thing is to call it a thing of such and such a kind: to bring it under a conception, to classify it. Expression, on the contrary, individualizes. The anger which I feel here and now, with a certain person, for a certain cause, is no doubt an instance of anger, and in describing it as anger one is telling truth about it; but it is much more than mere anger: it is a peculiar anger, not quite like any anger that I ever felt before, and probably not quite like any anger I shall ever feel again. To become fully conscious of it means becoming conscious of it not merely as an instance of anger, but as this quite peculiar anger. Expressing it, we saw, has something to do with becoming conscious of it; therefore, if being fully conscious of it means being conscious of all its peculiarities, fully expressing it means expressing all its peculiarities. The poet, therefore, in proportion as he understands his business, gets as far away as possible from merely labelling his emotions as instances of this or that general kind, and takes enormous pains to individualize them by expressing them in terms which reveal their difference from any other emotion of the same sort.

This is a point in which art proper, as the expression of emotion, differs sharply and obviously from any craft whose aim it is to arouse emotion. The end which a craft sets out to realize is always conceived in general terms, never individualized. However accurately defined it may be, it is always defined as the production of a thing having characteristics that could be shared by other things. A joiner, making a table out of these pieces of wood and no others, makes it to measurements and specifications which, even if actually shared by no other table, might in principle be shared by other tables. A physician treating a patient for a certain complaint is trying to produce in him a condition which might be, and probably has been, often produced in others, namely, the condition of recovering from that complaint. So an 'artist' setting out to produce a certain emotion in his audience is setting out to produce not an individual emotion, but an emotion of a certain kind. It follows that the means appropriate to its production will be not individual means but means of a certain kind: that is to say, means which are always in principle replaceable by other similar means. As every good craftsman insists, there is always a 'right way' of performing any operation. A 'way' of acting is a general pattern to which various individual actions may conform. In order that the 'work of art' should produce its intended psychological effect, therefore, whether this effect be magical or merely amusing, what is necessary is that it should satisfy certain conditions, possess certain characteristics: in other words be, not this work and no other, but a work of this kind and of no other. . . .

Art proper, as expression of emotion, has nothing to do with all this. The artist proper is a person who, grappling with the problem of expressing a certain emotion, says, 'I want to get this clear.' It is no use to him to get something else clear, however like it this other thing may be. Nothing will serve as a substitute.

He does not want a thing of a certain kind, he wants a certain thing.

This is why the kind of person who takes his literature as psychology, saying 'How admirably this writer depicts the feelings of women, or bus-drivers, or homosexuals . . .', necessarily misunderstands every real work of art with which he comes into contact, and takes for good art, with infallible precision, what is not art at all.

SELECTION AND AESTHETIC EMOTION

It has sometimes been asked whether emotions can be divided into those suitable for expression by artists and those unsuitable. If by art one means art proper, and identifies this with expression, the only possible answer is that there can be no such distinction. Whatever is expressible is expressible. There may be ulterior motives in special cases which make it desirable to express some emotions and not others; but only if by 'express' one means express publicly, that is, allow people to overhear one expressing oneself. This is because one cannot possibly decide that a certain emotion is one which for some reason it would be undesirable to express thus publicly, unless one first becomes conscious of it; and doing this, as we saw, is somehow bound up with expressing it. If art means the expression of emotion, the artist as such must be absolutely candid; his speech must be absolutely free. This is not a precept, it is a statement. It does not mean that the artist ought to be candid, it means that he is an artist only in so far as he is candid. Any kind of selection, any decision to express this emotion and not that, is inartistic not in the sense that it damages the perfect sincerity which distinguishes good art from bad, but in the sense that it represents a further process of a non-artistic kind, carried out when the work of expression proper is already complete. For until that work is complete one does not know what emotions one feels; and is therefore not in a position to pick and choose, and give one of them preferential treatment.

From these considerations a certain corollary follows about the division of art into distinct arts. Two such divisions are current: one according to the medium in which the artist works, into painting, poetry, music, and the like; the other according to the kind of emotion he expresses, into tragic, comic, and so forth. We are concerned with the second. If the difference between tragedy and comedy is a difference between the emotions they express, it is not a difference that can be present to the artist's mind when he is beginning his work; if it were, he would know what emotion he was going to express before he had expressed it. No artist, therefore, so far as he is an artist proper, can set out to write a comedy, a tragedy, an elegy, or the like. . . .

The same considerations provide an answer to the question whether there is such a thing as a specific 'aesthetic emotion'. If it is said that there is such an emotion independently of its expression in art, and that the business of artists is to express it, we must answer that such a view is nonsense. It implies, first, that artists have emotions of various kinds, among which is this peculiar aesthetic emotion; secondly, that they select this aesthetic emotion for expression. If the first proposition were true, the second would have to be false. If artists only find out what their emotions are in the course of finding out how to express them, they cannot begin the work of expression by deciding what emotion to express.

In a different sense, however, it is true that there is a specific aesthetic emotion. As we have seen, an unexpressed emotion is accompanied by a feeling of oppression; when it is expressed and thus comes into consciousness the same emotion is accompanied by a new feeling of alleviation or easement, the sense that this oppression is removed. It resembles the feeling of relief that comes when a burdensome intellectual or moral problem has been solved. We may call it, if we like, the specific feeling of having successfully expressed ourselves; and there is no reason why it should not be called a specific aesthetic emotion. But it is not a specific kind of emotion pre-existing to the expression of it, and having the peculiarity that when it comes to be expressed it is expressed artistically. It is an emotional colouring which attends the expression of any emotion whatever. . . .

EXPRESSING EMOTION AND BETRAYING EMOTION

Finally, the expressing of emotion must not be confused with what may be called the betraying of it, that is, exhibiting symptoms of it. When it is said that the artist in the proper sense of that word is a person who expresses his emotions, this does not mean that if he is afraid he turns pale and stammers; if he is angry he turns red and bellows; and so forth. These things are no doubt called expressions; but just as we distinguish proper and improper senses of the word 'art', so we must distinguish proper and improper senses of the word 'expression', and in the context of a discussion about art this sense of expression is an improper sense. The characteristic mark of expression proper is lucidity or intelligibility; a person who expresses something thereby becomes conscious of what it is that he is expressing, and enables others to become conscious of it in himself and in them. Turning pale and stammering is a natural accompaniment of fear, but a person who in addition to being afraid also turns pale and stammers does not thereby become conscious of the precise quality of his emotion. About that he is as much in the dark as he would be if (were that possible) he could feel fear without also exhibiting these symptoms of it.

Confusion between these two senses of the word 'expression' may easily lead to false critical estimates, and so to false aesthetic theory. It is sometimes thought a merit in an actress that when she is acting a pathetic scene she can work herself up to such an extent as to weep real tears. There may be some ground for that opinion if acting is not an art but a craft, and if the actress's object in that scene is to produce grief in her audience; and even then the conclusion would follow only if it were true that grief cannot be produced in the audience unless symptoms of grief are exhibited by the performer. And no doubt this is how most people think of the actor's work. But if his business is not amusement but art, the object at which he is aiming is not to produce a preconceived emotional effect on his audience but by means of a system of expressions, or language, composed partly of speech and partly of gesture, to explore his own emotions: to discover emotions in himself of which he was unaware, and, by permitting the audience to witness the discovery, enable them to make a similar discovery about themselves. In that case it is not her ability to weep real tears that would mark out a good actress; it is her ability to make it clear to herself and her audience what the tears are about.

This applies to every kind of art. The artist never rants. . . .

THE WORK OF ART AS IMAGINARY OBJECT

If the making of a tune is an instance of imaginative creation, a tune is an imaginary thing. And the same applies to a poem or a painting or any other work of art. This seems paradoxical; we are apt to think that a tune is not an imaginary thing but a real thing, a real collection of noises; that a painting is a real piece of canvas covered with real colours; and so on. I hope to show, if the reader will have patience, that there is no paradox here; that both these propositions express what we do as a matter of fact say about works of art; and that they do not contradict one another, because they are concerned with different things.

When, speaking of a work of art (tune, picture, &c.), we mean by art a specific craft, intended as a stimulus for producing specific emotional effects in an audience, we certainly mean to designate by the term 'work of art' something that we should call real. The artist as magician or purveyor of amusement is necessarily a craftsman making real things, and making them out of some material according to some plan. His works are as real as the works of an engineer, and for the same reason.

But it does not at all follow that the same is true of an artist proper. His business is not to produce an emotional effect in an audience, but, for example, to make a tune. This tune is already complete and perfect when it exists merely as a tune in his head, that is, an imaginary tune. Next, he may arrange for the tune to be played before an audience. Now there comes into existence a real tune, a collection of noises. But which of these two things is the work of art? Which of them is the music? The answer is implied in what we have already said: the music, the work of art, is not the collection of noises, it is the tune in the composer's head. The noises made by the performers, and heard by the audience, are not the music at all; they are only means by which the audience, if they listen intelligently (not otherwise), can reconstruct for themselves the imaginary tune that existed in the composer's head.

This is not a paradox. It is not something παραλδξαυ [paradoxical], contrary to what we ordinarily believe and express in our ordinary speech. We all know perfectly well, and remind each other often enough, that a person who hears the noises the instruments make is not thereby possessing himself of the music. Perhaps no one can do that unless he does hear the noises; but there is something else which he must do as well. Our ordinary word for this other thing is listening; and the listening which we have to do when we hear the noises made by musicians is in a way rather like the thinking we have to do when we hear the noises made, for example, by a person lecturing on a scientific subject. We hear the sound of his voice; but what he is doing is not simply to make noises, but to develop a scientific thesis. The noises are meant to assist us in achieving what he assumes to be our purpose in coming to hear him lecture, that is, thinking this same scientific thesis for ourselves. The lecture, therefore, is not a collection of noises made by the lecturer with his organs of speech; it is a collection of scientific thoughts related to those noises in such a way that a person who not only hears but thinks as well becomes able to think these thoughts for himself. We may call this the communication of thought by means of speech, if we like; but if we do, we must think of communication not as an 'imparting' of thought by the speaker to the hearer, the speaker somehow planting his thought in the hearer's receptive mind, but as a 'reproduction' of the speaker's thought by the hearer, in virtue of his own active thinking.

The parallel with listening to music is not complete. The two cases are similar at one point, dissimilar at another. They are dissimilar in that a concert and a scientific lecture are different things, and what we are trying to 'get out of' the concert is a thing of a different kind from the scientific thoughts we are trying to 'get out of' the lecture. But they are similar in this: that just as what we get out of the lecture is something other than the noises we hear proceeding from the lecturer's mouth, so what we get out of the concert is something other than the noises made by the performers. In each case, what we get out of it is something which we have to reconstruct in our own minds, and by our own efforts; something which remains for ever inaccessible to a person who cannot or will not make efforts of the right kind, however completely he hears the sounds that fill the room in which he is sitting.

This, I repeat, is something we all know perfectly well. And because we all know it, we need not trouble to examine or criticize the ideas of aestheticians (if there are any left to-day—they were common enough at one time) who say that what we get out of listening to music, or looking at paintings, or the like, is some peculiar kind of sensual pleasure. When we do these things, we certainly may, in so far as we are using our senses, enjoy sensual pleasures. It would be odd if we did not. A colour, or a shape, or an instrumental timbre may give us an exquisite pleasure of a purely sensual kind. It may even be true (though this is not so certain) that no one would become a lover of music unless he were more susceptible than other people to the sensual pleasure of sound. But even if a special susceptibility to this pleasure may at first lead some people towards music, they must, in proportion as they are more susceptible, take the more pains to prevent that susceptibility from interfering with their power of listening. For any concentration on the pleasantness of the noises themselves concentrates the mind on hearing, and makes it hard or impossible to listen. There is a kind of person who goes to concerts mainly for the sensual pleasure he gets from the sheer sounds; his presence may be good for the box-office, but it is as bad for music as the presence of a person who went to a scientific lecture for the sensual pleasure he got out of the tones of the lecturer's voice would be for science. And this, again, everybody knows.

It is unnecessary to go through the form of applying what has been said about music to the other arts. We must try instead to make in a positive shape the point that has been put negatively. Music does not consist of heard noises, paintings do not consist of seen colours, and so forth. Of what, then, do these things consist? Not, clearly, of a 'form', understood as a pattern or a system of relations between the various noises we hear or the various colours we see. Such 'forms' are nothing but the perceived structures of bodily 'works of art', that is to say, 'works of art' falsely so called; and these formalistic theories of art, popular though they have been and are, have no relevance to art proper and will not be further considered. . . . The distinction between form and matter, on which they are based, is a distinction belonging to the philosophy of craft, and not applicable to the philosophy of art.

The work of art proper is something not seen or heard, but something imagined. But what is it that we imagine? We have suggested that in music the work of art proper is an imagined tune. Let us begin by developing this idea.

Everybody must have noticed a certain discrepancy between what we actually see when looking at a picture or statue or play and what we see imaginatively; what we actually see when listening to music or speech and what we imaginatively hear. To take an obvious example: in watching a puppet-play we could (as we say) swear that we have seen the expression on the puppets' faces change with their changing gestures and the puppet-man's changing words and tones of voice. Knowing that they are only puppets, we know that their facial expression cannot change; but that makes no difference; we continue to see imaginatively the expressions which we know that we do not see actually. The same thing happens in the case of masked actors like those of the Greek stage. In listening to the pianoforte, again, we know from evidence of the same kind that we must be hearing every note begin with a *sforzando* [accent—T.E.W.], and fade away for the whole length of time that it continues to sound. But our imagination enables us to read into this experience something quite different.

As we seem to see the puppets' features move, so we seem to hear a pianist producing a *sostenuto* [prolonged—T.E.W.] tone, almost like that of a horn; and in fact notes of the horn and the pianoforte are easily mistaken one for the other. Still stranger, when we hear a violin and pianoforte playing together in the key, say, of G, the violin's F sharp is actually played a great deal sharper than the pianoforte's. Such a discrepancy would sound intolerably out of tune except to a person whose imagination was trained to focus itself on the key of G, and silently corrected every note of the equally tempered pianoforte to suit it. The corrections which imagination must thus carry out, in order that we should be able to listen to an entire orchestra, beggar description. When we listen to a speaker or singer, imagination is constantly supplying articulate sounds which actually our ears do not catch. In looking at a drawing in pen or pencil, we take a series of roughly parallel lines for the tint of a shadow. And so on.

Conversely, in all these cases imagination works negatively. We disimagine, if I may use the word, a great deal which actually we see and hear. The street noises at a concert, the noises made by our breathing and shuffling neighbours, and even some of the noises made by the performers, are thus shut out of the picture unless by their loudness or in some other way they are too obtrusive to be ignored. At the theatre, we are strangely able to ignore the silhouettes of the people sitting in front of us, and a good many things that happen on the stage. Looking at a picture, we do not notice the shadows that fall on it or, unless it is excessive, the light reflected from its varnish.

All this is commonplace. And the conclusion has already been stated by Shakespeare's Theseus: 'the best in this kind ['works of art', as things actually perceived by the senses—R.G.C.] are but shadows, and the worst are no worse if imagination amend them.' The music to which we listen is not the heard sound, but that sound as amended in various ways by the listener's imagination, and so with the other arts.

But this does not go nearly far enough. Reflection will show that the imagination with which we listen to music is something more, and more complex, than any inward ear; the imagination with which we look at paintings is something more than 'the mind's eye'. . . .

12

ART AS EXPERIENCE: JOHN DEWEY

The central claim of John Dewey's (1859–1952) theory of art is that art should not be conceived as a radically distinct aspect of human life. Too many theories of art fail, he insists, just because they treat art as a fundamentally different kind of human endeavor. Although admittedly endowing certain features of these endeavors with a special prominence, art must nonetheless be seen as continuous with more prosaic forms of human activity. Thus, the very features often cited as those that distinguish art from other spheres of human life—such as form and rhythm—are, according to Dewey, found throughout our ordinary experience. Dewey's view of art thus puts him at odds with such diverse theorists as Kant (Chapter 4), Bell (Chapter 10), and Collingwood (Chapter 11).

But if art is continuous with the rest of what we do, according to Dewey, wherein lies its distinctiveness? Dewey's answer is that art results when the desire to create an object whose perceptible properties will yield immediate satisfaction controls the process of its production. Although we may be pleased with the products of many different kinds of activities, only art making is guided by the aim of producing just such pleasure.

An important feature of this definition is that it unites various aspects of art often treated as distinct. For example, both artist and audience play equally important roles in this definition. An art object must be produced by an artist in anticipation of the satisfaction her audience will receive. Similarly, the artistic and the aesthetic refer, for Dewey, to two aspects of the same process, which he sometimes calls "aesthetic artistic" to indicate that neither of the two terms is primary. For him, "artistic" refers to the physical object, whereas "aesthetic" refers to the way in which it is experienced. Art, to be art, must be both artistic and aesthetic, have both an objective and a subjective side. There is, for Dewey, no art that is not aesthetic.

But what "aesthetic" means for Dewey is not what it often means for other theorists of art, for he holds that any experience can have an aesthetic dimension—as is, for example, the satisfaction a mathematician experiences in constructing a proof or a cobbler does in finishing a shoe. It is this sense of conscious completion that Dewey refers to as the aesthetic component of experience and that he sees as attainable in all realms of human endeavor. What is distinctive about art is that it is produced with just this feature in mind, whereas other goals structure the practices of the scientist or craftsperson.

Although Dewey views artistic activity as continuous with other forms of human production, he does think that art is not only a distinctive form of such production but also its apex. That is, because of its focus on our conscious appreciation of the complete process of creation—what Dewey calls "*an* experience"—art is, for him, exemplary of the possibilities inherent in human productive life.

STUDY QUESTIONS ON THE READING

1.   Why does Dewey see art and normal human activity as intimately linked?

2.   Why does Dewey think that art has come to be seen as involving a type of experience radically separate from the normal course of human life?

3.   Why does Dewey think that art is "the greatest intellectual achievement in the history of humanity"?

4.   Unlike many theorists, Dewey sees art and craft as intimately related. Do you think he is right? Why?

5.   What does Dewey mean by "*an* experience"? Why is this term relevant to his conception of art?

6.   According to Dewey, what is unusual about an artist? How does his view differ from Collingwood's?

7.   Do you agree that all areas of human experience can have an aesthetic component? If so, what, then, makes art unique?

8.   Dewey and Bell have radically different conceptions of art's place in human life. Whom do you agree with, if either? Why?

❖

JOHN DEWEY: ART AS EXPERIENCE

By one of the ironic perversities that often attend the course of affairs, the existence of the works of art upon which formation of an esthetic theory depends has become an obstruction to theory about them. For one reason, these works are products that exist externally and physically. In common conception, the work of art is often identified with the building, book, painting, or statue in its existence apart from human experience. Since the actual work of art is what the product does with and in experience, the result is not favorable to understanding. In addition, the very perfection of some of these products, the prestige they possess because of a long history of unquestioned admiration, creates conventions that get in the way of fresh insight. When an art product once attains classic status, it somehow becomes isolated from the human conditions under which it was brought into being and from the human consequences it engenders in actual life-experience. . . .

In order to *understand* the esthetic in its ultimate and approved forms, one must begin with it in the raw; in the events and scenes that hold the attentive eye and ear of man, arousing his interest and affording him enjoyment as he looks and listens: the sights that hold the crowd—the fire-engine rushing by; the machines excavating enormous holes in the earth; the human-fly climbing the steeple-side; the men perched high in air on girders, throwing and catching red-hot bolts. The sources of art in human experience will be learned by him who sees how the tense grace of the ball-player infects the onlooking crowd; who notes the delight of the housewife in tending her plants, and the intent interest of her goodman in tending the patch of green in front of the house; the zest of the spectator in poking the wood burning on the hearth and in watching the darting flames and crumbling coals. These people, if questioned as to the reason for their actions, would doubtless return reasonable answers. The man who poked the sticks of burning wood would say he did it to make the fire burn better; but he is none the less fascinated by the colorful drama of change enacted before his eyes and imaginatively partakes in it. He does not remain a cold spectator. What Coleridge said of the reader of poetry is true in its way of all who are happily absorbed in their activities of mind and body: "The reader should be carried forward, not merely or chiefly by the mechanical impulse of curiosity, not by a restless desire to arrive at the final solution, but by the pleasurable activity of the journey itself." . . .

So extensive and subtly pervasive are the ideas that set Art upon a remote pedestal, that many a person would be repelled rather than pleased if told that he enjoyed his casual recreations, in part at least, because of their esthetic quality. The arts which today have most vitality for the average person are things he does not take to be arts: for instance, the movie, jazzed music, the comic strip, and, too frequently, newspaper accounts of lovenests, murders, and exploits of bandits. For, when what he knows as art is relegated to the museum and gallery, the unconquerable impulse towards experiences enjoyable in themselves finds such outlet as the daily environment provides. Many a person who protests against the museum conception of art, still shares the fallacy from which that conception springs. For the popular notion comes from a separation of art from the objects and scenes of ordinary experience that many theorists and critics pride themselves upon holding and even elaborating. The times when select and distinguished objects are closely connected with the products of usual vocations are the times when appreciation of the former is most rife and most keen. When, because of their remoteness, the objects acknowledged by the cultivated to be works of fine art seem anemic to the mass of people, esthetic hunger is likely to seek the cheap and the vulgar.

The factors that have glorified fine art by setting it upon a far-off pedestal did not arise within the realm of art nor is their influence confined to the arts. For many persons an aura of mingled awe and unreality encompasses the "spiritual" and the "ideal" while "matter" has become by contrast a term of depreciation, something to be explained away or apologized for. The forces at work are those that have removed religion as well as fine art from the scope of the common or community life. The forces have historically produced so many of the dislocations and divisions of modern life and thought that art could not escape their influence. We do not have to travel to the ends of the earth nor return many millennia in time to find peoples for whom everything that intensifies the sense of immediate living is an object of intense admiration. Bodily scarification, waving feathers, gaudy robes, shining ornaments of gold and silver, of emerald and jade, formed the contents of esthetic arts, and, presumably, without the vulgarity of class exhibitionism that attends their analogues today. Domestic utensils, furnishings of tent and house, rugs, mats, jars, pots, bows, spears, were wrought with such delighted care that today we hunt them out and give them places of honor in our art museums. Yet in their own time and place, such things were enhancements of the processes of everyday life. Instead of being elevated to a niche apart, they belonged to display of prowess, the manifestation of group and clan membership, worship of gods, feasting and fasting, fighting, hunting, and all the rhythmic crises that punctuate the stream of living. . . .

Because of changes in industrial conditions the artist has been pushed to one side from the main streams of active interest. Industry has been mechanized and an artist cannot work mechanically for mass production. He is less integrated than formerly in the normal flow of social services. A peculiar esthetic "individualism" results. Artists find it incumbent upon them to betake themselves to their work as an isolated means of "self-expression." In order not to cater to the trend of economic forces, they often feel obliged to exaggerate their separateness to the point of eccentricity. Consequently artistic products take on to a still greater degree the air of something independent and esoteric.

Put the action of all such forces together, and the conditions that create the gulf which exists generally between producer and consumer in modern society operate to create also a chasm between ordinary and esthetic experience. Finally we have, as the record of this chasm, accepted as if it were normal, the philosophies of art that locate it in a region inhabited by no other creature, and that emphasize beyond all reason the merely contemplative character of the esthetic. Confusion of values enters in to accentuate the separation. Adventitious matters, like the pleasure of collecting, of exhibiting, of ownership and display, simulate esthetic values. Criticism is affected. There is much applause for the wonders of appreciation and the glories of the transcendent beauty of art indulged in without much regard to capacity for esthetic perception in the concrete.

My purpose, however, is not to engage in an economic interpretation of the history of the arts, much less to argue that economic conditions are either invariably or directly relevant to perception and enjoyment, or even to interpretation of individual works of art. It is to indicate that *theories* which isolate art and its appreciation by placing them in a realm of their own, disconnected from other modes of experiencing, are not inherent in the subject-matter but arise because of specifiable extraneous conditions. Embedded as they are in institutions and in habits of life, these conditions operate effectively because they work so unconsciously. Then the theorist assumes they are embedded in the nature of things. Nevertheless, the influence of these conditions is not confined to theory. As I have already indicated, it deeply affects the practice of living, driving away esthetic perceptions that are necessary ingredients of happiness, or reducing them to the level of compensating transient pleasurable excitations. . . .

Many theories about art already exist. If there is justification for proposing yet another philosophy of the esthetic, it must be found in a new mode of approach. Combinations and permutations among existing theories can easily be brought forth by those so inclined. But, to my mind, the trouble with existing theories is that they start from a ready-made compartmentalization, or from a conception of art that "spiritualizes" it out of connection with the objects of concrete experience. The alternative, however, to such spiritualization is not a degrading and Philistinish materialization of works of fine art, but a conception that discloses the way in which these works idealize qualities found in common experience. Were works of art placed in a directly human context in popular esteem, they would have a much wider appeal than they can have when pigeon-hole theories of art win general acceptance.

A conception of fine art that sets out from its connection with discovered qualities of ordinary experience will be able to indicate the factors and forces that favor the normal development of common human activities into matters of artistic value. It will also be able to point out those conditions that arrest its normal growth. Writers on esthetic theory often raise the question of whether esthetic philosophy can aid in cultivation of esthetic appreciation. The question is a branch of the general theory of criticism, which, it seems to me, fails to accomplish its full office if it does not indicate what to look for and what to find in concrete esthetic objects. But, in any case, it is safe to say that a philosophy of art is sterilized unless it makes us aware of the function of art in relation to other modes of experience, and unless it indicates why this function is so inadequately realized, and unless it suggests the conditions under which the office would be successfully performed.

The comparison of the emergence of works of art out of ordinary experiences to the refining of raw materials into valuable products may seem to some unworthy, if not an actual attempt to reduce works of art to the status of articles manufactured for commercial purposes. The point, however, is that no amount of ecstatic eulogy of finished works can of itself assist the understanding or the generation of such works. Flowers can be enjoyed without knowing about the interactions of soil, air, moisture, and seeds of which they are the result. But they cannot be *understood* without taking just these interactions into account—and theory is a matter of understanding. Theory is concerned with discovering the nature of the production of works of art and of their enjoyment in perception. How is it that the everyday making of things grows into that form of making which is genuinely artistic? How is it that our everyday enjoyment of scenes and situations develops into the peculiar satisfaction that attends the experience which is emphatically esthetic? These are the questions theory must answer. The answers cannot be found, unless we are willing to find the germs and roots in matters of experience that we do not currently regard as esthetic. Having discovered these active seeds, we may follow the course of their growth into the highest forms of finished and refined art. . . .

Art is thus prefigured in the very processes of living. A bird builds its nest and a beaver its dam when internal organic pressures coöperate with external materials so that the former are fulfilled and the latter are transformed in a satisfying culmination. We may hesitate to apply the word "art," since we doubt the presence of directive intent. But all deliberation, all conscious intent, grows out of things once performed organically through the interplay of natural energies. Were it not so, art would be built on quaking sands, nay, on unstable air.

The distinguishing contribution of man is consciousness of the relations found in nature. Through consciousness, he converts the relations of cause and effect that are found in nature into relations of means and consequence. Rather, consciousness itself is the inception of such a transformation. What was mere shock becomes an invitation; resistance becomes something to be used in changing existing arrangements of matter; smooth facilities become agencies for executing an idea. In these operations, an organic stimulation becomes the bearer of meanings, and motor responses are changed into instruments of expression and communication; no longer are they mere means of locomotion and direct reaction. Meanwhile, the organic substratum remains as the quickening and deep foundation. Apart from relations of cause and effect in nature, conception and invention could not be. Apart from the relation of processes of rhythmic conflict and fulfillment in animal life, experience would be without design and pattern. Apart from organs inherited from animal ancestry, idea and purpose would be without a mechanism of realization. The primeval arts of nature and animal life are so much the material, and, in gross outline, so much the model for the intentional achievements of man, that the theologically minded have imputed conscious intent to the structure of nature—as man, sharing many activities with the ape, is wont to think of the latter as imitating his own performances.

The existence of art is the concrete proof of what has just been stated abstractly. It is proof that man uses the materials and energies of nature with intent to expand his own life, and that he does so in accord with the structure of his organism—brain, sense-organs, and muscular system. Art is the living and concrete proof that man is capable of restoring consciously, and thus on the plane of meaning, the union of sense, need, impulse and action characteristic of the live creature. The intervention of consciousness adds regulation, power of selection, and redisposition. Thus it varies the arts in ways without end. But its intervention also leads in time to the *idea* of art as a conscious idea—the greatest intellectual achievement in the history of humanity.

The variety and perfection of the arts in Greece led thinkers to frame a generalized conception of art and to project the ideal of an art of organization of human activities as such—the art of politics and morals as conceived by Socrates and Plato. The ideas of design, plan, order, pattern, purpose emerged in distinction from and relation to the materials employed in their realization. The conception of man as the being that uses art became at once the ground of the distinction of man from the rest of nature and of the bond that ties him to nature. When the conception of art as the distinguishing trait of man was made explicit, there was assurance that, short of complete relapse of humanity below even savagery, the possibility of invention of new arts would remain, along with use of old arts, as the guiding ideal of mankind. Although recognition of the fact still halts, because of traditions established before the power of art was adequately recognized, science itself is but a central art auxiliary to the generation and utilization of other arts.

It is customary, and from some points of view necessary, to make a distinction between fine art and useful or technological art. But the point of view from which it is necessary is one that is extrinsic to the work of art itself. The customary distinction is based simply on acceptance of certain existing social conditions. I suppose the fetiches of the negro sculptor were taken to be useful in the highest degree to his tribal group, more so even than spears and clothing. But now they are fine art, serving in the twentieth century to inspire renovations in arts that had grown conventional. But they are fine art only because the anonymous artist lived and experienced so fully during the process of production. An angler may eat his catch without thereby losing the esthetic satisfaction he experienced in casting and playing. It is this degree of completeness of living in the experience of making and of perceiving that makes the difference between what is fine or esthetic in art and what is not. Whether the thing made is put to use, as are bowls, rugs, garments, weapons, is, *intrinsically* speaking, a matter of indifference. That many, perhaps most, of the articles and utensils made at present for use are not genuinely esthetic happens, unfortunately, to be true. But it is true for reasons that are foreign to the relation of the "beautiful" and "useful" as such. Wherever conditions are such as to prevent the act of production from being an experience in which the whole creature is alive and in which he possesses his living through enjoyment, the product will lack something of being esthetic. No matter how useful it is for special and limited ends, it will not be useful in the ultimate degree—that of contributing directly and liberally to an expanding and enriched life. The story of the severance and final sharp opposition of the useful and the fine is the history of that industrial development through which so much of production has become a form of postponed living and so much of consumption a superimposed enjoyment of the fruits of the labor of others. . . .

EXPERIENCE occurs continuously, because the interaction of live creature and environing conditions is involved in the very process of living. Under conditions of resistance and conflict, aspects and elements of the self and the world that are implicated in this interaction qualify experience with emotions and ideas so that conscious intent emerges. Oftentimes, however, the experience had is inchoate. Things are experienced but not in such a way that they are composed into *an* experience. There is distraction and dispersion; what we observe and what we think, what we desire and what we get, are at odds with each other. We put our hands to the plow and turn back; we start and then we stop, not because the experience has reached the end for the sake of which it was initiated but because of extraneous interruptions or of inner lethargy.

In contrast with such experience, we have *an* experience when the material experienced runs its course to fulfillment. Then and then only is it integrated within and demarcated in the general stream of experience from other experiences. A piece of work is finished in a way that is satisfactory; a problem receives its solution; a game is played through; a situation, whether that of eating a meal, playing a game of chess, carrying on a conversation, writing a book, or taking part in a political campaign, is so rounded out that its close is a consummation and not a cessation. Such an experience is a whole and carries with it its own individualizing quality and self-sufficiency. It is *an* experience. . . .

We have no word in the English language that unambiguously includes what is signified by the two words "artistic" and "esthetic." Since "artistic" refers primarily to the act of production and "esthetic" to that of perception and enjoyment, the absence of a term designating the two processes taken together is unfortunate. Sometimes, the effect is to separate the two from each other, to regard art as something superimposed upon esthetic material, or, upon the other side, to an assumption that, since art is a process of creation, perception and enjoyment of it have nothing in common with the creative act. In any case, there is a certain verbal awkwardness in that we are compelled sometimes to use the term "esthetic" to cover the entire field and sometimes to limit it to the receiving perceptual aspect of the whole operation. I refer to these obvious facts as preliminary to an attempt to show how the conception of conscious experience as a perceived relation between doing and undergoing enables us to understand the connection that art as production and perception and appreciation as enjoyment sustain to each other.

Art denotes a process of doing or making. This is as true of fine as of technological art. Art involves molding of clay, chipping of marble, casting of bronze, laying on of pigments, construction of buildings, singing of songs, playing of instruments, enacting rôles on the stage, going through rhythmic movements in the dance. Every art does something with some physical material, the body or something outside the body, with or without the use of intervening tools, and with a view to production of something visible, audible, or tangible. So marked is the active or "doing" phase of art, that the dictionaries usually define it in terms of skilled action, ability in execution. The Oxford Dictionary illustrates by a quotation from John Stuart Mill: "Art is an endeavor after perfection in execution" while Matthew Arnold calls it "pure and flawless workmanship."

The word "esthetic" refers, as we have already noted, to experience as appreciative, perceiving, and enjoying. It denotes the consumer's rather than the producer's standpoint. It is Gusto, taste; and, as with cooking, overt skillful action is on the side of the cook who prepares, while taste is on the side of the consumer, as in gardening there is a distinction between the gardener who plants and tills and the householder who enjoys the finished product.

These very illustrations, however, as well as the relation that exists in having an experience between doing and undergoing, indicate that the distinction between esthetic and artistic cannot be pressed so far as to become a separation.

Perfection in execution cannot be measured or defined in terms of execution; it implies those who perceive and enjoy the product that is executed. The cook prepares food for the consumer and the measure of the value of what is prepared is found in consumption. Mere perfection in execution, judged in its own terms in isolation, can probably be attained better by a machine than by human art. By itself, it is at most technique, and there are great artists who are not in the first ranks as technicians (witness Cezanne), just as there are great performers on the piano who are not great esthetically, and as Sargent is not a great painter.

Craftsmanship to be artistic in the final sense must be "loving"; it must care deeply for the subject matter upon which skill is exercised. A sculptor comes to mind whose busts are marvelously exact. It might be difficult to tell in the presence of a photograph of one of them and of a photograph of the original which was of the person himself. For virtuosity they are remarkable. But one doubts whether the maker of the busts had an experience of his own that he was concerned to have those share who look at his products. To be truly artistic, a work must also be esthetic—that is, framed for enjoyed receptive perception. Constant observation is, of course, necessary for the maker while he is producing. But if his perception is not also esthetic in nature, it is a colorless and cold recognition of what has been done, used as a stimulus to the next step in a process that is essentially mechanical.

In short, art, in its form, unites the very same relation of doing and undergoing, outgoing and incoming energy, that makes an experience to be an experience.

Because of elimination of all that does not contribute to mutual organization of the factors of both action and reception into one another, and because of selection of just the aspects and traits that contribute to their interpenetration of each other, the product is a work of esthetic art. Man whittles, carves, sings, dances, gestures, molds, draws and paints. The doing or making is artistic when the perceived result is of such a nature that *its* qualities *as perceived* have controlled the question of production. The act of producing that is directed by intent to produce something that is enjoyed in the immediate experience of perceiving has qualities that a spontaneous or uncontrolled activity does not have. The artist embodies in himself the attitude of the perceiver while he works.

Suppose, for the sake of illustration, that a finely wrought object, one whose texture and proportions are highly pleasing in perception, has been believed to be a product of some primitive people. Then there is discovered evidence that proves it to be an accidental natural product. As an external thing, it is now precisely what it was before. Yet at once it ceases to be a work of art and becomes a natural "curiosity." It now belongs in a museum of natural history, not in a museum of art. And the extraordinary thing is that the difference that is thus made is not one of just intellectual classification. A difference is made in appreciative perception and in a direct way. The esthetic experience— in its limited sense—is thus seen to be inherently connected with the experience of making. . . .

The process of art in production is related to the esthetic in perception organically—as the Lord God in creation surveyed his work and found it good.

Until the artist is satisfied in perception with what he is doing, he continues shaping and reshaping. The making comes to an end when its result is experienced as good—and that experience comes not by mere intellectual and outside judgment but in direct perception. An artist, in comparison with his fellows, is one who is not only especially gifted in powers of execution but in unusual sensitivity to the qualities of things. This sensitivity also directs his doings and makings.

As we manipulate, we touch and feel, as we look, we see; as we listen, we hear. The hand moves with etching needle or with brush. The eye attends and reports the consequence of what is done. Because of this intimate connection, subsequent doing is cumulative and not a matter of caprice nor yet of routine. In an emphatic artistic-esthetic experience, the relation is so close that it controls simultaneously both the doing and the perception. Such vital intimacy of connection cannot be had if only hand and eye are engaged. When they do not, both of them, act as organs of the whole being, there is but a mechanical sequence of sense and movement, as in walking that is automatic. Hand and eye, when the experience is esthetic, are but instruments through which the entire live creature, moved and active throughout, operates. Hence the expression is emotional and guided by purpose.

Because of the relation between what is done and what is undergone, there is an immediate sense of things in perception as belonging together or as jarring; as reenforcing or as interfering. The consequences of the act of making as reported in sense show whether what is done carries forward the idea being executed or marks a deviation and break. In as far as the development of an experience is *controlled* through reference to these immediately felt relations of order and fulfillment, that experience becomes dominantly esthetic in nature. The urge to action becomes an urge to that kind of action which will result in an object satisfying in direct perception. The potter shapes his clay to make a bowl useful for holding grain; but he makes it in a way so regulated by the series of perceptions that sum up the serial acts of making, that the bowl is marked by enduring grace and charm. The general situation remains the same in painting a picture or molding a bust. Moreover, at each stage there is anticipation of what is to come. This anticipation is the connecting link between the next doing and its outcome for sense. What is done and what is undergone are thus reciprocally, cumulatively, and continuously instrumental to each other.

The doing may be energetic, and the undergoing may be acute and intense. But unless they are related to each other to form a whole in perception, the thing done is not fully esthetic. The making for example may be a display of technical virtuosity, and the undergoing a gush of sentiment or a revery. If the artist does not perfect a new vision in his process of doing, he acts mechanically and repeats some old model fixed like a blue print in his mind. An incredible amount of observation and of the kind of intelligence that is exercised in perception of qualitative relations characterizes creative work in art. The relations must be noted not only with respect to one another, two by two, but in connection with the whole under construction; they are exercised in imagination as well as in observation. Irrelevancies arise that are tempting distractions; digressions suggest themselves in the guise of enrichments. There are occasions when the grasp of the dominant idea grows faint, and then the artist is moved unconsciously to fill in until his thought grows strong again. The real work of an artist is to build up an experience that is coherent in perception while moving with constant change in its development. . . .

THE considerations that have been presented imply both the community and the unlikeness, because of specific emphasis, of *an* experience, in its pregnant sense, and esthetic experience. The former has esthetic quality; otherwise its materials would not be rounded out into a single coherent experience. It is not possible to divide in a vital experience the practical, emotional, and intellectual from one another and to set the properties of one over against the characteristics of the others. The emotional phase binds parts together into a single whole; "intellectual" simply names the fact that the experience has meaning; "practical" indicates that the organism is interacting with events and objects which surround it. The most elaborate philosophic or scientific inquiry and the most ambitious industrial or political enterprise has, when its different ingredients constitute an integral experience, esthetic quality. For then its varied parts are linked to one another, and do not merely succeed one another. And the parts through their experienced linkage move toward a consummation and close, not merely to cessation in time. This consummation, moreover, does not wait in consciousness for the whole undertaking to be finished. It is anticipated throughout and is recurrently savored with special intensity.

Nevertheless, the experiences in question are dominantly intellectual or practical, rather than *distinctively* esthetic, because of the interest and purpose that initiate and control them. In an intellectual experience, the conclusion has value on its own account. It can be extracted as a formula or as a "truth," and can be used in its independent entirety as factor and guide in other inquiries. In a work of art there is no such single self-sufficient deposit. The end, the terminus, is significant not by itself but as the integration of the parts. It has no other existence. A drama or novel is not the final sentence, even if the characters are disposed of as living happily ever after. In a distinctively esthetic experience, characteristics that are subdued in other experiences are dominant; those that are subordinate are controlling—namely, the characteristics in virtue of which the experience is an integrated complete experience on its own account.

In every integral experience there is form because there is dynamic organization. I call it the organization dynamic because it takes time to complete it, because it is a growth. There is inception, development, fulfillment. Material is ingested and digested through interaction with that vital organization of the results of prior experience that constitutes the mind of the worker. Incubation goes on until what is conceived is brought forth and is rendered perceptible as part of the common world. An esthetic experience can be crowded into a moment only in the sense that a climax of prior long enduring processes may arrive in an outstanding movement which so sweeps everything else into it that all else is forgotten. That which distinguishes an experience as esthetic is conversion of resistance and tensions, of excitations that in themselves are temptations to diversion, into a movement toward an inclusive and fulfilling close.

Experiencing like breathing is a rhythm of intakings and outgivings. Their succession is punctuated and made a rhythm by the existence of intervals, periods in which one phase is ceasing and the other is inchoate and preparing. William James aptly compared the course of a conscious experience to the alternate flights and perchings of a bird. The flights and perchings are intimately connected with one another; they are not so many unrelated lightings succeeded by a number of equally unrelated hoppings. Each resting place in experience is an undergoing in which is absorbed and taken home the consequences of prior doing, and, unless the doing is that of utter caprice or sheer routine, each doing carries in itself meaning that has been extracted and conserved. As with the advance of an army, all gains from what has been already effected are periodically consolidated, and always with a view to what is to be done next. If we move too rapidly, we get away from the base of supplies—of accrued meanings—and the experience is flustered, thin, and confused. If we dawdle too long after having extracted a net value, experience perishes of inanition.

The *form* of the whole is therefore present in every member. Fulfilling, consummating, are continuous functions, not mere ends, located at one place only. An engraver, painter, or writer is in process of completing at every stage of his work. He must at each point retain and sum up what has gone before as a whole and with reference to a whole to come. Otherwise there is no consistency and no security in his successive acts. The series of doings in the rhythm of experience give variety and movement; they save the work from monotony and useless repetitions. The undergoings are the corresponding elements in the rhythm, and they supply unity; they save the work from the aimlessness of a mere succession of excitations. An object is peculiarly and dominantly esthetic, yielding the enjoyment characteristic of esthetic perception, when the factors that determine anything which can be called *an* experience are lifted high above the threshold of perception and are made manifest for their own sake.

13

ART AS TRUTH: MARTIN HEIDEGGER

Martin Heidegger (1889–1976) was one of the outstanding philosophers of the 20th century. Although *Being and Time,* his magnum opus published in 1927, remained unfinished, Heidegger wrote and lectured prolifically throughout his life, leaving behind a wealth of material both published and unpublished. Revelations surrounding his membership in the Nazi party and his brief stint as rector (president) of the University of Heidelberg under the Nazis have tarnished his reputation; nonetheless, he remains a dominant figure in Continental thought, a decisive influence on both existentialist and postmodern philosophic currents.

Heidegger's analysis of art is complex and the logic of his argument difficult to discern. We can get a better sense of his overall position if we consider the question that guides his efforts: What is the *origin* of the work of art? Exactly what is being asked here becomes clear once Heidegger's answer—that "art is the origin of the work of art"—is understood. Rather than yet another puzzling turn in a difficult argument, this assertion clarifies Heidegger's idea. Heidegger has a holistic understanding of art. That is, every aspect of the complex phenomenon known as art—the art object itself, the artist (or "creator" in Heidegger's terminology), the audience (or "preserver"), and the work (in the sense of effect) of art—is equally crucial to understanding what art is. Even though he does not explicitly mention other theories of art, Heidegger is implicitly critical of all those accounts that anoint one or another of its multiple components as *the* essential one. So the work of art—itself an ambiguous term that refers both to the art object and to its effects—can only be understood with reference to its role in that complex phenomenon.

Once Heidegger's holism is grasped, it is easier to analyze his more specific claims. Probably the most important among these is the assertion that art reveals the truth of Being. Many philosophers have linked art and truth, but Heidegger's unique conception of truth as the disclosure of Being is decisive for understanding his view.

Heidegger begins his analysis by asking what distinguishes an artwork from other types of things, especially from what he calls "equipment." An item of equipment (for example, a pencil or a hammer) plays a role in the various purposive projects we undertake—writing, building, and so forth. Superficially, equipment and artworks seem similar, for both are created complexes of form and matter. Just as a statue is a piece of marble on which a sculptor has imposed a form, a pencil is composed of wood and graphite, joined to make a useful object. But Heidegger argues that such a view passes over the essential nature of the artwork: its ability to reveal truth.

How does an artwork reveal truth? By getting us to see objects outside their customary settings, revealing the broader contexts within which they exist. Two of Heidegger's examples of artworks are the painting *Shoes* by Vincent van Gogh and an ancient Greek temple. (In a passage not included in this selection, he also discusses a poem about a Roman fountain.) Although the "worlds" disclosed by each of these works are very different from one another—the mundane world of the peasant is a far cry from the divinely animated world that the temple consecrates—both works make available to their viewers the specific worlds, the historical cultures, in which they were produced. As such, each work is an example of the essential nature of the artwork.

Heidegger's more specific account of what works of art reveal is difficult, but even if the details of his analysis remain unclear, we can see that he uses a triad of terms—"world," "earth," and "strife"—to explain the rise and fall of human cultures. "World" is the easiest of the three to understand, for we use it in much the same way as Heidegger when we talk of the world of the student or the world of the criminal. Heidegger's use of the term "earth" is harder to interpret, but in this sense the earth is that material underpinning on which cultures erect their worlds. Finally, "strife" refers to the essential conflict between world and earth, the fact that cultures create worlds but earth is not a passive element in the relationship. Rather, according to Heidegger, earth fights with world, eventually bringing culture down, thus allowing for historical development.

If the bulk of Heidegger's essay is concerned with exploring art's function, his holism requires that he also pay attention to other aspects of art. The essay thus includes analyses of the nature of the art object, the role of the artist, and the role of the audience. In discussing the nature of the art object, Heidegger tries to distinguish artworks from equipment by asserting that the former proclaim their creation as part of their content. Although the usefulness of items of equipment draws our attention away from the fact that they are produced—when writing or drawing with a pencil we scarcely notice it at all—works of art proclaim their status as creations.

A final aspect of Heidegger's account is its analysis of the role of both "creators" (artists) and "preservers" (audiences) in the constitution of artworks. Heidegger's holism requires that he view the latter as equally basic to the phenomenon of art as a whole. Otherwise, without them, there would be no works of art, only perhaps the material objects persisting as relics of times gone by.

Heidegger's discussion of the origin of the work of art indicts many of the standard Western conceptions, from Plato (Chapter 1) to Kant (Chapter 4), for bypassing art's essential nature. Despite the difficulty and obscurity of his argument, his view is important both for its holism and for its emphasis on art's cognitive function.

STUDY QUESTIONS ON THE READING

1.   How does Heidegger distinguish works of art from "mere things"? Which different types of "things" does he differentiate?

2.   Why does Heidegger deny that a work of art can be thought of as the result of the imposition of form on matter? Of the theorists you have read, which hold something like this view of art? Is Heidegger's criticism valid? Explain.

3.   What is the point of the example of Van Gogh's painting?

4.   Compare Heidegger's understanding of art as revelation of truth with that of other philosophers you have read. What is distinctive about his view? Do you find it plausible? Why or why not?

5.   Heidegger treats a painting and a building as paradigms of works of art. Do you think that these two very different types of things have a common status as works of art? Why or why not?

6.   Heidegger's talk of "preservers" makes it seem as if the existence of art is threatened. What do you make of this claim? Is there any validity to it? Explain.

7.   Why does Heidegger think that all art is, in its essence, poetry? Would you agree? Why or why not?

8.   Can Heidegger's view of art function as a general criterion for distinguishing works of art from other things, as he seems to think? Are there examples of works of art that do not fit his account? If so, what are they and why don't they satisfy his criterion?

9.   Aristotle and Heidegger share the view that art is related to truth. How similar are their overall accounts of art? How different?

❖

MARTIN HEIDEGGER: THE ORIGIN OF THE WORK OF ART

Origin here means that from and by which something is what it is and as it is. What something is, as it is, we call its essence or nature. The origin of something is the source of its nature. The question concerning the origin of the work

---

"The Origin of the Work of Art" from *Poetry, Language, Thought* by Martin Heidegger. Translation and Introduction by Albert Hofstadter. Copyright © 1971 by Martin Heidegger. Reprinted by permission of HarperCollins Publishers, Inc.

of art asks about the source of its nature. On the usual view, the work arises out of and by means of the activity of the artist. But by what and whence is the artist what he is? By the work; for to say that the work does credit to the master means that it is the work that first lets the artist emerge as a master of his art. The artist is the origin of the work. The work is the origin of the artist. Neither is without the other. Nevertheless, neither is the sole support of the other. In themselves and in their interrelations artist and work *are* each of them by virtue of a third thing which is prior to both, namely that which also gives artist and work of art their names—art. . . .

. . . [T]he question of the origin of the work of art becomes a question about the nature of art. Since the question whether and how art in general exists must still remain open, we shall attempt to discover the nature of art in the place where art undoubtedly prevails in a real way. Art is present in the art work. But what and how is a work of art? . . .

Works of art are familiar to everyone. Architectural and sculptural works can be seen installed in public places, in churches, and in dwellings. Art works of the most diverse periods and peoples are housed in collections and exhibitions. If we consider the works in their untouched actuality and do not deceive ourselves, the result is that the works are as naturally present as are things. The picture hangs on the wall like a rifle or a hat. A painting, e.g., the one by Van Gogh that represents a pair of peasant shoes, travels from one exhibition to another. Works of art are shipped like coal from the Ruhr and logs from the Black Forest. During the First World War Hölderlin's hymns were packed in the soldier's knapsack together with cleaning gear. Beethoven's quartets lie in the storerooms of the publishing house like potatoes in a cellar.

All works have this thingly character. What would they be without it? But perhaps this rather crude and external view of the work is objectionable to us. Shippers or charwomen in museums may operate with such conceptions of the work of art. We, however, have to take works as they are encountered by those who experience and enjoy them. But even the much-vaunted aesthetic experience cannot get around the thingly aspect of the art work. There is something stony in a work of architecture, wooden in a carving, colored in a painting, spoken in a linguistic work, sonorous in a musical composition. The thingly element is so irremovably present in the art work that we are compelled rather to say conversely that the architectural work is in stone, the carving is in wood, the painting in color, the linguistic work in speech, the musical composition in sound. "Obviously," it will be replied. No doubt. But what is this self-evident thingly element in the work of art? . . .

Our aim is to arrive at the immediate and full reality of the work of art, for only in this way shall we discover real art also within it. Hence we must first bring to view the thingly element of the work. To this end it is necessary that we should know with sufficient clarity what a thing is. Only then can we say whether the art work is a thing, but a thing to which something else adheres; only then can we decide whether the work is at bottom something else and not a thing at all.

THING AND WORK

What in truth is the thing, so far as it is a thing? When we inquire in this way, our aim is to come to know the thing-being (thingness) of the thing. The point is to discover the thingly character of the thing. To this end we have to be acquainted with the sphere to which all those entities belong which we have long called by the name of thing.

The stone in the road is a thing, as is the clod in the field. A jug is a thing, as is the well beside the road. But what about the milk in the jug and the water in the well? These too are things if the cloud in the sky and the thistle in the field, the leaf in the autumn breeze and the hawk over the wood, are rightly called by the name of thing. All these must indeed be called things, if the name is applied even to that which does not, like those just enumerated, show itself, i.e., that which does not appear. According to Kant, the whole of the world, for example, and even God himself, is a thing of this sort, a thing that does not itself appear, namely, a "thing-in-itself." In the language of philosophy both things-in-themselves and things that appear, all beings that in any way are, are called things.

Airplanes and radio sets are nowadays among the things closest to us, but when we have ultimate things in mind we think of something altogether different. Death and judgment—these are ultimate things. On the whole the word "thing" here designates whatever is not simply nothing. In this sense the work of art is also a thing, so far as it is not simply nothing. Yet this concept is of no use to us, at least immediately, in our attempt to delimit entities that have the mode of being of a thing, as against those having the mode of being of a work. And besides, we hesitate to call God a thing. In the same way we hesitate to consider the peasant in the field, the stoker at the boiler, the teacher in the school as things. A man is not a thing. It is true that we speak of a young girl who is faced with a task too difficult for her as being a young thing, still too young for it, but only because we feel that being human is in a certain way missing here and think that instead we have to do here with the factor that constitutes the thingly character of things. We hesitate even to call the deer in the forest clearing, the beetle in the grass, the blade of grass a thing. We would sooner think of a hammer as a thing, or a shoe, or an ax, or a clock. But even these are not mere things. Only a stone, a clod of earth, a piece of wood are for us such mere things. Lifeless beings of nature and objects of use. Natural things and utensils are the things commonly so called.

We thus see ourselves brought back from the widest domain, within which everything is a thing (thing = *re* = *ens* = an entity), including even the highest and last things, to the narrow precinct of mere things. "Mere" here means, first, the pure thing, which is simply a thing and nothing more; but then, at the same time, it means that which is only a thing, in an almost pejorative sense. It is mere things, excluding even use-objects, that count as things in the strict sense. What does the thingly character of these things, then, consist in? It is in reference to these that the thingness of things must be determinable. This determination enables us to characterize what it is that is thingly as such. Thus prepared, we are able to characterize the almost palpable reality of works, in which something else inheres. . . .

The interpretations of the thingness of the thing which, predominant in the course of Western thought, have long become self-evident and are now in everyday use, may be reduced to three.

This block of granite, for example, is a mere thing. It is hard, heavy, extended, bulky, shapeless, rough, colored, partly dull, partly shiny. We can take note of all these features in the stone. Thus we acknowledge its characteristics. But still, the traits signify something proper to the stone itself. They are its properties. The thing has them. The thing? What are we thinking of when we now have the thing in mind? Obviously a thing is not merely an aggregate of traits, nor an accumulation of properties by which that aggregate arises. A thing, as everyone thinks he knows, is that around which the properties have assembled. We speak in this connection of the core of things. . . .

Our reliance on the current interpretation of the thing is only seemingly well founded. But in addition this thing-concept (the thing as bearer of its characteristics) holds not only of the mere thing in its strict sense, but also of any being whatsoever. Hence it cannot be used to set apart thingly beings from non-thingly beings. Yet even before all reflection, attentive dwelling within the sphere of things already tells us that this thing-concept does not hit upon the thingly element of the thing, its independent and self-contained character. Occasionally we still have the feeling that violence has long been done to the thingly element of things and that thought has played a part in this violence, for which reason people disavow thought instead of taking pains to make it more thoughtful. But in defining the nature of the thing, what is the use of a feeling, however certain, if thought alone has the right to speak here? Perhaps however what we call feeling or mood, here and in similar instances, is more reasonable—that is, more intelligently perceptive—because more open to Being than all that reason which, having meanwhile become *ratio*, was misinterpreted as being rational. The hankering after the irrational, as abortive offspring of the unthought rational, therewith performed a curious service. To be sure, the current thing-concept always fits each thing. Nevertheless it does not lay hold of the thing as it is in its own being, but makes an assault upon it.

Can such an assault perhaps be avoided—and how? Only, certainly, by granting the thing, as it were, a free field to display its thingly character directly. Everything that might interpose itself between the thing and us in apprehending and talking about it must first be set aside. Only then do we yield ourselves to the undisguised presence of the thing. But we do not need first to call or arrange for this situation in which we let things encounter us without mediation. The situation always prevails. In what the senses of sight, hearing, and touch convey, in the sensations of color, sound, roughness, hardness, things move us bodily, in the literal meaning of the word. The thing is the *aistheton*, that which is perceptible by sensations in the senses belonging to sensibility. Hence the concept later becomes a commonplace according to which a thing is nothing but the unity of a manifold of what is given in the senses. Whether this unity is conceived as sum or as totality or as form alters nothing in the standard character of this thing-concept.

Now this interpretation of the thingness of the thing is as correct and demonstrable in every case as the previous one. This already suffices to cast doubt on its truth. If we consider moreover what we are searching for, the thingly character of the thing, then this thing-concept again leaves us at a loss. We never really first perceive a throng of sensations, e.g., tones and noises, in the appearance of things—as this thing-concept alleges; rather we hear the storm whistling in the chimney, we hear the three-motored plane, we hear the Mercedes in immediate distinction from the Volkswagen. Much closer to us than all sensations are the things themselves. We hear the door shut in the house and never hear acoustical sensations or even mere sounds. In order to hear a bare sound we have to listen away from things, divert our ear from them, i.e., listen abstractly.

In the thing-concept just mentioned there is not so much an assault upon the thing as rather an inordinate attempt to bring it into the greatest possible proximity to us. But a thing never reaches that position as long as we assign as its thingly feature what is perceived by the senses. Whereas the first interpretation keeps the thing at arm's length from us, as it were, and sets it too far off, the second makes it press too hard upon us. In both interpretations the thing vanishes. It is therefore necessary to avoid the exaggerations of both. The thing itself must be allowed to remain in its self-containment. It must be accepted in its own constancy. This the third interpretation seems to do, which is just as old as the first two.

That which gives things their constancy and pith but is also at the same time the source of their particular mode of sensuous pressure—colored, resonant, hard, massive—is the matter in things. In this analysis of the thing as matter (*hule*), form (*morphe*) is already coposited. What is constant in a thing, its consistency, lies in the fact that matter stands together with a form. The thing is formed matter. This interpretation appeals to the immediate view with which the thing solicits us by its looks (*eidos*). In this synthesis of matter and form a thing-concept has finally been found which applies equally to things of nature and to use-objects.

This concept puts us in a position to answer the question concerning the thingly element in the work of art. The thingly element is manifestly the matter of which it consists. Matter is the substrate and field for the artist's formative action. But we could have advanced this obvious and well-known definition of the thingly element at the very outset. Why do we make a detour through other current thing-concepts? Because we also mistrust this concept of the thing, which represents it as formed matter.

But is not precisely this pair of concepts, matter-form, usually employed in the domain in which we are supposed to be moving? To be sure. The distinction of matter and form is *the conceptual schema which is used, in the greatest variety of ways, quite generally for all art theory and aesthetics.* This incontestable fact, however, proves neither that the distinction of matter and form is adequately founded, nor that it belongs originally to the domain of art and the art work. Moreover, the range of application of this pair of concepts has long extended far beyond the field of aesthetics. Form and content are the most hackneyed concepts under which anything and everything may be subsumed.

And if form is correlated with the rational and matter with the irrational; if the rational is taken to be the logical and the irrational the alogical; if in addition the subject-object relation is coupled with the conceptual pair form-matter; then representation has at its command a conceptual machinery that nothing is capable of withstanding.

If, however, it is thus with the distinction between matter and form, how then shall we make use of it to lay hold of the particular domain of mere things by contrast with all other entities? But perhaps this characterization in terms of matter and form would recover its defining power if only we reversed the process of expanding and emptying these concepts. Certainly, but this presupposes that we know in what sphere of beings they realize their true defining power. That this is the domain of mere things is so far only an assumption. Reference to the copious use made of this conceptual framework in aesthetics might sooner lead to the idea that matter and form are specifications stemming from the nature of the art work and were in the first place transferred from it back to the thing. Where does the matter-form structure have its origin—in the thingly character of the thing or in the workly character of the art work?

The self-contained block of granite is something material in a definite if unshapely form. Form means here the distribution and arrangement of the material parts in spatial locations, resulting in a particular shape, namely that of a block. But a jug, an ax, a shoe are also matter occurring in a form. Form as shape is not the consequence here of a prior distribution of the matter. The form, on the contrary, determines the arrangement of the matter. Even more, it prescribes in each case the kind and selection of the matter—impermeable for a jug, sufficiently hard for an ax, firm yet flexible for shoes. The interfusion of form and matter prevailing here is, moreover, controlled beforehand by the purposes served by jug, ax, shoes. Such usefulness is never assigned or added on afterward to a being of the type of a jug, ax, or pair of shoes. But neither is it something that floats somewhere above it as an end.

Usefulness is the basic feature from which this entity regards us, that is, flashes at us and thereby is present and thus is this entity. Both the formative act and the choice of material—a choice given with the act—and therewith the dominance of the conjunction of matter and form, are all grounded in such usefulness. A being that falls under usefulness is always the product of a process of making. It is made as a piece of equipment for something. As determinations of beings, accordingly, matter and form have their proper place in the essential nature of equipment. This name designates what is produced expressly for employment and use. Matter and form are in no case original determinations of the thingness of the mere thing.

A piece of equipment, a pair of shoes for instance, when finished, is also self-contained like the mere thing, but it does not have the character of having taken shape by itself like the granite boulder. On the other hand, equipment displays an affinity with the art work insofar as it is something produced by the human hand. However, by its self-sufficient presence the work of art is similar rather to the mere thing which has taken shape by itself and is self-contained. Nevertheless we do not count such works among mere things. As a rule it is the use-objects around us that are the nearest and authentic things. Thus the piece of equipment is half thing, because characterized by thingliness, and yet it is something more; at the same time it is half art work and yet something less, because lacking the self-sufficiency of the art work. Equipment has a peculiar position intermediate between thing and work, assuming that such a calculated ordering of them is permissible. . . .

The situation stands revealed as soon as we speak of things in the strict sense as mere things. The "mere," after all, means the removal of the character of usefulness and of being made. The mere thing is a sort of equipment, albeit equipment denuded of its equipmental being. Thing-being consists in what is then left over. But this remnant is not actually defined in its ontological character. It remains doubtful whether the thingly character comes to view at all in the process of stripping off everything equipmental. Thus the third mode of interpretation of the thing, that which follows the lead of the matter-form structure, also turns out to be an assault upon the thing.

These three modes of defining thingness conceive of the thing as a bearer of traits, as the unity of a manifold of sensations, as formed matter. . . .

. . . [W]e risk the attempt to bring to view and express in words the thingly character of the thing, the equipmental character of equipment, and the workly character of the work. To this end, however, only one element is needful: to keep at a distance all the preconceptions and assaults of the above modes of thought, to leave the thing to rest in its own self, for instance, in its thing-being. What seems easier than to let a being be just the being that it is? Or does this turn out to be the most difficult of tasks, particularly if such an intention—to let a being be as it is—represents the opposite of the indifference that simply turns its back upon the being itself in favor of an unexamined concept of being? We ought to turn toward the being, think about it in regard to its being, but by means of this thinking at the same time let it rest upon itself in its very own being.

This exertion of thought seems to meet with its greatest resistance in defining the thingness of the thing; for where else could the cause lie of the failure of the efforts mentioned? The unpretentious thing evades thought most stubbornly. Or can it be that this self-refusal of the mere thing, this self-contained independence, belongs precisely to the nature of the thing? Must not this strange and uncommunicative feature of the nature of the thing become intimately familiar to thought that tries to think the thing? If so, then we should not force our way to its thingly character.

That the thingness of the thing is particularly difficult to express and only seldom expressible is infallibly documented by the history of its interpretation indicated above. This history coincides with the destiny in accordance with which Western thought has hitherto thought the Being of beings. However, not only do we now establish this point; at the same time we discover a clue in this history. Is it an accident that in the interpretation of the thing the view that takes matter and form as guide attains to special dominance? This definition of the thing derives from an interpretation of the equipmental being of equipment. And equipment, having come into being through human making, is particularly familiar to human thinking. At the same time, this familiar being has a peculiar intermediate position between thing and work. We shall follow this clue and search first for the equipmental character of equipment. . . .

We choose as example a common sort of equipment—a pair of peasant shoes. We do not even need to exhibit actual pieces of this sort of useful article in order to describe them. Everyone is acquainted with them. But since it is a matter here of direct description, it may be well to facilitate the visual realization of them. For this purpose a pictorial representation suffices. We shall choose a well-known painting by Van Gogh, who painted such shoes several times. But what is there to see here? Everyone knows what shoes consist of. If they are not wooden or bast shoes, there will be leather soles and uppers, joined together by thread and nails. Such gear serves to clothe the feet. Depending on the use to which the shoes are to be put, whether for work in the field or for dancing, matter and form will differ.

Such statements, no doubt correct, only explicate what we already know. The equipmental quality of equipment consists in its usefulness. But what about this usefulness itself? In conceiving it, do we already conceive along with it the equipmental character of equipment? In order to succeed in doing this, must we not look out for useful equipment in its use? The peasant woman wears her shoes in the field. Only here are they what they are. They are all the more genuinely so, the less the peasant woman thinks about the shoes while she is at work, or looks at them at all, or is even aware of them. She stands and walks in them. That is how shoes actually serve. It is in this process of the use of equipment that we must actually encounter the character of equipment.

As long as we only imagine a pair of shoes in general, or simply look at the empty, unused shoes as they merely stand there in the picture, we shall never discover what the equipmental being of the equipment in truth is. From Van Gogh's painting we cannot even tell where these shoes stand. There is nothing surrounding this pair of peasant shoes in or to which they might belong—only an undefined space. There are not even clods of soil from the field or the field-path sticking to them, which would at least hint at their use. A pair of peasant shoes and nothing more. And yet—

From the dark opening of the worn insides of the shoes the toilsome tread of the worker stares forth. In the stiffly rugged heaviness of the shoes there is the accumulated tenacity of her slow trudge through the far-spreading and ever-uniform furrows of the field swept by a raw wind. On the leather lie the dampness and richness of the soil. Under the soles slides the loneliness of the field-path as evening falls. In the shoes vibrates the silent call of the earth, its quiet gift of the ripening grain and its unexplained self-refusal in the fallow desolation of the wintry field. This equipment is pervaded by uncomplaining anxiety as to the certainty of bread, the wordless joy of having once more withstood want, the trembling before the impending childbed and shivering at the surrounding menace of death. This equipment belongs to the *earth,* and it is protected in the *world* of the peasant woman. From out of this protected belonging the equipment itself rises to its resting-within-itself.

But perhaps it is only in the picture that we notice all this about the shoes. The peasant woman, on the other hand, simply wears them. If only this simple wearing were so simple. When she takes off her shoes late in the evening, in deep but healthy fatigue, and reaches out for them again in the still dim dawn, or passes them by on the day of rest, she knows all this without noticing or reflecting. The equipmental quality of the equipment consists indeed in its usefulness. But this usefulness itself rests in the abundance of an essential being of the equipment. We call it reliability. By virtue of this reliability the peasant woman is made privy to the silent call of the earth; by virtue of the reliability of the equipment she is sure of her world. World and earth exist for her, and for those who are with her in her mode of being, only thus—in the equipment. We say "only" and therewith fall into error; for the reliability of the equipment first gives to the simple world its security and assures to the earth the freedom of its steady thrust.

The equipmental being of equipment, reliability, keeps gathered within itself all things according to their manner and extent. The usefulness of equipment is nevertheless only the essential consequence of reliability. The former vibrates in the latter and would be nothing without it. A single piece of equipment is worn out and used up; but at the same time the use itself also falls into disuse, wears away, and becomes usual. Thus equipmentality wastes away, sinks into mere stuff. In such wasting, reliability vanishes. This dwindling, however, to which use-things owe their boringly obtrusive usualness, is only one more testimony to the original nature of equipmental being. The worn-out usualness of the equipment then obtrudes itself as the sole mode of being, apparently peculiar to it exclusively. Only blank usefulness now remains visible. It awakens the impression that the origin of equipment lies in a mere fabricating that impresses a form upon some matter. Nevertheless, in its genuinely equipmental being, equipment stems from a more distant source. Matter and form and their distinction have a deeper origin.

The repose of equipment resting within itself consists in its reliability. Only in this reliability do we discern what equipment in truth is. But we still know nothing of what we first sought: the thing's thingly character. And we know nothing at all of what we really and solely seek: the workly character of the work in the sense of the work of art.

Or have we already learned something unwittingly, in passing so to speak, about the work-being of the work?

The equipmental quality of equipment was discovered. But how? Not by a description and explanation of a pair of shoes actually present; not by a report about the process of making shoes; and also not by the observation of the actual use of shoes occurring here and there; but only by bringing ourselves before Van Gogh's painting. This painting spoke. In the vicinity of the work we were suddenly somewhere else than we usually tend to be.

The art work lets us know what shoes are in truth. It would be the worst self-deception to think that our description, as a subjective action, had first depicted everything thus and then projected it into the painting. If anything is questionable here, it is rather that we experienced too little in the neighborhood of the work and that we expressed the experience too crudely and too literally. But above all, the work did not, as it might seem at first, serve merely for a better visualizing of what a piece of equipment is. Rather, the equipmentality of equipment first genuinely arrives at its appearance through the work and only in the work.

What happens here? What is at work in the work? Van Gogh's painting is the disclosure of what the equipment, the pair of peasant shoes, *is* in truth. This entity emerges into the unconcealedness of its being. The Greeks called the unconcealedness of beings *aletheia*. We say "truth" and think little enough in using this word. If there occurs in the work a disclosure of a particular being, disclosing what and how it is, then there is here an occurring, a happening of truth at work.

In the work of art the truth of an entity has set itself to work. "To set" means here: to bring to a stand. Some particular entity, a pair of peasant shoes, comes in the work to stand in the light of its being. The being of the being comes into the steadiness of its shining.

The nature of art would then be this: the truth of beings setting itself to work. . . .

We seek the reality of the art work in order to find there the art prevailing within it. The thingly substructure is what proved to be the most immediate reality in the work. But to comprehend this thingly feature the traditional thing-concepts are not adequate; for they themselves fail to grasp the nature of the thing. The currently predominant thing-concept, thing as formed matter, is not even derived from the nature of the thing but from the nature of equipment. It also turned out that equipmental being generally has long since occupied a peculiar preeminence in the interpretation of beings. This preeminence of equipmentality, which however did not actually come to mind, suggested that we pose the question of equipment anew while avoiding the current interpretations.

We allowed a work to tell us what equipment is. By this means, almost clandestinely, it came to light what is at work in the work: the disclosure of the particular being in its being, the happening of truth. If, however, the reality of the work can be defined solely by means of what is at work in the work, then what about our intention to seek out the real art work in its reality? As long as we supposed that the reality of the work lay primarily in its thingly substructure we were going astray. We are now confronted by a remarkable result of our considerations—if it still deserves to be called a result at all. Two points become clear:

First: the dominant thing-concepts are inadequate as means of grasping the thingly aspect of the work.

Second: what we tried to treat as the most immediate reality of the work, its thingly substructure, does not belong to the work in that way at all.

As soon as we look for such a thingly substructure in the work, we have unwittingly taken the work as equipment, to which we then also ascribe a superstructure supposed to contain its artistic quality. But the work is not a piece of equipment that is fitted out in addition with an aesthetic value that adheres to it. The work is no more anything of the kind than the bare thing is a piece of equipment that merely lacks the specific equipmental characteristics of usefulness and being made.

Our formulation of the question of the work has been shaken because we asked, not about the work but half about a thing and half about equipment.

Still, this formulation of the question was not first developed by us. It is the formulation native to aesthetics. The way in which aesthetics views the art work from the outset is dominated by the traditional interpretation of all beings. But the shaking of this accustomed formulation is not the essential point. What matters is a first opening of our vision to the fact that what is workly in the work, equipmental in equipment, and thingly in the thing comes closer to us only when we think the Being of beings. To this end it is necessary beforehand that the barriers of our preconceptions fall away and that the current pseudo concepts be set aside. That is why we had to take this detour. But it brings us directly to a road that may lead to a determination of the thingly feature in the work. The thingly feature in the work should not be denied; but if it belongs admittedly to the work-being of the work, it must be conceived by way of the work's workly nature. If this is so, then the road toward the determination of the thingly reality of the work leads not from thing to work but from work to thing.

The art work opens up in its own way the Being of beings. This opening up, i.e., this deconcealing, i.e., the truth of beings, happens in the work. In the art work, the truth of what is has set itself to work. Art is truth setting itself to work. What is truth itself, that it sometimes comes to pass as art? What is this setting-itself-to-work?

THE WORK AND TRUTH

. . . Where does a work belong? The work belongs, as work, uniquely within the realm that is opened up by itself. For the work-being of the work is present in, and only in, such opening up. We said that in the work there was a happening of truth at work. The reference to Van Gogh's picture tried to point to this happening. With regard to it there arose the question as to what truth is and how truth can happen.

We now ask the question of truth with a view to the work. But in order to become more familiar with what the question involves, it is necessary to make visible once more the happening of truth in the work. For this attempt let us deliberately select a work that cannot be ranked as representational art.

A building, a Greek temple, portrays nothing. It simply stands there in the middle of the rock-cleft valley. The building encloses the figure of the god, and in this concealment lets it stand out into the holy precinct through the open portico. By means of the temple, the god is present in the temple. This presence of the god is in itself the extension and delimitation of the precinct as a holy precinct. The temple and its precinct, however, do not fade away into the indefinite. It is the temple-work that first fits together and at the same time gathers around itself the unity of those paths and relations in which birth and death, disaster and blessing, victory and disgrace, endurance and decline acquire the shape of destiny for human being. The all-governing expanse of this open relational context is the world of this historical people. Only from and in this expanse does the nation first return to itself for the fulfillment of its vocation.

Standing there, the building rests on the rocky ground. This resting of the work draws up out of the rock the mystery of that rock's clumsy yet spontaneous support. Standing there, the building holds its ground against the storm raging above it and so first makes the storm itself manifest in its violence. The luster and gleam of the stone, though itself apparently glowing only by the grace of the sun, yet first brings to light the light of the day, the breadth of the sky, the darkness of the night. The temple's firm towering makes visible the invisible space of air. The steadfastness of the work contrasts with the surge of the surf, and its own repose brings out the raging of the sea. Tree and grass, eagle and bull, snake and cricket first enter into their distinctive shapes and thus come to appear as what they are. The Greeks early called this emerging and rising in itself and in all things *phusis*. It clears and illuminates, also, that on which and in which man bases his dwelling. We call this ground the *earth*. What this word says is not to be associated with the idea of a mass of matter deposited somewhere, or with the merely astronomical idea of a planet. Earth is that whence the arising brings back and shelters everything that arises without violation. In the things that arise, earth is present as the sheltering agent.

The temple-work, standing there, opens up a world and at the same time sets this world back again on earth, which itself only thus emerges as native ground. But men and animals, plants and things, are never present and familiar as unchangeable objects, only to represent incidentally also a fitting environment for the temple, which one fine day is added to what is already there. We shall get closer to what *is*, rather, if we think of all this in reverse order, assuming of course that we have, to begin with, an eye for how differently everything then faces us. Mere reversing, done for its own sake, reveals nothing.

The temple, in its standing there, first gives to things their look and to men their outlook on themselves. This view remains open as long as the work is a work, as long as the god has not fled from it. It is the same with the sculpture of the god, votive offering of the victor in the athletic games. It is not a portrait whose purpose is to make it easier to realize how the god looks; rather, it is a work that lets the god himself be present and thus *is* the god himself. The same holds for the linguistic work. In the tragedy nothing is staged or displayed theatrically, but the battle of the new gods against the old is being fought. The linguistic work, originating in the speech of the people, does not refer to this battle; it transforms the people's saying so that now every living word fights the battle and puts up for decision what is holy and what unholy, what great and what small, what brave and what cowardly, what lofty and what flighty, what master and what slave (cf. Heraclitus, Fragment 53).

In what, then, does the work-being of the work consist? Keeping steadily in view the points just crudely enough indicated, two essential features of the work may for the moment be brought out more distinctly. We set out here, from the long familiar foreground of the work's being, the thingly character which gives support to our customary attitude toward the work.

When a work is brought into a collection or placed in an exhibition we say also that it is "set up." But this setting up differs essentially from setting up in the sense of erecting a building, raising a statue, presenting a tragedy at a holy festival. Such setting up is erecting in the sense of dedication and praise. Here "setting up" no longer means a bare placing. To dedicate means to consecrate, in the sense that in setting up the work the holy is opened up as holy and the god is invoked into the openness of his presence. Praise belongs to dedication as doing honor to the dignity and splendor of the god. Dignity and splendor are not properties beside and behind which the god, too, stands as something distinct, but it is rather in the dignity, in the splendor that the god is present. In the reflected glory of this splendor there glows, i.e., there lightens itself, what we called the word. To e-rect means: to open the right in the sense of a guiding measure, a form in which what belongs to the nature of being gives guidance. But why is the setting up of a work an erecting that consecrates and praises? Because the work, in its work-being, demands it. How is it that the work comes to demand such a setting up? Because it itself, in its own work-being, is something that sets up. What does the work, as work, set up? Towering up within itself, the work opens up a *world* and keeps it abidingly in force.

To be a work means to set up a world. But what is it to be a world? The answer was hinted at when we referred to the temple. On the path we must follow here, the nature of world can only be indicated. What is more, this indication limits itself to warding off anything that might at first distort our view of the world's nature.

The world is not the mere collection of the countable or uncountable, familiar and unfamiliar things that are just there. But neither is it a merely imagined framework added by our representation to the sum of such given things. The *world worlds,* and is more fully in being than the tangible and perceptible realm in which we believe ourselves to be at home. World is never an object that stands before us and can be seen. World is the ever-nonobjective to which we are subject as long as the paths of birth and death, blessing and curse keep us transported into Being. Wherever those decisions of our history that relate to our very being are made, are taken up and abandoned by us, go unrecognized and are rediscovered by new inquiry, there the world worlds. A stone is worldless. Plant and animal likewise have no world; but they belong to the covert throng of a surrounding into which they are linked. The peasant woman, on the other hand, has a world because she dwells in the overtness of beings, of the things that are. Her equipment, in its reliability, gives to this world a necessity and nearness of its own. By the opening up of a world, all things gain their lingering and hastening, their remoteness and nearness, their scope and limits. In a world's worlding is gathered that spaciousness out of which the protective grace of the gods is granted or withheld. Even this doom of the god remaining absent is a way in which world worlds.

A work, by being a work, makes space for that spaciousness. "To make space for" means here especially to liberate the Open and to establish it in its structure. This installing occurs through the erecting mentioned earlier. The work as work sets up a world. The work holds open the Open of the world. But the setting up of a world is only the first essential feature in the work-being of a work to be referred to here. Starting again from the foreground of the work, we shall attempt to make clear in the same way the second essential feature that belongs with the first.

When a work is created, brought forth out of this or that work-material—stone, wood, metal, color, language, tone—we say also that it is made, set forth out of it. But just as the work requires a setting up in the sense of a consecrating-praising erection, because the work's work-being consists in the setting up of a world, so a setting forth is needed because the work-being of the work itself has the character of setting forth. The work as work, in its presencing, is a setting forth, a making. But what does the work set forth? We come to know about this only when we explore what comes to the fore and is customarily spoken of as the making or production of works.

To work-being there belongs the setting up of a world. Thinking of it within this perspective, what is the nature of that in the work which is usually called the work material? Because it is determined by usefulness and serviceability, equipment takes into its service that of which it consists: the matter. In fabricating equipment—e.g., an ax—stone is used, and used up. It disappears into usefulness. The material is all the better and more suitable the less it resists perishing in the equipmental being of the equipment. By contrast the temple-work, in setting up a world, does not cause the material to disappear, but rather causes it to come forth for the very first time and to come into the Open of the work's world. The rock comes to bear and rest and so first becomes rock; metals come to glitter and shimmer, colors to glow, tones to sing, the word to speak. All this comes forth as the work sets itself back into the massiveness and heaviness of stone, into the firmness and pliancy of wood, into the hardness and luster of metal, into the lighting and darkening of color, into the clang of tone, and into the naming power of the word.

That into which the work sets itself back and which it causes to come forth in this setting back of itself we called the earth. Earth is that which comes forth and shelters. Earth, self-dependent, is effortless and untiring. Upon the earth and in it, historical man grounds his dwelling in the world. In setting up a world, the work sets forth the earth. This setting forth must be thought here in the strict sense of the word. The work moves the earth itself into the Open of a world and keeps it there. *The work lets the earth be an earth.* . . .

The setting up of a world and the setting forth of earth are two essential features in the work-being of the work. They belong together, however, in the unity of work-being. This is the unity we seek when we ponder the self-subsistence of the work and try to express in words this closed, unitary repose of self-support. . . .

The world is the self-disclosing openness of the broad paths of the simple and essential decisions in the destiny of an historical people. The earth is the spontaneous forthcoming of that which is continually self-secluding and to that extent sheltering and concealing. World and earth are essentially different from one another and yet are never separated. The world grounds itself on the earth, and earth juts through world. But the relation between world and earth does not wither away into the empty unity of opposites unconcerned with one another. The world, in resting upon the earth, strives to surmount it. As self-opening it cannot endure anything closed. The earth, however, as sheltering and concealing, tends always to draw the world into itself and keep it there.

The opposition of world and earth is a striving. But we would surely all too easily falsify its nature if we were to confound striving with discord and dispute, and thus see it only as disorder and destruction. In essential striving, rather, the opponents raise each other into the self-assertion of their natures. Self-assertion of nature, however, is never a rigid insistence upon some contingent state, but surrender to the concealed originality of the source of one's own being. In the struggle, each opponent carries the other beyond itself. Thus the striving becomes ever more intense as striving, and more authentically what it is. The more the struggle overdoes itself on its own part, the more inflexibly do the opponents let themselves go into the intimacy of simple belonging to one another. The earth cannot dispense with the Open of the world if it itself is to appear as earth in the liberated surge of its self-seclusion. The world, again, cannot soar out of the earth's sight if, as the governing breadth and path of all essential destiny, it is to ground itself on a resolute foundation.

In setting up a world and setting forth the earth, the work is an instigating of this striving. This does not happen so that the work should at the same time settle and put an end to the conflict in an insipid agreement, but so that the strife may remain a strife. Setting up a world and setting forth the earth, the work accomplishes this striving. The work-being of the work consists in the fighting of the battle between world and earth. It is because the struggle arrives at its high point in the simplicity of intimacy that the unity of the work comes about in the fighting of the battle. The fighting of the battle is the continually self-overreaching gathering of the work's agitation. The repose of the work that rests in itself thus has its presencing in the intimacy of striving.

From this repose of the work we can now first see what is at work in the work. Until now it was a merely provisional assertion that in an art work the truth is set to work. In what way does truth happen in the work-being of the work, i.e., now, how does truth happen in the fighting of the battle between world and earth? What is truth?

How slight and stunted our knowledge of the nature of truth is, is shown by the laxity we permit ourselves in using this basic word. By truth is usually meant this or that particular truth. That means: something true. A cognition articulated in a proposition can be of this sort. However, we call not only a proposition true, but also a thing, true gold in contrast with sham gold. True here means genuine, real gold. What does the expression "real" mean here? To us it is what is in truth. The true is what corresponds to the real, and the real is what is in truth. The circle has closed again.

What does "in truth" mean? . . .

Truth means the nature of the true. We think this nature in recollecting the Greek word *aletheia,* the unconcealedness of beings. . . .

If here and elsewhere we conceive of truth as unconcealedness, we are not merely taking refuge in a more literal translation of a Greek word. We are reminding ourselves of what, unexperienced and unthought, underlies our familiar and therefore outworn nature of truth in the sense of correctness. . . .

But it is not we who presuppose the unconcealedness of beings; rather, the unconcealedness of beings (Being) puts us into such a condition of being that in our representation we always remain installed within and in attendance upon unconcealedness. Not only must that in *conformity* with which a cognition orders itself be already in some way unconcealed. The entire *realm* in which this "conforming to something" goes on must already occur as a whole in the unconcealed; and this holds equally of that *for* which the conformity of a proposition to fact becomes manifest. With all our correct representations we would get nowhere, we could not even presuppose that there already is manifest something to which we can conform ourselves, unless the unconcealedness of beings had already exposed us to, placed us in that lighted realm in which every being stands for us and from which it withdraws. . . .

This Open happens in the midst of beings. It exhibits an essential feature which we have already mentioned. To the Open there belong a world and the earth. But the world is not simply the Open that corresponds to clearing, and the earth is not simply the Closed that corresponds to concealment. Rather, the world is the clearing of the paths of the essential guiding directions with which all decision complies. Every decision, however, bases itself on something not mastered, something concealed, confusing; else it would never be a decision. The earth is not simply the Closed but rather that which rises up as self-closing. World and earth are always intrinsically and essentially in conflict, belligerent by nature. Only as such do they enter into the conflict of clearing and concealing.

Earth juts through the world and world grounds itself on the earth only so far as truth happens as the primal conflict between clearing and concealing. But how does truth happen? We answer: it happens in a few essential ways. One of these ways in which truth happens is the work-being of the work. Setting up a world and setting forth the earth, the work is the fighting of the battle in which the unconcealedness of beings as a whole, or truth, is won.

Truth happens in the temple's standing where it is. This does not mean that something is correctly represented and rendered here, but that what is as a whole is brought into unconcealedness and held therein. To hold (*halten*) originally means to tend, keep, take care (*hüten*). Truth happens in Van Gogh's painting. This does not mean that something is correctly portrayed, but rather that in the revelation of the equipmental being of the shoes, that which is as a whole—world and earth in their counterplay—attains to unconcealedness.

Thus in the work it is truth, not only something true, that is at work. The picture that shows the peasant shoes, the poem that says the Roman fountain,[1] do not just make manifest what this isolated being as such is—if indeed they manifest anything at all; rather, they make unconcealedness as such happen in regard to what is as a whole. The more simply and authentically the shoes are engrossed in their nature, the more plainly and purely the fountain is engrossed in its nature—the more directly and engagingly do all beings attain to a greater degree of being along with them. That is how self-concealing being is illuminated. Light of this kind joins its shining to and into the work. This shining, joined in the work, is the beautiful. *Beauty is one way in which truth occurs as unconcealedness.*

---

[1] Heidegger had earlier used the poem as another example of a work of art. [T.E.W.]

We now, indeed, grasp the nature of truth more clearly in certain respects. What is at work in the work may accordingly have become more clear. . . .

TRUTH AND ART

Art is the origin of the art work and of the artist. Origin is the source of the nature in which the being of an entity is present. What is art? We seek its nature in the actual work. The actual reality of the work has been defined by that which is at work in the work, by the happening of truth. This happening we think of as the fighting of the conflict between world and earth. Repose occurs in the concentrated agitation of this conflict. The independence or self-composure of the work is grounded here. . . .

The work's createdness, however, can obviously be grasped only in terms of the process of creation. Thus, constrained by the facts, we must consent after all to go into the activity of the artist in order to arrive at the origin of the work of art. The attempt to define the work-being of the work purely in terms of the work itself proves to be unfeasible.

In turning away now from the work to examine the nature of the creative process, we should like nevertheless to keep in mind what was said first of the picture of the peasant shoes and later of the Greek temple.

We think of creation as a bringing forth. But the making of equipment, too, is a bringing forth. Handicraft—a remarkable play of language—does not, to be sure, create works, not even when we contrast, as we must, the hand-made with the factory product. But what is it that distinguishes bringing forth as creation from bringing forth in the mode of making? It is as difficult to track down the essential features of the creation of works and the making of equipment as it is easy to distinguish verbally between the two modes of bringing forth. Going along with first appearances we find the same procedure in the activity of potter and sculptor, of joiner and painter. The creation of a work requires craftsmanship. Great artists prize craftsmanship most highly. They are the first to call for its painstaking cultivation, based on complete mastery. They above all others constantly strive to educate themselves ever anew in thorough craftsmanship. . . .

The readiness of equipment and the createdness of the work agree in this, that in each case something is produced. But in contrast to all other modes of production, the work is distinguished by being created so that its createdness is part of the created work. But does not this hold true for everything brought forth, indeed for anything that has in any way come to be? Everything brought forth surely has this endowment of having been brought forth, if it has any endowment at all. Certainly. But in the work, createdness is expressly created into the created being, so that it stands out from it, from the being thus brought forth, in an expressly particular way. If this is how matters stand, then we must also be able to discover and experience the createdness explicitly in the work.

The emergence of createdness from the work does not mean that the work is to give the impression of having been made by a great artist. The point is not that the created being be certified as the performance of a capable person, so that the producer is thereby brought to public notice. It is not the "N. N. fecit" that is to be made known. Rather, the simple "factum est" is to be held forth into the Open by the work: namely this, that unconcealedness of what is has happened here, and that as this happening it happens here for the first time; or, that such a work *is* at all rather than is not. The thrust that the work as this work is, and the uninterruptedness of this plain thrust, constitute the steadfastness of the work's self-subsistence. Precisely where the artist and the process and the circumstances of the genesis of the work remain unknown, this thrust, this "*that* it is" of createdness, emerges into view most purely from the work.

To be sure, "that" it is made is a property also of all equipment that is available and in use. But this "that" does not become prominent in the equipment; it disappears in usefulness. The more handy a piece of equipment is, the more inconspicuous it remains that, for example, such a hammer is and the more exclusively does the equipment keep itself in its equipmentality. In general, of everything present to us, we can note that it *is;* but this also, if it is noted at all, is noted only soon to fall into oblivion, as is the wont of everything commonplace. And what is more commonplace than this, that a being is? In a work, by contrast, this fact, that it *is* as a work, is just what is unusual. The event of its being created does not simply reverberate through the work; rather, the work casts before itself the eventful fact that the work is as this work, and it has constantly this fact about itself. The more essentially the work opens itself, the more luminous becomes the uniqueness of the fact that it is rather than is not. The more essentially this thrust comes into the Open, the stronger and more solitary the work becomes. In the bringing forth of the work there lies this offering "that it be." . . .

The more solitarily the work, fixed in the figure, stands on its own and the more cleanly it seems to cut all ties to human beings, the more simply does the thrust come into the Open that such a work *is,* and the more essentially is the extraordinary thrust to the surface and the long-familiar thrust down. But this multiple thrusting is nothing violent, for the more purely the work is itself transported into the openness of beings—an openness opened by itself—the more simply does it transport us into this openness and thus at the same time transport us out of the realm of the ordinary. To submit to this displacement means: to transform our accustomed ties to world and to earth and henceforth to restrain all usual doing and prizing, knowing and looking, in order to stay within the truth that is happening in the work. Only the restraint of this staying lets what is created be the work that it is. This letting the work be a work we call the preserving of the work. It is only for such preserving that the work yields itself in its createdness as actual, i.e., now: present in the manner of a work.

Just as a work cannot be without being created but is essentially in need of creators, so what is created cannot itself come into being without those who preserve it. . . .

To determine the thing's thingness neither consideration of the bearer of properties is adequate, nor that of the manifold of sense data in their unity, and least of all that of the matter-form structure regarded by itself, which is derived from equipment. Anticipating a meaningful and weighty interpretation of the thingly character of things, we must aim at the thing's belonging to the earth. The nature of the earth, in its free and unhurried bearing and self-closure, reveals itself, however, only in the earth's jutting into a world, in the opposition of the two. This conflict is fixed in place in the figure of the work and becomes manifest by it. What holds true of equipment—namely that we come to know its equipmental character specifically only through the work itself—also holds of the thingly character of the thing. The fact that we never know thingness directly, and if we know it at all, then only vaguely and thus require the work—this fact proves indirectly that in the work's work-being the happening of truth, the opening up or disclosure of what is, is at work. . . .

In the work, the happening of truth is at work and, indeed, at work according to the manner of a work. Accordingly the nature of art was defined to begin with as the setting-into-work of truth. Yet this definition is intentionally ambiguous. It says on the one hand: art is the fixing in place of a self-establishing truth in the figure. This happens in creation as the bringing forth of the unconcealedness of what is. Setting-into-work, however, also means: the bringing of work-being into movement and happening. This happens as preservation. Thus art is: the creative preserving of truth in the work. *Art then is the becoming and happening of truth.* Does truth, then, arise out of nothing? It does indeed if by nothing is meant the mere not of that which is, and if we here think of that which is as an object present in the ordinary way, which thereafter comes to light and is challenged by the existence of the work as only presumptively a true being. Truth is never gathered from objects that are present and ordinary. Rather, the opening up of the Open, and the clearing of what is, happens only as the openness is projected, sketched out, that makes its advent in thrownness. . . .

Art is the setting-into-work of truth. In this proposition an essential ambiguity is hidden, in which truth is at once the subject and the object of the setting. But subject and object are unsuitable names here. They keep us from thinking precisely this ambiguous nature, a task that no longer belongs to this consideration. Art is historical, and as historical it is the creative preserving of truth in the work. Art happens as poetry. Poetry is founding in the triple sense of bestowing, grounding, and beginning. Art, as founding, is essentially historical. This means not only that art has a history in the external sense that in the course of time it, too, appears along with many other things, and in the process changes and passes away and offers changing aspects for historiology. Art is history in the essential sense that it grounds history.

Art lets truth originate. Art, founding preserving, is the spring that leaps to the truth of what is, in the work. To originate something by a leap, to bring something into being from out of the source of its nature in a founding leap—this is what the word origin [German *Ursprung,* literally, primal leap] means.

The origin of the work of art—that is, the origin of both the creators and the preservers, which is to say of a people's historical existence, is art. This is so because art is by nature an origin: a distinctive way in which truth comes into being, that is, becomes historical.

We inquire into the nature of art. Why do we inquire in this way? We inquire in this way in order to be able to ask more truly whether art is or is not an origin in our historical existence, whether and under what conditions it can and must be an origin.

Such reflection cannot force art and its coming-to-be. But this reflective knowledge is the preliminary and therefore indispensable preparation for the becoming of art. Only such knowledge prepares its space for art, their way for the creators, their location for the preservers.

In such knowledge, which can only grow slowly, the question is decided whether art can be an origin and then must be a head start, or whether it is to remain a mere appendix and then can only be carried along as a routine cultural phenomenon.

Are we in our existence historically at the origin? Do we know, which means do we give heed to, the nature of the origin? Or, in our relation to art, do we still merely make appeal to a cultivated acquaintance with the past?

For this either-or and its decision there is an infallible sign. Hölderlin, the poet—whose work still confronts the Germans as a test to be stood—named it in saying:

Schwer verlässt was nahe dem Ursprung wohnet, den Ort.
[Reluctantly that which dwells near its origin departs.]

— "THE JOURNEY," VERSES 18–19

14

ART AS AURATIC: WALTER BENJAMIN

No 20th-century philosopher of art has reflected more deeply on how changes in modern art have affected our understanding of art itself than Walter Benjamin (1892–1940). For Benjamin, a German Marxist philosopher and literary critic, photography and film have had a revolutionary impact on art. In his essay, "The Work of Art in the Age of Mechanical Reproduction," from which this selection is drawn, Benjamin theorizes the artwork's loss of aura and how this alters the function of art in society. At the same time, Benjamin is concerned with the relationship between art and politics. Writing as Hitler came to power in Germany, Benjamin, a Jew, maintained hope that art could be used in the struggle against fascism.

Benjamin is less concerned to provide a general definition of art than to understand how the function of art has changed under capitalism and its technological innovations. In particular, he wants to understand how "mechanical reproduction," the ability to copy works of art through purely technical means changes art's social function. Central in this regard is the development of photography, with its ability to produce unlimited numbers of accurate copies, and film, the art form whose photographic basis makes it seem to reproduce the world in time as well as space.

Benjamin's thesis is that the reproducibility of artworks has caused their aura to decline. By using the term "aura," Benjamin attempts to capture the reverence that people in earlier societies, often in religious contexts, had for works of art. In establishing his claim, Benjamin draws an analogy between the structure of art objects and commodities or goods produced for the market. In the first volume of *Das Kapital,* Karl Marx (1818–1883) had distinguished between the ability of a commodity to satisfy a human need (its use value) and its value in the market place (its exchange value), arguing that exchange value had come to predominate under capitalism. Analogously, Benjamin first distinguishes the cult value of the artwork—its place within a cult as a unique object often hidden from view—from its exhibition value—its worth as an object that is accessible to all. Technological reproduction, he then argues, makes the cult value of art recede in favor of its exhibition value.

For Benjamin, this means that many of the ways philosophers have attempted to characterize art are no longer valid—for example, art can no longer be regarded as autonomous, that is, a realm in which specific social interests play no part, as Kant (Chapter 4) and other philosophers of art had asserted. The burning question for Benjamin is whether art can have a positive political function, inducing people to join a revolution against fascism. Benjamin famously remarks that fascists such as Hitler have *aestheticized* politics with their mass demonstrations and rallies; he proposes instead art be *politicized* as a weapon in the fight for social justice.

Benjamin's assessment of the impact of technology on art is thus suitably *dialectical*. On the one hand, he sees the reproducibility of art in the modern world as destructive of its aura; on the other hand, this very loss of aura makes possible a use of art heretofore unthinkable: promoting socialist revolution.

STUDY QUESTIONS ON THE READING

1. Why does Benjamin think that artworks traditionally had aura? Do you agree? Why or why not?

2. Is Benjamin right that mechanical reproduction has destroyed the aura of works of art? Explain.

3. Benjamin thinks that art is no longer autonomous. How does this make his view of art different from the views of other philosophers you have read? How might Kant react to his claim?

4. Explain Benjamin's distinction between distraction and concentration as two ways of relating to art. Do you think this distinction is helpful in thinking about the difference between high and low culture, esoteric and mass art? Explain.

5. Do you think that modern arts like the cinema can be a political force in the way Benjamin intends? Can you think of any films that have had a political impact?

❖

WALTER BENJAMIN: THE WORK OF ART IN THE AGE OF MECHANICAL REPRODUCTION

. . . [T]heses about the art of the proletariat after its assumption of power or about the art of a classless society would have less bearing on these demands [for prognostication] than theses about the developmental tendencies of art

---

under present conditions of production. Their dialectic is no less noticeable in the superstructure than in the economy. It would therefore be wrong to underestimate the value of such theses as a weapon. They brush aside a number of outmoded concepts, such as creativity and genius, eternal value and mystery—concepts whose uncontrolled (and at present almost uncontrollable) application would lead to a processing of data in the Fascist sense. The concepts which are introduced into the theory of art in what follows differ from the more familiar terms in that they are completely useless for the purposes of Fascism. They are, on the other hand, useful for the formulation of revolutionary demands in the politics of art.

I

In principle a work of art has always been reproducible. Manmade artifacts could always be imitated by men. Replicas were made by pupils in practice of their craft, by masters for diffusing their works, and, finally, by third parties in the pursuit of gain. Mechanical reproduction of a work of art, however, represents something new. Historically, it advanced intermittently and in leaps at long intervals, but with accelerated intensity. The Greeks knew only two procedures of technically reproducing works of art: founding and stamping. Bronzes, terra cottas, and coins were the only art works which they could produce in quantity. All others were unique and could not be mechanically reproduced.

With the woodcut graphic art became mechanically reproducible for the first time, long before script became reproducible by print. The enormous changes which printing, the mechanical reproduction of writing, has brought about in literature are a familiar story. However, within the phenomenon which we are here examining from the perspective of world history, print is merely a special, though particularly important, case. During the Middle Ages engraving and etching were added to the woodcut; at the beginning of the nineteenth century lithography made its appearance.

With lithography the technique of reproduction reached an essentially new stage. This much more direct process was distinguished by the tracing of the design on a stone rather than its incision on a block of wood or its etching on a copperplate and permitted graphic art for the first time to put its products on the market, not only in large numbers as hitherto, but also in daily changing forms. Lithography enabled graphic art to illustrate everyday life, and it began to keep pace with printing. But only a few decades after its invention, lithography was surpassed by photography. For the first time in the process of pictorial reproduction, photography freed the hand of the most important artistic functions which henceforth devolved only upon the eye looking into a lens. Since the eye perceives more swiftly than the hand can draw, the process of pictorial reproduction was accelerated so enormously that it could keep pace with speech. A film operator shooting a scene in the studio captures the images at the speed of an actor's speech. Just as lithography virtually implied the illustrated newspaper, so did photography foreshadow the sound film. The technical reproduction of sound was tackled at the end of the last century. These convergent endeavors made predictable a situation which Paul Valéry pointed up in this sentence: "Just as water, gas, and electricity are brought into our houses from far off to satisfy our needs in response to a minimal effort, so we shall be supplied with visual or auditory images, which will appear and disappear at a simple movement of the hand, hardly more than a sign."[1] Around 1900 technical reproduction had reached a standard that not only permitted it to reproduce all transmitted works of art and thus to cause the most profound change in their impact upon the public; it also had captured a place of its own among the artistic processes. For the study of this standard nothing is more revealing than the nature of the repercussions that these two different manifestations—the reproduction of works of art and the art of the film—have had on art in its traditional form.

II

Even the most perfect reproduction of a work of art is lacking in one element: its presence in time and space, its unique existence at the place where it happens to be. This unique existence of the work of art determined the history to which it was subject throughout the time of its existence. This includes the changes which it may have suffered in physical condition over the years as well as the various changes in its ownership. The traces of the first can be revealed only by chemical or physical analyses which it is impossible to perform on a reproduction; changes of ownership are subject to a tradition which must be traced from the situation of the original.

The presence of the original is the prerequisite to the concept of authenticity. Chemical analyses of the patina of a bronze can help to establish this, as does the proof that a given manuscript of the Middle Ages stems from an archive of the fifteenth century. The whole sphere of authenticity is outside technical— and, of course, not only technical—reproducibility. Confronted with its manual reproduction, which was usually branded as a forgery, the original preserved all its authority; not so *vis à vis* technical reproduction. The reason is twofold. First, process reproduction is more independent of the original than manual reproduction. For example, in photography, process reproduction can bring out those aspects of the original that are unattainable to the naked eye yet accessible to the lens, which is adjustable and chooses its angle at will. And photographic reproduction, with the aid of certain processes, such as enlargement or slow motion, can capture images which escape natural vision. Secondly, technical reproduction can put the copy of the original into situations which would be out of reach for the original itself. Above all, it enables the original to meet the beholder halfway, be it in the form of a photograph or a phonograph record. The cathedral leaves its locale to be received in the studio of a lover of art; the choral production, performed in an auditorium or in the open air, resounds in the drawing room.

---

[1] Paul Valéry, *Pièces sur L'Art* (Paris: Gallimard, 1934), 226.

The situations into which the product of mechanical reproduction can be brought may not touch the actual work of art, yet the quality of its presence is always depreciated. This holds not only for the art work but also, for instance, for a landscape which passes in review before the spectator in a movie. In the case of the art object, a most sensitive nucleus—namely, its authenticity—is interfered with whereas no natural object is vulnerable on that score. The authenticity of a thing is the essence of all that is transmissible from its beginning, ranging from its substantive duration to its testimony to the history which it has experienced. Since the historical testimony rests on the authenticity, the former, too, is jeopardized by reproduction when substantive duration ceases to matter. And what is really jeopardized when the historical testimony is affected is the authority of the object.

One might subsume the eliminated element in the term "aura" and go on to say: that which withers in the age of mechanical reproduction is the aura of the work of art. This is a symptomatic process whose significance points beyond the realm of art.

One might generalize by saying: the technique of reproduction detaches the reproduced object from the domain of tradition. By making many reproductions it substitutes a plurality of copies for a unique existence. And in permitting the reproduction to meet the beholder or listener in his own particular situation, it reactivates the object reproduced. These two processes lead to a tremendous shattering of tradition which is the obverse of the contemporary crisis and renewal of mankind. Both processes are intimately connected with the contemporary mass movements. Their most powerful agent is the film. Its social significance, particularly in its most positive form, is inconceivable without its destructive, cathartic aspect, that is, the liquidation of the traditional value of the cultural heritage. This phenomenon is most palpable in the great historical films. It extends to ever new positions. In 1927 Abel Gance exclaimed enthusiastically: "Shakespeare, Rembrandt, Beethoven will make films . . . all legends, all mythologies and all myths, all founders of religion, and the very religions . . . await their exposed resurrection, and the heroes crowd each other at the gate."[2] Presumably without intending it, he issued an invitation to a far-reaching liquidation.

III

. . . The concept of aura which was proposed above with reference to historical objects may usefully be illustrated with reference to the aura of natural ones. We define the aura of the latter as the unique phenomenon of a distance, however close it may be. If, while resting on a summer afternoon, you follow with your eyes a mountain range on the horizon or a branch which casts its shadow over you, you experience the aura of those mountains, of that branch.

---

[2] Abel Gance, "Le Temps de l'image est venu," *L'Art cinématographique*, Vol. 2 (Paris: Librairie Felix Alcan, 1927), 94f.

This image makes it easy to comprehend the social bases of the contemporary decay of the aura. It rests on two circumstances, both of which are related to the increasing significance of the masses in contemporary life. Namely, the desire of contemporary masses to bring things "closer" spatially and humanly, which is just as ardent as their bent toward overcoming the uniqueness of every reality by accepting its reproduction. Every day the urge grows stronger to get hold of an object at very close range by way of its likeness, its reproduction. Unmistakably, reproduction as offered by picture magazines and newsreels differs from the image seen by the unarmed eye. Uniqueness and permanence are as closely linked in the latter as are transitoriness and reproducibility in the former. To pry an object from its shell, to destroy its aura, is the mark of a perception whose "sense of the universal equality of things" has increased to such a degree that it extracts it even from a unique object by means of reproduction. Thus is manifested in the field of perception what in the theoretical sphere is noticeable in the increasing importance of statistics. The adjustment of reality to the masses and of the masses to reality is a process of unlimited scope, as much for thinking as for perception.

IV

The uniqueness of a work of art is inseparable from its being imbedded in the fabric of tradition. This tradition itself is thoroughly alive and extremely changeable. An ancient statue of Venus, for example, stood in a different traditional context with the Greeks, who made it an object of veneration, than with the clerics of the Middle Ages, who viewed it as an ominous idol. Both of them, however, were equally confronted with its uniqueness, that is, its aura. Originally the contextual integration of art in tradition found its expression in the cult. We know that the earliest art works originated in the service of a ritual—first the magical, then the religious kind. It is significant that the existence of the work of art with reference to its aura is never entirely separated from its ritual function. In other words, the unique value of the "authentic" work of art has its basis in ritual, the location of its original use value. This ritualistic basis, however remote, is still recognizable as secularized ritual even in the most profane forms of the cult of beauty. The secular cult of beauty, developed during the Renaissance and prevailing for three centuries, clearly showed that ritualistic basis in its decline and the first deep crisis which befell it. With the advent of the first truly revolutionary means of reproduction, photography, simultaneously with the rise of socialism, art sensed the approaching crisis which has become evident a century later. At the time, art reacted with the doctrine of *l'art pour l'art,* [art for art's sake] that is, with a theology of art. This gave rise to what might be called a negative theology in the form of the idea of "pure" art, which not only denied any social function of art but also any categorizing by subject matter. (In poetry, Mallarmé was the first to take this position.)

An analysis of art in the age of mechanical reproduction must do justice to these relationships, for they lead us to an all-important insight: for the first time in world history, mechanical reproduction emancipates the work of art from its parasitical dependence on ritual. To an ever greater degree the work of art reproduced becomes the work of art designed for reproducibility. From a photographic negative, for example, one can make any number of prints; to ask for the "authentic" print makes no sense. But the instant the criterion of authenticity ceases to be applicable to artistic production, the total function of art is reversed. Instead of being based on ritual, it begins to be based on another practice—politics.

V

Works of art are received and valued on different planes. Two polar types stand out: with one, the accent is on the cult value; with the other, on the exhibition value of the work. Artistic production begins with ceremonial objects destined to serve in a cult. One may assume that what mattered was their existence, not their being on view. The elk portrayed by the man of the Stone Age on the walls of his cave was an instrument of magic. He did expose it to his fellow men, but in the main it was meant for the spirits. Today the cult value would seem to demand that the work of art remain hidden. Certain statues of gods are accessible only to the priest in the cella; certain Madonnas remain covered nearly all year round; certain sculptures on medieval cathedrals are invisible to the spectator on ground level. With the emancipation of the various art practices from ritual go increasing opportunities for the exhibition of their products. It is easier to exhibit a portrait bust that can be sent here and there than to exhibit the statue of a divinity that has its fixed place in the interior of a temple. The same holds for the painting as against the mosaic or fresco that preceded it. And even though the public presentability of a mass originally may have been just as great as that of a symphony, the latter originated at the moment when its public presentability promised to surpass that of the mass.

With the different methods of technical reproduction of a work of art, its fitness for exhibition increased to such an extent that the quantitative shift between its two poles turned into a qualitative transformation of its nature. This is comparable to the situation of the work of art in prehistoric times when, by the absolute emphasis on its cult value, it was, first and foremost, an instrument of magic. Only later did it come to be recognized as a work of art. In the same way today, by the absolute emphasis on its exhibition value the work of art becomes a creation with entirely new functions, among which the one we are conscious of, the artistic function, later may be recognized as incidental. This much is certain: today photography and the film are the most serviceable exemplifications of this new function. . . .

VII

The nineteenth-century dispute as to the artistic value of painting versus photography today seems devious and confused. This does not diminish its importance, however; if anything, it underlines it. The dispute was in fact the symptom of a historical transformation the universal impact of which was not realized by either of the rivals. When the age of mechanical reproduction separated art from its basis in cult, the semblance of its autonomy disappeared forever. The resulting change in the function of art transcended the perspective of the century; for a long time it even escaped that of the twentieth century, which experienced the development of the film.

Earlier much futile thought had been devoted to the question of whether photography is an art. The primary question—whether the very invention of photography had not transformed the entire nature of art—was not raised. . . .

XV

The mass is a matrix from which all traditional behavior toward works of art issues today in a new form. Quantity has been transmuted into quality. The greatly increased mass of participants has produced a change in the mode of participation. The fact that the new mode of participation first appeared in a disreputable form must not confuse the spectator. Yet some people have launched spirited attacks against precisely this superficial aspect. Among these, Duhamel has expressed himself in the most radical manner. What he objects to most is the kind of participation which the movie elicits from the masses. Duhamel calls the movie "a pastime for helots, a diversion for uneducated, wretched, worn-out creatures who are consumed by their worries . . . , a spectacle which requires no concentration and presupposes no intelligence . . . , which kindles no light in the heart and awakens no hope other than the ridiculous one of someday becoming a 'star' in Los Angeles."[3] Clearly, this is at bottom the same ancient lament that the masses seek distraction whereas art demands concentration from the spectator. That is a commonplace. The question remains whether it provides a platform for the analysis of the film. A closer look is needed here. Distraction and concentration form polar opposites which may be stated as follows: A man who concentrates before a work of art is absorbed by it. He enters into this work of art the way legend tells of the Chinese painter when he viewed his finished painting. In contrast, the distracted mass absorbs the work of art. This is most obvious with regard to buildings. Architecture has always represented the prototype of a work of art the reception of which is consummated by a collectivity in a state of distraction. The laws of its reception are most instructive.

Buildings have been man's companions since primeval times. Many art forms have developed and perished. Tragedy begins with the Greeks, is extinguished with them, and after centuries its "rules" only are revived. The epic poem, which had its origin in the youth of nations, expires in Europe at the end of the Renaissance. Panel painting is a creation of the Middle Ages, and nothing guarantees its uninterrupted existence. But the human need for shelter is lasting. Architecture has never been idle. Its history is more ancient than that of any other art, and its claim to being a living force has significance in every

---

[3] Georges Duhamel, *Scènes de la vie future* (Paris: Mercure de France, 1930), 58.

attempt to comprehend the relationship of the masses to art. Buildings are appropriated in a twofold manner: by use and by perception—or rather, by touch and sight. Such appropriation cannot be understood in terms of the attentive concentration of a tourist before a famous building. On the tactile side there is no counterpart to contemplation on the optical side. Tactile appropriation is accomplished not so much by attention as by habit. As regards architecture, habit determines to a large extent even optical reception. The latter, too, occurs much less through rapt attention than by noticing the object in incidental fashion. This mode of appropriation, developed with reference to architecture, in certain circumstances acquires canonical value. For the tasks which face the human apparatus of perception at the turning points of history cannot be solved by optical means, that is, by contemplation, alone. They are mastered gradually by habit, under the guidance of tactile appropriation.

The distracted person, too, can form habits. More, the ability to master certain tasks in a state of distraction proves that their solution has become a matter of habit. Distraction as provided by art presents a covert control of the extent to which new tasks have become soluble by apperception. Since, moreover, individuals are tempted to avoid such tasks, art will tackle the most difficult and most important ones where it is able to mobilize the masses. Today it does so in the film. Reception in a state of distraction, which is increasing noticeably in all fields of art and is symptomatic of profound changes in apperception, finds in the film its true means of exercise. The film with its shock effect meets this mode of reception halfway. The film makes the cult value recede into the background not only by putting the public in the position of the critic, but also by the fact that at the movies this position requires no attention. The public is an examiner, but an absent-minded one. . . .

EPILOGUE

. . ."*Fiat ars—pereat mundus,*" [Let there be art—let the world perish. —T.E.W.] says Fascism, and, as Marinetti admits, expects war to supply the artistic gratification of a sense perception that has been changed by technology. This is evidently the consummation of *"l'art pour l'art."* Mankind, which in Homer's time was an object of contemplation for the Olympian gods, now is one for itself. Its self-alienation has reached such a degree that it can experience its own destruction as an aesthetic pleasure of the first order. This is the situation of politics which Fascism is rendering aesthetic. Communism responds by politicizing art.

15

ART AS LIBERATORY: THEODOR ADORNO

Theodor Adorno (1903–1969) was a dominant figure in the Frankfurt School, a group of Marxist philosophers and social theorists that also included Max Horkheimer and Herbert Marcuse. Many of them emigrated to the United States from Hitler's Germany in the 1930s. For Adorno as for his colleagues, capitalism is not simply an economic system based on exploitation but also a social and cultural system that usurps human freedom. Nowhere is this view more clearly elaborated than in his wide-ranging and subtle philosophy of art.

On the one hand, Adorno thinks of art as one of the few domains in which the human subject is able to attain "something like freedom in the midst of unfreedom." Art can bring to consciousness the aspiration for freedom even in societies that systematically attempt to deny it. Thus, Adorno emphasizes art's presentation of the *contradiction* between the possibility of reconciliation—by which he means transcendence of conflict—and the society in which such reconciliation is not only absent but deemed unattainable. His example, given in section 3 of his essay "Is Art Lighthearted?" is the music of Mozart. According to Adorno, when we listen to Mozart's music, we are not simply aware of its beautiful harmonies or, as he would say, its presentation of reconciliation; we also compare this with the social world in which we live, one notable, according to Adorno, for not even attempting to meet the needs of all. Art lets us see both what is possible and how distant that possibility actually is.

At the same time, Adorno is conscious that art is not immune to the influence of the market economy. Indeed, he is highly critical of what he calls the "Culture Industry" for subverting the liberatory possibilities of art in favor of entertainments that merely assuage the exhaustion of those who labor under capitalist exploitation. Indeed, this perverted form of art does not honor the aspiration for freedom and reconciliation, but instead portrays unfreedom as inevitable, as desirable even.

In our selection, Adorno structures his discussion of art through the opposition of seriousness and lightheartedness. Because art arouses our pleasure, it is intimately connected with the concept of the lighthearted. Indeed, its lightheartedness stands as a reproach to reality and its "seriousness." Yet art is also serious in its attempt to represent the contradiction between reality and the desire for freedom. Art must embody both or it is no longer genuine. The failure to maintain seriousness is precisely the accusation Adorno lodges against the Culture Industry, under whose domination the message of art becomes: Enjoy! Acquiesce!

The need to contest the Culture Industry's domination of art is made all the more pressing for Adorno by the Holocaust, which threatens to make genuine art, with its commitment to incorporating lightheartedness, a profanity: After all, how could one tolerate jesting on the graves of those millions of innocent victims? What is called for, Adorno asserts, is a new type of art, one that transcends the lighthearted-serious dichotomy, and he finds it exemplified in the theater of Samuel Beckett. Beckett's plays mark the advent of a form of art beyond the duality of comedy and tragedy, allowing art to survive the devastations of the 20th century.

STUDY QUESTIONS ON THE READING

1. Why does Adorno think that art allows human beings to realize their own possibilities?

2. How does the Culture Industry demean the nature of art? What does Adorno mean by its "forced cheerfulness"?

3. What differences do you see between Benjamin's views of art and Adorno's? Which, if either, do you feel is superior? Why?

4. What is kitsch?

5. Why, for Adorno, must Auschwitz change the nature of art? Are there any events that make it impossible for art to go on as before?

6. Do you agree with Adorno's assessment of the need for a new form of art, beyond comedy and tragedy, as realized, for example, in such Beckett plays as *Waiting for Godot*?

THEODOR ADORNO: IS ART LIGHTHEARTED?

The prologue to Schiller's *Wallenstein* ends with the line, "Ernst ist das Leben, heiter ist die Kunst"—life is serious, art is lighthearted. It is modeled on a line from Ovid's *Tristia:* "Vita verecunda est, Musa jocosa mihi" (II, 354), or "My life is modest and sober, my muse is gay." Perhaps one may impute an intent to

From *Notes to Literature* by Theodor Adorno. Copyright © 1991 Columbia University Press. Reprinted by permission of the publisher.

Ovid, the charming and artful classical writer. He, whose life was so light-hearted that the Augustinian establishment could not tolerate it, was winking at his patrons, composing his lightheartedness back into the literary gaiety of the *Ars amandi* and repentantly letting it be seen that he personally was concerned with the serious conduct of life. For Ovid it was a matter of being pardoned. Schiller, the court poet of German Idealism, wanted nothing to do with this sort of Latin cunning. His maxim wags its finger with no end in mind. It thereby becomes totally ideological and is incorporated into the household stock of the bourgeoisie, ready for citation on the appropriate occasion. For it affirms the established and popular distinction between work and leisure. Something that has its roots in the torments of prosaic and unfree labor and the well-justified aversion to it is declared to be an eternal law of two cleanly separated spheres. Neither is to mingle with the other. Precisely by virtue of its edifying lack of cogency, art is to be incorporated into and subordinated to bourgeois life as its antagonistic complement. One can already see the organization of leisure time this will eventually result in. It is the Garden of Elysium, where the heavenly roses grow, to be woven by women into earthly life, which is so loathsome. The possibility that things might sometime become truly different is hidden from Schiller the idealist. He is concerned with the effects of art. For all the noblesse of his gesture, Schiller secretly anticipates the situation under the culture industry in which art is prescribed to tired businesspeople as a shot in the arm. Hegel was the first to object, at the height of German Idealism, to an aesthetics of effect [*Wirkungsaesthetik*] dating back to the eighteenth century and including Kant, and with it to this view of art: art was not, he stated, a mechanism for delight and instruction à la Horace.

2

Still, there is a measure of truth in the platitude about art's lightheartedness. If art were not a source of pleasure for people, in however mediated a form, it would not have been able to survive in the naked existence it contradicts and resists. This is not something external to it, however, but part of its very definition. Although it does not refer to society, the Kantian formulation "purposefulness without purpose" alludes to this. Art's purposelessness consists in its having escaped the constraints of self-preservation. It embodies something like freedom in the midst of unfreedom. The fact that through its very existence it stands outside the evil spell that prevails allies it to a promise of happiness, a promise it itself somehow expresses in its expression of despair. Even in Beckett's plays the curtain rises the way it rises on the room with the Christmas presents. In its attempt to divest itself of its element of semblance, art labors in vain to rid itself of the residue of the pleasure-giving element, which it suspects of betraying it to yea-saying. For all that, the thesis of art's lightheartedness is to be taken in a very precise sense. It holds for art as a whole, not for individual works. Those may be thoroughly devoid of lightheartedness, in accordance with the horrors of reality. What is lighthearted in art is, if you like, the opposite of what one might easily assume it to be: not its content but its demeanor, the abstract fact that it is art at all, that it opens out over the reality to whose violence it bears witness at the same time. This confirms the idea expressed by the philosopher Schiller, who saw art's lightheartedness in its playfulness and not in its stating of intellectual contents, even those that went beyond Idealism. A priori, prior to its works, art is a critique of the brute seriousness that reality imposes upon human beings. Art imagines that by naming this fateful state of affairs it is loosening its hold. That is what is lighthearted in it; as a change in the existing mode of consciousness, that is also, to be sure, its seriousness.

3

But art, which, like knowledge, takes all its material and ultimately its forms from reality, indeed from social reality, in order to transform them, thereby becomes entangled in reality's irreconcilable contradictions. It measures its profundity by whether or not it can, through the reconciliation that its formal law brings to contradictions, emphasize the real lack of reconciliation all the more. Contradiction vibrates through its most remote mediations, just as the din of the horrors of reality sounds in music's most extreme pianissimo. Where faith in culture vainly sings the praises of music's harmony, as in Mozart, that harmony sounds a dissonance to the harsh tones of reality and has them as its substance. That is Mozart's sadness. Only through the transformation of something that is in any case preserved in negative form, the contradictory, does art accomplish what is then betrayed the moment it is glorified as a Being beyond what exists, independent of its opposite. Though attempts to define kitsch usually fail, still not the worst definition would be one that made the criterion of kitsch whether an art product gives form to consciousness of contradiction—even if it does so by stressing its opposition to reality—or dissembles it. In this respect seriousness should be demanded of any work of art. As something that has escaped from reality and is nevertheless permeated with it, art vibrates between this seriousness and lightheartedness. It is this tension that constitutes art.

4

The significance of this contradictory movement between lightheartedness and seriousness in art—its dialectic—can be clarified in a simple way through two distiches by Hölderlin, which the poet, no doubt intentionally, placed close together. The first, entitled "Sophocles," reads: "Viele versuchen umsonst das Freudigste freudig zu sagen / Hier spricht endlich es mir, hier in der Trauer sich aus" ["Many attempt, vainly, to say the most joyful thing joyfully / Here it finally expresses itself to me, here, in sorrow"]. The tragedian's lightheartedness should be sought not in the mythical content of his dramas, perhaps not even in the reconciliation he confers upon myth, but rather in his saying [*sagen*] it, in its expressing itself [*aussprechen*]; both expressions are employed, with emphasis, in Hölderlin's lines. The second distichon bears the title "Die Scherzhaften," or "The Ones Who Make Jokes": "Immer spielt ihr und scherzt? ihr müsst! O Freunde! mir geht diss / In die Seele, denn diss müssen Verzweifelte nur" ["Are you always playing and joking? You have to! Oh friends, this affects me deeply, for only the desperate have to do that"]. Where art tries of its own accord to be lighthearted and thereby tries to adapt itself to a use which, according to Hölderlin, nothing holy can serve any longer, it is reduced to the level of a human need and its truth content is betrayed. Its ordained cheerfulness fits into the way of the world. It encourages people to submit to what is decreed, to comply. This is the form of objective despair. If one takes the distichon seriously enough, it passes judgment on the affirmative character of art. Since then, under the dictates of the culture industry, that affirmative character has become omnipresent, and the joke has become the smirking caricature of advertising pure and simple.

5

For the relationship between the serious and the lighthearted in art is subject to a historical dynamic. Whatever may be called lighthearted in art is something that has come into being, something unthinkable either in archaic works or in works with a strictly theological context. What is lighthearted in art presupposes something like urban freedom, and it does not appear for the first time in the early bourgeoisie, as in Boccaccio, Chaucer, Rabelais, and Don Quixote, but is already present as the element, known to later periods as classical, that distinguishes itself from the archaic. The means by which art frees itself of myth, of the dark and aporetic, is essentially a process, not an invariant fundamental choice between the serious and the lighthearted. It is in the lightheartedness of art that subjectivity first comes to know and become conscious of itself. Through lightheartedness it escapes from entanglement and returns to itself. There is something of bourgeois personal freedom in lightheartedness, though it also shares thereby in the historical fate of the bourgeoisie. What was once humor becomes irretrievably dull; the later variety degenerates into the hearty contentment of complicity. In the end it becomes intolerable. After that, however, who could still laugh at Don Quixote and its sadistic mockery of the man who breaks down in the face of the bourgeois reality principle? What is supposed to be funny about the comedies of Aristophanes—which are as brilliant today as they were then—has become a mystery; the equation of the coarse with the comical can now be appreciated only in the provinces. The more profoundly society fails to deliver the reconciliation that the bourgeois spirit promised as the enlightenment of myth, the more irresistibly humor is pulled down into the netherworld, and laughter, once the image of humanness, becomes a regression to inhumanity.

6

Since art has been taken in hand by the culture industry and placed among the consumer goods, its lightheartedness has become synthetic, false, and bewitched. No lightheartedness is compatible with the arbitrarily contrived. The

pacified relationship of lightheartedness and nature excludes anything that ma-
nipulates and calculates nature. The distinction language makes between the
joke and the wisecrack captures this quite precisely. Where we see lightheartedness today, it is distorted by being decreed, down to the ominous "nevertheless" of the sort of tragedy that consoles itself with the idea that that's just how
life is. Art, which is no longer possible if it is not reflective, must renounce
lightheartedness of its own accord. It is forced to do so above all by what has
recently happened. The statement that it is not possible to write poetry after
Auschwitz does not hold absolutely, but it is certain that after Auschwitz, because Auschwitz was possible and remains possible for the foreseeable future,
lighthearted art is no longer conceivable. Objectively, it degenerates into cynicism, no matter how much it relies on kindness and understanding. In fact, this
impossibility was sensed by great literature, first by Baudelaire almost a century before the European catastrophe, and then by Nietzsche as well and in the
George School's abstention from humor. Humor has turned into polemical
parody. There it finds a temporary refuge as long as it remains unreconciled,
taking no notice of the concept of reconciliation that was once allied to the
concept of humor. By now the polemical form of humor has become questionable as well. It can no longer count on being understood, and polemic, of all
artistic forms, cannot survive in a vacuum. Several years ago there was a
debate about whether fascism could be presented in comic or parodistic form
without that constituting an outrage against its victims. The silly, farcical,
second-rate quality is unmistakable, the kinship between Hitler and his followers on the one hand and the gutter press and stool pigeons on the other. One
cannot laugh at it. The bloody reality was not the spirit [*Geist*], or evil spirit
[*Ungeist*] that spirit could make fun of. Times were still good when Hašek
wrote *Schweyk*, with nooks and crannies and sloppiness right in the middle of
the system of horror. But comedies about fascism would become accomplices
of the silly mode of thinking that considered fascism beaten in advance because
the strongest battalions in world history were against it. Least of all should the
position of the victors be taken by the opponents of fascism, who have a duty
not to resemble in any way those who entrench themselves in that position. The
historical forces that produced the horror derive from the inherent nature of
the social structure. They are not superficial forces, and they are much too
powerful for anyone to have the prerogative of treating them as though he had
world history behind him and the Führers actually were the clowns whose
nonsense their murderous talk came to resemble only afterwards.

7

Because, moreover, the moment of lightheartedness inheres in art's freedom
from mere existence, which even works that are desperate—and those works
all the more—demonstrate, the moment of lightheartedness or humor is not
simply expelled from them in the course of history. It survives in their self-
critique, as humor about humor. The artful meaninglessness and silliness characteristic of radical contemporary works of art, characteristics that are so
irritating to those with a positive outlook, represent not so much the regression

of art to an infantile stage as its humorous judgment on humor. Wedekind's *pièce à clef* directed against the publisher of *Simplizissimus* bears the subtitle: satire on satire. There is something similar in Kafka, whose shock-prose was experienced by some of his interpreters, Thomas Mann among them, as humor, and whose relationship to Hašek is being studied by Slovakian authors. In the face of Beckett's plays especially, the category of the tragic surrenders to laughter, just as his plays cut off all humor that accepts the status quo. They bear witness to a state of consciousness that no longer admits the alternative of seriousness and lightheartedness, nor the composite tragi- comedy. Tragedy evaporates because the claims of the subjectivity that was to have been tragic are so obviously inconsequential. A dried up, tearless weeping takes the place of laughter. Lamentation has become the mourning of hollow, empty eyes. Humor is salvaged in Beckett's plays because they infect the spectator with laughter about the absurdity of laughter and laughter about despair. This process is linked with that of artistic reduction, a path leading to a survival minimum as the minimum of existence remaining. This minimum discounts the historical catastrophe, perhaps in order to survive it.

8

A withering away of the alternative between lightheartedness and seriousness, between the tragic and the comic, almost between life and death, is becoming evident in contemporary art. With this, art negates its whole past, doubtless because the familiar alternative expresses a situation divided between the happiness of survival and the catastrophe that forms the medium for that survival. Given the complete disenchantment of the world, art that is beyond lightheartedness and seriousness may be as much a figure of reconciliation as a figure of horror. Such art corresponds both to disgust with the ubiquity, both overt and covert, of advertisements for existence, and resistance to the cothurne, which by its exorbitant elevation of suffering once again sides with immutability. In view of the recent past, art can no more be completely serious than it can still be lighthearted. One begins to doubt whether art was ever as serious as culture had convinced people it was. Art can no longer equate the expression of mourning with what is most joyful, as Hölderlin's poem, which considered itself in tune with the *Weltgeist,* once did. The truth content of joy seems to have become unattainable. The fact that the genres are becoming blurred, that the tragic gesture seems comic and the comic dejected, is connected with that. The tragic is decaying because it raises a claim to the positive meaning of negativity, the meaning that philosophy called positive negation. This claim cannot be made good. The art that moves ahead into the unknown, the only art now possible, is neither lighthearted nor serious; the third possibility, however, is cloaked in obscurity, as though embedded in a void the figures of which are traced by advanced works of art.

16

ART AS INDEFINABLE: MORRIS WEITZ

Austrian-born Ludwig Wittgenstein (1889–1951) was an enormously influential figure in 20th-century Anglo-American analytic philosophy. In his *Philosophical Investigations,* he argued that, heretofore, philosophers had misunderstood the nature of language, believing that every word had an associated, sharply defined meaning. Instead, Wittgenstein proposed that we think of words on the analogy with family. If we look at photographs of a large family over a number of generations, we notice there is no single characteristic, not even a small set of characteristics such as having curly hair and a large nose, that all family members share. Instead, there is a set of overlapping yet different resemblances among the individuals who make up the family. So Aunt Mary and Uncle Joe may both have curly hair, which Grandma Rose does not have; but she may have the large nose in common with Uncle Joe that Aunt Mary lacks, and so on. Words are governed by the logic of family resemblance, according to Wittgenstein, for we can see a set of overlapping but differing criteria that explain how a word functions in a language.

In his essay "The Role of Theory in Aesthetics," Morris Weitz (1916–1981) adapts this Wittgensteinian view of language to the concept of art. But instead of simply applying Wittgenstein's general claims about language to the case at hand, Weitz argues that the very nature of art as a practice makes definition impossible. Because art inherently evolves, innovative artworks constantly disrupt prior categories. Whether these new works sufficiently resemble old ones to justify their being classified as instances of the same general concept is a question open to debate, and one that cannot be settled by appeal to definition. Rather, it calls for a decision based on one's understanding of the works and their relation to a tradition.

Because he believes art's definition is based on a mistaken understanding of the concept, does Weitz therefore conclude that traditional theories should simply be discarded? Not at all: Instead of providing definitions of "art," these theories have constantly reformulated criteria of artistic excellence, despite the intentions of their proponents. And in so doing, they have helped us appreciate works of art that challenge settled opinion.

STUDY QUESTIONS ON THE READING

1.   Weitz lists a number of different definitions of art and then goes on to criticize them. What are the different definitions, and what does Weitz claim is wrong with them?

2.   What is an open concept? Why are open concepts indefinable?

3.   Do you agree with Weitz that "art" is an open concept? Why or why not?

4.   Weitz distinguishes between a descriptive and an evaluative use of the concept "art." What does he mean by these two uses? Is one of the two more central? Why or why not?

5.   Weitz claims that previous definitions of art, however they may have been intended, actually function to provide criteria of artistic excellence. Do you agree with Weitz's recommendation about how to reconceive the various theories in this book? Explain.

❖

MORRIS WEITZ: THE ROLE OF
THEORY IN AESTHETICS

Is aesthetic theory, in the sense of a true definition or set of necessary and sufficient properties of art, possible? If nothing else does, the history of aesthetics itself should give one enormous pause here. For, in spite of the many theories, we seem no nearer our goal today than we were in Plato's time. Each age, each art-movement, each philosophy of art, tries over and over again to establish the stated ideal only to be succeeded by a new or revised theory, rooted, at least in part, in the repudiation of preceding ones. Even today, almost everyone interested in aesthetic matters is still deeply wedded to the hope that the correct theory of art is forthcoming. We need only examine the numerous new books on art in which new definitions are proffered; or, in our own country especially, the basic textbooks and anthologies to recognize how strong the priority of a theory of art is.

In this essay I want to plead for the rejection of this problem. I want to show that theory—in the requisite classical sense—is *never* forthcoming in aesthetics, and that we would do much better as philosophers to supplant the question, "What is the nature of art?," by other questions, the answers to which will provide us with all the understanding of the arts there can be. I want

"The Role of Theory in Aesthetics" by Morris Weitz from the *Journal of Aesthetics and Art Criticism*. Copyright © 1956. Reprinted with the permission of Blackwell Publishing.

to show that the inadequacies of the theories are not primarily occasioned by any legitimate difficulty such e.g., as the vast complexity of art, which might be corrected by further probing and research. Their basic inadequacies reside instead in a fundamental misconception of art. Aesthetic theory—all of it—is wrong in principle in thinking that a correct theory is possible because it radically misconstrues the logic of the concept of art. Its main contention that "art" is amenable to real or any kind of true definition is false. Its attempt to discover the necessary and sufficient properties of art is logically misbegotten for the very simple reason that such a set and, consequently, such a formula about it, is never forthcoming. Art, as the logic of the concept shows, has no set of necessary and sufficient properties, hence a theory of it is logically impossible and not merely factually difficult. Aesthetic theory tries to define what cannot be defined in its requisite sense. But in recommending the repudiation of aesthetic theory I shall not argue from this, as too many others have done, that its logical confusions render it meaningless or worthless. On the contrary, I wish to reassess its role and its contribution primarily in order to show that it is of the greatest importance to our understanding of the arts. . . .

The problem with which we must begin is not "What is art?," but "What sort of concept is 'art'?" Indeed, the root problem of philosophy itself is to explain the relation between the employment of certain kinds of concepts and the conditions under which they can be correctly applied. If I may paraphrase Wittgenstein, we must not ask, What is the nature of any philosophical x?, or even, according to the semanticist, What does "x" mean?, a transformation that leads to the disastrous interpretation of "art" as a name for some specifiable class of objects; but rather, What is the use or employment of "x"? What does "x" do in the language? This, I take it, is the initial question, the begin-all if not the end-all of any philosophical problem and solution. Thus, in aesthetics, our first problem is the elucidation of the actual employment of the concept of art, to give a logical description of the actual functioning of the concept, including a description of the conditions under which we correctly use it or its correlates.

My model in this type of logical description or philosophy derives from Wittgenstein. It is also he who, in his refutation of philosophical theorizing in the sense of constructing definitions of philosophical entities, has furnished contemporary aesthetics with a starting point for any future progress. In his new work, *Philosophical Investigations*,[1] Wittgenstein raises as an illustrative question, What is a game? The traditional philosophical, theoretical answer would be in terms of some exhaustive set of properties common to all games. To this Wittgenstein says, let us consider what we call "games": "I mean boardgames, card-games, ball-games, Olympic games, and so on. What is common to them all?—Don't say: 'there *must* be something common, or they would not be called "games"' but *look and see* whether there is anything common to all.—For if you look at them you will not see something that is common to *all*, but similarities, relationships, and a whole series of them at that. . . ."

---

[1] L. Wittgenstein, *Philosophical Investigations* (Oxford, 1953), trans. E. Anscombe; see esp. Part I, Sections 65–75. All quotations are from these sections.

Card games are like board games in some respects but not in others. Not all games are amusing, nor is there always winning or losing or competition. Some games resemble others in some respects—that is all. What we find are no necessary and sufficient properties, only "a complicated network of similarities overlapping and crisscrossing," such that we can say of games that they form a family with family resemblances and no common trait. If one asks what a game is, we pick out sample games, describe these, and add, "This and *similar things* are called 'games'." This is all we need to say and indeed all any of us knows about games. Knowing what a game is is not knowing some real definition or theory but being able to recognize and explain games and to decide which among imaginary and new examples would or would not be called "games." The problem of the nature of art is like that of the nature of games, at least in these respects: If we actually look and see what it is that we call "art," we will also find no common properties—only strands of similarities. Knowing what art is is not knowing some real definition or theory but being able to recognize and explain games and to decide which among imaginary and new examples would or would not be called "games."

The problem of the nature of art is like that of the nature of games, at least in these respects: If we actually look and see what it is that we call "art," we will also find no common properties—only strands of similarities. Knowing what art is is not apprehending some manifest or latent essence but being able to recognize, describe, and explain those things we call "art" in virtue of these similarities.

But the basic resemblance between these concepts is their open texture. In elucidating them, certain (paradigm) cases can be given, about which there can be no question as to their being correctly described as "art" or "game," but no exhaustive set of cases can be given. I can list some cases and some conditions under which I can apply correctly the concept of art but I cannot list all of them, for the all-important reason that unforeseeable or novel conditions are always forthcoming or envisageable.

A concept is open if its conditions of application are emendable and corrigible; i.e., if a situation or case can be imagined or secured which would call for some sort of *decision* on our part to extend the use of the concept to cover this, or to close the concept and invent a new one to deal with the new case and its new property. If necessary and sufficient conditions for the application of a concept can be stated, the concept is a closed one. But this can happen only in logic or mathematics where concepts are constructed and completely defined. It cannot occur with empirically-descriptive and normative concepts unless we arbitrarily close them by stipulating the ranges of their uses.

I can illustrate this open character of "art" best by examples drawn from its sub-concepts. Consider questions like "Is Dos Passos' *U. S. A.* a novel?," "Is V. Woolf's *To the Lighthouse* a novel?," "Is Joyce's *Finnegan's Wake* a novel?" On the traditional view, these are construed as factual problems to be answered yes or no in accordance with the presence or absence of defining properties. But certainly this is not how any of these questions is answered. Once it arises, as it has many times in the development of the novel from Richardson to Joyce (e.g., "Is Gide's *The School for Wives* a novel or a diary?"), what is at stake is no factual analysis concerning necessary and sufficient properties but a decision as to whether the work under examination is similar in certain respects to other works, already called "novels," and consequently warrants the extension of the concept to cover the new case. The new work is narrative, fictional, contains character delineation and dialogue but (say) it has no regular time-sequence in the plot or is interspersed with actual newspaper reports. It is like recognized novels, A, B, C . . . , in some respects but not like them in others. But then neither were B and C like A in some respects when it was decided to extend the concept applied to A to B and C. Because work N + 1 (the brand new work) is like A, B, C . . . N in certain respects—has strands of similarity to them—the concept is extended and a new phase of the novel engendered. "Is N + 1 a novel?," then, is no factual, but rather a decision problem, where the verdict turns on whether or not we enlarge our set of conditions for applying the concept.

What is true of the novel is, I think, true of every sub-concept of art: "tragedy," "comedy," "painting," "opera," etc., of "art" itself. No "Is X a novel, painting, opera, work of art, etc.?" question allows of a definitive answer in the sense of a factual yes or no report. "Is this *collage* a painting or not?" does not rest on any set of necessary and sufficient properties of painting but on whether we decide—as we did!—to extend "painting" to cover this case.

"Art," itself, is an open concept. New conditions (cases) have constantly arisen and will undoubtedly constantly arise; new art forms, new movements will emerge, which will demand decisions on the part of those interested, usually professional critics, as to whether the concept should be extended or not. Aestheticians may lay down similarity conditions but never necessary and sufficient ones for the correct application of the concept. With "art" its conditions of application can never be exhaustively enumerated since new cases can always be envisaged or created by artists, or even nature, which would call for a decision on someone's part to extend or to close the old or to invent a new concept. (E.g., "It's not a sculpture, it's a mobile.")

What I am arguing, then, is that the very expansive, adventurous character of art, its ever-present changes and novel creations, makes it logically impossible to ensure any set of defining properties. We can, of course, choose to close the concept. But to do this with "art" or "tragedy" or "portraiture," etc., is ludicrous since it forecloses on the very conditions of creativity in the arts.

Of course there are legitimate and serviceable closed concepts in art. But these are always those whose boundaries of conditions have been drawn for a *special* purpose. Consider the difference, for example, between "tragedy" and "(extant) Greek tragedy." The first is open and must remain so to allow for the possibility of new conditions, e.g., a play in which the hero is not noble or fallen or in which there is no hero but other elements that are like those of plays we already call "tragedy." The second is closed. The plays it can be applied to, the conditions under which it can be correctly used are all in, once the boundary, "Greek," is drawn. Here the critic can work out a theory or real definition in which he lists the common properties at least of the extant Greek tragedies. Aristotle's definition, false as it is as a theory of all the plays of

Aeschylus, Sophocles, and Euripides, since it does not cover some of them,[2] properly called "tragedies," can be interpreted as a real (albeit incorrect) definition of this closed concept; although it can also be, as it unfortunately has been, conceived as a purported real definition of "tragedy," in which case it suffers from the logical mistake of trying to define what cannot be defined—of trying to squeeze what is an open concept into an honorific formula for a closed concept.

What is supremely important, if the critic is not to become muddled, is to get absolutely clear about the way in which he conceives his concepts; otherwise he goes from the problem of trying to define "tragedy," etc., to an arbitrary closing of the concept in terms of certain preferred conditions or characteristics which he sums up in some linguistic recommendation that he mistakenly thinks is a real definition of the open concept. Thus, many critics and aestheticians ask, "What is tragedy?," choose a class of samples for which they may give a true account of its common properties, and then go on to construe this account of the chosen closed class as a true definition or theory of the whole open class of tragedy. This, I think, is the logical mechanism of most of the so-called theories of the sub-concepts of art: "tragedy," "comedy," "novel," etc. In effect, this whole procedure, subtly deceptive as it is, amounts to a transformation of correct criteria for *recognizing* members of certain legitimately closed classes of works of art into recommended criteria for *evaluating* any putative member of the class.

The primary task of aesthetics is not to seek a theory but to elucidate the concept of art. Specifically, it is to describe the conditions under which we employ the concept correctly. Definition, reconstruction, patterns of analysis are out of place here since they distort and add nothing to our understanding of art. What, then, is the logic of "X is a work of art"?

As we actually use the concept, "Art" is both descriptive (like "chair") and evaluative (like "good"); i.e., we sometimes say, "This is a work of art," to describe something and we sometimes say it to evaluate something. Neither use surprises anyone. What, first, is the logic of "X is a work of art," when it is a descriptive utterance? What are the conditions under which we would be making such an utterance correctly? There are no necessary and sufficient conditions but there are the strands of similarity conditions, i.e., bundles of properties, none of which need be present but most of which are, when we describe things as works of art. I shall call these the "criteria of recognition" of works of art. All of these have served as the defining criteria of the individual traditional theories of art; so we are already familiar with them. Thus, mostly, when we describe something as a work of art, we do so under the conditions of there being present some sort of artifact, made by human skill, ingenuity, and imagination, which embodies in its sensuous, public medium—stone, wood, sounds, words, etc.—certain distinguishable elements and relations. Special theorists would add conditions like satisfaction of wishes, objectification or expression of emotion, some act of empathy, and so on; but these latter conditions seem to

---

[2] See H. D. F. Kitto, *Greek Tragedy* (London, 1939), on this point.

be quite adventitious, present to some but not to other spectators when things are described as works of art. "*X* is a work of art and contains *no* emotion, expression, act of empathy, satisfaction, etc.," is perfectly good sense and may frequently be true. "*X* is a work of art and . . . was made by no one," or . . . "exists only in the mind and not in any publicly observable thing," or . . . "was made by accident when he spilled the paint on the canvas," in each case of which a normal condition is denied, are also sensible and capable of being true in certain circumstances. None of the criteria of recognition is a defining one, either necessary or sufficient, because we can sometimes assert of something that it is a work of art and go on to deny any one of these conditions, even the one which has traditionally been taken to be basic, namely, that of being an artifact: Consider, "This piece of driftwood is a lovely piece of sculpture." Thus, to say of anything that it is a work of art is to commit oneself to the presence of *some* of these conditions. One would scarcely describe *X* as a work of art if *X* were not an artifact, or a collection of elements sensuously presented in a medium, or a product of human skill, and so on. If none of the conditions were present, if there were no criteria present for recognizing something as a work of art, we would not describe it as one. But, even so, no one of these or any collection of them is either necessary or sufficient.

The elucidation of the descriptive use of "Art" creates little difficulty. But the elucidation of the evaluative use does. For many, especially theorists, "This is a work of art" does more than describe; it also praises. Its conditions of utterance, therefore, include certain preferred properties or characteristics of art. I shall call these "criteria of evaluation." Consider a typical example of this evaluative use, the view according to which to say of something that it is a work of art is to imply that it is a *successful* harmonization of elements. Many of the honorific definitions of art and its sub-concepts are of this form. What is at stake here is that "Art" is construed as an evaluative term which is either identified with its criterion or justified in terms of it. "Art" is defined in terms of its evaluative property, e.g., successful harmonization. On such a view, to say "*X* is a work of art" is (1) to say something which is taken *to mean* "*X* is a successful harmonization" (e.g., "Art *is* significant form") or (2) to say something praiseworthy *on the basis* of its successful harmonization. Theorists are never clear whether it is (1) or (2) which is being put forward. Most of them, concerned as they are with this evaluative use, formulate (2), i.e., that feature of art that *makes* it art in the praise-sense, and then go on to state (1), i.e., the definition of "Art" in terms of its art-making feature. And this is clearly to confuse the conditions under which we say something evaluatively with the meaning of what we say. "This is a work of art," said evaluatively, cannot mean "This is a successful harmonization of elements"—except by stipulation—but at most is said in virtue of the art-making property, which is taken as a (the) criterion of "Art," when "Art" is employed to assess. "This is a work of art," used evaluatively, serves to praise and not to affirm the reason why it is said.

The evaluative use of "Art," although distinct from the conditions of its use, relates in a very intimate way to these conditions. For, in every instance of "This is a work of art" (used to praise), what happens is that the criterion of evaluation (e.g., successful harmonization) for the employment of the concept of art is converted into a criterion of recognition. This is why, on its evaluative use, "This is a work of art" implies "This has P," where "P" is some chosen art-making property. Thus, if one chooses to employ "Art" evaluatively, as many do, so that "This is a work of art and not (aesthetically) good" makes no sense, he uses "Art" in such a way that he refuses to *call* anything a work of art unless it embodies his criterion of excellence.

There is nothing wrong with the evaluative use; in fact, there is good reason for using "Art" to praise. But what cannot be maintained is that theories of the evaluative use of "Art" are true and real definitions of the necessary and sufficient properties of art. Instead they are honorific definitions, pure and simple, in which "Art" has been redefined in terms of chosen criteria.

But what makes them—these honorific definitions—so supremely valuable is not their disguised linguistic recommendations; rather it is the *debates* over the reasons for changing the criteria of the concept of art which are built into the definitions. In each of the great theories of art, whether correctly understood as honorific definitions or incorrectly accepted as real definitions, what is of the utmost importance are the reasons proffered in the argument for the respective theory, that is, the reasons given for the chosen or preferred criterion of excellence and evaluation. It is this perennial debate over these criteria of evaluation which makes the history of aesthetic theory the important study it is. The value of each of the theories resides in its attempt to state and to justify certain criteria which are either neglected or distorted by previous theories. Look at the Bell-Fry theory again. Of course, "Art is significant form" cannot be accepted as a true, real definition of art; and most certainly it actually functions in their aesthetics as a redefinition of art in terms of the chosen condition of significant form. But what gives it its aesthetic importance is what lies behind the formula: In an age in which literary and representational elements have become paramount in painting, *return* to the plastic ones since these are indigenous to painting. Thus, the role of the theory is not to define anything but to use the definitional form, almost epigrammatically, to pinpoint a crucial recommendation to turn our attention once again to the plastic elements in painting.

Once we, as philosophers, understand this distinction between the formula and what lies behind it, it behooves us to deal generously with the traditional theories of art; because incorporated in every one of them is a debate over and argument for emphasizing or centering upon some particular feature of art which has been neglected or perverted. If we take the aesthetic theories literally, as we have seen, they all fail; but if we reconstrue them, in terms of their function and point, as serious and argued-for recommendations to concentrate on certain criteria of excellence in art, we shall see that aesthetic theory is far from worthless. Indeed, it becomes as central as anything in aesthetics, in our understanding of art, for it teaches us what to look for and how to look at it in art. What is central and must be articulated in all the theories are their debates over the reasons for excellence in art—debates over emotional depth, profound truths, natural beauty, exactitude, freshness of treatment, and so on, as criteria of evaluation—the whole of which converges on the perennial problem of what makes a work of art good. To understand the role of aesthetic theory is not to conceive it as definition, logically doomed to failure, but to read it as summaries of seriously made recommendations to attend in certain ways to certain features of art.

17

ART AS EXEMPLIFICATION: NELSON GOODMAN

In his provocatively entitled essay "When Is Art?" Nelson Goodman (1906–1998) argues that the central question in the philosophy of art is not *what* makes an object a work of art, but *when* an object becomes a work of art. Goodman's point is that an object is a work of art in virtue not of some special property it possesses, but rather of how it is employed. Goodman's view is pragmatic, because it attributes a work's status to the uses to which it is put.

The target of Goodman's argument is formalism, a view we have seen represented by Bell (Chapter 10). The formalist distinguishes properties intrinsic to a work from those that are not, arguing that only the former are aesthetically relevant. In particular, formalists assert that whatever symbolic properties a work may possess, such as its being a representation of a real object, are irrelevant to its aesthetic merit: Works that aim to represent reality have, by virtue of their accuracy alone, no claim to value as art. Against this view, Goodman holds that all works of art have symbolic properties relevant to their status as artworks. (He eschews questions of merit.) Central to his argument is the claim that exemplification is a common symbolic property. A work of art exemplifies a property when it not only possesses that property but also makes a kind of selective reference to that property. Thus, a Mondrian painting may *be* non-representational, but it exemplifies or "showcases" the property of being geometrical, a property it possesses in virtue of its obvious geometrical and pointed shapes, which call attention to its geometricality.

We can then say, according to Goodman, that a work expresses any property it exemplifies, but only metaphorically; a musical work, for example, may exemplify sadness, but it cannot literally *be* sad. But this means that even paintings declared to be nonrepresentational or purely formal symbolize because they, like the samples you find in a fabric store, exemplify some of their properties. This is something they do in certain contexts but not something that sets them apart from other types of objects in the world, for exemplification is something that ordinary things can share with artworks.

For an object to be a work of art, then, it must function as a symbol, something that it can do in some contexts but not in others. As Goodman quips, a

Rembrandt may be a work of art when it hangs in a museum but not when it is used "to replace a broken window or as a blanket." This is why the question for him is *when*—and not *what*—is art.

To this question, he supplies a tentative answer: An object is an art object when it has five characteristics: both syntactic and semantic density (all differences in an object's structure may be relevant symbolically), relative repleteness (many features of a symbol are significant), exemplification (a symbol's serving as a sample of a property it possesses), and multiple and complex reference (a symbol's performing a variety of referential functions). The details of this account are less important for our purposes than its general tenor: For Goodman, works of art do not constitute a special class of object, although they do have certain types of properties that single them out; rather, they are objects we approach in a unique way.

STUDY QUESTIONS ON THE READING

1.   What distinguishes the purist or formalist approach to works of art? What theorists have you read that are examples of such an approach? Why does Goodman think this view is mistaken? What about it does he think is correct?

2.   Why does Goodman discuss samples?

3.   Explain what Goodman means by exemplification. How can this concept explain the meaning of works that are nonrepresentational?

4.   How does Goodman's account of art help us understand why "found art" and conceptual art qualify as art? Why do such works pose a problem for traditional theories of art? Do you find Goodman's account of them satisfactory? Explain.

5.   Do you think that something can be a work of art at one time and not at another, as Goodman suggests? Why or why not?

❖

NELSON GOODMAN: WHEN IS ART?

1. THE PURE IN ART

If attempts to answer the question "What is art?" characteristically end in frustration and confusion, perhaps—as so often in philosophy—the question is the wrong one. A reconception of the problem, together with application of some results of a study of the theory of symbols, may help to clarify such moot matters as the role of symbolism in art and the status as art of the 'found object' and so-called 'conceptual art'.

One remarkable view of the relation of symbols to works of art is illustrated in an incident bitingly reported by Mary McCarthy:[1]

> Seven years ago, when I taught in a progressive college, I had a pretty girl student in one of my classes who wanted to be a short-story writer. She was not studying with me, but she knew that I sometimes wrote short stories, and one day, breathless and glowing, she came up to me in the hall, to tell me that she had just written a story that her writing teacher, a Mr. Converse, was terribly excited about. "He thinks it's wonderful" she said, "and he's going to help me fix it up for publication."
>
> I asked what the story was about; the girl was a rather simple being who loved clothes and dates. Her answer had a deprecating tone. It was about a girl (herself) and some sailors she had met on the train. But then her face, which had looked perturbed for a moment, gladdened.
>
> "Mr. Converse is going over it with me and we're going to put in the symbols."

Today the bright-eyed art student will more likely be told, with equal subtlety, to keep out the symbols; but the underlying assumption is the same: that symbols, whether enhancements or distractions, are extrinsic to the work itself. A kindred notion seems to be reflected in what we take to be symbolic art. We think first of such works as Bosch's *Garden of Delight* or Goya's *Caprichos* or the Unicorn tapestries or Dali's drooping watches, and then perhaps of religious paintings, the more mystical the better. What is remarkable here is less the association of the symbolic with the esoteric or unearthly than the classification of works as symbolic upon the basis of their having symbols as their subject matter—that is, upon the basis of their depicting rather than of being symbols. This leaves as nonsymbolic art not only works that depict nothing but also portraits, still-lifes, and landscapes where the subjects are rendered in a straightforward way without arcane allusions and do not themselves stand as symbols.

On the other hand, when we choose works for classification as nonsymbolic, as art without symbols, we confine ourselves to works without subjects; for example, to purely abstract or decorative or formal paintings or buildings or musical compositions. Works that represent anything, no matter what and no matter how prosaically, are excluded; for to represent is surely to refer, to stand for, to symbolize. Every representational work is a symbol; and art without symbols is restricted to art without subject.

That representational works are symbolic according to one usage and nonsymbolic according to another matters little so long as we do not confuse the two usages. What matters very much, though, according to many contemporary artists and critics, is to isolate the work of art as such from whatever it symbolizes or refers to in any way. Let me set forth in quotation marks, since I am offering it

---

[1] "Settling the Colonel's Hash," *Harper's Magazine*, 1954; reprinted in *On the Contrary* (Farrar, Straus and Cudahy, 1961), 225.

for consideration without now expressing any opinion of it, a composite statement of a currently much advocated program or policy or point of view:

> "What a picture symbolizes is external to it, and extraneous to the picture as a work of art. Its subject if it has one, its references—subtle or obvious—by means of symbols from some more or less well-recognized vocabulary, have nothing to do with its aesthetic or artistic significance or character. Whatever a picture refers to or stands for in any way, overt or occult, lies outside it. What really counts is not any such relationship to something else, not what the picture symbolizes, but what it is in itself—what its own intrinsic qualities are. Moreover, the more a picture focuses attention on what it symbolizes, the more we are distracted from its own properties. Accordingly, any symbolization by a picture is not only irrelevant but disturbing. Really pure art shuns all symbolization, refers to nothing, and is to be taken for just what it is, for its inherent character, not for anything it is associated with by some such remote relation as symbolization."

Such a manifesto packs punch. The counsel to concentrate on the intrinsic rather than the extrinsic, the insistence that a work of art is what it is rather than what it symbolizes, and the conclusion that pure art dispenses with external reference of all kinds have the solid sound of straight thinking, and promise to extricate art from smothering thickets of interpretation and commentary.

2. A DILEMMA

But a dilemma confronts us here. If we accept this doctrine of the formalist or purist, we seem to be saying that the content of such works as the *Garden of Delight* and the *Caprichos* doesn't really matter and might better be left out. If we reject the doctrine, we seem to be holding that what counts is not just what a work is but lots of things it isn't. In the one case we seem to be advocating lobotomy on many great works; in the other we seem to be condoning impurity in art, emphasizing the extraneous.

The best course, I think, is to recognize the purist position as all right and all wrong. But how can that be? Let's begin by agreeing that what is extraneous is extraneous. But is what a symbol symbolizes always external to it? Certainly not for symbols of all kinds. Consider the symbols:

(a) "this string of words", which stands for itself;
(b) "word", which applies to itself among other words;
(c) "short", which applies to itself and some other words and many other things; and
(d) "having seven syllables", which has seven syllables.

Obviously what some symbols symbolize does not lie entirely outside the symbols. The cases cited are, of course, quite special ones, and the analogues among pictures—that is, pictures that are pictures of themselves or include themselves in what they depict can perhaps be set aside as too rare and idiosyncratic to carry any weight. Let's agree for the present that what a work represents, except in a few cases like these, is external to it and extraneous.

Does this mean that any work that represents nothing meets the purist's demands? Not at all. In the first place, some surely symbolic works such as Bosch's paintings of weird monsters, or the tapestry of a unicorn, represent nothing; for there are no such monsters or demons or unicorns anywhere but in such pictures or in verbal descriptions. To say that the tapestry 'represents a unicorn' amounts only to saying that it is a unicorn-picture, not that there is any animal, or anything at all that it portrays. These works, even though there is nothing they represent, hardly satisfy the purist. Perhaps, though, this is just another philosopher's quibble; and I won't press the point. Let's agree that such pictures, though they represent nothing, are representational in character, hence symbolic and so not 'pure'. All the same, we must note in passing that their being representational involves no representation of anything outside them, so that the purist's objection to them cannot be on that ground. His case will have to be modified in one way or another, with some sacrifice of simplicity and force.

In the second place, not only representational works are symbolic. An abstract painting that represents nothing and is not representational at all may express, and so symbolize, a feeling or other quality, or an emotion or idea. Just because expression is a way of symbolizing something outside the painting—which does not itself sense, feel or think—the purist rejects abstract expressionist as well as representational works.

For a work to be an instance of 'pure' art, of art without symbols, it must on this view neither represent nor express nor even be representational or expressive. But is that enough? Granted, such a work does not stand for anything outside it; all it has are its own properties. But of course if we put it that way, all the properties any picture or anything else has—even such a property as that of representing a given person—are properties of the picture, not properties outside it.

The predictable response is that the important distinction among the several properties a work may have lies between its internal or intrinsic and its external or extrinsic properties; that while all are indeed its own properties, some of them obviously relate the picture to other things; and that a nonrepresentational, nonexpressive work has only internal properties.

This plainly doesn't work; for under any even faintly plausible classification of properties into internal and external, any picture or anything else has properties of both kinds. That a picture is in the Metropolitan Museum, that it was painted in Duluth, that it is younger than Methuselah, would hardly be called internal properties. Getting rid of representation and expression does not give us something free of such external or extraneous properties.

Furthermore, the very distinction between internal and external properties is a notoriously muddled one. Presumably the colors and shapes in a picture must be considered internal; but if an external property is one that relates the picture or object to something else, then colors and shapes obviously must be counted as external; for the color or shape of an object not only may be shared by other objects but also relates the object to others having the same or different colors or shapes.

Sometimes, the terms "internal" and "intrinsic" are dropped in favor of "formal". But the formal in this context cannot be a matter of shape alone. It must include color, and if color, what else? Texture? Size? Material? Of course, we may at will enumerate properties that are to be called formal; but the 'at will' gives the case away. The rationale, the justification, evaporates. The properties left out as nonformal can no longer be characterized as all and only those that relate the picture to something outside it. So we are still faced with the question what if any *principle* is involved—the question how the properties that matter in a nonrepresentational, nonexpressive painting are distinguished from the rest.

I think there is an answer to the question; but to approach it, we'll have to drop all this high-sounding talk of art and philosophy, and come down to earth with a thud.

3. SAMPLES

Consider again an ordinary swatch of textile in a tailor's or upholsterer's sample book. It is unlikely to be a work of art or to picture or express anything. It's simply a sample—a simple sample. But what is it a sample of? Texture, color, weave, thickness, fiber content . . . ; the whole point of this sample, we are tempted to say, is that it was cut from a bolt and has all the same properties as the rest of the material. But that would be too hasty.

Let me tell you two stories—or one story with two parts. Mrs. Mary Tricias studied such a sample book, made her selection, and ordered from her favorite textile shop enough material for her overstuffed chair and sofa—insisting that it be exactly like the sample. When the bundle came she opened it eagerly and was dismayed when several hundred 2″ × 3″ pieces with zigzag edges exactly like the sample fluttered to the floor. When she called the shop, protesting loudly, the proprietor replied, injured and weary, "But Mrs. Tricias, you said the material must be exactly like the sample. When it arrived from the factory yesterday, I kept my assistants here half the night cutting it up to match the sample."

This incident was nearly forgotten some months later, when Mrs. Tricias, having sewed the pieces together and covered her furniture, decided to have a party. She went to the local bakery, selected a chocolate cupcake from those on display and ordered enough for fifty guests, to be delivered two weeks later. Just as the guests were beginning to arrive, a truck drove up with a single huge cake. The lady running the bake-shop was utterly discouraged by the complaint. "But Mrs. Tricias, you have no idea how much trouble we went to. My husband runs the textile shop and he warned me that your order would have to be in one piece."

The moral of this story is not simply that you can't win, but that a sample is a sample of some of its properties but not others. The swatch is a sample of texture, color, etc. but not of size or shape. The cupcake is a sample of color, texture, size, and shape, but still not of all its properties. Mrs. Tricias would have complained even more loudly if what was delivered to her was like the sample in having been baked on that same day two weeks earlier.

Now in general which of its properties is a sample a sample of? Not all its properties; for then the sample would be a sample of nothing but itself. And not its 'formal' or 'internal' or, indeed, any one specifiable set of properties. The kind of property sampled differs from case to case: the cupcake but not the swatch is a sample of size and shape; a specimen of ore may be a sample of what was mined at a given time and place. Moreover, the sampled properties vary widely with context and circumstance. Although the swatch is normally a sample of its texture, etc. but not of its shape or size, if I show it to you in answer to the question "What is an upholsterer's sample?" it then functions not as a sample of the material but as a sample of an upholsterer's sample, so that its size and shape are now among the properties it is a sample of.

In sum, the point is that a sample is a sample of—or *exemplifies*—only some of its properties, and that the properties to which it bears this relationship of exemplification vary with circumstances and can only be distinguished as those properties that it serves, under the given circumstances, as a sample of. Being a sample of or exemplifying is a relationship something like that of being a friend; my friends are not distinguished by any single identifiable property or cluster of properties, but only by standing, for a period of time, in the relationship of friendship with me.

The implications for our problem concerning works of art may now be apparent. The properties that count in a purist painting are those that the picture makes manifest, selects, focuses upon, exhibits, heightens in our consciousness—those that it shows forth—in short, those properties that it does not merely possess but *exemplifies*, stands as a sample of.

If I am right about this, then even the purist's purest painting symbolizes. It exemplifies certain of its properties. But to exemplify is surely to symbolize—exemplification no less than representation or expression is a form of reference. A work of art, however free of representation and expression, is still a symbol even though what it symbolizes be not things or people or feelings but certain patterns of shape, color, texture that it shows forth.

What, then, of the purist's initial pronouncement that I said facetiously is all right and all wrong? It is all right in saying that what is extraneous is extraneous, in pointing out that what a picture represents often matters very little, in arguing that neither representation nor expression is required of a work, and in stressing the importance of so-called intrinsic or internal or 'formal' properties. But the statement is all wrong in assuming that representation and expression are the only symbolic functions that paintings may perform, in supposing that what a symbol symbolizes is always outside it, and in insisting that what counts in a painting is the mere possession rather than the exemplification of certain properties.

Whoever looks for art without symbols, then, will find none—if all the ways that works symbolize are taken into account. Art without representation or expression or exemplification—yes; art without all three—*no*.

To point out that purist art consists simply in the avoidance of certain kinds of symbolization is not to condemn it but only to uncover the fallacy in the usual manifestos advocating purist art to the exclusion of all other kinds.

I am not debating the relative virtues of different schools or types or ways of painting. What seems to me more important is that recognition of the symbolic function of even purist painting gives us a clue to the perennial problem of when we do and when we don't have a work of art.

The literature of aesthetics is littered with desperate attempts to answer the question "What is art?" This question, often hopelessly confused with the question "What is good art?", is acute in the case of found art—the stone picked out of the driveway and exhibited in a museum—and is further aggravated by the promotion of so-called environmental and conceptual art. Is a smashed automobile fender in an art gallery a work of art? What of something that is not even an object, and not exhibited in any gallery or museum—for example, the digging and filling-in of a hole in Central Park as prescribed by Oldenburg? If these are works of art, then are all stones in the driveway and all objects and occurrences works of art? If not, what distinguishes what is from what is not a work of art? That an artist calls it a work of art? That it is exhibited in a museum or gallery? No such answer carries any conviction.

As I remarked at the outset, part of the trouble lies in asking the wrong question—in failing to recognize that a thing may function as a work of art at some times and not at others. In crucial cases, the real question is not "What objects are (permanently) works of art?" but "When is an object a work of art?"—or more briefly, as in my title, "When is art?"

My answer is that just as an object may be a symbol—for instance, a sample—at certain times and under certain circumstances and not at others, so an object may be a work of art at some times and not at others. Indeed, just by virtue of functioning as a symbol in a certain way does an object become, while so functioning, a work of art. The stone is normally no work of art while in the driveway, but may be so when on display in an art museum. In the driveway, it usually performs no symbolic function. In the art museum, it exemplifies certain of its properties—e.g., properties of shape, color, texture. The hole-digging and filling functions as a work insofar as our attention is directed to it as an exemplifying symbol. On the other hand, a Rembrandt painting may cease to function as a work of art when used to replace a broken window or as a blanket.

Now, of course, to function as a symbol in some way or other is not in itself to function as a work of art. Our swatch, when serving as a sample, does not then and thereby become a work of art. Things function as works of art only when their symbolic functioning has certain characteristics. Our stone in a museum of geology takes on symbolic functions as a sample of the stones of a given period, origin, or composition, but it is not then functioning as a work of art.

The question just what characteristics distinguish or are indicative of the symbolizing that constitutes functioning as a work of art calls for careful study in the light of a general theory of symbols. That is more than I can undertake here, but I venture the tentative thought that there are five symptoms of the aesthetic: (1) syntactic density, where the finest differences in certain respects constitute a difference between symbols—for example, an ungraduated mercury thermometer as contrasted with an electronic digital read-out instrument; (2) semantic density, where symbols are provided for things distinguished by the finest differences in certain respects—for example, not only the ungraduated thermometer again but also ordinary English, though it is not syntactically dense; (3) relative repleteness, where comparatively many aspects of a symbol are significant—for example, a single-line drawing of a mountain by Hokusai where every feature of shape, line, thickness, etc. counts, in contrast with perhaps the same line as a chart of daily stockmarket averages, where all that counts is the height of the line above the base; (4) exemplification, where a symbol, whether or not it denotes, symbolizes by serving as a sample of properties it literally or metaphorically possesses; and finally (5) multiple and complex reference, where a symbol performs several integrated and interacting referential functions,[2] some direct and some mediated through other symbols.

These symptoms provide no definition, much less a full-blooded description or a celebration. Presence or absence of one or more of them does not qualify or disqualify anything as aesthetic; nor does the extent to which these features are present measure the extent to which an object or experience is aesthetic.[3] Symptoms, after all, are but clues; the patient may have the symptoms without the disease, or the disease without the symptoms. And even for these five symptoms to come somewhere near being disjunctively necessary and conjunctively (as a syndrome) sufficient might well call for some redrawing of the vague and vagrant borderlines of the aesthetic. Still, notice that these properties tend to focus attention on the symbol rather than, or at least along with, what it refers to. Where we can never determine precisely just which symbol of a system we have or whether we have the same one on a second occasion, where the referent is so elusive that properly fitting a symbol to it requires endless care, where more rather than fewer features of the symbol count, where the symbol is an instance of properties it symbolizes and may perform many interrelated simple and complex referential functions, we cannot merely look through the symbol to what it refers to as we do in obeying traffic lights or reading scientific texts, but must attend constantly to the symbol itself as in seeing paintings or reading poetry. This emphasis upon the nontransparency of a work of art, upon the primacy of the work over what it refers to, far from involving denial or disregard of symbolic functions, derives from certain characteristics of a work as a symbol.[4]

Quite apart from specifying the particular characteristics differentiating aesthetic from other symbolization, the answer to the question "When is art?" thus seems to me clearly to be in terms of symbolic function. Perhaps to say that an object is art when and only when it so functions is to overstate the case or to speak elliptically. The Rembrandt painting remains a work of art, as it remains a painting, while functioning only as a blanket; and the stone from the

---

[2] This excludes ordinary ambiguity, where a term has two or more quite independent denotations at quite different times and in quite different contexts.

[3] That poetry, for example, which is not syntactically dense, is less art or less likely to be art than painting that exhibits all four symptoms thus does not at all follow. Some aesthetic symbols may have fewer of the symptoms than some nonaesthetic symbols. This is sometimes misunderstood.

[4] This is another version of the dictum that the purist is all right and all wrong.

driveway may not strictly become art by functioning as art.[5] Similarly, a chair remains a chair even if never sat on, and a packing case remains a packing case even if never used except for sitting on. To say what art does is not to say what art is; but I submit that the former is the matter of primary and peculiar concern. The further question of defining stable property in terms of ephemeral function—the what in terms of the when—is not confined to the arts but is quite general, and is the same for defining chairs as for defining objects of art. The parade of instant and inadequate answers is also much the same: that whether an object is art—or a chair—depends upon intent or upon whether it sometimes or usually or always or exclusively functions as such. Because all this tends to obscure more special and significant questions concerning art, I have turned my attention from what art is to what art does.

A salient feature of symbolization, I have urged, is that it may come and go. An object may symbolize different things at different times, and nothing at other times. An inert or purely utilitarian object may come to function as art, and a work of art may come to function as an inert or purely utilitarian object. Perhaps, rather than art being long and life short, both are transient.

---

[5] Just as what is not red may look or be said to be red *at certain times,* so what is not art may function as or be said to be art at certain times. That an object functions as art at a given time, that it has the status of art at that time, and that it is art at that time may all be taken as saying the same thing—so long as we take none of these as ascribing to the object any stable status.

18

ART AS THEORY: ARTHUR DANTO

Post-World War II developments offered a distinct challenge to previous theories of art. Abstract expressionism, pop art, minimalism—these and many other schools produced works that seemed to violate the boundary between art and non-art. How could a large painting consisting of nothing more than two large criss-crossing black brushstrokes on a white background be called art? What about a carton that looks, to all intents and purposes, just like the Brillo carton in the storage area of your local supermarket? Was there anything that could *not* be art? And if anything could be art, was art itself still a meaningful concept?

One of the first philosophers to take up the challenge proffered by contemporary art was Arthur Danto (b. 1924), philosopher and much admired art critic for *The Nation* magazine. His essay, "The Artworld," not only takes contemporary art seriously, but also changed the terms of debate about the nature of art.

Central to Danto's work is the question "What distinguishes an artwork—such as Warhol's *Brillo Box*—from the real thing, in this case a carton containing boxes of soap pads?" This is the problem of perceptually indistinguishable counterparts. It asks, if we can't see any perceptible difference between an artwork and the real thing, why isn't the box on the supermarket shelf also artwork?

Danto's answer has two important elements: The first has to do with theories of art; the second, with what he calls "the artworld."

The role of a theory of art in validating something as an artwork goes like this: Object A, although perceptually indistinguishable from object B, is an artwork because of the existence of a theory and interpretation under which A is an artwork. Although Danto talks in this essay of artistic theories, his meaning becomes clearer if we substitute the idea of artistic interpretations.

The reason that Warhol's *Brillo Box* is a work of art, whereas the actual box is not, is that there is an interpretation of the former under which it possesses distinctive ontological properties. For example, the Warhol box may have the property of referring to the mass production of consumer goods in postwar America. The Brillo box, while perceptually indistinguishable from Warhol's, is just a box and lacks that property. According to Danto, works of art, themselves real objects, also have properties their counterparts lack.

The second element of Danto's solution to the problem of perceptually indistinguishable counterparts—the artworld—is comprised of "an atmosphere of artistic theory, a knowledge of the history of art." This is not a very precise claim, but it can be unpacked as follows: To understand an object as a work of art, one has to have knowledge of both the history and theory of art. This is because to be an artwork requires that the object occupy a place in the history of art, something that it does in virtue of the presence of a theory (or interpretation). Without a prior understanding of art history and theory—in short, of the artworld—a viewer could not see an object *as* a work of art.

Danto's claim here mirrors Heidegger's in "The Origin of the Work of Art" (Chapter 13): What Heidegger refers to as "art" and posits as the origin of the *work* of art is akin to what Danto refers to as the artworld. Both suggest that individual works of art can be identified as such only because of the existence of a prior set of norms governing their production and interpretation.

Danto's theory has been enormously influential. For many philosophers, it marks a new beginning in the attempt to understand art's nature, restoring the work to its world.

STUDY QUESTIONS ON THE READING

1. What is the imitation theory of art (IT)? Of the philosophers you have read, which hold it? What criticisms does Danto make of it? Do you agree?

2. What is the realist theory of art (RT)? Of the philosophers you have read, which hold it? Which artworks does Danto see as having established its validity?

3. Danto invents a character called Testadura who mistakes an artwork for a real thing. How does Danto explain Testadura's mistake?

4. What does Danto mean by the "*is* of artistic identification"? How is this sense of *is* different from other senses of that word?

5. What is the artworld? What role does it have in constituting works of art?

6. What role does Danto see for artistic theories in constituting works of art?

7. What does Danto see as Andy Warhol's significance? Do you agree? Why or why not?

ARTHUR DANTO: THE ARTWORLD

HAMLET: Do you see nothing there?
THE QUEEN: Nothing at all; yet all that is I see.

SHAKESPEARE: HAMLET, ACT III, SCENE IV

Hamlet and Socrates, though in praise and deprecation respectively, spoke of art as a mirror held up to nature. As with many disagreements in attitude, this one has a factual basis. Socrates saw mirrors as but reflecting what we can already see; so art, insofar as mirrorlike, yields idle accurate duplications of the appearances of things, and is of no cognitive benefit whatever. Hamlet, more acutely, recognized a remarkable feature of reflecting surfaces, namely that they show us what we could not otherwise perceive—our own face and form—and so art, insofar as it is mirrorlike, reveals us to ourselves, and is, even by socratic criteria, of some cognitive utility after all. As a philosopher, however, I find Socrates' discussion defective on other, perhaps less profound grounds than these. If a mirror-image of *o* is indeed an imitation of *o*, then, if art is imitation, mirror-images are art. But in fact mirroring objects no more is art than returning weapons to a madman is justice; and reference to mirrorings would be just the sly sort of counterinstance we would expect Socrates to bring forward in rebuttal of the theory he instead uses them to illustrate. If that theory requires us to class *these* as art, it thereby shows its inadequacy: "is an imitation" will not do as a sufficient condition for "is art." Yet, perhaps because artists *were* engaged in imitation, in Socrates' time and after, the insufficiency of the theory was not noticed until the invention of photography. Once rejected as a sufficient condition, mimesis was quickly discarded as even a necessary one; and since the achievement of Kandinsky, mimetic features have been relegated to the periphery of critical concern, so much so that some works survive in spite of possessing those virtues, excellence in which was once celebrated as the essence of art narrowly escaping demotion to mere illustrations.

It is, of course, indispensable in socratic discussion that all participants be masters of the concept up for analysis, since the aim is to match a real defining expression to a term in active use, and the test for adequacy presumably consists in showing that the former analyzes and applies to all and only those things of which the latter is true. The popular disclaimer notwithstanding, then, Socrates' auditors purportedly knew what art was as well as what they liked; and a theory of art, regarded here as a real definition of 'Art', is accordingly not to be of great use in helping men to recognize instances of its application. Their antecedent ability to do this is precisely what the adequacy of the theory is to be tested against, the problem being only to make explicit what they already know. It is *our* use of the term that the theory allegedly means to capture, but we are supposed able, in the words of a recent writer, "to separate those objects which are works of art from those which are not, because . . . we know how correctly to use the word 'art' and to apply the phrase 'work of art'." Theories, on this account, are somewhat like mirror-images on Socrates' account, showing forth what we already know, wordy reflections of the actual linguistic practice we are masters in.

But telling artworks from other things is not so simple a matter, even for native speakers, and these days one might not be aware he was on artistic terrain without an artistic theory to tell him so. And part of the reason for this lies in the fact that terrain is constituted artistic in virtue of artistic theories, so that one use of theories, in addition to helping us discriminate art from the rest, consists in making art possible. Glaucon and the others could hardly have known what was art and what not: otherwise they would never have been taken in by mirror-images.

I

Suppose one thinks of the discovery of a whole new class of artworks as something analogous to the discovery of a whole new class of facts anywhere, viz., as something for theoreticians to explain. In science, as elsewhere, we often accommodate new facts to old theories via auxiliary hypotheses, a pardonable enough conservatism when the theory in question is deemed too valuable to be jettisoned all at once. Now the Imitation Theory of Art (IT) is, if one but thinks it through, an exceedingly powerful theory, explaining a great many phenomena connected with the causation and evaluation of artworks, bringing a surprising unity into a complex domain. Moreover, it is a simple matter to shore it up against many purported counterinstances by such auxiliary hypotheses as that the artist who deviates from mimeticity is perverse, inept, or mad. Ineptitude, chicanery, or folly are, in fact, testable predications. Suppose, then, tests reveal that these hypotheses fail to hold, that the theory, now beyond repair, must be replaced. And a new theory is worked out, capturing what it can of the old theory's competence, together with the heretofore recalcitrant facts. One might, thinking along these lines, represent certain episodes in the history of art as not dissimilar to certain episodes in the history of science, where a conceptual revolution is being effected and where refusal to countenance certain facts, while in part due to prejudice, inertia, and self-interest, is due also to the fact that a well-established, or at least widely credited theory is being threatened in such a way that all coherence goes.

Some such episode transpired with the advent of post-impressionist paintings. In terms of the prevailing artistic theory (IT), it was impossible to accept these as art unless inept art: otherwise they could be discounted as hoaxes, self-advertisements, or the visual counterparts of madmen's ravings. So to get them accepted *as* art, on a footing with the *Transfiguration* (not to speak of a

Landseer stag), required not so much a revolution in taste as a theoretical revision of rather considerable proportions, involving not only the artistic enfranchisement of these objects, but an emphasis upon newly significant features of accepted artworks, so that quite different accounts of their status as artworks would now have to be given. As a result of the new theory's acceptance, not only were post-impressionist paintings taken up as art, but numbers of objects (masks, weapons, etc.) were transferred from anthropological museums (and heterogeneous other places) to *musées des beaux arts,* though, as we would expect from the fact that a criterion for the acceptance of a new theory is that it account for whatever the older one did, nothing had to be transferred out of the *musée des beaux arts*—even if there were internal rearrangements as between storage rooms and exhibition space. Countless native speakers hung upon suburban mantelpieces innumerable replicas of paradigm cases for teaching the expression 'work of art' that would have sent their Edwardian forebears into linguistic apoplexy.

To be sure, I distort by speaking of a theory: historically, there were several, all, interestingly enough, more or less defined in terms of the IT. Art-historical complexities must yield before the exigencies of logical exposition, and I shall speak as though there were one replacing theory, partially compensating for historical falsity by choosing one which was actually enunciated. According to it, the artists in question were to be understood not as unsuccessfully imitating real forms but as successfully creating new ones, quite as real as the forms which the older art had been thought, in its best examples, to be creditably imitating. Art, after all, had long since been thought of as creative (Vasari says that God was the first artist), and the post-impressionists were to be explained as genuinely creative, aiming, in Roger Fry's words, "not at illusion but reality." This theory (RT) furnished a whole new mode of looking at painting, old and new. Indeed, one might almost interpret the crude drawing in Van Gogh and Cézanne, the dislocation of form from contour in Rouault and Dufy, the arbitrary use of color planes in Gauguin and the Fauves, as so many ways of drawing attention to the fact that these were *nonimitations,* specifically intended not to deceive. Logically, this would be roughly like printing "Not Legal Tender" across a brilliantly counterfeited dollar bill, the resulting object (counterfeit *cum* inscription) rendered incapable of deceiving anyone. It is not an illusory dollar bill, but then, just because it is non-illusory it does not automatically become a real dollar bill either. It rather occupies a freshly opened area between real objects and real facsimiles of real objects: it is a non-facsimile, if one requires a word, and a new contribution to the world. Thus, Van Gogh's *Potato Eaters,* as a consequence of certain unmistakable distortions, turns out to be a non-facsimile of real-life potato eaters; and inasmuch as these are not facsimiles of potato eaters, Van Gogh's picture, as a non-imitation, had as much right to be called a real object as did its putative subjects. By means of this theory (RT), artworks re-entered the thick of things from which socratic theory (IT) had sought to evict them: if no *more* real than what carpenters wrought, they were at least no *less* real. The Post-Impressionist won a victory in ontology.

It is in terms of RT that we must understand the artworks around us today. Thus Roy Lichtenstein paints comic-strip panels, though ten or twelve feet high. These are reasonably faithful projections onto a gigantesque scale of the homely frames from the daily tabloid, but it is precisely the scale that counts. A skilled engraver might incise *The Virgin and the Chancellor Rollin* on a pin-head, and it would be recognizable as such to the keen of sight, but an engraving of a Barnett Newman on a similar scale would be a blob, disappearing in the reduction. A *photograph* of a Lichtenstein is indiscernible from a photograph of a counterpart panel from *Steve Canyon;* but the photograph fails to capture the scale, and hence is as inaccurate a reproduction as a black-and-white engraving of Botticelli, scale being essential here as color there. Lichtensteins, then, are not imitations but *new entities,* as giant whelks would be. Jasper Johns, by contrast, paints objects with respect to which questions of scale are irrelevant. Yet his objects cannot be imitations, for they have the remarkable property that any intended copy of a member of this class of objects is automatically a member of the class itself, so that these objects are logically inimitable. Thus, a copy of a numeral just *is* that numeral: a painting of 3 is a 3 made of paint. Johns, in addition, paints targets, flags, and maps. Finally, in what I hope are not unwitting footnotes to Plato, two of our pioneers—Robert Rauschenberg and Claes Oldenburg—have made genuine beds.

Rauschenberg's bed hangs on a wall, and is streaked with some desultory housepaint. Oldenburg's bed is a rhomboid, narrower at one end than the other, with what one might speak of as a built-in perspective: ideal for small bedrooms. As beds, these sell at singularly inflated prices, but one *could* sleep in either of them: Rauschenberg has expressed the fear that someone might just climb into his bed and fall asleep. Imagine, now, a certain Testadura—a plain speaker and noted philistine—who is not aware that these are art, and who takes them to be reality simple and pure. He attributes the paintstreaks on Rauschenberg's bed to the slovenliness of the owner, and the bias in the Oldenburg bed to the ineptitude of the builder or the whimsy, perhaps, of whoever had it "custom-made." These would be mistakes, but mistakes of rather an odd kind, and not terribly different from that made by the stunned birds who pecked the sham grapes of Zeuxis. They mistook art for reality, and so has Testadura. But it was meant to *be* reality, according to RT. Can one have mistaken reality for reality? How shall we describe Testadura's error? What, after all, prevents Oldenburg's creation from being a misshapen bed? This is equivalent to asking what makes it art, and with this query we enter a domain of conceptual inquiry where native speakers are poor guides: *they* are lost themselves.

II

To mistake an artwork for a real object is no great feat when an artwork is the real object one mistakes it for. The problem is how to avoid such errors, or to remove them once they are made. The artwork is a bed, and not a bed-illusion; so there is nothing like the traumatic encounter against a flat surface that brought it home to the birds of Zeuxis that they had been duped. Except for the guard cautioning Testadura not to sleep on the artworks, he might never have discovered that this was an artwork and not a bed; and since, after all, one cannot discover that a bed is not a bed, how is Testadura to realize that he has made an error? A certain sort of explanation is required, for the error here is a curiously philosophical one, rather like, if we may assume as correct some well-known views of P. F. Strawson, mistaking a person for a material body when the truth is that a person *is* a material body in the sense that a whole class of predicates, sensibly applicable to material bodies, are sensibly, and by appeal to no different criteria, applicable to persons. So you cannot *discover* that a person is not a material body.

We begin by explaining, perhaps, that the paintstreaks are not to be explained away, that they are *part* of the object, so the object is not a mere bed with—as it happens—streaks of paint spilled over it, but a complex object fabricated out of a bed and some paintstreaks: a paint-bed. Similarly, a person is not a material body with—as it happens—some thoughts superadded, but is a complex entity made up of a body and some conscious states: a conscious-body. Persons, like artworks, must then be taken as irreducible to *parts* of themselves, and are in that sense primitive. Or, more accurately, the paintstreaks are not part of the real object—the bed—which happens to be part of the artwork, but are, *like* the bed, part of the artwork as such. And this might be generalized into a rough characterization of artworks that happen to contain real objects as parts of themselves: not every part of an artwork A is part of a real object R when R is part of A and can, moreover, be detached from A and seen *merely* as R. The mistake thus far will have been to mistake A for *part* of itself, namely R, even though it would not be incorrect to say that A is R, that the artwork is a bed. It is the 'is' which requires clarification here.

There is an *is* that figures prominently in statements concerning artworks which is not the *is* of either identity or predication; nor is it the *is* of existence, of identification, or some special *is* made up to serve a philosophic end. Nevertheless, it is in common usage, and is readily mastered by children. It is the sense of *is* in accordance with which a child, shown a circle and a triangle and asked which is him and which his sister, will point to the triangle saying "That is me"; or, in response to my question, the person next to me points to the man in purple and says "That one is Lear"; or in the gallery I point, for my companion's benefit, to a spot in the painting before us and say "That white dab is Icarus." We do not mean, in these instances, that whatever is pointed to stands for, or represents, what it is said to be, for the *word* 'Icarus' stands for or represents Icarus: yet I would not in the same sense of *is* point to the word and say "That is Icarus." The sentence "That *a* is *b*" is perfectly compatible with "That *a* is not *b*" when the first employs this sense of *is* and the second employs some other, though *a* and *b* are used nonambiguously throughout. Often, indeed, the truth of the first *requires* the truth of the second. The first, in fact, is incompatible with "That *a* is not *b*" only when the *is* is used nonambiguously throughout. For want of a word I shall designate this the *is of artistic identification*; in each case in which it is used, the *a* stands for some specific physical property of, or physical part of, an object; and, finally, it is a necessary condition for something to be an artwork that some part or property of it be designable by the subject of a sentence that employs this special *is*. It is an *is*, incidentally, which has near-relatives in marginal and mythical pronouncements. (Thus, one *is* Quetzalcoatl; those *are* the Pillars of Hercules.)

Let me illustrate. Two painters are asked to decorate the east and west walls of a science library with frescoes to be respectively called *Newton's First Law* and *Newton's Third Law*. These paintings, when finally unveiled, look, scale apart, as follows:

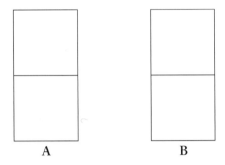

A   B

As objects I shall suppose the works to be indiscernible: a black, horizontal line on a white ground, equally large in each dimension and element. *B* explains his work as follows: a mass, pressing downward, is met by a mass pressing upward: the lower mass reacts equally and oppositely to the upper one. *A* explains his work as follows: the line through the space is the path of an isolated particle. The path goes from edge to edge, to give the sense of its *going beyond*. If it ended or began within the space, the line would be curved: and it is parallel to the top and bottom edges, for if it were closer to one than to another, there would have to be a force accounting for it, and this is inconsistent with its being the path of an *isolated* particle.

Much follows from these artistic identifications. To regard the middle line as an edge (mass meeting mass) imposes the need to identify the top and bottom half of the picture as rectangles, and as two distinct parts (not necessarily as two masses, for the line could be the edge of *one* mass jutting up—or down—into empty space). If it is an edge, we cannot thus take the entire area of the painting as a single space: it is rather composed of two forms, or one form and a non-form. We could take the entire area as a single space only by taking the middle horizontal as a *line* which is not an edge. But this almost requires a three-dimensional identification of the whole picture: the area can be a flat surface which the line is *above* (*Jet-flight*), or *below* (*Submarine-path*), or *on* (*Line*), or *in* (*Fissure*), or *through* (*Newton's First Law*)—though in this last case the area is not a flat surface but a transparent cross section of absolute space. We could make all these prepositional qualifications clear by imagining perpendicular cross sections to the picture plane. Then, depending upon the applicable prepositional clause, the area is (artistically) interrupted or not by the horizontal element. If we take the line as *through* space, the edges of the picture are not really the edges of the space: the space goes beyond the picture if the line itself does; and we are in the same space as the line is. As *B*, the edges of the picture can be *part* of the picture in case the masses go right to the edges, so that the edges of the picture are *their* edges. In that case, the vertices of the picture would be the vertices of the masses, except that the masses have four vertices more than the picture itself does: here four vertices would be part of the art work which were not part of the real object. Again, the faces of the masses could be the face of the picture, and in looking at the picture, we are looking at these faces: but *space* has no face, and on the reading of *A* the work has to be read as faceless, and the face of the physical object would not be part of the artwork. Notice here how one artistic identification engenders another artistic identification, and how, consistently with a given identification, we are *required* to give others and *precluded* from still others: indeed, a given identification determines how many elements the work is to contain. These different identifications are incompatible with one another, or generally so, and each might be said to make a different artwork, even though each artwork contains the identical real object as part of itself—or at least parts of the identical real object as parts of itself. There are, of course, senseless identifications: no one could, I think, sensibly read the middle horizontal as *Love's Labour's Lost* or *The Ascendency of St. Erasmus.* Finally, notice how acceptance of one identification rather than another is in effect to exchange one *world* for another. We could, indeed, enter a quiet poetic world by identifying the upper area with a clear and cloudless sky, reflected in the still surface of the water below, whiteness kept from whiteness only by the unreal boundary of the horizon.

And now Testadura, having hovered in the wings throughout this discussion, protests that *all he sees is paint*: a white painted oblong with a black line painted across it. And how right he really is: that is all he sees or that anybody can, we aesthetes included. So, if he asks us to show him what there is further to see, to demonstrate through pointing that this is an artwork (*Sea and Sky*), we cannot comply, for he has overlooked nothing (and it would be absurd to suppose he had, that there was something tiny we could point to and he, peering closely, say "So it is! A work of art after all!"). We cannot help him until he has mastered the *is of artistic identification* and so *constitutes* it a work of art. If he cannot achieve this, he will never look upon artworks: he will be like a child who sees sticks as sticks.

But what about pure abstractions, say something that looks just like *A* but is entitled No. 7? The 10th Street abstractionist blankly insists that there is nothing here but white paint and black, and none of our literary identifications need apply. What then distinguishes him from Testadura, whose philistine utterances are indiscernible from his? And how can it be an artwork for him and not for Testadura, when they agree that there is nothing that does not meet the eye? The answer, unpopular as it is likely to be to purists of every variety, lies in the fact that this artist has returned to the physicality of paint through an atmosphere compounded of artistic theories and the history of recent and remote painting, elements of which he is trying to refine out of his own work; and as a consequence of this his work belongs in this atmosphere and is part of this history. He has achieved abstraction through rejection of artistic identifications, returning to the real world from which such identifications remove us (he thinks), somewhat in the mode of Ch'ing Yuan, who wrote:

> Before I had studied Zen for thirty years, I saw mountains as mountains and waters as waters. When I arrived at a more intimate knowledge, I came to the point where I saw that mountains are not mountains, and waters are not waters. But now that I have got the very substance I am at rest. For it is just that I see mountains once again as mountains, and waters once again as waters.

His identification of what he has made is logically dependent upon the theories and history he rejects. The difference between his utterance and Testadura's "This is black paint and white paint and nothing more" lies in the fact that he is still using the *is* of artistic identification, so that his use of "That black paint is black paint" is not a tautology. Testadura is not at that stage. To see something as art requires something the eye cannot decry—an atmosphere of artistic theory, a knowledge of the history of art: an artworld.

III

Mr. Andy Warhol, the Pop artist, displays facsimiles of Brillo cartons, piled high, in neat stacks, as in the stockroom of the supermarket. They happen to be of wood, painted to look like cardboard, and why not? To paraphrase the critic of the *Times,* if one may make the facsimile of a human being out of bronze, why not the facsimile of a Brillo carton out of plywood? The cost of these boxes happens to be 2×10^3 that of their homely counterparts in real life—a differential hardly ascribable to their advantage in durability. In fact the Brillo people might, at some slight increase in cost, make their boxes out of plywood without these becoming artworks, and Warhol might make *his* out of cardboard without their ceasing to be art. So we may forget questions of intrinsic value, and ask why the Brillo people cannot manufacture art and why Warhol cannot *but* make artworks. Well, his are made by hand, to be sure. Which is like an insane reversal of Picasso's strategy in pasting the label from a bottle of Suze onto a drawing, saying as it were that the academic artist, concerned with exact imitation, must always fall short of the real thing: so why not just *use* the real thing? The Pop artist laboriously reproduces machinemade objects by hand, e.g., painting the labels on coffee cans (one can hear the familiar commendation "Entirely made by hand" falling painfully out of the guide's vocabulary when confronted by these objects). But the difference cannot consist in craft: a man who carved pebbles out of stones and carefully constructed a work called *Gravel Pile* might invoke the labor theory of value to account for the price he demands; but the question is, What makes it art? And why need Warhol *make* these things anyway? Why not just scrawl his signature across one? Or crush one up and display it as *Crushed Brillo Box* ("A protest against mechanization . . .") or simply display a Brillo carton as *Uncrushed Brillo Box* ("A bold affirmation of the plastic authenticity of industrial . . .")? Is this man a kind of Midas, turning whatever he touches into the gold of pure art? And the whole world consisting of latent artworks waiting, like the bread and wine of reality, to be transfigured, through some dark mystery, into the indiscernible flesh and blood of the sacrament? Never mind that the Brillo box may not be good, much less great art. The impressive thing is that it is art at all. But if it is, why are not the indiscernible Brillo boxes that are in the stockroom? Or *has* the whole distinction between art and reality broken down?

Suppose a man collects objects (ready-mades), including a Brillo carton; we praise the exhibit for variety, ingenuity, what you will. Next he exhibits nothing but Brillo cartons, and we criticize it as dull, repetitive, self-plagiarizing—or (more profoundly) claim that he is obsessed by regularity and repetition, as in *Marienbad*. Or he piles them high, leaving a narrow path; we tread our way through the smooth opaque stacks and find it an unsettling experience, and write it up as the closing in of consumer products, confining us as prisoners: or we say he is a modern pyramid builder. True, we don't say these things about the stockboy. But then a stockroom is not an art gallery, and we cannot readily separate the Brillo cartons from the gallery they are in, any more than we can separate the Rauschenberg bed from the paint upon it. Outside the gallery, they are pasteboard cartons. But then, scoured clean of paint, Rauschenberg's bed is a bed, just what it was before it was transformed into art. But then if we think this matter through, we discover that the artist has failed, really and of necessity, to produce a mere real object. He has produced an artwork, his use of real Brillo cartons being but an expansion of the resources available to artists, a contribution to *artists' materials,* as oil paint was, or *tuche.*

What in the end makes the difference between a Brillo box and a work of art consisting of a Brillo Box is a certain theory of art. It is the theory that takes it up into the world of art, and keeps it from collapsing into the real object which it is (in a sense of *is* other than that of artistic identification). Of course, without the theory, one is unlikely to see it as art, and in order to see it as part of the artworld, one must have mastered a good deal of artistic theory as well as a considerable amount of the history of recent New York painting. It could not have been art fifty years ago. But then there could not have been, everything being equal, flight insurance in the Middle Ages, or Etruscan typewriter erasers. The world has to be ready for certain things, the artworld no less than the real one. It is the role of artistic theories, these days as always, to make the artworld, and art, possible. It would, I should think, never have occurred to the painters of Lascaux that they were producing *art* on those walls. Not unless there were neolithic aestheticians.

IV

The artworld stands to the real world in something like the relationship in which the City of God stands to the Earthly City. Certain objects, like certain individuals, enjoy a double citizenship, but there remains, the RT notwithstanding, a fundamental contrast between artworks and real objects. Perhaps this was already dimly sensed by the early framers of the IT who, inchoately realizing the nonreality of art, were perhaps limited only in supposing that the sole way objects had of being other than real is to be sham, so that artworks necessarily had to be imitations of real objects. This was too narrow. So Yeats saw in writing "Once out of nature I shall never take / My bodily form from any natural thing." It is but a matter of choice: and the Brillo box of the artworld may be just the Brillo box of the real one, separated and united by the *is* of artistic identification. But I should like to say some final words about the theories that make artworks possible, and their relationship to one another. In so doing, I shall beg some of the hardest philosophical questions I know.

*　*　*

I shall now think of pairs of predicates related to each other as "opposites," conceding straight off the vagueness of this *demodé* term. Contradictory predicates are not opposites, since one of each of them must apply to every object in the universe, and neither of a pair of opposites need apply to some objects in the universe. An object must first be of a certain kind before either of a pair of opposites applies to it, and then at most and at least one of the opposites must apply to it. So opposites are not contraries, for contraries may both be false of some objects in the universe, but opposites cannot both be false; for of some objects, neither of a pair of opposites *sensibly* applies, unless the object is of the right sort. Then, if the object is of the required kind, the opposites behave as contradictories. If F and non-F are opposites, an object o must be of a certain kind K before either of these sensibly applies; but if o is a member of K, then o either is F or non-F, to the exclusion of the other. The class of pairs of opposites that sensibly apply to the ($\hat{o}$) Ko I shall designate as the class of K-*relevant predicates*. And a necessary condition for an object to be of a kind K is that at least one pair of K-relevant opposites be sensibly applicable to it. But, in fact, if an object is of kind K, at least and at most one of each K-relevant pair of opposites applies to it.

I am now interested in the K-relevant predicates for the class K of artworks. And let F and non-F be an opposite pair of such predicates. Now it might happen that, throughout an entire period of time, every artwork is non-F. But since nothing thus far is both an artwork and F, it might never occur to anyone that non-F is an artistically relevant predicate. The non-F-ness of artworks goes unmarked. By contrast, all works up to a given time might be G, it never occurring to anyone until that time that something might both be an artwork and non-G; indeed, it might have been thought that G was a *defining trait* of artworks when in fact something might first have to be an artwork before G is sensibly predicable of it—in which case non-G might also be predicable of artworks, and G itself then could not have been a defining trait of this class.

Let F be 'is representational' and let G be 'is expressionist'. At a given time, these and their opposites are perhaps the only art-relevant predicates in critical use. Now letting '+' stand for a given predicate P and '−' for its opposite non-P, we may construct a style matrix more or less as follows:

F	G
+	+
+	−
−	+
−	−

The rows determine available styles, given the active critical vocabulary: representational expressionistic (e.g., Fauvism); representational nonexpressionistic (Ingres); nonrepresentational expressionistic (Abstract Expressionism); nonrepresentational nonexpressionist (hard-edge abstraction). Plainly, as we add art-relevant predicates, we increase the number of available styles at the rate of 2^n. It is, of course, not easy to see in advance which predicates are going to be added or replaced by their opposites, but suppose an artist determines that *H* shall henceforth be artistically relevant for his paintings. Then, in fact, both *H* and non-*H* become artistically relevant for *all* painting, and if his is the first and only painting that is *H*, every other painting in existence becomes non-*H*, and the entire community of paintings is enriched, together with a doubling of the available style opportunities. It is this retroactive enrichment of the entities in the artworld that makes it possible to discuss Raphael and De Kooning together, or Lichtenstein and Michelangelo. The greater the variety of artistically relevant predicates, the more complex the individual members of the artworld become; and the more one knows of the entire population of the artworld, the richer one's experience with any of its members.

In this regard, notice that, if there are *m* artistically relevant predicates, there is always a bottom row with *m* minuses. This row is apt to be occupied by purists. Having scoured their canvasses clear of what they regard as inessential, they credit themselves with having distilled out the essence of art. But this is just their fallacy: exactly as many artistically relevant predicates stand true of their square monochromes as stand true of any member of the Artworld, and they can *exist* as artworks only insofar as "impure" paintings exist. Strictly speaking, a black square by Reinhardt is artistically as rich as Titian's *Sacred and Profane Love*. This explains how less is more.

Fashion, as it happens, favors certain rows of the style matrix: museums, connoisseurs, and others are makeweights in the Artworld. To insist, or seek to, that all artists become representational, perhaps to gain entry into a specially prestigious exhibition, cuts the available style matrix in half: there are then $2^n/2$ ways of satisfying the requirement, and museums then can exhibit all these "approaches" to the topic they have set. But this is a matter of almost purely sociological interest: one row in the matrix is as legitimate as another. An artistic breakthrough consists, I suppose, in adding the possibility of a column to the matrix. Artists then, with greater or less alacrity, occupy the positions thus opened up: this is a remarkable feature of contemporary art, and for those unfamiliar with the matrix, it is hard, and perhaps impossible, to recognize certain positions as occupied by artworks. Nor would these things be artworks without the theories and the histories of the Artworld.

Brillo boxes enter the artworld with that same tonic incongruity the *commedia dell'arte* characters bring into *Ariadne auf Naxos*. Whatever is the artistically relevant predicate in virtue of which they gain their entry, the rest of the Artworld becomes that much the richer in having the opposite predicate available and applicable to its members. And, to return to the views of Hamlet with which we began this discussion, Brillo boxes may reveal us to ourselves as well as anything might: as a mirror held up to nature, they might serve to catch the conscience of our kings.

19

ART AS INSTITUTION: GEORGE DICKIE

George Dickie (b. 1926), whose institutional theory of art takes its inspiration from Arthur Danto (Chapter 18), conceives the artworld as an institution conferring artistic status on objects. Dickie outlines this view in the following selection, taken from his 1974 book *Art and the Aesthetic*.

A central impetus for the institutional theory is the inability of its predecessors—the imitation and expression theories (see Chapters 1 and Chapter 10)—to provide necessary and sufficient conditions for something to be a work of art. This failure had led many philosophers of art to agree with Weitz (Chapter 16) that, in principle, no such definition could be devised. Dickie believes that the institutional theory answers the traditional demand for a definition of art while avoiding Weitz's objections.

The central claim of the institutional theory is that what makes an object a work of art is its being viewed as such by functionaries of the artworld. For Dickie, the artworld is a *social institution,* like the police or the church, but operates to perpetuate artistic practice. Although it lacks clearly stated rules and prescribed social roles, Dickie believes there are enough parallels between it and such explicitly defined social institutions to justify the attribution. The artworld, then, is constituted by the practices of artists, gallery owners, critics, art historians, philosophers of art, and so forth. By exhibiting works of art, teaching about art, and other actions, these members of the artworld perpetuate the social institution of art.

How is artistic status conferred by the artworld? To see how this is done, Dickie, following one of Danto's suggestions, asks us to consider Marcel Duchamp's *Fountain,* an ordinary urinal that Duchamp signed "R. Mutt," gave a title, and submitted for exhibition. The question raised by *Fountain,* for both Dickie and Danto, is what distinguishes it from its perceptually indistinguishable counterpart in a men's room so that *it,* and not the latter, is a work of art, no matter how inferior a work one might judge it to be. Dickie's answer is that *Fountain* is art because Duchamp's actions confer artistic status on it. Duchamp, acting on behalf of the artworld, made *Fountain* a work of art when he signed, named, and exhibited it, because, in so doing, he made it something that other actors in the artworld would treat *as* a work of art.

Dickie explains how a person can confer artistic status on a physical object by analogy with how someone occupying a recognized role within a well-defined social institution can confer special status. For example, a justice of the peace who says, "I now pronounce you husband and wife," *confers* the status of husband on a man and of wife on a woman (in the usual circumstances, anyway). The justice of the peace represents the state in conferring on the two individuals their status as married. Similarly, Dickie claims that Duchamp transforms a commonplace object into a work of art by his actions.

In response to extensive criticism of the argument presented here, Dickie has modified his account of how artistic status is conferred by the artworld. Nonetheless, the essentials of his view remain: Being a work of art is not a property inherent in an object and perceptually available to a viewer, but a relational property consequent upon that object's role within the artworld. Dickie's view, together with Danto's, has become a focus of discussion in contemporary philosophy of art. With their emphasis on the artworld, and its role in the constitution of the artwork, both views situate art within a broader social context than is acknowledged by traditional theories.

STUDY QUESTIONS ON THE READING

1. Do you agree with Dickie that being an artifact is a necessary condition of something's being a work of art? Why or why not?

2. What are the differences between Danto's understanding of the artworld and Dickie's? Which theory do you find superior? Why?

3. Do you see any problems with Dickie's assimilation of the artworld to highly formalized social institutions? Explain.

4. Does Dickie give artists too much power? Can any object produced by an artist count as art? Explain.

5. Do you think that the institutional theory of art solves the problems that Weitz raises? Why or why not?

6. Is being a work of art a relational property of physical objects? Explain.

GEORGE DICKIE, ART AND THE AESTHETIC: AN INSTITUTIONAL ANALYSIS

The attempt to define "art" by specifying its necessary and sufficient conditions is an old endeavor. The first definition—the imitation theory—despite

---

what now seem like obvious difficulties, more or less satisfied everyone until some time in the nineteenth century. After the expression theory of art broke the domination of the imitation theory, many definitions purporting to reveal the necessary and sufficient conditions of art appeared. In the mid-1950's, several philosophers, inspired by Wittgenstein's talk about concepts, began arguing that there are no necessary and sufficient conditions for art. Until recently, this argument had persuaded so many philosophers of the futility of trying to define art that the flow of definitions had all but ceased. Although I will ultimately try to show that "art" can be defined, the denial of that possibility has had the very great value of forcing us to look deeper into the concept of "art." The parade of dreary and superficial definitions that had been presented was, for a variety of reasons, eminently rejectable. The traditional attempts to define "art," from the imitation theory on, may be thought of as Phase I and the contention that "art" cannot be defined as Phase II. I want to supply Phase III by defining "art" in such a way as to avoid the difficulties of the traditional definitions and to incorporate the insights of the later analysis. I should note that the imitation theory of the fine arts seems to have been adopted by those who held it without much serious thought and perhaps cannot be considered as a self-conscious theory of art in the way that the later theories can be.

The traditional attempts at definition have sometimes failed to see beyond prominent but accidental features of works of art, features that have characterized art at a particular stage in its historical development. For example, until quite recently the works of art clearly recognizable as such were either obviously representational or assumed to be representational. Paintings and sculptures were obviously so, and music was widely assumed in some sense also to be representational. Literature was representational in that it described familiar scenes of life. It was, then, easy enough to think that imitation must be the essence of art. The imitation theory focused on a readily evident relational property of works of art, namely, art's relation to subject matter. The development of nonobjective art showed that imitation is not even an always accompanying property of art, much less an essential one.

The theory of art as the expression of emotion has focused on another relational property of works of art, the relation of a work to its creator. The expression theory also has proved inadequate, and no other subsequent definition has been satisfactory. Although not fully satisfying as definitions, the imitation and expression theories do provide a clue: both singled out *relational* properties of art as essential. As I shall try to show, the two defining characteristics of art are indeed relational properties, and one of them turns out to be exceedingly complex. . . .

Although he does not attempt to formulate a definition, Arthur Danto in his provocative article, "The Artworld," has suggested the direction that must be taken by an attempt to define "art." [See Chapter 18—T.E.W.] In reflecting on art and its history together with such present-day developments as Warhol's *Brillo Carton* and Rauschenberg's *Bed*, Danto writes, "To see something as art requires something the eye cannot descry—an atmosphere of artistic theory, a knowledge of history of art: an artworld." Admittedly, this stimulating comment is in need of elucidation, but it is clear that in speaking of "something the eye cannot descry" Danto is [claiming] that nonexhibited properties are of great importance in constituting something as art. In speaking of atmosphere and history, . . . Danto points to the rich structure in which particular works of art are embedded: he indicates *the institutional nature of art.*

I shall use Danto's term "artworld" to refer to the broad social institution in which works of art have their place. But is there such an institution? George Bernard Shaw speaks somewhere of the apostolic line of succession stretching from Aeschylus to himself. Shaw was no doubt speaking for effect and to draw attention to himself, as he often did, but there is an important truth implied by his remark. There is a long tradition or continuing institution of the theater having its origins in ancient Greek religion and other Greek institutions. That tradition has run very thin at times and perhaps even ceased to exist altogether during some periods, only to be reborn out of its memory and the need for art. The institutions associated with the theater have varied from time to time: in the beginning it was Greek religion and the Greek state; in medieval times, the church; more recently, private business and the state (national theater). What has remained constant with its own identity throughout its history is the theater itself as an established way of doing and behaving, what I shall call . . . the primary convention of the theater. This institutionalized behavior occurs on both sides of the "footlights": both the players and the audience are involved and go to make up the institution of the theater. The roles of the actors and the audience are defined by the traditions of the theater. What the author, management, and players present is art, and it is art because it is presented within the theater-world framework. Plays are written to have a place in the theater system and they exist as plays, that is, as art, within that system. Of course, I do not wish to deny that plays also exist as literary works, that is, as art within the literary system: the theater system and the literary system overlap. Let me make clear what I mean by speaking of the artworld as an institution. Among the meanings of "institution" in *Webster's New Collegiate Dictionary* are the following: "3. That which is instituted as: a. An established practice, law, custom, etc. b. An established society or corporation." When I call the artworld an institution I am saying that it is an established practice. Some persons have thought that an institution must be an established society or corporation and, consequently, have misunderstood my claim about the artworld.

Theater is only one of the systems within the artworld. Each of the systems has had its own origins and historical development. We have some information about the later stages of these developments, but we have to guess about the origins of the basic art systems. I suppose that we have complete knowledge of certain recently developed subsystems or genres such as Dada and happenings. Even if our knowledge is not as complete as we wish it were, however, we do have substantial information about the systems of the artworld as they currently exist and as they have existed for some time. One central feature all of the systems have in common is that each is a framework for the *presenting* of particular works of art. Given the great variety of the systems of the artworld it is not surprising that works of art have no exhibited properties in common.

If, however, we step back and view the works in their institutional setting, we will be able to see the essential properties they share.

Theater is a rich and instructive illustration of the institutional nature of art. But it is a development within the domain of painting and sculpture—Dadaism—that most easily reveals the institutional essence of art. Duchamp and friends conferred the status of art on "ready-mades" (urinals, hatracks, snow shovels, and the like), and when we reflect on their deeds we can take note of a kind of human action which has until now gone unnoticed and unappreciated—the action of conferring the status of art. Painters and sculptors, of course, have been engaging all along in the action of conferring this status on the objects they create. As long, however, as the created objects were conventional, given the paradigms of the times, the objects themselves and their fascinating exhibited properties were the focus of the attention of not only spectators and critics but of philosophers of art as well. When an artist of an earlier era painted a picture, he did some or all of a number of things: depicted a human being, portrayed a certain man, fulfilled a commission, worked at his livelihood, and so on. In addition he also acted as an agent of the artworld and conferred the status of art on his creation. Philosophers of art attended to only some of the properties the created object acquired from these various actions, for example, to the representational or to the expressive features of the objects. They entirely ignored the nonexhibited property of status. When, however, the objects are bizarre, as those of the Dadaists are, our attention is forced away from the objects' obvious properties to a consideration of the objects in their social context. As works of art Duchamp's "ready-mades" may not be worth much, but as examples of art they are very valuable for art theory. I am not claiming that Duchamp and friends invented the conferring of the status of art; they simply used an existing institutional device in an unusual way. Duchamp did not invent the artworld, because it was there all along.

The artworld consists of a bundle of systems: theater, painting, sculpture, literature, music, and so on, each of which furnishes an institutional background for the conferring of the status on objects within its domain. No limit can be placed on the number of systems that can be brought under the generic conception of art, and each of the major systems contains further subsystems. These features of the artworld provide the elasticity whereby creativity of even the most radical sort can be accommodated. A whole new system comparable to the theater, for example, could be added in one fell swoop. What is more likely is that a new subsystem would be added within a system. For example, junk sculpture added within sculpture, happenings added within theater. Such additions might in time develop into full-blown systems. Thus, the radical creativity, adventuresomeness, and exuberance of art of which Weitz speaks [See Chapter 16—T.E.W.] is possible within the concept of art, even though it is closed by the necessary and sufficient conditions of artifactuality and conferred status.

Having now briefly described the artworld, I am in a position to specify a definition of "work of art." The definition will be given in terms of artifactuality and the conferred status of art or, more strictly speaking, the conferred status of candidate for appreciation. Once the definition has been stated, a great deal will still remain to be said by way of clarification: A work of art in the classificatory sense is (1) an artifact (2) a set of the aspects of which has had conferred upon it the status of candidate for appreciation by some person or persons acting on behalf of a certain social institution (the artworld).

The second condition of the definition makes use of four variously interconnected notions: (1) acting on behalf of an institution, (2) conferring of status, (3) being a candidate, and (4) appreciation. The first two of these are so closely related that they must be discussed together. I shall first describe paradigm cases of conferring status outside the artworld and then show how similar actions take place within the artworld. The most clear-cut examples of the conferring of status are certain legal actions of the state. A king's conferring of knighthood, a grand jury's indicting someone, the chairman of the election board certifying that someone is qualified to run for office, or a minister's pronouncing a couple man and wife are examples in which a person or persons acting on behalf of a social institution (the state) confer(s) *legal* status on persons. The congress or a legally constituted commission may confer the status of national park or monument on an area or thing. The examples given suggest that pomp and ceremony are required to establish legal status, but this is not so, although of course a legal system is presupposed. For example, in some jurisdictions common-law marriage is possible—a legal status acquired without ceremony. The conferring of a Ph.D. degree on someone by a university, the election of someone as president of the Rotary, and the declaring of an object as a relic of the church are examples in which a person or persons confer(s) nonlegal status on persons or things. In such cases some social system or other must exist as the framework within which the conferring takes place, but, as before, ceremony is not required to establish status: for example, a person can acquire the status of wise man or village idiot within a community without ceremony.

Some may feel that the notion of conferring status within the artworld is excessively vague. Certainly this notion is not as clear-cut as the conferring of status within the legal system, where procedures and lines of authority are explicitly defined and incorporated into law. The counterparts in the artworld to specified procedures and lines of authority are nowhere codified, and the artworld carries on its business at the level of customary practice. Still there *is* a practice and this defines a social institution. A social institution need not have a formally established constitution, officers, and bylaws in order to exist and have the capacity to confer status—some social institutions are formal and some are informal. The artworld could become formalized, and perhaps has been to some extent in certain political contexts, but most people who are interested in art would probably consider this a bad thing. Such formality would threaten the freshness and exuberance of art. The core personnel of the artworld is a loosely organized, but nevertheless related, set of persons including artists (understood to refer to painters, writers, composers), producers, museum directors, museum-goers, theater-goers, reporters for newspapers, critics for publications of all sorts, art historians, art theorists, philosophers of art, and others. These are the people who keep the machinery of the artworld working and thereby provide for its continuing existence. In addition, every person who sees himself as a member of the artworld is thereby a member. Although I have called the persons just listed the core personnel of the art-world, there is a minimum core within that core without which the artworld would not exist. This essential core consists of artists who create the works, "presenters" to present the works, and "goers" who appreciate the works. This minimum core might be called "the presentation group," for it consists of artists whose activity is necessary if anything is to be presented, the presenters (actors, stage managers, and so on), and the goers whose presence and cooperation is necessary in order for anything to be presented. A given person might play more than one of these essential roles in the case of the presentation of a particular work. Critics, historians, and philosophers of art become members of the artworld at some time after the minimum core personnel of a particular art system get that system into operation. All of these roles are institutionalized and must be learned in one way or another by the participants. For example, a theater-goer is not just someone who happens to enter a theater; he is a person who enters with certain expectations and knowledge about what he will experience and an understanding of how he should behave in the face of what he will experience.

Assuming that the existence of the artworld has been established or at least made plausible, the problem is now to see how status is conferred by this institution. My thesis is that, in a way analogous to the way in which a person is certified as qualified for office, or two persons acquire the status of common-law marriage within a legal system, or a person is elected president of the Rotary, or a person acquires the status of wise man within a community, so an artifact can acquire the status of candidate for appreciation within the social system called "the artworld." How can one tell when the status has been conferred? An artifact's hanging in an art museum as part of a show and a performance at a theater are sure signs. There is, of course, no guarantee that one can always know whether something is a candidate for appreciation, just as one cannot always tell whether a given person is a knight or is married. When an object's status depends upon nonexhibited characteristics, a simple look at the object will not necessarily reveal that status. The nonexhibited relation *may* be symbolized by some badge, for example, by a wedding ring, in which case a simple look will reveal the status.

The more important question is that of how the status of candidate for appreciation is conferred. The examples just mentioned, display in a museum and a performance in a theater, seem to suggest that a number of persons are required for the actual conferring of the status. In one sense a number of persons are required but in another sense only one person is required: a number of persons are required to make up the social institution of the artworld, but only one person is required to act on behalf of the artworld and to confer the status of candidate for appreciation. In fact, many works of art are seen only by one person—the one who creates them—but they are still art. The status in question may be acquired by a single person's acting on behalf of the artworld and *treating an artifact as a candidate for appreciation*. Of course, nothing prevents a group of persons from conferring the status, but it is usually conferred by a single person, the artist who creates the artifact. It may be helpful to compare and contrast the notion of conferring the status of candidate for appreciation with a case in which something is simply presented for appreciation: hopefully this will throw light on the notion of status of candidate. Consider the case of a salesman of plumbing supplies who spreads his wares before us. "Placing before" and "conferring the status of candidate for appreciation" are very different notions, and this difference can be brought out by comparing the salesman's action with the superficially similar act of Duchamp in entering a urinal which he christened *Fountain* in that now-famous art show. The difference is that Duchamp's action took place within the institutional setting of the artworld and the plumbing salesman's action took place outside of it. The salesman could do what Duchamp did, that is, convert a urinal into a work of art, but such a thing probably would not occur to him. Please remember that *Fountain*'s being a work of art does not mean that it is a good one, nor does this qualification insinuate that it is a bad one either. The antics of a particular present-day artist serve to reinforce the point of the Duchamp case and also to emphasize a significance of the practice of naming works of art. Walter de Maria has in the case of one of his works even gone through the motions, no doubt as a burlesque, of using a procedure used by many legal and some nonlegal institutions—the procedure of licensing. His *High Energy Bar* (a stainless-steel bar) is accompanied by a certificate bearing the name of the work and stating that the bar is a work of art only when the certificate is present. In addition to highlighting the status of art by "certifying" it on a document, this example serves to suggest a significance of the act of naming works of art. An object may acquire the status of art without ever being named but giving it a title makes clear to whomever is interested that an object is a work of art. Specific titles function in a variety of ways—as aids to understanding a work or as a convenient way of identifying it, for example—but any title at all (even *Untitled*) is a badge of status.

The third notion involved in the second condition of the definition is candidacy: a member of the artworld confers the status of candidate for appreciation. The definition does not require that a work of art actually be appreciated, even by one person. The fact is that many, perhaps most, works of art go unappreciated. It is important not to build into the definition of the classificatory sense of "work of art" value properties such as actual appreciation: to do so would make it impossible to speak of unappreciated works of art. Building in value properties might even make it awkward to speak of bad works of art. A theory of art must preserve certain central features of the way in which we talk about art, and we do find it necessary sometimes to speak of unappreciated art and of bad art. Also, not every aspect of a work is included in the candidacy for appreciation; for example, the color of the back of a painting is not ordinarily considered to be something which someone might think it appropriate to appreciate. . . . The definition of "work of art" should not, therefore, be understood as asserting that every aspect of a work is included within the candidacy for appreciation.

The fourth notion involved in the second condition of the definition is appreciation itself. Some may assume that the definition is referring to a special kind of *aesthetic* appreciation. . . . I do not think there is any reason to think that there is a special kind of aesthetic appreciation. All that is meant by "appreciation" in the definition is something like "in experiencing the qualities of a thing one finds them worthy or valuable," and this meaning applies quite generally both inside and outside the domain of art. Several persons have felt that my account of the institutional theory of art is incomplete because of what they see as my insufficient analysis of appreciation. They have, I believe, thought that there are different kinds of appreciation and that the appreciation in the appreciation of art is somehow typically different from the appreciation in the appreciation of nonart. But the only sense in which there is a difference between the appreciation of art and the appreciation of nonart is that the appreciations have different *objects*. The institutional structure in which the art object is embedded, not different kinds of appreciation, makes the difference between the appreciation of art and the appreciation of nonart. . . .

The definition I have given contains a reference to the artworld. Consequently, some may have the uncomfortable feeling that my definition is viciously circular. Admittedly, in a sense the definition is circular, but it is not viciously so. If I had said something like "A work of art is an artifact on which a status has been conferred by the artworld" and then said of the artworld only that it confers the status of candidacy for appreciation, then the definition would be viciously circular because the circle would be so small and *uninformative*. I have, however, devoted a considerable amount of space in this chapter to describing and analyzing the historical, organizational, and functional intricacies of the artworld, and if this account is accurate the reader has received a considerable amount of *information* about the artworld. The circle I have run is not small and it is not uninformative. If, in the end, the artworld cannot be described independently of art, that is, if the description contains references to art historians, art reporters, plays, theaters, and so on, then the definition strictly speaking is circular. It is not, however, viciously so, because the whole account in which the definition is embedded contains a great deal of information about the artworld. One must not focus narrowly on the definition alone: for what is important to see is that art is an institutional concept and this requires seeing the definition in the context of the whole account. I suspect that the "problem" of circularity will arise frequently, perhaps always, when institutional concepts are dealt with. . . .

20

ART AS AESTHETIC PRODUCTION:
MONROE C. BEARDSLEY

We have sampled some of the newer views developed by analytic philosophers—for example, that the term *art* cannot be defined (see Chapter 16) or that it is the artworld that confers the status of artwork (see Chapter 19). Against this, Monroe C. Beardsley (1915–1985) defends the primacy of the artist's "art-making" intention. An artwork is such because of the artist's intention that what he or she is fashioning be a work of art, that what he of she creates satisfy an aesthetic interest.

We have already encountered the linkage between art and aesthetic interest or emotion. What is distinctive about Beardsley's position is that he makes the artist's intention to satisfy an aesthetic interest a necessary condition of something's being a work of art.

In many ways, this view appeals to common sense. It emphasizes the importance of the artist and the artist's goal in creating the artwork. It also limits art to products of human activity, thus drawing a sharp distinction between those things that happen to satisfy our aesthetic interest and those that are made with this purpose in mind.

Beardsley begins his argument by clarifying why it is important to define art. As he points out, a definition of art can be put to many uses: the critic needs to decide which objects are worth reviewing; funding agencies, which projects are worthy of grant money; the historian of art, which art is historically consequential. According to Beardsley, without an adequate definition, it would be impossible to make such decisions rationally.

Foremost among those who require a definition of art, Beardsley continues, is the anthropologist. Because of the discipline's broad, cross-cultural orientation, the anthropologist needs a way of deciding which activities to count as artistic. But this gives rise to a puzzle: Given the pair of concepts—artwork and artistic activity—which is to receive definitional priority, and why?

Although it might seem we should begin with the artwork itself—as had such diverse philosophers as Plato (Chapter 1) and Danto (Chapter 18)—Beardsley argues that the concept of artistic production must be given priority in our search for a definition. The reason is that artistic production has two clearly defined aspects: the productive activity itself and its reception. An artwork is not only something that is produced, it is also something received or appreciated by an audience. This, then, provides the basic structure for Beardsley's definition of art: "An artwork is something produced with the intention of giving it the capacity to satisfy the aesthetic interest." Both roles—producer and receiver of the artwork—are central to this definition.

Two features of the definition require a bit of explanation. The first is the importance of the artist's intention in producing the work. That this is necessary for something to be a work of art is a highly contentious claim, but Beardsley thinks it crucial. (Curiously, he is also well known for criticizing the intentional fallacy of assuming the author's intentions are relevant for understanding the meaning of the artwork!) Only something that is produced with a very specific intention on the part of its producer—that the work satisfy an aesthetic interest—will count as a work of art. But what is this aesthetic interest? Here, Beardsley again endorses a now controversial idea, one that goes back to Hume (Chapter 3) and Kant (Chapter 4)—namely, that there is a distinctive type of pleasure that we desire to experience and artists create to satisfy.

Beardsley's account of art, then, is important because it vigorously rearticulates, for a contemporary public, classical ideas about the nature of art. Whether his defense meets the objections that have been raised against them is something for you to decide.

STUDY QUESTIONS ON THE READING

1. Why does Beardsley think it important to develop a definition of art? Do you agree? Why or why not?

2. What makes an experience *aesthetic* for Beardsley? Can you think of examples of aesthetic experiences you have had? Do you agree with Beardsley's characterization of them? Explain.

3. Does it make sense for the "art-making" intention to be central to the definition of art? Why or why not? What problems does this linkage present?

4. Is there a problem with Beardsley's coupling the intentionality thesis with the anthropological point of view? Why or why not?

5. Could there be art, according to Beardsley's definition, in a society that lacked a concept of art? Why or why not? What about in a society lacking the concept of aesthetic interest?

6. In the third section of this reading, Beardsley lists a number of objections to his definition of art. What are they? Do you think he answers them satisfactorily? Explain.

7. Compare Beardsley's definition of art with those of Bell and Danto. Which type of approach do you find best? Why?

❖

MONROE C. BEARDSLEY: AN AESTHETIC DEFINITION OF ART

Like other questions of the same syntactic form, the question "What is art?" invites analysis of words and thoughts as well as the phenomena they refer to. But, being a philosophical question, it will not be satisfied by lexicography or psychology. I don't suppose that my task here is to inquire how various people commonly, or uncommonly, use the word "art" in English, or corresponding words in other languages, nor to canvas popular, or unpopular, opinion about what art is or ought to be. Taken philosophically, the question calls for decisions and proposals: What are the noteworthy features of the phenomena to which the word in question seems, however loosely, to call our attention? What are the significant distinctions that need to be marked for the purposes of theoretical understanding, and that the word "art" or one of its cognates ("artwork," "artistic," "artistry," etc.) is most apt and suitable for marking? How does art, defined in a comparatively clear, if somewhat unorthodox, way, differ from closely related things? Of course it will be a merit in any proposed definition of art if it matches reasonably well at least one fairly widespread use of the term, but it will not necessarily be a merit if the match is close, since philosophical reflection is expected to yield definitions and distinctions rather more valuable—to philosophy—than casual familiar ones.

I proclaim these assumptions or biasses at the start, to show my conception of my task—for which no further defense or apology will be forthcoming. What I will try to defend is a definition of art—actually, a rather old-fashioned one in essentials—that I have come to regard as best adapted to the requirements of a sound philosophy of art.

I

It should not be necessary to argue that we have need for a definition of art, but since this has been vigorously denied, some argument must be given. The point of a definition is, of course, to fix a meaning—to establish and stabilize it for some range of contexts—and thus mark out a class of things to be referred to by some group of people. One would think the philosopher of art could use a definition, since he should be curious to know what he is philosophizing about. Not that he can *begin* with an adequate definition—he only needs some uncontested examples of art, which are surely not hard to come by—but at some point he will want to say why these are examples of art, and how we are

From Monroe C. Beardsley, *Art as Aesthetic Production*. Reprinted by permission of Haven Publications.

to tell what future things his philosophical conclusions are supposed to apply to. The critic of an art may be a similar case; it should be useful to him to have criteria for deciding what sorts of thing he is to criticize. The historian of an art—of dance, drama, architecture, or whatever—will surely have use for a definition to tell him what belongs in his history and what does not: Should the dance historian deal with parades and with cavorting bears?

Should the architecture historian deal with igloos and Macdonald's [sic] eateries? If so, why? If not, why not? To answer such questions well requires a defensible definition. Even the practical legislator or administrator may have use for a definition, in deciding, for example, which imported objects to exempt from duties, or which allegedly artistic projects should be funded by the National Endowment for the Arts.

But we must expecially note the needs of the anthropologist, and indeed as we move on we should keep in mind this broad cross-cultural perspective. Essential to our understanding of any culture is a grasp of the various forms of activity that it manifests, and of distinctions that are most significant to the members of the society that has that culture. When we observe someone carving wood or moving about in a circle with others, we must ask whether the activity is religious, political, economic, medical, etc.—or artistic. What function do the participants think of themselves as fulfilling, and how does it relate to other activities in which they engage? Even when the same act of carving or dancing in a ring has more than one character—it is both religious and artistic, say—we don't understand it unless we make this distinction and see that both descriptions apply. Distinction does not entail separation, and it is the distinction that is basic—though of course it may also be important to note that in one society these two forms of activity are always combined (the artists are the priests), while in another society they are kept apart and assigned to specialized persons. In a very few societies, horribly deprived or nearing destruction, we may be able to discern no activities to label "artistic," but there seems to be an ingredient or dimension of culture that runs across most societies, however varied, and whose nature we would like to articulate as well as we can. In other words, we want to define.

There are two definition questions that spring up when we take this anthropological point of view. We may, as I said, observe activities, and want to know which activities are artistic ones (allowing that they may also be political or pedagogical, etc.). We may notice certain objects that seem to engage the attention of many persons in the society from time to time, and want to know which of them, if any, are artworks (again allowing that they may also be sacred objects or economic objects, etc.). Here are two paired concepts, that of *artistic activity* and that of *artwork;* and already we are faced with one of the definitional decisions we must make. If we have an independent definition of "artwork," it is easy to define "artistic activity" as "activity that involves dealing with artworks." But it may turn out to be impossible, or inconvenient, to give a satisfactory definition of "artwork" without making reference to *some* form of artistic activity, either on the part of those who create artworks or those who receive them or both. . . .

II

Once we know what things are artworks in a particular society (and anything that is an artwork in some society is an artwork *tout court*), we can identify artistic activities by discovering which activities involve interaction with artworks. Artistic activities, so conceived, may be extremely varied, especially in a complex society, though we might want to draw some useful lines to separate interactions from more remote or indirect relationships. Thus editors of novels and dance coaches are plainly engaged in artistic activities, but typesetters of novels and doctors who strive to keep dancers in a state of physical repair are plainly not. Interesting as it might be to pause for a discussion of this distinction, and how to make it, we must stick to more central matters. And highly central are two artistic activities in particular, for they enable us to define "artwork," which can be used in turn to define the other artistic activities.

The first of these central activities is art-making or art-creating—what I shall call, very broadly, *art-production*. Again, tempting problems turn up, but we have to set them aside: they concern the concept of art-creation and the difference between making and creating. I use "production" generously, trying to slip around these puzzles: it includes making, altering, assembling, joining, arranging, and other distinguishable actions, including certain kinds of doing (as in dancing). What is produced, I think, is always something physical (an object or event) and perceptual, in that it has some properties that can be perceived. Often what is produced also has properties that are not perceptual or physical—such as meanings, messages, the capacity to evoke emotions or images, etc. Thus even an alleged work of conceptual art—one that is no more than a closed art gallery with a sign on it saying that the artwork being exhibited that week is just the closed art gallery itself—is a product in my sense (though whether it is an artwork is a question of the sort I expect my definition to clarify and help resolve). Since art-production is a species of production in general, if we are going to distinguish it from the rest, we shall need to specify a differentia. One plausible candidate for such a differentia, is *mode of production*. But this is barred to us, by the fact that the same process of production, as we said, may result in an object that is both an artwork and a religious object. Another plausible candidate is *intention*: that it is the presence of a certain kind of intention that makes production, art-production. This suggestion is immune to the counter-argument just given, for something can be produced with more than one intention—say, both an artistic and a religious intention. Another plausible candidate is *result*: that it is the achievement of a product of a certain kind that makes the production artistic. But this seems to lead to saying that production is artistic when it results in an artwork; and I do not want to adopt this definition since I want to be able to define "artwork" (partly) in terms of its production.

Thus we seem to be beckoned toward adopting a definition of "art-production" that will make use of the concept of intention. But to characterize the specific type of intention needed we must turn to the second central artistic activity, which I have (for want of a better word) called *reception*. Reception comprises a variety of activities engaged in, in the presence of—or perhaps in response to reproductions or reports or memories of—sculpture, oral performances of literature, films, operas, etc. We view, listen to, contemplate, apprehend, watch, read, think about, peruse, and so forth. Sometimes in this receptive interaction we find that our experience (including all that we are aware of: perceptions, feelings, emotions, impulses, desires, beliefs, thoughts) is lifted in a certain way that is hard to describe and especially to summarize: it takes on a sense of freedom from concern about matters outside the thing received, an intense affect that is nevertheless detached from practical ends, the exhilarating sense of exercising powers of discovery, integration of the self and its experiences. When experience has some or all of these properties, I say it has an *aesthetic character,* or is, for short, aesthetic experience. Much more, of course, ought really to be said to fill out this mere sketch; and much more could be said, were room available. To say no more leaves, I am aware, a soft place in my definitional scheme, but if it proves to be the softest place, I shall have to be content.

When we voluntarily receive those things that are the result of art-production, we often do so with the intention of obtaining aesthetic experience—in other words, we have an *aesthetic interest* in those things. (We can have an aesthetic interest in other things as well—such as products of nature or technology.) I use the term "interest" in its fuller sense, which includes two ideas: (1) we *take* an interest in something, when approaching it and interacting with it, and we take an interest in the aesthetic character of the experience we hope to gain from it; but also (2) we *have* an interest in that experience, in the sense that it is *in our interest* to obtain it, since it is worthwhile. I do not defend this claim here, but I believe myself to be justified in making the assumption that aesthetic experience is desirable, has value, satisfies a genuine human interest.

We have now the makings of the definition I am after, and I propose that:

> An artwork is something produced with the intention of giving it the capacity to satisfy the aesthetic interest.

Admirably terse, but therefore in need of exegesis, which I hope will guard it against misreading. It is an *aesthetic* definition of art, that is, a definition using the concept of the aesthetic, and though it is not the only possible aesthetic definition, it is the one I shall henceforth refer to.

To begin at the end, I have to assume that the concept of aesthetic interest is good enough for present purposes, even though it is defined in terms of aesthetic experience, which is the subject of lively and unabated controversy. It is important that the word "capacity" appears where it does: there are of course intimate cases of artistic activity in which the artist (i.e., artwork-producer) directly aims to provide aesthetic experience to some particular person or group of persons; but I say that it is enough if (as is more widely the case) he or she intends to fashion something that aesthetic experience *can* be obtained from. The artist may have no idea who, if anyone, will be able to obtain aesthetic experience from it, and maybe no one will (for example, if it is immediately destroyed). Appropriate interaction with the artwork may be extremely demanding or may depend on rare talents and extensive knowledge. The artist may be content to put his painting away or paint it over, once he is satisfied with what he has done—that is, believes that if someone with the requisite qualifications *were* to take an aesthetic interest in it, that interest would be satisfied to some degree. "Satisfaction," it should be noted, allows of degrees; it does not mean *complete* satisfaction.

The artist who works solely for his or her own enjoyment is an extreme case, no doubt; art-production is normally a social activity in which the producer and receiver are different persons. The impulse to make something capable of satisfying the aesthetic interest and to share it must be a very elementary one in very many societies, and must be present before there is a further desire to establish a continuing group (an institution) with an explicitly acknowledged group aim to foster artistic activity. In time there will emerge a tradition, a conviction that there are approved and disapproved ways, or better and worse ways, of carrying on the activity. But I can't see how tradition is essential to it, and I see no good reason to withhold the label "artwork" from art-production undertaken before or independently of a tradition. Artistic innovations involve rejection of at least some elements of a tradition, a striking out on one's own, but they must be counted within art as much as less adventurous works.

When I use the word "intention," I mean a combination of desire and belief: intending to produce a work capable of satisfying the aesthetic interest involves both (a) desiring to produce such a work and (b) believing that one will produce, or is in the process of producing, such a work. So normally the artist has a serious purpose: there is something he wants to do in producing what he produces; and he will have reason to believe that success is possible. If, for example, it is unlikely that a painter could believe that by closing the art gallery and placing a sign on it he would produce something capable of satisfying the aesthetic interest, then it is unlikely that in closing the art gallery and placing a sign on it he was producing an artwork. We must of course allow for far-out beliefs, however unreasonable; there are painters quite capable of believing that closing the art gallery and placing a sign on it might provide aesthetic experience to someone who came to the gallery, found the sign, and meditated on the symbolic significance of this higher order of art that is so self-effacing, so sublimely self-sacrificial that it denies itself its own existence (like Keats's unheard melodies that are sweeter than the heard ones). If this was indeed an intention the painter had in closing the gallery and placing the sign, then I am prepared to classify the closed and labelled gallery an artwork. There is, of course, no implication here about the degree of success; it is enough that something was intended. This places the painter's activity in a significant class of human activities, the artistic ones; it decides the kind of social enterprise he is engaged in, and it determines the primary (not the only) way in which his product is to be judged.

The example points up a problem in the application of this definition, though not, in my opinion, a fatal one. To identify the artistic activities and the artworks of a society we must make correct inferences about intentions. And intentions, being private, are difficult to know. But artistic activities are no different in this respect from all other significant activities of a society; if the anthropologist cannot understand what the observable behavior means to the people so behaving, what their desires and beliefs, purposes and motives, are, then he does not understand their culture. We must make use of available verbal testimony, but inferences can legitimately reach beyond that. Once we discover that people in a given society have the *idea* of satisfying an aesthetic interest, and once we know at least some of their ways of satisfying this interest, we can reasonably infer the aesthetic intention (that is, the intention to produce something capable of satisfying the aesthetic interest) from properties of the product. A painting with a religious subject and evident power to move believers to religious devotion may also give evidence of extreme care in the composition, color harmony, subtle variations in light and texture; then we have a good reason to believe that *one* of the intentions with which the painter worked was the aesthetic one. The fact that a product belongs to a genre that already contains indubitable artworks also counts as evidence of aesthetic intention: hence, for example, some rather inferior statues of the Buddha sometimes find their way into art museums.

According to the definition I propose, and am defending, the aesthetic intention need not be the only one, or even the dominant one; it must have been present and at least to some degree effective—that is, it played a causal or explanatory role with respect to some features of the work. Again, even if we know that a Chinookan story, such as "Seal and Her Younger Brother Lived There," is told mainly to children to teach them a lesson (and so has primarily a pedagogical intention), the presence of aesthetically satisfying formal features and its success in satisfying the aesthetic interest is enough to stamp it as a work of literary art. It is sometimes said that Paleolithic cave-drawings were not produced with any aesthetic intention at all, or aesthetically enjoyed, because they had a magical or religious function. One argument seems to be that no one in the culture could have had an aesthetic interest because the culture left no pure art-works (that is, works produced solely with an aesthetic intention). My view is that we know far too little about what was going on in the minds of Paleolithic people to be at all dogmatic about this, or to use their drawings as a counter-example to the aesthetic definition of art. Moreover—although this is a matter of interesting dispute, too—it seems highly probable to me that early human beings developed a capacity for aesthetic experience and a relish for it *before* they deliberately fashioned objects or actions for the purpose of providing aesthetic experience—just as they must have learned to use fire they found before they learned to make fires, and used found rocks as tools before they shaped rocks into better tools, and caves as housing before they built houses.

It is easy to point out vaguenesses in my definition; borderline cases can be found. This is true of most definitions, especially of cultural activities and objects. How pronounced must the aesthetic intention be? (It may be very subordinate to other intentions.) How much activity on the part of the artist is required in order to say that he is producing? (He may merely bring the snowflakes indoors and let them melt as they will.) How much of a sense of integration must an experience have to be aesthetic? (It may involve only a momentary pulling together of pleased attention to a particularly pregnant pothole.) There will inevitably be things we can cover by the definition if we are charitable but exclude if we want to be severe. Fuller explanation might tighten up the definition in some respects, but a rigorous line of demarcation is not to be expected—or even desired, perhaps, except by the legislator or administrator faced with practical decisions, and even he may have to decide some cases a bit arbitrarily, thinking mainly of precedents that will be set and untoward legal consequences to be avoided. Of course, if my definition is deemed hopelessly vague, so that it marks no useful distinction at all, it must be rejected; but surely, even as it stands, it clearly and decisively admits a large number of things and rules out a large number of other things. I would incline toward generosity and a welcoming attitude toward novelty—but I would look for evidence of some aesthetic intention, and I see no reason to twist my definition to make room for something like, say Edward T. Cone's one hundred metronomes running down with nobody silly enough to wait around for them—even if this "musical composition" is titled "Poème symphonique."

There will always be room for debate about such distinctions as that between producing art and kidding art—and perhaps the closed art gallery is a case in point. Kidding is a kind of message, and when done well certainly does not disqualify the kidding object from being itself an artwork; the enjoyment of wit can be an aesthetic experience. But common sense should not be abandoned along with philosophical acumen in these matters. The fuss that has been made about Duchamp's *Fountain* has long amazed me. It does not seem that in submitting that object to the art show and getting it more or less hidden from view, Duchamp or anyone else thought of it either as art or as having an aesthetic capacity. He did not establish a new meaning of "artwork," nor did he really inaugurate a tradition that led to the acceptance of plumbing figures (or other "readymades") as artworks today. If there was a point, it was surely to prove to the jury that even their tolerance had limits, and that they would *not* accept anything—at least gracefully. This small point was made effectively, but the episode doesn't seem to me to provide the slightest reason to regard the aesthetic definition as inadequate. Many objects exhibited today by the avantgarde evidently do make comments of some kind on art itself, but these objects may or may not be artworks. To classify them as artworks just because they make comments on art would be to classify a lot of dull and sometimes unintelligible magazine articles and newspaper reviews as artworks, and where is the advantage of that? To classify them as artworks just because they are exhibited is, to my mind, intellectually spineless, and results in classifying the exhibits at commercial expositions, science museums, stamp clubs and World's Fairs as artworks. Where is the advantage of that? To classify them as artworks just because they are called art by those who are called artists because they make things they call art is not to classify at all, but to think in circles. Perhaps these objects deserve a special name, but not the name of art. The distinction between objects that do and those that do not enter into artistic activities by reason of their connection with the aesthetic interest is still vital to preserve, and no other word than "art" is as suitable to mark it.

III

It remains to consider some of the reasonable objections that may occur to the reader—partly to dispose (if I can) of the more obvious ones, thus encouraging potential critics of the aesthetic definition to concentrate on raising more surprising and far-reaching ones, and partly to suggest some guidelines for constructing alternative proposals to replace the definition with a better one. My method will be to consider briefly some propositions that may be suspected of being untoward consequences of the definition; some of them, I argue, do not really follow from it and the others are quite acceptable.

1. If we take artworks as I have characterized them, then it is possible for children, even quite young children, to create artworks. This consequence is unacceptable to philosophers whose definitions assign to artworks an essential dependence on institutions, traditions, or aesthetic theories, for we may suppose that seven-year-olds, say, when they draw pictures, write poems, or make up songs, do not yet participate in what is called the "artworld." But it seems to me invidious to deny children this capability, especially on rather a priori grounds. The basic social activity, as I see it, is one in which a person produces something that he or she finds aesthetically enjoyable and shares it with others who may be able to appreciate it. Once this concept arises, we can have artworks, however simple and crude they may be. This does not mean making pictures of Thanksgiving turkeys according to the directions of a teacher, and seeking commendation for doing the assignment right. But developmental psychologists who have studied the "artful scribbles" of children (notably Howard Gardner) discern a frequent ability to use pictorial symbol systems for aesthetic purposes.

2. The question arises whether, on the aesthetic definition, forgeries of artworks can themselves be artworks. My answer is that some are and some are not: it all depends on the effective presence of an aesthetic intention. To begin with one extreme, a mechanical reproduction of an artwork (such as a picture-postcard sold in an art-museum shop) should probably not be classified as an artwork, even though it may be capable of affording some aesthetic satisfaction. At the other extreme, we have free copies (such as a Reubens copy of a Titian) that are plainly painted with an aesthetic intention. But of course neither of these is a forgery, strictly speaking, because there is no intent to deceive, no misrepresentation of producership. Now we can imagine a person making an exact copy of a painting by Chirico for the purpose (that is, with the intention) of passing it off as a genuine Chirico; and we can imagine that his method of working is tediously atomistic: he uses instruments to make sure that each small area matches the original perfectly. In that case he might execute the forgery without any aesthetic intention at all. This is hard to believe; it is far more likely that he will paint with an eye to capturing the

peculiar quality of the empty, lonely, ominous space in the Chirico in order to make sure the forgery is good enough as a painting to fool a connoisseur. In that case the forger is producing an artwork. This conclusion will strike art historians as a reductio ad absurdum of the proposed definition, for they make no room in their history for forgeries. I agree that forgeries do not belong to the history of art, any more than any other copies or reproductions, because they have no significance for the development of art. But I do not see why a careful copyist, though thoroughly unoriginal, cannot be producing an artwork; and I do not see how the addition of another intention (to deceive someone) makes the product less an artwork—expecially since the very success of the deception may depend on the painter's having the intention to make his work as capable as the original one of satisfying the aesthetic interest.

3. It follows from my definition that once an artwork, always an artwork. Anyone who holds that something can become an artwork and cease to be an artwork will object to my definition, and be inclined to adopt an institutional definition. It is sometimes said that, for example, a spinning wheel or snow shovel may begin life as a nonartwork, tied down to its lowly function; that at some point the artworld (prodded by an enterprising museum curator or by a maverick painter like Duchamp) may open its arms to embrace it, placing it on display and thus converting it into an artwork; and that at a still later time this designation or status may be withdrawn, so that the spinning wheel or snow shovel reverts to its original state. If some versions of the institutional theory are right, and there is an implicit or explicit performative act by which nonart can be given art-status, then it seems the process should be reversible by a converse act, as marriages can be annulled, names changed, contracts declared void, cabinet appointments rescinded, votes overturned, priests defrocked, and so forth. But the notion of taking away an object's property of being art is prima facie puzzling, and this puzzlingness is accounted for on the aesthetic definition. Something that is not an artwork can of course be exhibited, can become the object of aesthetic interest, can fall from fashion as people lose aesthetic interest in it. But since what makes art, art is an intention with which it was produced, nothing can be art that was not art from the start, and nothing that is art can cease to be art. And this seems to me a more intelligible and less misleading way to talk than to say, for example, that the Victorian paintings now stored in the art-museum's basement have ceased to be art, just because they are no longer much admired.

4. If it is the intention that counts in art-production, does it follow that one cannot *fail* to produce an artwork, if one intends to? That might seem an unfortunate consequence of the proposed definition, if it is a consequence. To straighten out the difficulty here requires some careful attention to certain features of actions and intentions. I do not say that the aesthetic intention is the intention to produce an artwork,

but the intention to produce something capable of satisfying the aesthetic interest. To intend to produce an artwork is to intend to produce something produced with the intention of producing something capable of satisfying the aesthetic interest; and this second-order intention, though it does occur, is not the usual one, I think. Thus in a certain rather innocuous sense artworks are often produced unintentionally—that is, without the intention to produce an artwork. But of course an artwork cannot be produced without any intention, and in this sense there can be no unintentional artworks. Paint may be spilled and pottery cracked unintentionally, and the pattern of paint or of the cracks may be capable of satisfying the aesthetic interest; but that alone does not make an artwork. One can fail in various ways in trying to produce an artwork: the work may not be as original as was hoped (the box of Kitty-Litter submitted to the avant-garde show turns out to be the second one submitted), or the work may not be the kind of work hoped for (the poem is not nearly as ironic as had been expected). But as far as I can see, the only way one can fail to produce an artwork after setting out to produce something capable of satisfying the aesthetic interest is by failing to make the physical object one tries to make (the clay is defective or the temperature of the kiln not right, so the pot falls apart), or to do the deed one tries to do (the dancer slips and falls instead of completing the pirouette). As long as *something* is produced with the aesthetic intention, an artwork is produced.

5. It is a consequence of my aesthetic definition, then, that tawdry and negligible objects will be classified as artworks. In such a sorting there is no implication of worth or value. Admittedly, this insistence on preserving a value-neutral sense of "artwork," for the purposes sketched at the start of this essay, runs counter to a familiar use of "work of art" for artistic praise. But we need a term for the classification; indeed, without it we will not even be able to make sense of the evaluative expression "a good artwork." And there are other terms to do the job of evaluating—indeed, a large number, because we call artworks not only "good" but many other things, both kind and unkind.

Before the anthropologist could hope to discover which objects in a society are its "artworks" in the normative sense (that is, what I would call its good or great artworks), it seems that he or she will first have to gain some notion of the class of things in reference to which some of its members are judged superior or supreme. And the anthropologist (since he is not necessarily an art historian) may be as interested in the failed products of a society's artistic activities as in its successes—especially if he can come to understand the causes and the consequences of these failures. Moreover, when we take an anthropological interest in our own society, or others of a comparable level of civilization, we have to study a vast and highly significant phenomenon that is generally labelled "popular art." Part of my aim in providing a definition of art that has no builtin value-judgments ranking decorative designs, stories, dances, songs, etc. is to encompass the popular arts as well as those for which we lack a convenient label—I suppose because they have been thought of as the real thing: portraits in oil, epic poems, ballet, lieder, etc. To gather popular and "esoteric" artworks (using the latter term with some diffidence) in the same broad class is not, of course, to deny differences in value, but it is to invite study of continuities and degrees of accessibility, of complexity, of training in taste, of seriousness in affect, and so forth. I don't see any good reason for not regarding *Guys and Dolls* and *The Pirates of Penzance* as artworks, along with *Tannhäuser* and *The Marriage of Figaro*. When it comes to other sorts of product now much studied by scholars—bed-quilts, cigarstore Indians, Dixieland jazz, old Tarzan movies—it may strike some people that we have wandered to the edge of art, if not beyond. There will, of course, always be a question whether something was indeed produced with an aesthetic intention, but even when this intention was probably minimal and the skill to carry it out deficient, the social function served may be the same as that of clearly artistic activities, or closely related to it. So a broad definition of art that still retains its essential connection with the aesthetic interest has much to recommend it.

21

Art as Make-Believe: Kendall Walton

As children, all of us played various games that involved pretending. Whether it was cowboys and Indians or a tea party of grass and mudcakes, such games were an integral part of everyone's childhood.

The provocative claim made by Kendall Walton (b. 1939) is that all representational art involves similar pretense. By using colored shapes on a canvas or words printed on a page, such works of art involve us in the complex games of make-believe we call "art."

Despite being an analytic philosopher, Walton is not interested in defining art, in specifying exactly which objects in the world fall under that concept. Rather, his concern—articulated forcefully in his magnum opus, *Mimesis as Make-Believe*, from which this selection is drawn—is to explore one mechanism that he takes to be basic to very many works of art, that of making believe or pretending. As I have said, the core idea of his theory is that art involves the same cognitive processes that structure many children's games, pretending that one thing is really something else.

Although this view might seem overly reductive at first sight—"Is Walton saying that art is nothing but a child's game?" a puzzled reader might wonder—it really is not, for Walton is not trying to reduce art to the simple games of pretense that we all engaged in as children. Rather, he is saying that some of the same basic cognitive processes are involved both in children's simple games and in complex works of art. This claim is intended to give us a handle on how works of art function in our lives.

Key to Walton's argument is the notion of a *prop*. Props are the basic elements in all games of pretense. Taking a stick to be an arrow or a stone to be a lump of sugar are two examples of how real things in the world functions as props for our imaginative games. In playing cowboys and Indians, young boys and girls in less politically sensitive times used sticks as props that helped structure their play. Without a stick in your hand, you simply couldn't shoot at someone else, whose body was also a prop that turned into an imaginary cowboy or Indian. What props do, according to Walton, is to structure the imaginary world that a game creates. Thus, "James is a cowboy" helps describe what is going on in the imagination of James and his young playmates, where a young boy fictionally becomes a skilled adult tender of bovine creatures.

But how does this view help us understand works of art? Let's consider the tried and true example of the *Mona Lisa*. If we look at the painting not as a representation—that is, consider it as only colored pigments on a canvas rather than as a painting of a young woman—then it is made up of an arrangement of colored pigments on a flat surface. Now, if we focus on one patch of color—say, the fleshy tones in the bottom center of the canvas—we are irresistibly drawn into a game of make-believe when we pretend that patch of canvas is a hand. And similarly for other parts of the canvas. When we look at any of them and see them as elements of a human being, we are, according to Walton, taking part in a game of make-believe in which we pretend that we are seeing an actual human being and not just colored paint on a canvas. Of course, we also know that we are pretending. It's not that we are completely fooled, as many viewers of *trompe l'oeil* paintings were; at the same time that we think to ourselves, "What an enigmatic smile that woman has," we are aware that we are entertaining that thought only fictionally, for there is no real woman there at all. It's all pretense, not reality.

Using the idea of games of make-believe as the key to understanding art is as innovative as it is surprising. Once one gets past the initial puzzlement that the idea generates, it seems to provide a key to understanding both how works of art function and why we enjoy them.

STUDY QUESTIONS ON THE READING

1. Central to Walton's argument is the notion of a prop. Explain what he means by this term. Can you think of a game of make-believe that involves an interesting use of a prop?

2. What does Walton mean by "fictional" and "fictional truth"? What role do props have in generating fictional truths? What is the relationship between fictional truths and imagination?

3. In a footnote, Walton states that the idea of fictionality makes Danto's notion of an "is" of artistic identification (see Chapter 18) superfluous. Recall what Danto meant by this term. Why is it made unnecessary by Walton's concept of fictionality?

4. How does Walton define "representation"? Are all props representations? What makes a prop a representation?

5. Walton distinguishes between nonfigurative art and nonrepresentational art. Explain the difference. Do you find his account of abstract art as representational convincing? Why or why not?

6. Do you find Walton's account of representational art as make-believe convincing? Why or why not?

❖

KENDALL WALTON: MIMESIS AS MAKE-BELIEVE

In order to understand paintings, plays, films, and novels, we must look first at dolls, hobbyhorses, toy trucks, and teddy bears. The activities in which representational works of art are embedded and which give them their point are best seen as continuous with children's games of make-believe. Indeed, I advocate regarding these activities as games of make-believe themselves, and I shall argue that representational works function as props in such games, as dolls and teddy bears serve as props in children's games.

Children devote enormous quantities of time and effort to make-believe activities. And this preoccupation seems to be nearly universal, not peculiar to any particular cultures or social groups. The urge to engage in make-believe and the needs such activities address would seem to be very fundamental ones. If they are, one would not expect children simply to outgrow them when they grow up; it would be surprising if make-believe disappeared without a trace at the onset of adulthood.

It doesn't. It continues, I claim, in our interaction with representational works of art (which of course itself begins in childhood). The forms make-believe activities take do change significantly as we mature. They become more subtle, more sophisticated, less overt. The games children play with dolls and toy trucks are in some ways more transparent and easier to understand than their more sophisticated successors. This is one reason why children's games will help illuminate the games adults play with representational works of art.

It goes without saying that in speaking of "games" of make-believe we must disavow any implication that they are mere frivolity. Children's games serve purposes far more significant than that of keeping them happy and out of mischief. It is generally recognized, I believe, that such games—and imaginative activities generally—do indeed, as their prevalence suggests, have a profound role in our efforts to cope with our environment. Children in the Auschwitz concentration camp played a game called "going to the gas chamber." Some may be horrified at the thought of treating such a tragic matter so lightly. But this "game" is probably best regarded as an earnest attempt by the participants to comprehend and come to grips with their terrible situation. In "playing" it they were, I suspect, facing the reality of genocide with the utmost seriousness.

Much needs to be learned about the benefits of make-believe, about just what needs it serves and how it serves them. But suggestions come easily to mind: that engaging in make-believe provides practice in roles one might someday assume in real life, that it helps one to understand and sympathize with others, that it enables one to come to grips with one's own feelings, that it broadens one's perspectives. An advantage of regarding paintings, plays, and

Reprinted by permission of the publisher from *Mimesis as Make-Believe: On the Foundations of the Representational Arts* by Kendall L. Walton, p. 1–12, 35–43, 51–57, 67–69, Cambridge, Mass.: Harvard University Press, copyright © 1990 by the President and Fellows of Harvard College.

the like as props in games of make-believe is that whatever we may learn about the functions of children's games of make-believe, and whatever we may feel we know already, are likely to help explain how and why such representational works are valuable and important.

Games of make-believe are one species of imaginative activity; specifically, they are exercises of the imagination involving *props*. . . .

PROPS AND FICTIONAL TRUTHS

Let us turn now to the settings in which imaginings occur . . .—to dreams, day-dreams, games of make-believe, and the experiencing of representational works of art.

When it is "true in a game of make-believe," as we say, that Jules goes on a buffalo hunt, the proposition that he goes on a buffalo hunt is *fictional,* and the fact that it is fictional is a *fictional truth*. In general, whatever is the case "in a fictional world"—in the world of a game of make-believe or dream or day-dream or representational work of art—is fictional. When Fred dreams of fame and riches, it is fictional that he is rich and famous. In Seurat's *Sunday on the Island of La Grande Jatte* a couple is strolling in a park; fictionally this is so. It is fictional that there is a society of six-inch-tall people called Lilliputians, and also that a certain Gregor Samsa was transformed into an insect.[1]

To call a proposition fictional amounts to saying only that it is "true in some fictional world or other." Sometimes we will want to specify which "world" something is "true in." So let's say that the proposition that there is a society of six-inch-tall people is not only fictional but, more specifically, fictional in *Gulliver's Travels,* or *Gulliver's Travels*–fictional. It is *Gulliver's Travels*–fictional also that a war was fought over whether eggs should be broken on the large or the small end. But the proposition that a couple is strolling in a park belongs to a different world; it is *La Grande Jatte*–fictional. "It is fictional that *p*" can be thought of as analogous to "It is believed (or desired, or claimed, or denied) by *someone or other* that *p*," and "It is *Gulliver's Travels*–fictional that *p*" as analogous to "It is believed (desired, claimed, denied) *by Jones* that *p*." So much for terminology. . . .

What is fictionality? We understand intuitively what it is for something to be "true in a fictional world"; if we didn't, criticism as we know it would be impossible. But how is fictionality to be analyzed? The first step toward an analysis is to investigate the relation between fictionality and the imagination. In doing so we shall see, finally, what props are and how they are important.

Being fictional and being imagined are characteristics that many propositions share. Readers of *Gulliver's Travels* imagine that there is a society of six-inch-tall people. Fred imagines that he is rich and famous. But it would be a serious mistake

---

[1] The notion of fictionality obviates the need for Danto's "is's" of artistic and other special sorts of identification (*Transfiguration,* pp. 126–27). It is fictional that a doll is a person or an actor Hamlet, in the usual sense of "is." (The identities in some of Danto's examples are fictional only in what I will call "unofficial" games of make-believe.)

simply to identify the fictional with what is imagined. What is fictional need not be imagined, and perhaps what is imagined need not be fictional.

"Let's say that stumps are bears," Eric proposes. Gregory agrees, and a game of make-believe is begun, one in which stumps—all stumps, not just one or a specified few—"count as" bears. Coming upon a stump in the forest, Eric and Gregory imagine a bear. Part of what they imagine is that there is a bear at a certain spot—the spot actually occupied by the stump. "Hey, there's a bear over there!" Gregory yells to Eric. Susan, who is not in on the game but overhears, is alarmed. So Eric reassures her that it is only "in the game" that there is a bear at the place indicated. The proposition that there is a bear there is fictional in the game.

Or so Eric and Gregory think. They approach the bear cautiously, but only to discover that the stump is not a stump at all but a moss-covered boulder. "False alarm. There isn't a bear there after all," Gregory observes with surprise and relief. And for the benefit of outsiders, "We were mistaken in thinking that, in the world of the game, there was a bear there." Eric and Gregory did imagine that a bear was there, but this did not make it fictional in their game. They do not say that fictionally there was a bear which evaporated when they approached, nor that it is *no longer* fictional that a bear was there at the earlier time. Gregory takes back his previous claim that fictionally a bear was in the place indicated, and he is right to do so.

Meanwhile, however, unbeknownst to anyone, there is an actual stump buried in a thicket not twenty feet behind Eric. Fictionally a bear is lurking in the thicket, although neither Eric nor Gregory realizes the danger. No one imagines a bear in the thicket; it is not fictional that a bear is there because somebody imagines that there is. But it is fictional. What makes it fictional? The stump. Thus does the stump generate a fictional truth. It is a prop. Props are generators of fictional truths, things which, by virtue of their nature or existence, make propositions fictional. A snow fort is a prop. It is responsible for the fictionality of the proposition that there is a (real) fort with turrets and a moat. A doll makes it fictional in a child's game that there is a blonde baby girl.

Representational works of art are props also. What makes it fictional in *La Grande Jatte* that a couple is strolling in a park is the painting itself, the pattern of paint splotches on the surface of the canvas. It is because of the words constituting *Gulliver's Travels* that fictionally there is a society of six-inch-tall people who go to war over how eggs are to be broken.

Props generate fictional truths independently of what anyone does or does not imagine. But they do not do so entirely on their own, apart from any (actual or potential) imaginers. Props function only in a social, or at least human, setting. The stump in the thicket makes it fictional that a bear is there only because there is a certain convention, understanding, agreement in the game of make-believe, one to the effect that wherever there is a stump, fictionally there is a bear. I will call this a *principle of generation*. This principle was established by explicit stipulation: "Let's say that stumps are bears." But not all principles are established thus. Some, including most involving works of art, are never explicitly agreed on or even formulated, and imaginers may be unaware of them, at least in the sense of being unable to spell them out. I do not assume that principles of generation are, in general or even normally, "conventional" or "arbitrary," nor that they must be learned. Nevertheless, what principles of generation there are depends on which ones people accept in various contexts. The principles that are in force are those that are understood, at least implicitly, to be in force.

Props are often prompters or objects of imagining also; even all three. Any stumps Eric and Gregory discover during their game have all three roles; they prompt Eric and Gregory to imagine certain things, and among the imaginings they prompt are imaginings about themselves (imaginings, of the stumps, that they are bears). But the three functions are distinct. It is clear already that props need not be prompters or objects of any imaginings. An undiscovered stump prompts no imaginings and is not imagined about, although it is a prop. Nor must prompters or objects be props. Suppose Eric associates raspberries with poison ivy; it was after picking raspberries that he suffered his worst outbreak of poison ivy, and he hasn't forgotten. He sees raspberry bushes in the forest and imagines poison ivy. Let's say that he also imagines of the raspberry bushes that they are poison ivy plants. This does not make it fictional in his game that poison ivy is growing in the forest, for there is as yet no principle of generation in effect, no even implicit understanding, whereby the raspberry bushes "count as" poison ivy. No such principle need be in force even if it happens that Gregory too associates raspberry bushes with poison ivy for some reason and is prompted to imagine as Eric does. Without the relevant understanding, Eric's and Gregory's imaginations simply wander—in similar directions, as it happens. They interrupt the game to engage in their own personal fantasies.

We are still lacking a positive account of fictionality. We know that being fictional is not the same as being imagined, and we have seen how some fictional truths are established—by props working in conjunction with principles of generation. But what is thus established? The answer will emerge when we consider what connections do obtain between fictionality and imagination.

Imagining is easily thought of as a free, unregulated activity, subject to no constraints save whim, happenstance, and the obscure demands of the unconscious. The imagination is meant to explore, to wander at will through our conceptual universes. In this respect imagination appears to contrast sharply with belief. Beliefs, unlike imaginings, are correct or incorrect. Belief aims at truth. What is true and only what is true is to be believed. We are not free to believe as we please. We are free to imagine as we please.

So it may seem, but it isn't quite so. Imaginings are constrained also; some are proper, appropriate in certain contexts, and others not. Herein lies the key to the notion of fictional truth. Briefly, a fictional truth consists in there being a prescription or mandate in some context to imagine something. Fictional propositions are propositions that are *to be* imagined—whether or not they are in fact imagined.

The agreements which participants in a collective daydream make about what to imagine can be thought of as rules prescribing certain imaginings. It is a rule of a certain joint fantasy that participants are to imagine traveling to Saturn in a rocket, or that they are to imagine of a particular stump that it is a bear. True, the agreements are made, the rules established voluntarily, and their prescriptions are relative to one's role as a participant in the imaginative activity in question. But they do prescribe. Anyone who refuses to imagine what was agreed on refuses to "play the game" or plays it improperly. He breaks a rule.

These rules are categorical. But I shall be interested mostly in conditional rules, ones to the effect that *if* certain circumstances obtain, certain things are to be imagined. The principle of generation in Eric's and Gregory's game is a conditional rule—the rule that if there is a stump at a certain place, one is to imagine that there is a bear there. Given that a stump does occupy a certain spot, imagining that a bear occupies that spot is mandated. Of course if participants in the game are unaware of a particular stump—because it is buried in a thicket, for example—their failure to imagine as prescribed is understandable; one can only do one's best to follow the rule. But to refuse to imagine that there is a bear where there is a stump in full view would be to flout the rule, to refuse to play the game.

The fictionality of the proposition that there is a bear at a certain place consists in the fact that imagining it is prescribed by a rule of the game. The rule is conditional, its prescription dependent on the presence of a stump. Thus does the stump generate the fictional truth.

Is there, for *every* fictional proposition, a requirement that it be imagined? If a stump is exactly 4 feet $5^1/_2$ inches tall, presumably it is fictional ("true in the game") that there is a bear of precisely that height. Must Eric and Gregory imagine *that*, on pain of playing the game improperly? Must they imagine (even nonoccurrently) that, like all bears, this one has a heart that pumps blood through its body, and that it likes blueberries? Is the appreciator of a picture of a flock of birds required to notice that fictionally there are exactly forty-seven birds in the flock and to imagine accordingly? To do *that* might well be to view the picture inappropriately, to let trivial details distract one from what is important about it. A proposition is fictional, let's say, if it is to be imagined (in the relevant context) *should the question arise,* it being understood that often the question *shouldn't* arise. In normal cases the qualification can be understood thus: If *p* is fictional, then should one be forced to choose between imagining *p* and imagining not-*p*, one is to do the former. When I speak of prescriptions to imagine in what follows, I will take them to be so qualified.

Principles of generation can in general be construed as rules about what is to be imagined in what circumstances, but only if we are careful to disavow certain likely implications of this term. Calling them rules may suggest that they are established by explicit fiat or agreement and consciously borne in mind in the contexts in which they are operative, as is the rule of Eric's and Gregory's game. I repeat: I make no such assumptions. A principle is in force in a particular context if it is understood in that context that, given such-and-such circumstances, so and so is to be imagined. The understanding need not be explicit or conscious. I do not assume that it must be "arbitrary" or "conventional." It may be so ingrained that we scarcely notice it, so natural that it is hard to envision not having it. We may have been born with it, or with a nearly irresistible disposition to acquire it. Nevertheless, principles of generation, whether or not we call them rules, constitute conditional prescriptions about what is to be imagined in what circumstances. And the propositions that are to be imagined are fictional.

Fictionality has turned out to be analogous to truth in some ways; the relation between fictionality and imagining parallels that between truth and belief. Imagining aims at the fictional as belief aims at the true. What is true is to be believed; what is fictional is to be imagined.

There is a persistent temptation to go one step further and to think of fictionality as a species of truth. (Imagining might then be regarded as a kind of believing, one appropriate to this species of truth.) The temptation is both reflected in and nourished by the fact that what is fictional is colloquially described as *"true* in a fictional world." "Fictional worlds" are easily thought of as remote corners of the universe where unicorns really do roam, where a war is actually fought over how eggs should be broken, where it is true that a bear hides in a thicket a few feet from Eric. Moreover, we often feel free to omit phrases such as "It is true in a fictional world that" entirely, just as we omit "It is true that" thereby asserting what is true rather than describing it as true. We say, simply, "A bear was hiding in the thicket" instead of "It is true in the game of make-believe that a bear was hiding in the thicket," and we say it in an assertive tone of voice. "A unicorn has been captured," we declare, in place of, "In (the world of) the Unicorn Tapestries a unicorn has been captured." "We are on our way to Saturn" does the job of "We are on our way to Saturn, in the world of our daydream." Thus we *seem* to assert that a bear was (really) hiding in the thicket, and so forth; we talk as though fictional propositions are true. Could it be that they are? Granted, they do not generally enjoy the kind of truth possessed, for example, by the proposition that there are no unicorns and the proposition that children sometimes play games of make-believe. "Truth in a fictional world" must be distinguished from "truth in the real world." But the temptation to regard both as species of a single genus is manifest.

I resist. What we call truth in a fictional world is not a kind of truth. The phrase "In the world of the Unicorn Tapestries," preceding "a unicorn was captured," does not indicate in what manner or where or in what realm it is true that a unicorn was captured, or anything of the sort. This is *not* true, *period.* "It is believed (desired, claimed, denied) that *p*" is used not to assert that *p* is true but to attribute a different property *to* it, to assert that this proposition is believed, or that someone desires or claims or denies it to be true. Likewise, "It is fictional that *p*" and its colloquial variants attribute not truth but fictionality to *p*.

My reasons for rejecting the temptation to construe fictionality as a variety of truth will emerge only when we begin to understand why we are tempted. Understanding the temptation is in any case at least as important as combating it. It is no accident that we speak as we do—as though there really are unicorns, as though a war actually was fought over how to break eggs—and an explanation is needed of why we do. The explanation and the source of the temptation lie at the very foundation of the human institution of fiction.

Although fictionality is not truth, the two are perfectly compatible. We noted earlier that people often imagine what is true and what they know to be true. Such imaginings are sometimes prescribed. It is fictional in Fred's daydream that he likes warm climates, as he actually does. It is *Tom Sawyer*–fictional, and true as well, that the Mississippi River runs alongside the state of Missouri. This point would seem to be too obvious to need emphasis. But it does.

The role of props in generating fictional truths is enormously important. They give fictional worlds and their contents a kind of objectivity, an independence from cognizers and their experiences which contributes much to the excitement of our adventures with them. This objectivity constitutes another affinity between fictionality, insofar as it derives from props, and truth. The stump game shows that what is fictional, when props are involved, is detached not only from our imaginings but also from what people think and what they take to be fictional. We can be unaware of fictional truths or mistaken about them as easily as we can about those aspects of the real world on which they depend. Eric and Gregory are genuinely surprised to discover that fictionally a bear is lurking in the thicket. It is not thinking that makes it so; the prop does. Fictional worlds, like reality, are "out there," to be investigated and explored if we choose and to the extent that we are able. To dismiss them as "figments of people's imaginations" would be to insult and underestimate them.

One final note: It is by mandating the imagining of *propositions* that props generate fictional truths. But imagining is not exclusively propositional. *Imagining a bear* goes beyond imagining that there is one. To imagine swimming or climbing or giving a speech is not just to imagine of oneself that one swims or climbs or gives a speech, if it is even partly that. Props prescribe nonpropositional imaginings as well as propositional ones. They do not thereby generate fictional truths, but the mandated nonpropositional imaginings are a distinctive and important part of our games of make-believe. . . .

REPRESENTATIONS

La Grande Jatte, Michelangelo's *David, Gulliver's Travels, Macbeth,* and representational works of art generally are props in games of make-believe. So are dolls, toy trucks, the stumps in Eric's and Gregory's game, and also cloud formations and constellations of stars when we "see" animals or faces in them, if we understand them to prescribe the imaginings they prompt. The differences among these various props need to be seen against the background of their commonality, the fact that all prescribe imaginings, generate fictional truths. But the differences are important. One of them merits early consideration. The stumps and cloud formations especially are likely to seem oddly sorted with representational works of art. I propose to understand "representation" in a way that will exclude them.

The stumps are ad hoc props, pressed into service for a single game of make-believe on a single occasion. Dolls and toy trucks, by contrast, are designed to be props; they were made specifically for that purpose. That is their function, what they are for, as it is the function of chairs to be sat in and of bicycles to be ridden. Moreover, dolls and toy trucks are meant to be not just props but props in games of certain kinds, ones in which they generate certain sorts of fictional truths: dolls are intended to "count as" babies and toy trucks as trucks. I will call games of the kind a given prop has the function of serving in *authorized* ones for it. A given doll is not designed for any *particular* game (token), of course, and it is expected to serve in many different ones; it will play its part in the games of several generations of children if it hangs together long enough. (A snow fort, however, may be built with just one specific game in mind.)

La Grande Jatte and other representational works of art are more like dolls than stumps. They are made specifically for the purpose of being used as props in games of certain kinds, indefinitely many of them played by different appreciators on different occasions.

Some might prefer to classify only things *created* to be props, things whose function in *that* sense is to be props, as representations. This would exclude not only stumps but also constellations of stars such as Ursa Major and natural objects generally (unless one wants to count the intentions of a creative deity), as well as artifacts created for other purposes (a table used as a "house" in a game of make-believe, for instance).

I favor limiting "representation" to things whose function is to be props, but in a looser and less restrictive sense of "function," which I will not define rigidly. A thing may be said to have the function of serving a certain purpose, regardless of the intentions of its maker, if things of that *kind* are typically or normally meant by their makers to serve that purpose. This may allow one to say that a pattern of cracks in a rock or a doodle drawn unthinkingly but which happens to resemble a drawing of a face has the function of making it fictional in games of make-believe that there is a face. Or something might be said to have a given function (for a certain social group) if there is a tradition or common practice or convention (in that social group) of using it or things like it for that purpose. Thus the function of coal may be to heat houses, of gold to serve as a medium of exchange, of Ursa Major to make it fictional that there is a bear.

(Even if we do understand a thing's function to be linked to the objectives of its creator, this may be so only because there happens to be a tradition or convention or understanding whereby this is so.)

Functions may in some cases be thought of as a matter of rules about how things are to be used. There may be rules that certain things, or things of certain kinds, or things made with certain intentions or in certain social contexts are to be used as props of certain sorts in games of make-believe. Such rules must not be confused with the rules of any particular games. They are rather meta-rules—rules about what sorts of games, games with what rules, are to be played with the things in question. I suggest that meta-rules of this sort (implicit ones) apply to standard instances of representational works.

It can be something's function to serve as a prop even if it never actually does so, even if the relevant game is never actually played. So representations needn't actually be used as props. A painting that is never seen and a forever unread novel will count as representations. (Such works are props in game *types* which, given their functions, they establish, even if the types have no instances or tokens.)

Functions are society relative. Coal and gold and constellations and dolls have functions only with reference to a given social context. An object may have a make-believe function for one social group but not for another, and so may be a representation for the one but not the other. Stumps that are merely ad hoc props relative to our society as a whole might have the function of serving as props in a more local context; a few children might constitute a temporary society relative to which the stumps are full-fledged representations.

It is the function, in any reasonable sense of the term, of ordinary representational works of art to serve as props in games of make-believe. This is a notable fact about them, quite apart from how "representation" is defined. If it is understood that a given object's function is to be a prop in games of certain sorts, the games do not need to be set up anew each time they are played. Stipulations are not required to establish the relevant principles of generation. This is like having an established language available to use for any conversation, rather than having to set up an ad hoc code for each one: The gain is not only in convenience, however. Insofar as it is the object's recognized function to be a prop in certain kinds of games, the principles are likely to seem natural, to be accepted automatically, to be internalized, and the prescribed imaginings are likely to occur spontaneously. Moreover, creators of props can predict how their creations will be used, and so can direct people's imaginings by designing props appropriately.

Appreciating paintings and novels is largely a matter of playing games of make-believe with them of the sort it is their function to be props in. But sometimes we are interested in the props themselves, apart from any particular game. And we are interested, sometimes, in seeing what contributions it is their *function* to make to games of make-believe, what fictional truths it is their function to generate, and what sorts of games would accord with their function, without necessarily actually playing such games. This is often the interest of critics, those who seek to understand and evaluate representations. It is also the interest of those who would draw inferences from a work about the artist, about his personality, style, talent, or originality. . . . [A]ppreciation as well as criticism often involves interest of this kind. But no such interest is appropriate to ad hoc props like stumps—those lacking the function of being props.

Characterizing representations as things with the function of being props in games of make-believe leaves unsettled many questions about what qualifies. Is the listener to imagine that Stravinsky's *Pulcinella Suite* was written in the late baroque period, or does she just note that its style is in some ways like that of baroque works? Do live television broadcasts have the function of prescribing imaginings? The bread and wine used in communion? A child's bronzed boots? Some questionable examples need to be understood more fully, but others will never submit to anything but arbitrary and pointless stipulation. That is no objection to our theory. The illumination claimed for it does not depend on the sharpness of the lines it inscribes. But there should now be less mystery in the uncertainty.

. . . [L]et us turn to what is called "nonrepresentational" or "nonobjective" or "nonfigurative" art, including the paintings of such artists as Albers, Malevich, Mondrian, Pollock, Rothko, and Stella.

NONFIGURATIVE ART

"To see something as a representation," Richard Wollheim contends,

> is intrinsically bound up with, and even in its highest reaches is merely an elaboration or extension of, the way in which, when the black paint is applied to

white canvas, we can see the black on the white, or behind the white, or level with it. [An objection:] things like diagrams, arabesques, doodles, . . . are cases where we see one thing on another, [but] surely [they] are not representational. We see one line cross *over* another, we see one edge of the cube stick out *in front of* another. . . . I agree: but then I do not see why we should not regard these as cases where we see something as a representation. Indeed, the only reason I can think of for not doing so is a prejudice: . . . that is, the crude identification of the representational with the figurative. For, of course, we cannot see the diagram of a cube, or a grid-like doodle, . . . as something figurative.[2]

In Kasimir Malevich's *Suprematist Painting* (1915) we "see," in the upper part of the canvas, a diagonally positioned yellow rectangular shape in front of a horizontal green line (or elongated rectangle), and that in turn in front of a large black trapezoid oriented on the opposite diagonal. This is how we see the painting, not how it is. Actually the yellow, green, and black are all on (virtually) the same plane; there are not one but two horizontal green shapes, separated by a corner of the yellow rectangle; and the black is not a trapezoid but a complex shape surrounding an assortment of rectangular areas. To see the painting this way is, in part, to imagine (nondeliberately) a yellow rectangle in front of an elongated green one, and so on. And this is how the painting is supposed to be seen; imagining the yellow in front of the green is prescribed by virtue of actual features of the canvas. So the painting is a prop; it makes it fictional in games of make-believe played by viewers that there is a yellow rectangle in front of a green one. Surely, also, it is the painting's function, in any reasonable sense, to serve as such a prop. So *Suprematist Painting* is representational.

I see no way around this argument. It might be thought that what we have here is simply an illusion—it *appears* to the viewer that there is a yellow rectangle, in front of a long green one, in front of a black trapezoid—not a case of imagining. But, in the first place, it is not clear that this is a full-fledged illusion. For there is a sense in which the painting appears to be a flat surface, with no part of it significantly in front of any other. We can easily tell by looking that this is so, even while we "see" the yellow in front of the green. And even if there is an illusion, this does not mean that viewers do not imagine the yellow in front of the green. The illusion, if such it is, does not fool us; we realize full well that the painting's surface is flat. Why not say that it induces an imagining instead? Saying this will be especially reasonable if, rather than ignoring or trying to escape the "illusion," the "appearance" of the yellow's being in front of the green and so on, the viewer cultivates it, dwells on it.

But if *Suprematist Painting* is representational, there will be few if any paintings that are not. Any "nonfigurative" or "nonobjective" painting that is to be seen in some figure-ground configuration will qualify. So, probably, will any design making use of what Gestalt psychologists call *closure*: such a design will mandate our imagining a square, for example, when it contains only hints of one. Jackson Pollock's dripped and splashed paintings may turn out to generate fictional truths about drippings and splashings. Most or even all music will likely have to be considered representational for analogous reasons.

---

[2] Wollheim, "On Drawing an Object," in *On Art and the Mind* (Cambridge, MA: Harvard University Press, 1974), pp. 27–28.

I do not find these conclusions distressing. They underscore easily over-looked but important similarities which supposedly "nonobjective" works do indeed bear to obviously representational ones. But they also leave us with a problem: There is a significant discontinuity between works like *Suprematist Painting* and works like *La Grande Jatte* that needs to be accounted for, even if both qualify as "representations." Wollheim offers some terminology; for him *Suprematist Painting*, though "representational," is not "figurative," whereas *La Grande Jatte* is both. But it is not clear how he would spell this out.

Here is a suggestion: The imaginings *Suprematist Painting* prescribes are imaginings about parts of that work itself. We are to imagine of the actual rec-tangular patch of yellow on the canvas that it is in front of the green, and so on. This distinguishes *Suprematist Painting* from *La Grande Jatte* and aligns it with dolls and sculptures. We are not to imagine anything of *La Grande Jatte* or its parts, but we are to imagine of a doll that it is a baby and (I presume) of a bronze bust of Napoleon that it is (part of) Napoleon. But in each of the lat-ter two cases the object of our imaginings is imagined to be something very dif-ferent from what it is, something which (arguably) it *necessarily* is not. A molded piece of plastic, for example, is imagined to be a flesh-and-blood baby. The yellow rectangle in *Suprematist Painting*, however, is imagined to be what it is: a yellow rectangle. It is also imagined to be related to other things in ways in which it isn't actually—to be in front of a horizontal green rectangle, for in-stance. But it *could* have been related to such other things in these ways. The yellow rectangle in *Suprematist Painting* is more like the actual mirror in Juan Gris's collage *The Marble Console* than the doll. The mirror is imagined to be a mirror, which it is, and to be attached to a marble tabletop, which it is not. (It is attached to a depiction of a marble tabletop.)

We might express this suggestion by saying that figurative paintings "point beyond" themselves in a way that *Suprematist Painting* does not. *La Grande Jatte* portrays people and objects distinct from the painting itself (fictitious ones perhaps), whereas *Suprematist Painting* merely depicts its own elements in a certain manner. *La Grande Jatte* induces and prescribes imaginings about things external to the canvas; *Suprematist Painting* calls merely for imaginative rearrangement of the marks on its surface. This formulation of the difference will not stand if we decide not to recognize fictitious objects. Nevertheless, we think of *La Grande Jatte* as portraying fictitious things beyond itself and *Suprematist Painting* as not doing so. . . .

THE MAGIC OF MAKE-BELIEVE

Make-believe—the use of (external) props in imaginative activities—is a truly remarkable invention. We have seen how props insulate fictional worlds from what people do and think, conferring on them a kind of objective integrity worthy of the real world and making their exploration an adventure of dis-covery and surprise. Yet worlds of make-believe are much more malleable than reality is. We can arrange their contents as we like by manipulating props or even, if necessary, altering principles of generation. We can make people turn into pumpkins, or make sure the good guys win, or see what it is like for the bad guys to win. The excitement of exploring the unknown will be lost to the extent that we construct the worlds ourselves. But if we let others (artists) construct them for us, we can enjoy not only the excitement but also the benefits of any special talent and insight they may bring to the task.

There is a price to pay in real life when the bad guys win, even if we learn from the experience. Make-believe provides the experience—something like it anyway—for free. Catastrophes don't really occur (usually) when it is fictional that they do. The divergence between fictionality and truth spares us pain and suffering we would have to expect in the real world. We realize some of the benefits of hard experience without having to undergo it.

This last advantage is common to imaginative activities generally. But only make-believe offers the remarkable combination of other features I am claiming for it. Worlds of deliberate daydreams (like Fred's) are amenable to human control, but they do not enjoy the independence that make-believe worlds do. Dreams and spontaneous daydreams can boast a certain independence; the dreamer waits to see what will happen, and is sometimes surprised. But neither he nor anyone else can effectively manipulate them. (Drugs or mushrooms or spicy food may have some, mostly unpredictable, effects.) One must accept dream worlds as they come.

Dreaming is, moreover, inevitably a solitary activity. One may have lots of company *within* a dream; one may dream about others as well as oneself. And the dreamer can share his experiences at breakfast. But what he shares then is merely his reflections on the dream from outside of it. We do not do the dreaming together; we do not join with others in experiencing a dream. Deliberate daydreams, by contrast, can be social. But they sacrifice not only the objectivity of their fictional worlds but also the vivacity of spontaneous imaginings. Games of make-believe, however, are easily shared; we play them together. And doing so neither compromises the objectivity of the fictional worlds nor lessens the spontaneity of participants' imaginings.

Objectivity, control, the possibility of joint participation, spontaneity, all on top of a certain freedom from the cares of the real world: it looks as though make-believe has everything. There are reasons for engaging in other modes of imagining, no doubt, purposes they serve that make-believe does not. But the magic of make-believe is an extraordinarily promising basis on which to explain the representational arts—their power, their complexity and diversity, their capacity to enrich our lives.

Representations, I have said, are things possessing the social function of serving as props in games of make-believe, although they also *prompt* imaginings and are sometimes *objects* of them as well. A prop is something which, by virtue of conditional *principles of generation,* mandates imaginings. Propositions whose imaginings are mandated are *fictional,* and the fact that a given proposition is fictional is a *fictional truth. Fictional worlds* are associated with collections of fictional truths; what is fictional is fictional in a given world—the world of a game of make-believe, for example, or that of a representational work of art.

22

Art as Text: Roland Barthes

Roland Barthes (1915–1980) was one of the founders of a mode of cultural analysis known as structuralism, whose central insight derives from the work of Ferdinand de Saussure (1857–1913). Saussure argued that the individual speakers of a language do not determine the meanings of the words they utter; rather, the significance of their utterances is determined by the pre-existing system of meanings on which they draw.

In his essay "The Death of the Author," Barthes makes a statement intended to be as provocative as Nietzsche's famous pronouncement of the Death of God. He applies the general structuralist claim to critique the idea of the artist as creator or author of the artwork. For many theorists of literature and the arts, such as Monroe Beardsley (Chapter 20), it is the intentions of the artist that confer artistic status on the products of her activity.

According to Barthes, modernism forces a re-evaluation of this idea: When the production of meaning by modernist literary works—those of Mallarmé and Proust are his examples—are analyzed with techniques modeled on structural linguistics, reference to their authors' intentions becomes superfluous. And this result can be generalized: Rather than speak of *the work* with its associations to the author as the origin of a single, determinate meaning, Barthes prefers the notion of text, understood as an ensemble of competing "writings" (or, as people would now put it, discourses) that the scriptor—it is he or she who replaces the now-deceased author—does not create, but quotes. The scriptor can only quote, because his or her sole resources are the already existing discourses at hand. But rather than fashion them into a unified whole—as previous theorists conceived of the outcome of artistic creation—all that is left for the scriptor is to bind them into a mélange. The presence of such distinct, competing discourses in a single text is what the structuralist critic is interested in exposing to view.

In place of the author—no longer the source of meaning—Barthes enthrones the reader, who, by decoding the competing writings that constitute the text, achieves authority over it.

Although Barthes writes about literature, his claims can be readily generalized to the other arts. The idea of the artist as the origin of the work of art has had a venerable history, dating back to the rise of the modern individual in 16th-century Europe. For Barthes, the advent of modernism signals the demise of this idea.

Barthes's writings have had a major effect on artists and theorists. Designating this as a postmodern age, they no longer view art as the product of an authorizing intelligence ideally in control of the meanings it produces. Instead, they believe, the best one can do is place various existing ideas in competition with one another. This emphasis on quotation rather than originality is distinctive of Barthes and his followers.

STUDY QUESTIONS ON THE READING

1. Barthes claims that the author is a modern figure. What does he mean by this claim? When does he say the idea of the author began?

2. What does Barthes mean by the "death of the author"? If texts do not have authors, how could their authors die?

3. How has modern literature contributed to the death of the author, according to Barthes? Do you agree? Why or why not?

4. How does linguistics figure in establishing Barthes's case?

5. Barthes claims that a text is not a unity but a diversity of writings. What does this claim mean? Do you agree with it? Do certain types of texts seem to fit his characterization better than others? Which—and why?

6. Why does Barthes say that the reader has replaced the author? What difference does this make to the practice of literary criticism?

7. How would Barthes's claim have to be reformulated to apply to art in general? Do you think it makes sense? Is there such a thing as art without artists?

8. Beardsley clearly disagrees with Barthes's claims. How might he respond to Barthes? What might Barthes say in return? Whom do you agree with, if either? Explain.

ROLAND BARTHES: THE DEATH OF THE AUTHOR

In his story *Sarrasine* Balzac, describing a castrato disguised as a woman, writes the following sentence: '*This was woman herself, with her sudden fears, her irrational whims, her instinctive worries, her impetuous boldness, her fussings, and her delicious sensibility.'* Who is speaking thus? Is it the hero of the story bent on remaining ignorant of the castrato hidden beneath the woman? Is it Balzac the individual, furnished by his personal experience with a philosophy of Woman? Is it Balzac the author professing 'literary' ideas on femininity? Is it universal wisdom? Romantic psychology? We shall never know, for the good reason that writing is the destruction of every voice, of every point of origin. Writing is that neutral, composite, oblique space where our subject slips away, the negative where all identity is lost, starting with the very identity of the body writing.

No doubt it has always been that way. As soon as a fact is *narrated* no longer with a view to acting directly on reality but intransitively, that is to say, finally outside of any function other than that of the very practice of the symbol itself, this disconnection occurs, the voice loses its origin, the author enters into his own death, writing begins. The sense of this phenomenon, however, has varied; in ethnographic societies the responsibility for a narrative is never assumed by a person but by a mediator, shaman or relator whose 'performance'—the mastery of the narrative code—may possibly be admired but never his 'genius.' The author is a modern figure, a product of our society insofar as, emerging from the Middle Ages with English empiricism, French rationalism and the personal faith of the Reformation, it discovered the prestige of the individual, of, as it is more nobly put, the 'human person.' It is thus logical that in literature it should be this positivism, the epitome and culmination of capitalist ideology, which has attached the greatest importance to the 'person' of the author. The *author* still reigns in histories of literature, biographies of writers, interviews, magazines, as in the very consciousness of men of letters anxious to unite their person and their work through diaries and memoirs. The image of literature to be found in ordinary culture is tyrannically centred on the author, his person, his life, his tastes, his passions, while criticism still consists for the most part in saying that Baudelaire's work is the failure of Baudelaire the man, Van Gogh's his madness, Tchaikovsky's his vice. The *explanation* of a work is always sought in the man or woman who produced it, as if it were always in the end, through the more or less transparent allegory of the fiction, the voice of a single person, the *author* 'confiding' in us.

Though the sway of the Author remains powerful (the new criticism has often done no more than consolidate it), it goes without saying that certain writers have long since attempted to loosen it. In France, Mallarmé was doubtless the first to see and to foresee in its full extent the necessity to substitute language itself for the person who until then had been supposed to be its owner. For him, for us too, it is language which speaks, not the author; to write is, through a prerequisite impersonality (not at all to be confused with the castrating objectivity of the realist novelist), to reach that point where only language acts, 'performs,' and not 'me.' Mallarmé's entire poetics consists in suppressing the author in the interests of writing (which is, as will be seen, to restore the place of the reader). Valéry, encumbered by a psychology of the Ego, considerably diluted Mallarmé's theory but, his taste for classicism leading him to turn to the lessons of rhetoric, he never stopped calling into question and deriding the Author; he stressed the linguistic and, as it were, 'hazardous' nature of his activity, and throughout his prose works he militated in favour of the essentially verbal condition of literature, in the face of which all recourse to the writer's interiority seemed to him pure superstition. Proust himself, despite the apparently psychological character of what are called his *analyses*, was visibly concerned with the task of inexorably blurring, by an extreme subtilization, the relation between the writer and his characters; by making of the narrator not he who has seen and felt nor even he who is writing, but he who *is going to write* (the young man in the novel—but, in fact, how old is he and who is he?—wants to write but cannot; the novel ends when writing at last becomes possible), Proust gave modern writing its epic. By a radical reversal, instead of putting his life into his novel, as is so often maintained, he made of his very life a work for which his own book was the model; so that it is clear to us that Charlus does not imitate Montesquiou but that Montesquiou—in his anecdotal, historical reality—is no more than a secondary fragment, derived from Charlus. Lastly, to go no further than this prehistory of modernity, Surrealism, though unable to accord language a supreme place (language being system and the aim of the movement being, romantically, a direct subversion of codes—itself moreover illusory: a code cannot be destroyed, only 'played off'), contributed to the desacrilization of the image of the Author by ceaselessly recommending the abrupt disappointment of expectations of meaning (the famous surrealist 'jolt'), by entrusting the hand with the task of writing as quickly as possible what the head itself is unaware of (automatic writing), by accepting the principle and the experience of several people writing together. Leaving aside literature itself (such distinctions really becoming invalid), linguistics has recently provided the destruction of the Author with a valuable analytical tool by showing that the whole of the enunciation is an empty process, functioning perfectly without there being any need for it to be filled with the person of the interlocutors. Linguistically, the author is never more than the instance writing, just as *I* is nothing other than the instance saying *I*: language knows a 'subject,' not a 'person,' and this subject, empty outside of the very enunciation which defines it, suffices to make language 'hold together,' suffices, that is to say, to exhaust it.

The removal of the Author (one could talk here with Brecht of a veritable 'distancing,' the Author diminishing like a figurine at the far end of the literary stage) is not merely an historical fact or an act of writing; it utterly transforms the modern text (or—which is the same thing—the text is henceforth made and read in such a way that at all its levels the author is absent). The temporality is different. The Author, when believed in, is always conceived of as the past of his own book: book and author stand automatically on a single line divided into a *before* and an *after*. The Author is thought to *nourish* the book, which is to say that he exists before it, thinks, suffers, lives for it, is in the same relation of antecedence to his work as a father to his child. In complete contrast, the modern scriptor is born simultaneously with the text, is in no way equipped with a being preceding or exceeding the writing, is not the subject with the book as predicate; there is no other time than that of the enunciation and every text is eternally written *here and now*. The fact is (or, it follows) that *writing* can no longer designate an operation of recording, notation, representation, 'depiction' (as the Classics would say); rather, it designates exactly what linguists, referring to Oxford philosophy, call a performative, a rare verbal form (exclusively given in the first person and in the present tense) in which the enunciation has no other content (contains no other proposition) than the act by which it is uttered—something like the *I declare* of kings or the *I sing* of very ancient poets. Having buried the Author, the modern scriptor can thus no longer believe, as according to the pathetic view of his predecessors, that this hand is too slow for his thought or passion and that consequently, making a law of necessity, he must emphasize this delay and indefinitely 'polish' his form. For him, on the contrary, the hand, cut off from any voice, borne by a pure gesture of inscription (and not of expression), traces a field without origin—or which, at least, has no other origin than language itself, language which ceaselessly calls into question all origins.

We know now that a text is not a line of words releasing a single 'theological' meaning (the 'message' of the Author-God) but a multidimensional space in which a variety of writings, none of them original, blend and clash. The text is a tissue of quotations drawn from the innumerable centres of culture. Similar to Bouvard and Pécuchet, those eternal copyists, at once sublime and comic and whose profound ridiculousness indicates precisely the truth of writing, the writer can only imitate a gesture that is always anterior, never original. His only power is to mix writings, to counter the ones with the others, in such a way as never to rest on any one of them. Did he wish to *express himself*, he ought at least to know that the inner 'thing' he thinks to 'translate' is itself only a ready-formed dictionary, its words only explainable through other words, and so on indefinitely; something experienced in exemplary fashion by the young Thomas de Quincey, he who was so good at Greek that in order to translate absolutely modern ideas and images into that dead language, he had, so Baudelaire tells us (in *Paradis Artificiels*), 'created for himself an unfailing dictionary, vastly more extensive and complex than those resulting from the ordinary patience of purely literary themes.' Succeeding the Author, the scriptor no longer bears within him passions, humours, feelings, impressions, but rather this immense dictionary from which he draws a writing that can know no halt: life never does more than imitate the book, and the book itself is only a tissue of signs, an imitation that is lost, infinitely deferred.

Once the Author is removed, the claim to decipher a text becomes quite futile. To give a text an Author is to impose a limit on that text, to furnish it with a final signified, to close the writing. Such a conception suits criticism very well, the latter then allotting itself the important task of discovering the Author (or its hypostases: society, history, psyché, liberty) beneath the work: when the Author has been found, the text is 'explained'—victory to the critic. Hence there is no surprise in the fact that, historically, the reign of the Author has also been that of the Critic, nor again in the fact that criticism (be it new) is today undermined along with the Author. In the multiplicity of writing, everything is to be *disentangled*, nothing *deciphered*; the structure can be followed, 'run' (like the thread of a stocking) at every point and at every level, but there is nothing beneath: the space of writing is to be ranged over, not pierced; writing ceaselessly posits meaning ceaselessly to evaporate it, carrying out a systematic exemption of meaning. In precisely this way literature (it would be better from now on to say *writing*), by refusing to assign a 'secret,' an ultimate meaning, to the text (and to the world as text), liberates what may be called an anti-theological activity, an activity that is truly revolutionary since to refuse to fix meaning is, in the end, to refuse God and his hypostases— reason, science, law.

Let us come back to the Balzac sentence. No one, no 'person,' says it: its source, its voice, is not the true place of the writing, which is reading. Another—very precise—example will help to make this clear: recent research (J.-P. Vernant) has demonstrated the constitutively ambiguous nature of Greek tragedy, its texts being woven from words with double meanings that each character understands unilaterally (this perpetual misunderstanding is exactly the 'tragic'); there is, however, someone who understands each word in its duplicity and who, in addition, hears the very deafness of the characters speaking in front of him—this someone being precisely the reader (or here, the listener). Thus is revealed the total existence of writing: a text is made of multiple writings, drawn from many cultures and entering into mutual relations of dialogue, parody, contestation, but there is one place where this multiplicity is focused and that place is the reader, not, as was hitherto said, the author. The reader is the space on which all the quotations that make up a writing are inscribed without any of them being lost; a text's unity lies not in its origin but in its destination. Yet this destination cannot any longer be personal: the reader is without history, biography, psychology; he is simply that *someone* who holds together in a single field all the traces by which the written text is constituted. Which is why it is derisory to condemn the new writing in the name of a humanism hypocritically turned champion of the reader's rights. Classic criticism has never paid any attention to the reader; for it, the writer is the only person in literature. We are now beginning to let ourselves be fooled no longer by the arrogant antiphrastical recriminations of good society in favour of the very thing it sets aside, ignores, smothers, or destroys; we know that to give writing its future, it is necessary to overthrow the myth: the birth of the reader must be at the cost of the death of the Author.

23

ART AS FETISH: ADRIAN PIPER

In her essay, "Performance and the Fetishism of Art Objects," Adrian Piper (b. 1948), a socially conscious artist and philosopher, both critiques how we view art and argues for the special status of performance art. Although other philosophers, such as Arthur Danto (Chapter 18) and George Dickie (Chapter 19), have called attention to the role of the artworld as conferring artistic status on objects, they have not been critical of this process. Piper contends that such theories obscure the actual mechanisms by which art is produced and viewed.

To make her case, Piper begins with a familiar view of some modern works of art: that they seek to make the uniqueness of objects available to us as viewers. In this, her interest is somewhat different from Benjamin's (Chapter 14), who announced the destruction of aura as a consequence of modern techniques of reproduction. Indeed, Piper does not share the view that the auratic character of art has been eroded. She argues instead that the contemporary art world values artworks precisely for their uniqueness. Further, she attacks the view that it is their aura that endows artworks with their distinctive ontological character. Rather, she argues, such a conception of art mystifies the real nature of the artistic process.

According to Piper, much contemporary art involves the creation of objects intended to call attention to their own uniqueness, a self-consciously auratic art, so to speak. But all objects are unique, although we often ignore this about them. As Heidegger argued in *Being and Time*, objects are for the most part submerged in the routines in which we employ them to realize our purposes and projects. One way to think about art, especially contemporary art, Piper suggests, is as an attempt to pluck objects from their normal referential frames, to get us to ponder precisely their specialness, their uniqueness.

But, Piper argues, such a project—even if it does animate the production of a great deal of contemporary art—is misguided. When we look at works of art, even as we are moved by what she calls "the mystery of the object," we cannot be aware of them just in their singularity. After all, we do compare works of art, treat them as instances of a kind, in order to understand them.

There is, according to Piper, no way in which we can be brought face to face with the uniqueness of an object, not even in a museum display. To think that such an unmediated access to individuality is possible is to believe in what the philosopher Wilfrid Sellars (1912–1989) has called, "the myth of the given," the idea that we can gain access to a purely given content, without the interposition of any general conceptual element.

But why does it seem so plausible that the meaning and value of art objects depend on their uniqueness? Piper's answer is that they have an inherently fetishistic character. Marx used the concept of fetishism to explain the nature of the capitalist economy. Although constituted through human activity, the economy has the appearance of a realm in which *things* are in control, determining, for example, their own prices. According to Marx, such a view of the economy fetishizes the commodity, treats it as having mystical powers. Piper argues that the artworld is similarly fetishized, for it treats art objects as independent entities that have a destiny beyond our control.

One important consequence of Piper's view is that art criticism should, as one of its goals, expose the fetishistic character of art. That is, the critic should focus on the social structures determining the object's production and exhibition. Here, Piper is making a case for a more socially conscious criticism, one that does not treat art as an autonomous realm.

Having made her case for a transformed understanding of art, Piper then turns to performance art, which differs from other art forms in virtue of the artist's presence as a constituent of the art object. Piper thinks that this gives performance art a unique immediacy for its audiences and, hence, a distinctive critical power. Nonetheless, she remains concerned that our fetishized view of art will keep performance art from realizing its potential as a socially engaged form of art.

STUDY QUESTIONS ON THE READING

1.   What does Piper mean by "the mystery of objects"? How does it compare with what Benjamin calls the "aura" of works of art?

2.   What are Piper's arguments against the view that art objects are unique? Do you find them convincing? Why or why not?

3.   Why does Piper think that the purported uniqueness of art objects is more central to the way we value them than their aesthetic value? Do you agree? What would this say about the artworld?

4.   Is Piper's analysis of the fetishistic character of art convincing? Explain.

5.   Is "performance art" art? Why or why not? Which theories of art that you have read can account for its status? Explain.

6.   Do you agree with Piper about performance art's unique status? Do you think performance art has a greater potential for social criticism than other forms of art? Why or why not?

❖

ADRIAN PIPER: PERFORMANCE AND THE
FETISHISM OF ART OBJECTS

Let me begin by describing a certain desirable experience common to the viewing and producing of art objects, which I will call *the mystery of the object*. This consists in having such objects appear to one as massive, charged, seemingly impenetrable presences, with their own inner workings and unique qualities. They sometimes seem to be almost anthropomorphic presences, alive and percipient like human beings. Viewing them is then a process of searching out and understanding their peculiar logic and structure, and discerning whatever it is that makes them unique.

Objects in general, not only art objects, have certain features that help to explain their perceived mystery. They are three-dimensional, like human beings. And like human beings, they not only inhabit but arrogate the space they're in. They also have a unique spatiotemporal location and can move through space and behave in accordance with discernible laws (causal, cybernetic, logical, intentional, etc.); this fact holds out the illusory promise that one may one day come to understand them completely, if one only gathers enough information about their structures, context, creation, and function.

All this is to say that, like human beings, objects have identities; that is, they are particular collections of qualities and features, such that, together with the quality of having some particular spatiotemporal location, any such object is uniquely individuated from all other objects. These qualities and features may include all the same physical features we ascribe to human beings (such as anatomical features, tactile qualities, and principles of motion, etc.); in this sense, such objects may even seem to have their own personalities.

We are regularly blinded to the mystery of objects in daily life because we so often utilize them as tools or instruments for achieving our ends, or for satisfying our needs and desires. Under these conditions, the objects in question are not seen as self-subsistent entities in their own right; rather, they are perceived and conceptualized through the lens of the final ends they are utilized for. Those of their features that are useful to us are retained and registered in consciousness, while those which are irrelevant are forgotten or discarded. In this way, our plans, expectations, and prejudices about objects shape our perceptions of them. We subject them not merely to the categories of thought but to those of practical use and manipulation.

This means that objects tend to lose their unique identities in the very process of being perceived by us, for they are quickly absorbed into the plans and projects we view them as serving. And this does not happen only with those particular objects we actually happen to use for the particular ends we actually happen to have. The phenomenon occurs as well with all similar and

---

"Performance and the Fetishism of Art Objects" by Adrian Piper. Reprinted by courtesy of the author.

related objects. We may utilize some particular objects that we identify in terms of their function, and this shapes our expectations and perceptions of other objects like them. These then extend to similar or related objects that may have a similar or related pragmatic function under similar or related conditions, and this instrumentalizing conception is then extended to any new object we experience: In order to discriminate and classify a new entity at all, the first and most basic question is always, "What is it *for*?" Thus all objects we experience tend to lose their individuality for us, and this is a consequence of our practical ability to subordinate each and every one of them to some actual or possible human plan. Our projects render them useful but necessarily anonymous.

One easy way of understanding much modern art since Duchamp is through its attempt to resist this pragmatic co-optation of objects. Of course modern art can be interpreted in many other ways and has many other functions as well. But one of the things it seems to do is to attempt to restore to us the individuality of particular objects by resisting our instinctive inclination to classify them under categories of use and function. Consider some of the strategies that have been employed for doing this:

1. One may isolate functional objects from their functional contexts, as Sylvia Mangold's floor paintings or Donna Dennis's house facades do;
2. One may isolate parts of functional objects from the context created by the complete functional object itself, as Rosemary Mayer's draped and sewn material sculptures do;
3. One may isolate particular features of parts of functional objects from their larger context, as do the tactile surfaces of Lee Krasner's or Helen Frankenthaler's paintings, the rounded industrial forms of Eva Hesse, or the hard-edge architectural Plexiglas® sculptures of Sylvia Stone;
4. One may isolate particular subfeatures of parts of functional objects, as do Agnes Martin's grid paintings or Jo Baer's framed white paintings.

The strategy can be iterated infinitely, to increasingly minuscule sensory features of objects, such as texture, color, mass, detail of shape, etc., that render the resulting art object increasingly abstract and particularized the more completely the feature in question can be divorced from its functional context and connotations. Such features may then be combined in random or idiosyncratic ways in order further to increase their conceptual distance from the functional categories in terms of which we normally identify them. Ideally the result is an entity with which we are confronted that forces us to experience its unique identity and its mystery on its own terms; terms that are resistant to our functional categorizations and our attempts to appropriate the object into our plans and projects. This ideal result is an important one because it provides us, as viewers, with a fresh and wholly unique experience that forces us to revise our assumptions about the external world and calls into question the expectations we bring to it. It requires us to expand and refine our classificatory concepts in order to accommodate a new type of object for which there is, by definition, only one exemplar.

I now want to show why this particular purpose of much modern art cannot possibly be achieved.

First of all, as soon as art objects are presented to the viewer *in order to* restore the mystery and uniqueness of the object, or *in order to* stimulate a new and freshening perceptual experience, they become instrumental tools. There is no difference in status between the goal of making or viewing art in order to "learn something new," "expand one's range of perceptual or experiential possibilities," "see the world anew," and so on, and the more mundane goals of making or using objects in order to, for example, keep food from spoiling, or heat the house, or stay dry in the rain. They are all purposes to which objects are subordinate. Nor is there, therefore, any difference between art ideologies that claim that art should be created and experienced for its own sake (that is, for the sake of our enjoyment of it) and those that claim that art should be created and experienced in order to raise people's political consciousness, provide an innocuous therapeutic outlet, advance the revolution, or indoctrinate. "Art for art's sake" enthusiasts don't seem to realize that the purported purity of art is already sullied by its instrumental relation to their own aesthetic needs. Art is always instrumental to some end. The pressing question is whether artists and viewers are making the right choices about which ends their art ought to serve.

Because restoring the mystery of the object and thereby providing one with a new and valuable perceptual experience are themselves plans or ends to which art objects bear an instrumental relation, we can make the same observations about the effects of this plan on our perception of the object as about the effects of other plans. For example, art objects are then perceived through the obfuscating lens of these plans; we view the object largely in these terms and seek out the features of it that most promote them. These features are retained in consciousness, while those that are irrelevant are discarded. Consider, for instance, the critical responses to Jackson Pollock's later drip paintings. It is hard to find any serious art lover who is willing to take seriously and explore the ramifications of their similarity to a house painter's drop cloth. Similarly, that one of Oldenburg's giant lipstick monuments strongly resembles West Berlin's Kaiser Wilhelm Gedächtnis-Kirche, both in form and possible function (that is, place of worship, shelter, architectural monument) is largely ignored. Instead, one speaks of Pollock's innovative working of the surface of the canvas, the creation of depth vying with two-dimensional tactility, the psychoanalytic import of the forms, and so on. Similarly, in Oldenburg's work, one hears much about the outsize functional object as a nonfunctional disruption of the architectural environment through the manipulation of scale. In both cases, our attention is drawn to what is unusual and new about these works, rather than what is functionally familiar. To point out what is functionally familiar about them becomes a kind of sacrilege; one is accused of philistinism, or underdeveloped powers of aesthetic discrimination. But many of Pollock's paintings *do* resemble house painters' drop cloths; and Oldenburg's giant lipsticks do look like the Kaiser Wilhelm Gedächtnis-Kirche. Anyone who thinks these assertions reflect negatively on the works or artists in question is missing the point, which is merely that our expectations of a certain kind of aesthetic experience shape our perception of the object by selecting and highlighting certain of its features at the expense of others.

This implies that, just as with other types of objects to which we bring a different set of expectations, the objects presented in an art context lose for us those aspects of their individual identities that are irrelevant to or inconsistent with their aesthetic function. Hence they are deindividualized by the very intention to make them most fully individual for us. Presentation in the art context is ultimately no more successful in restoring to us the uniqueness of the object's identity than are other, more patently functional contexts. In either case, the identity of the object is lost and absorbed into our aesthetic plans for it.

A second reason why the attempt to restore the mystery of the object cannot succeed is that the desire for the unique experience of the object can be viewed as an instrumental means to the more final end of increasing the marginal utility of commodity consumption in general. Here some clarification of terminology is in order. By *consumption*, I will mean any use or experience of a possessed object that satisfies some desire or other. Some examples: We consume food in order to satisfy hunger; we consume records in order to satisfy our desire to hear music. Similarly, we consume art objects in order to satisfy our desire for new and innovative perceptual experience, or our desire to expand our perceptual sensitivity to our surroundings, or for aesthetic of intellectual stimulation, and so on. By *marginal utility*, I will mean simply the utility or desirability of the last in the series of commodities consumed. Thus, for example, suppose I have a desire to quench my thirst. The first glass of water I drink will be the most intensely enjoyable; this is what it means to say that it has the "highest utility." The second glass of water will be less enjoyable; it thus has lower utility. The third glass of water will be still less enjoyable—indeed, may be positively unpleasant, if my thirst is already quenched. Thus it has less utility. If the marginal utility of something is the utility of the last in the series of that commodity consumed, we can see that the marginal utility of water as a thirst quencher diminishes; the utility of the last glass consumed is considerably lower than that of the first. And this is also true in general: Marginal utility always diminishes. The more of some commodity one consumes, the less satisfying it becomes.

Now let us apply this general point to my claim about art objects. I said that the desire for the unique experience of the object can be viewed as an instrumental means to the more final end of *increasing* the marginal utility of commodity consumption in general. This is to suggest that the desire for newness and uniqueness in our experience of an art object can be interpreted as a desire to consume a series of objects that *do not* become less and less satisfying the more of them we consume. This can be seen to be true by definition of "newness and uniqueness." What we desire is a new experience that is not the last, and therefore least satisfying, of a series of such experiences; does not represent the point of satiation past which we have no desire to experience such objects at all. What we desire is the experience of an art object that is both the first and the last in the series of such objects.

But this desire can never be satisfied. For, first of all, we have already seen that it imposes a plan or purpose to which the object is instrumental, and that, like any such plan, the unique identity of the object—that which would bring us the brand of experience of it we desire—is submerged, absorbed, and ultimately lost in it. Second, art objects themselves form a series of consumable commodities. Even if each member of the series could satisfy our desire for uniqueness, this desire itself would reach the point of satiation, past which continued further experience of such objects would be perceived not as perceptual stimulation but rather as a perceptual assault. This is just to observe that, like any commodity, the marginal utility of art objects must diminish, upon pain of sensory overload.

There are additional reasons why contemporary art practice cannot restore to us the unique identity of the object. We must generalize over the series of art objects in order to understand and identify them at all. For to understand something is at the very least to connect it coherently with other similar things; to be able to compare and contrast it with other objects; and to be able to make meaningful statements about it in language. If we could not do these things, we could not differentiate the object uniquely at all. But language consists—must consist—in general concepts, and we need these in order to be able to say or recognize what features of the object make it unique or different from other objects. So if we did not generalize art objects, we could not identify them as art objects to begin with. But of course to generalize about an object is to resist the mystery of its uniqueness: It is to classify it in terms of the features it shares with other objects and to differentiate it in terms of those it does not. But we could not identify those features in the first place if they were not general in their application to more than one such object.

The consequence is that, once again, the uniqueness of the object is lost in the very attempt to specify it. It is absorbed in precisely those general categories independently of which we would have no way of identifying it at all. For example, consider some of the ways in which we generalize over the class of art objects:

1. as "art";
2. with respect to genre, that is, figurative painting, nonrepresentational art, pottery, "hard-edge" sculpture, and so on;
3. with respect to *movement,* for example, pop art, pointillism, minimalism, mannerism, conceptual art, and so on;
4. with respect to the development and/or influence of a particular artist's interests, such that that artist's own works are shown to have common themes or concerns over an extended period of time, or such that the work of other artists is understood in terms of its similarities to that of the artist in question.

There are, of course, many other ways we may generalize over art objects, although these are less popular in the particular art context and historical period to which this discussion is addressed: with respect to social impact, propagandistic or didactic value, therapeutic value, political orientation, and so on. All of these are general categories we employ or might employ for identifying particular works of art.

Now one might object to my claims on the grounds that these arguments show only that we cannot directly experience the full mystery of art objects because we are blinded by our implicitly generalizing cognitive capacities.

But they do not show that art objects in themselves are not unique. Indeed, quite the contrary, for I said at the beginning of this discussion that every object is uniquely individuated from every other, at least by its unique spatiotemporal location, and more often than not by other specific features that compose, for each object, a unique collection of features that identify that particular object.

But this objection is mistaken. To begin with, we can concede that each object is uniquely individuated by its spatiotemporal location. But it would be difficult to show that aesthetic value depended solely on the spatiotemporal location of an art object, quite independently of any other features it might have. So let us put aside the spatiotemporal uniqueness of objects as indices of their aesthetic status. This is to claim that the brand of aesthetic experience I have been describing does not attach to art objects in virtue of their spatiotemporal uniqueness alone.

But more important, the objection is mistaken because it is at least in theory possible to reproduce any object, hence any art object, an infinite number of times. We have the technological resources to replicate the color, shape, texture, and design of any object we can produce in the first place. This, I believe, is simply a fact about the resources and capacities we now have to reproduce our own culture.

Reactions to this fact tend to run the gamut from outrage to denial. For example, when Nelson Rockefeller chose some important pieces from his collection to be reproduced in large quantities and sold at prices greatly beneath that of the originals some years ago, the *New York Times* critic who wrote about this expressed the view that Rockefeller's decision represented a travesty of the value of art and that it cheapened the original value of the works to be replicated. On the other hand, Nelson Goodman, in *The Language of Art,* tries unsuccessfully to explain why it is that a good forgery does not have the same aesthetic value as the original of which it is a forgery. His argument essentially comes to a flat statement that there are some features of a work of art that *cannot* be reproduced, however microscopic; and by this he does not mean to refer to such features as "having been produced by artist X," which are originally extrinsic to the actual experience of the object, but rather to actual visual or tactile qualities of the object that may be too microscopic to be perceived by the naked eye. But surely *these* qualities are, if microscopic, also extrinsic to the aesthetic enjoyment of the object as well. And if they are not microscopic, then it is hard to see why we should suppose them impossible to replicate.

These responses are interesting because they demonstrate the depth of our resistance to detaching the aesthetic value of a work of art from our experience of its purported specialness and uniqueness. It seems that our knowledge that there are other, identical objects with the same features as those we are contemplating spoils our pleasure in those features. Our response, which is to aesthetically devalue such a work, bears more than a merely analogical relationship to the response of economically devaluing a stone or metal upon discovering that it is not a scarce commodity after all. It seems that our aesthetic appraisal of art objects depends more on the presumption of their uniqueness as commodities than it does on the actual features it happens to have. For to discover that an object is a reproduction is to discover that it is one of a general class of such objects. But to discover that it is reproducible is then to admit that it at least proves the existence of such a general class.

So if my arguments so far are sound, art objects in fact have no unique identities. They are not, after all, unique collections of features. Hence the experience I have described as the mystery of the art object must be explained in some other way.

To do this, let us return to that experience itself for further scrutiny. We observed that a feature of this experience is that the object seems to have a certain personality; to be opaque and impenetrable; to have a certain presence and power that seems to arrogate the space it is in. We said that the object appears to us as an independent entity, sometimes with its own life, logic, and intelligence, which it is the critic's (or critical viewer's) job to discern and clarify.

Another way of explaining this experience is to say that each feature of a humanly produced object, and more strongly of art objects, is the consequence of human thought and choice, and human beings are, in fact, unique in the specified sense. When artists make objects, they either create their features, or modify them, or uniquely recombine them, or decide to allow them to remain in their natural states; these are all decisions that art producers make. Creators of nonart objects make the same decisions, and one can experience the mystery of nonart objects too. But art objects remind us of their mystery through their isolation from their functional contexts. As I suggested earlier, this is a project to which the art object is subordinated just like any other project. And if its mystery were a function of its unique individuality, it would be inaccessible to us for the reasons already given. But if the mystery of art objects is rather to be explained by the fact they exhibit human intelligence and planning, and a human investiture of energy and thought, then such isolation from functional contests would serve to illuminate these facts about them rather than to obscure them. On this reading, the mystery and "presence" of art objects are derivative from the mystery and presence of human beings—of objects in each of our perceptual fields that contain histories, thoughts, motives, aspirations that are initially opaque to us until we have gotten to know them; that is, become familiar with their inner workings and logic.

This is to say that art objects are irreducibly fetishistic (in Marx's sense): As creators of them, we invest art objects with the human attributes of personality, presence, power, and individuality because human beings have these attributes and express them in the products of their labor (when that labor is freely chosen). And as viewers, we respond to these attributes because we recognize them as the products of human labor.

Now, Marx's conception of the fetishism of commodities was a critical one. He argued that it was a mistake to ascribe to objects their own logic and intelligence, supposed to be independent of human intervention, and to then suppose that the object was therefore subject to laws—the economic laws of the free market—that were beyond the ability of individual human beings to control, when in fact objects of human labor were merely catalysts for human interaction and existed within the context of human social and economic relations. We can apply the same criticism to this conception of art objects. That art objects have their mystery and their power to compel our attention is undeniable, and this is part of why they are important to us. They remind us of who we are and of the capacities for imagination and creativity that we have. But to infer from this that such objects are subject to laws and forces beyond human intervention or control is to make precisely the same mistake Marx rightly deplored. It is to abdicate responsibility for what happens to the object after it is made, and for how it is to be understood, and to forget that we, after all, and not the object itself, control the object's destiny. This then illegitimately licenses us to wring our hands over critical misinterpretations of the object, and unjust terms of exhibition and sale of the object, and—occasionally—even over the inflated pricing of art objects, all the while regarding the unfolding history of the object from the sidelines as though we were a passive theater audience, powerless to intervene in the course of the play.

These observations suggest the following conclusions. First, the aesthetic value of an art object cannot depend on its unique identity (it has none). Second, its aesthetic value must depend on its generality (judgments about art objects are necessarily general in character). Third, the aesthetic value of an art object *should* include recognition of its necessarily functional character as a catalyst of human interaction; as an instrument for achieving human plans; and as a communicator of human ideas, intelligence, and choices. Acceptance of this third, prescriptive point would, of course, put the burden on us to take control of the aesthetic and economic destiny of the object to a much greater degree than most artists and viewers are presently inclined to do; and to clarify to ourselves just what plans we have in mind to which the object is subject (fame and fortune? communicating a message? art-world superstardom? political revolution? or counterrevolution? etc.). Finally, it would require us to revise considerably the terms by which we evaluate and understand the object. We would need to pay much more attention than we do to the biographies and intentions of their creators and hence to the social and economic conditions that inform them. We would need to recognize that there are no features of such objects, such as their color, balance, distribution of space, or compositional unity, that can be fully detached from the plans and intentions of their creators or the socially determined expectations and presuppositions of their viewers.

We would need to take far less seriously than we do the purported newness and innovativeness of the object as a criterion for making aesthetic judgments, and to think instead much more about whether the object is sparking in us the kind of response we think it ought to, or that we think we need to have more of; whether it is forcing us to rethink basic and unexamined presuppositions about each other and the world in general, or merely reinforcing the ones we have; and whether it is conveying to us meaningful messages and experiences of a kind that might enable us to become better individuals. That is, it would require the transformation of our critical vocabulary from an entrepreneurial one to a humanist one.

Now I want to apply these perfectly general observations about art objects to the special case of performance art. Clearly, performances count as art objects too. They are discrete, organized entities that are the outcome of human intelligence and choice; they exist within the art context; they invite appraisal in terms of the same general critical vocabulary we apply to other kinds of contemporary art objects; and they are created by individuals who think of themselves as artists and who are recognized as such, in accordance with plans motivated by the intention to produce art.

In addition, they offer us the same experience of a mysterious, self-directed, compelling presence—not the presence of a single material entity but of a spatiotemporally unified entity that includes material and nonmaterial components. Performances are also subject to the same implicitly general judgments that are given of other kinds of object, and are instrumentally subject to human plans in much the same way.

But from these features we cannot and do not infer their implicit generality. For they contain actual human beings as components, and this makes them unreproducible. So performances are partially unique, whereas other kinds of art objects are not.

This gives performance art a dual character. On the one hand, as art objects, performances are instrumental, general, and if my suggestion is accepted, fetishistic in the sense already described. To this extent, performers function as parts of an art object and hence as art objects themselves. This makes them susceptible to the same constraints and observations we have made of other kinds of art objects: They are used as instruments, they take on a general role of character (we often speak of this as a "mythic" role when applying these features to human beings in the context of a work of art), and fetishistically express an investiture of human intelligence and choice as catalysts for the human social interactions that lie behind them. On the other hand, performers are unique human beings and invest their role as performers with their own personalities and energy. This makes performance art a unique social collaboration between audience and performers without the intervening (and Marx would say, obfuscating) presence of a catalytic medium about which we feel fully justified in claiming that they are alien presences out of our ability to control, and subject to their own mysterious laws and logic. We cannot claim this about performers because they are, of course, subject to the same logic, laws, and controlling forces to which we ourselves are subject.

The danger to which I should like to call attention is that we may incline to fully assimilate performance art to the first category and forget the special status conferred on it by the second; that is, we may objectify performance art and therefore treat and view it in the same essentially entrepreneurial terms we use with other kinds of art objects, with all the attendant mistakes and self-deceptions already catalogued. The consequence of such an assimilation would be the deliberate defusing of performance art's potentially vast power to confront its audience with substantive claims that can effect far-reaching changes in people's views about any of the very many substantive topics with which performance art deals. It would mean the reduction of this immense power to the same innocuous, inoffensive, and politically sanitized level as is already occupied by so much of contemporary art. And in view of the preceding conclusions, this would call into question our justification for encouraging the further development of performance art at all.

24

ART AS DECONSTRUCTABLE: JACQUES DERRIDA

Jacques Derrida (1930–2004), the founder of the philosophic method of deconstruction, is less interested in providing an account of what art is than in exhibiting the illicit yet inevitable assumptions that have guided theorizing about art within the Western tradition. Thus, his contribution to the debate about the nature of art is not so much another theory as it is a critique of the unacknowledged presuppositions that have structured this very debate.

Our selection, from the introduction to Derrida's book *The Truth in Painting*, begins his elaborate deconstruction of Western philosophy's reflections on art. Derrida asserts that the way in which philosophers have asked about art's nature already predetermines their answers. His goal is to deconstruct this way of understanding art, to show how the answers to the question are already contained in the way in which the questions are posed. (He also says that he would deconstruct the social practices through which this way of thinking is taught, but little of what he does here is addressed to that issue.)

At the most general level, Derrida asserts that in their inquiry into art, philosophers make two unjustified assumptions. The first is that there are undoubted works of art. The task then becomes only that of explaining why *they* are works of art. But, Derrida asks, why should we assume without dispute that there exists a set of things that are works of art? Isn't this itself something to be justified by a philosophy of art? Second, philosophers have also assumed that there is one thing that the word "art" refers to and that the philosophy of art will explain this unitary phenomenon. Again, Derrida asks whether this assumption is justified: Why not assume that "art" is polysemous, that there is a variety of meanings to this term that cannot be unified behind a single, undifferentiated, original meaning?

This latter assumption has important consequences, for it results in the belief that actual works of art are somehow simply embodiments of the univocal meaning that art has. Rather than seeing art as doing many different things, Derrida claims, philosophers see art as essentially always the same, despite its many instantiations in different works. Further, because this general meaning of art is something that can be formulated in language and, more specifically, in speech—one of the great illicit assumptions of Western philosophy, according to Derrida, is that speech is more basic than writing—all of the diverse arts are subordinated to "the authority of speech and the 'discursive' arts."

The claim that speech is more basic than writing lies at the heart of what Derrida terms the metaphysics of presence. All of Western metaphysics is contaminated by this idea: that it is possible to have a completely unmediated grasp of reality. Derrida's goal in deconstructing a philosophic text is to show how it is unconsciously structured by this fundamental assumption.

It is not clear how Derrida conceives of the alternative to Western metaphysics or what shape a philosophy beyond the metaphysics of presence would take. For our purposes, however, that is less important than seeing how Derrida proposes to deconstruct previous philosophic attempts to say what art it. Thus, in our selection, Derrida takes up the task of a provisional deconstruction of Hegel's (Chapter 6) and Heidegger's (Chapter 13) discussions of art, the two texts he sees as fundamental for Western aesthetics. He argues that, despite their manifest differences—Heidegger explicitly sets himself the task of going beyond Hegel's reflections on art—both texts embody this Western approach.

In his more specific discussions of Hegel and Heidegger, Derrida exposes the presence in both their works of a common, fundamental metaphor: that of the circle. As he points out, the circle is itself a figure whose history could be traced within Western art. It is therefore ironic, to say the least, that these two philosophers rely on it in their expositions of art's nature, for it creates a vicious circle. If defining art depends on having a clear concept of circularity—itself explicated with the history of art itself—then the attempt at definition cannot succeed.

Be that as it may, Derrida goes on to show how all the presuppositions of the Western approach to art are common to the two texts of the two great philosophers. Crucially, each selects exemplars from the Western canon whose status as works of art are uncontested and then sets out to create a theory to justify that status. As a result, according to Derrida, they are condemned to simply repeat the tradition's answer to the question "What is art?" or, more carefully, their reflections on art take place on a ground whose possibilities are already contained and constrained by the terms with which they set out.

The present selection is entitled "Parergon," a term that means a secondary or subordinate element in a work, such as its "ornamentation." One of Derrida's goals in the balance of his book is to undercut the idea that we have justification for distinguishing the primary and secondary aspects of works of art. Although this selection gives no more than a taste of Derrida's method, it provides a good example of the difficult and disjointed style of his later works, in which Derrida extends the scope of deconstruction to his own writing in an attempt to disrupt the familiar discursive strategies of Western metaphysics all the way down to the very typography of its texts. Hence, the sentences beginning and ending in midstream and the framelike brackets enclosing blank spaces separating portions of written text.

By violating norms of continuity previously taken to be necessary for philosophical argumentation, Derrida's text shows them to be dispensable. Indeed, for him, this fragmented text—both visually and linguistically—points toward the possibility of writing that is beyond or outside of Western metaphysics.

Derrida's deconstructive readings of the great texts of the Western tradition from Plato onward probe deeply into the assumptions that have guided them. Here, we can appreciate the trenchancy of such a reading applied to the debate about the nature of art. It remains to be seen, however, whether ultimately it proves telling.

STUDY QUESTIONS ON THE READING

1. What does Derrida see as problematic about the assumption that certain objects can unproblematically be designated works of art?

2. Why is it a mistake, according to Derrida, to assume that art is a unitary phenomenon? Do you agree with him?

3. How does thinking of art as unitary result in a hierarchy of arts? Why is this a problem? Should art involve a hierarchical categorization of different arts, like poetry and painting? Why or why not?

4. How, according to Derrida, is the circle metaphor present in Hegel's and Heidegger's theories of art? Why does he find this metaphor problematic? Do you think this is a fundamental weakness of these accounts? Explain.

5. Does it matter that Hegel and Heidegger privilege Western art? Why or why not?

❖

JACQUES DERRIDA: THE TRUTH IN PAINTING

[A note on typography: Derrida's text does not follow the usual linguistic or typographic style of academic prose. I have tried to follow his practice here as closely as possible. —T.E.W.]

PARERGON I. LEMMATA

it's enough

to say: abyss and satire of the abyss

begin and end with a "that's enough" which would have *nothing to do with* the sufficing or self-sufficing of sufficiency, *nothing to do with* satisfaction. Reconsider, further on, the whole syntax of these

---

untranslatable locutions, the *with* of the *nothing to do* . . . . Write, if possible, finally, without *with*, not *without* but without *with*, finally, *not even oneself.*

Opening with the *satis*, the *enough* (inside and outside, above and below, to left and right), satire, farce on the edge of excess

what is a title?

And what if *parergon* were the title?

Here the false title is art. A seminar would treat *of art*. Of art and the fine arts. It would thus answer to a program and to one of its great questions. These questions are all taken from a determinate set. Determined according to history and system. The history would be that of philosophy within which the history of the philosophy of art would be marked off, insofar as it treats of art and of the history of art: its models, its concepts, its problems have not fallen from the skies, they have been constituted according to determinate modes at determinate moments. This set forms a system, a greater logic and an encyclopedia within which the fine arts would stand out as a particular region. The *Agrégation de philosophie*[1] also forms a history and a system

how a question of this type—art—becomes inscribed in a program. We must not only turn to the history of philosophy, for example to the Greater Logic or the Encyclopedia of Hegel, to his *Lectures on Aesthetics* [see Chapter 6] which sketch out, precisely, one part of the encyclopedia, system of training for teaching and cycle of knowledge. We must take account of certain specific relays, for example those of so-called philosophy teaching in France, in the institution of its programs, its forms of examinations and competitions, its scenes and its rhetoric. Whoever undertook such an inquiry—and I do no more here than point out its stakes and its necessity—would no doubt have to direct herself, via a very overdetermined political history, toward the network indicated by the proper name of Victor Cousin, that very French philosopher and politician who thought himself very Hegelian and never stopped wanting to *transplant* (that is just about his word for it) Hegel into France, after having insistently asked him, in writing at least, to impregnate him, Cousin, and through him French philosophy . . . . . Strengthened, among other things, by this more or less hysterical pregnancy, he played a determinant role, or at least represented one, in the construction of the French University and its philosophical institution—all the teaching structures that we still inhabit. Here I do no more than name, with a proper name as one of the guiding threads, the necessity of a deconstruction. Following the consistency of its

[1] The *Agrégation de philosophie* is the highest degree awarded by French universities. It is the rough equivalent of the Ph.D. degree. —T.E.W.]

logic, it attacks not only the internal edifice, both semantic and formal, of philosophemes, but also what one would be wrong to assign to it as its external housing, its extrinsic conditions of practice: the historical forms of its pedagogy, the social, economic or political structures of this pedagogical institution. It is because deconstruction interferes with solid structures, "material" institutions, and not only with discourses or signifying representations, that it is always distinct from an analysis or a "critique." And in order to be pertinent, deconstruction works as strictly as possible in that place where the supposedly "internal" order of the philosophical is articulated by (internal *and* external) necessity with the institutional conditions and forms of teaching. To the point where the concept of institution itself would be subjected to the same deconstructive treatment. But I am already leading into next year's seminar (1974–5)

to delimit now a narrower entry into what I shall try to expound this year in the course. Traditionally, a course begins by the semantic analysis of its title, of the word or concept which entitles it and which can legitimate its discourse only by receiving its own legitimation from that discourse. Thus one would begin by asking oneself: What is *art*? Then: Where does it come from? What is the origin of art? This assumes that we reach agreement about what we understand by the word *art*. Hence: What is the origin of the *meaning* of "art"? For these questions, the *guiding thread* (but it is precisely toward the notion of the *thread* and the *interlacing* that I should like to lead you, from afar) will *always* have been the existence of "works," of "works of art." Hegel says so at the beginning of the *Lectures on Aesthetics*: we have before us but a single representation, namely, that there are works of art. This representation can furnish us with an appropriate point of departure. So the question then becomes: What is "the origin of the work of art"? And it is not without significance that this question gives its title to one of the last great discourses on art, that of Heidegger [see Chapter 13].

This protocol of the question installs us in a fundamental presupposition, and massively predetermines the system and combinatory possibilities of answers. What it begins by implying is that art—the word, the concept, the thing—has a unity and, what is more, an originary meaning, an *etymon*, a truth that is *one* and *naked* and that it would be sufficient to unveil it *through* history. It implies first of all that "art" can be reached following the three ways of word, concept, and thing, or again of signifier, signified, and referent, or even by some opposition between presence and representation.

Through history: the crossing can in this case just as well denote historicism, the determining character of the historicity of meaning, as it can denote ahistoricity, history crossed, transfixed in the direction of meaning, in the sense of a meaning in itself ahistorical. The syntagm "through history" could entitle all our questions without constraining them in advance. By presupposing the *etymon*—one and naked—a presupposition without which one would perhaps never open one's mouth, by beginning with a meditation on the apparent polysemy of *tékhne* in order to lay bare the simple kernel which supposedly lies hidden behind the multiplicity, one gives oneself to thinking that *art* has a meaning, one meaning. Better, that its history is *not* a history or that it is *one* history only in that it is governed by this one and naked meaning, under the regime of its internal meaning, as history of the meaning of art. If one were to consider the *physis/tékhne* opposition to be irreducible, if one were to accredit so hastily its translation as *nature/art* or *nature/technique,* one would easily commit oneself to thinking that art, being no longer nature, is history. The opposition nature/history would be the analogical relay of *physis/tékhne.* One can thus already say: as for history, we shall have to deal with the contradiction or the oscillation between two apparently incompatible motifs. They both ultimately come under one and the same logical formality: namely, that if the philosophy of art always has the greatest difficulty in dominating the history of art, a certain concept of the historicity of art, this is, paradoxically, because it too easily thinks of art as historical. What I am putting forward here obviously assumes the transformation of the concept of history, from one statement to the other. That will be the work of this seminar

If, therefore, one were to broach lessons on art or aesthetics by a question of this type ("What is art?" "What is the origin of art or of works of art?" "What is the meaning of art?" "What does art mean?" etc.), the form of the question would already provide an answer. Art would be predetermined or precomprehended in it. A conceptual opposition which has traditionally served to comprehend art would already, always, be at work there: for example the opposition between meaning, as inner content, and form. Under the apparent diversity of the historical forms of art, the concepts of art or the words which seem to translate "art" in Greek, Latin, the Germanic languages, etc. (but the closure of this list is already problematic), one would be seeking a one-and-naked meaning which would inform from the inside, like a content, while distinguishing itself from the forms which it informs. In order to think art in general, one thus accredits a series of oppositions (meaning/form, inside/outside, content/container, signified/signifier, represented/representer, etc.) which, precisely, structure the traditional interpretation of works of art. One makes of art in general an object in which one claims to distinguish an inner meaning, the invariant, and a multiplicity of external variations *through* which, as through so many veils, one would try to see or restore the true, full, originary meaning: one, naked. Or again, in an analogous gesture, by asking what art *means* (to say), one submits the mark "art" to a very determined regime of interpretation which has supervened in history: it consists, in its *tautology* without reserve, in interrogating the *vouloir-dire* [will to say—T.E.W.] of every work of so-called art, even if its form is not that of saying. In this way one wonders what a plastic or musical work means (to say), submitting all productions to the authority of speech and the "discursive" arts

such that by accelerating the rhythm a little one would go on to this collusion: between the question ("What is art?" "What is the origin of the work of art?" "What is the meaning of art or of the history of art?") and the hierarchical classification of the arts. When a philosopher repeats this question without transforming it, without destroying it in its form, its question-form, its onto-interrogative structure, he has already subjected the whole of *space* to the discursive arts, to voice and the *logos*. This can be verified: teleology and hierarchy are prescribed in the envelope of the question

the philosophical encloses art in its circle but its discourse on art is at once, by the same token, caught in a circle.

Like the figure of the third term, the figure of the circle asserts itself at the beginning of the *Lectures on Aesthetics* and the *Origin of the Work of Art*. So very different in their aim, their procedure, their style, these two discourses have in common, as a common interest, that they exclude—(that) which then comes to form, close and bound them from inside and outside alike. And if it were a frame

one of them, Hegel's, gives classical teleology its greatest deployment. He finishes off, as people say a little too easily, onto-theology. The other, Heidegger's, attempts, by taking a step backwards, to go back behind all the oppositions that have commanded the history of aesthetics. For example, in passing, that of form and matter, with all its derivatives. Two discourses, then, as different as could be, on either side of a line whose tracing we imagine to be simple and nondecomposable. Yet how can it be that they have in common this: the subordination of all the arts to speech, and, if not to poetry, at least to the poem, the said, language, speech, nomination . . . ? (Reread here the third and final part of the *Origin* . . . , "Truth and Art.")

not go any further, for the moment, in the reading of these two discourses. Keeping provisionally to their introductions, I notice the following: they both start out from a figure of the circle. And they stay there.

They stand in it even if their residence in the circle apparently does not have the same status in each case. For the moment I do not ask myself: What is a circle? I leave to one side the figure of the circle, its place, its privilege or its decadence in the history of art. Since the treatment of the circle is part of the history of art and is delimited in it as much as it delimits it, it is perhaps not a neutral gesture to apply to it something that is also nothing other than one of its figures. It is still a circle, which redoubles, re-marks, and places *en abyme*[2] the singularity of this figure. Circle of circles, circle in the encircled circle. How could a circle place itself *en abyme*?

   The circle and the abyss, that would be the title. On the way we will no doubt encounter the question of the title. What happens when one entitles a "work of art"? What is the *topos* of the title? Does it take place (and where?) in relation to the work? On the edge? Over the edge? On the internal border? In an overboard that is re-marked and reapplied, by invagination, within, between the presumed center and the circumference? Or between that which is framed and that which is framing in the frame? Does the *topos* of the title, like that of a *cartouche,* command the "work" from the discursive and juridical instance of an *hors-d'oeuvre,* a place outside the work, from the exergue of a more or less directly definitional statement, and even if the definition operates in the manner of a performative? Or else does the title play *inside* the space of the "work," inscribing the legend, with its definitional pretension, in an ensemble that it no longer commands and which constitutes it—the title—as a localized effect? If I say for example that the circle and the abyss will be the title of the play that I am performing today, as an introduction, what am I doing and what is happening? Will the circle and the abyss be the object of my discourse and defined by it? Or else do they describe the form which constrains my discourse, its scene rather than its object, and moreover a scene stolen away by the abyss from present representation? As if a discourse on the circle also had to *describe* a circle, and perhaps the very one that it describes, describe a circular movement at the very moment that it describes a circular movement, describe it displacing itself in its meaning; or else as if a discourse on the abyss had to know the abyss, in the sense that one knows something that happens to or affects one, as in "to know failure" or "to know success" rather than to know an object. The circle and the abyss, then, the circle *en abyme.* ⸻

beginning of the *Lectures on Aesthetics.* From the first pages of the introduction, Hegel poses, as always, the question of the point of departure. How is one to begin a philosophical discourse on aesthetics? Hegel had already linked the essence of the beautiful to the essence of art. According to the determinate opposition of nature and mind, and *thus* of nature and art, he had already posited that a

---

[2] This term was introduced into literary study by André Gide. When a concept is placed "en abyme," its instability is shown. T.E.W.

philosophical work devoted to aesthetics, the philosophy or science of the beautiful, must exclude natural beauty. It is in everyday life that one speaks of a beautiful sky. But there is no natural beauty. More precisely, artistic beauty is superior to natural beauty, as the mind that produces it is superior to nature. One must therefore say that absolute beauty, the *telos* or final essence of the beautiful, appears in art and not in nature as such. Now the problem of the introduction causes no difficulty in the case of the natural or mathematical sciences: their object is given or determined in advance, and with it the method that it requires. When, on the contrary, the sciences bear on the products of the mind, the "need for an introduction or preface makes itself felt." Since the object of such sciences is produced by the mind, by that which knows, the mind will have to have engaged in a self-knowledge, in the knowledge of what it produces, of the product of its own production. This autodetermination poses singular problems of priority. The mind must put itself into its own product, produce a discourse on what it produces, introduce itself of itself into itself. This circular duction, this intro-reduction to oneself, calls for what Hegel names a "presupposition". In the science of the beautiful, the mind presupposes itself, anticipates itself, precipitates itself. *Head first.* Everything with which it commences is already a result, a *work,* an effect of a projection of the mind, a *resultare.* Every foundation, every justification will have been a result—this is, as you know, the mainspring of the speculative dialectic. Presuppositions must proceed from a "proven and demonstrated necessity," explains Hegel. "In philosophy, nothing must be accepted which does not possess the character of necessity, which means that everything in philosophy must have the value of a result."

We are, right from the introduction, encircled.

No doubt art figures one of those productions of mind thanks to which the latter returns to itself, comes back to consciousness and cognizance and comes to its proper place by *returning* to it, in a circle. What is *called* mind is that which says to itself "come" only to hear *itself* already saying "come back." The mind is what it is, says what it means, only *by returning.* Retracing its steps, in a circle. But art forms only one of the circles in the great circle of the *Geist* or the revenant (this visitor can be called *Gast,* or *ghost, guest* or *Gespenst*). The end of art, and its truth, is religion, that other circle of which the end, the truth, will have been philosophy, and so on. And you know—we shall have to get the most out of this later on—the function of the ternary rhythm in this circulation. The fact remains that here art is studied from the point of view of its end. Its pastness is its truth. The philosophy of art is thus a circle in a circle of circles: a "ring" says Hegel, in the totality of philosophy. It turns upon itself and in annulling itself it links onto other rings. This annular concatenation forms the circle of circles of the philosophical encyclopedia. Art cuts out a circumscription or takes away a circumvolution from it. It encircles itself   ———

|

——   the inscription of a circle

in the circle does not necessarily *give* the abyss, onto the abyss, *en abyme.* In order to be abyssal, the smallest circle must inscribe in itself the figure of the largest. *Is there* any abyss in the Hegelian circulation? To the question posed in this form there is no decidable answer. What does the "there is" mean in these statements? Wherein does the "there is" differ from a "there exists," or "*X* is," "*X* presents itself," "*X* is present," etc.? Skirting round a necessary protocol here (it would proceed via the *gift* or the giving of the abyss, onto the abyss, *en abyme*, via the problematic of the *es gibt, il y a, it gives,* and of the *es gibt Sein,* opened by Heidegger), I note only this: the answer arrests the abyss, unless it be already dragged down into it in advance. And can be in it without knowing it, at the very moment that a proposition of the type "this is an abyss or a *mise en abyme*" appears to destroy the instability of the relations of whole to part, the indecision of the structures of inclusion which throws *en abyme*. The statement itself can *form part of the whole*

metaphor of the circle of circles, of training as philosophical encyclopedia. Organic metaphor, finalized as a whole whose parts conspire. Biological metaphor too. But it is also a metaphor, if it is a metaphor, for art and for the work of art. The totality of philosophy, the encyclopedic corpus is described *as* a living organism *or as* a work of art. It is represented on the model of one of its parts which thus becomes greater than the whole of which it forms part, which it makes into a part. As always, and Kant formalized this in an essential way, the communication between the problem of aesthetic judgment and that of organic finality is internal. At the moment of describing *lemmatic* precipitation, the need to treat the concept of *philosophy of art* in an anticipatory way, Hegel has to have recourse, certainly, to the metaphor of the circle and of the circle of circles which he says, moreover, is *only* a representation. But also to the metaphor of the organic whole. Only philosophy in its entirety gives us knowledge of the universe as a unique organic totality in itself, which develops "from its own concept." Without losing anything of what makes it a whole "which returns to itself," this "sole world of truth" is contained, retained, and gathered together in itself. In the "circlet" of this scientific necessity, each part represents a "circle returning into itself" and keeping a tie of solidarity with the others, a necessary and simultaneous interlacing. It is animated by a "backward movement" and by a "forward movement" by which it develops and reproduces itself in another in a fecund way. Thus it is that, for us, the concept of the beautiful and of art is "a presupposition given by the system of philosophy." Philosophy alone can pose the question "What is the beautiful?" and answer it: the beautiful is a production of art, i.e., of the mind. The idea of beauty is given to us by art, that circle inside the circle of the mind and of the philosophical encyclopedia, etc.

Before beginning to speak of the beautiful and of the fine arts, one ought therefore, by right, to develop the whole of the *Encyclopedia* and the *Greater Logic.* But since it is necessary, in fact, to begin "lemmatically, so to speak" by anticipation or precipitation of the circlet, Hegel recognizes that his point of departure is vulgar, and its philosophical justification insufficient. He will have begun by the "representation" of art and of the beautiful for the "common consciousness". The price to be paid may seem very heavy: it will be said for example that the whole aesthetics develops, explicates, and lays out the representations of naïve consciousness. But does not this negative cancel itself at once? On the immediately following page, Hegel explains that on a circle of circles, one is justified in starting from any point. "There is no absolute beginning in science." The chosen point of departure, in everyday representation: *there are* works of art, we have them *in front of us* in representation. But how are they to be recognized? This is not an abstract and juridical question. At each step, at each example, in the absence of enormous theoretical, juridical, political, etc. protocols, there is a trembling of the limit between the "there is" and the "there is not" "work of art," between a "thing" and a "work," a "work" in general and a "work of art." Let's leave it. What does "leave" [*laisser*] mean ((*laisser*) *voir* [allow to see (or be seen)], (*laisser*) *faire* [allow to do (or be done)], *voir faire, faire voir, faire faire* [cause (something) to be done], leave as a remainder, leave in one's will), what does "leave" do? etc.

certainly not insignificant that more than a century later, a meditation on art begins by turning in an analogous circle while pretending to take a step beyond or back behind the whole of metaphysics or western onto-theology. *The Origin of the Work of Art* will have taken a running start for an incommensurable leap. Certainly, and here are some dry indications of it, pending a more patient reading.

1. All the oppositions which support the metaphysics of art find themselves questioned, in particular that of form and matter, with all its derivatives. This is done in the course of a questioning on the being-work of the work and the being-thing of a thing in all the determinations of the thing that more or less implicitly support any philosophy of art (*hypokeimenon, aistheton, hyle*).
2. As the *Postface* indicates, it is from the possibility of its death that art can here be interrogated. It is possible that art is in its death throes, but "it will take a good few centuries" until it dies and is mourned (Heidegger does not mention mourning). The *Origin* is situated in the zone of resonance of Hegel's *Lectures on Aesthetics* in as much as they think of art as a "past": "In the most comprehensive . . . meditation which the West possesses on the essence of art— comprehensive because thought out from metaphysics—in Hegel's *Lectures on Aesthetics*, stands the following proposition: 'But we no longer have an absolute need to bring a content to presentation in the form of art. Art, from the aspect of its highest destination, is for us something past.'" After recalling that it would be laughable to elude

this proposition under the pretext that works have survived this verdict—a possibility which, one can be sure, did not escape its author—Heidegger continues: "But the question remains: is art still, or is it no longer, an essential and necessary mode according to which the decisive truth happens for our historical Dasein? But if it is no longer that, then the question remains: why? The decision about Hegel's proposition has not yet been reached." So Heidegger interrogates art and more precisely the work of art as the advent or as the history of truth, but of a truth which he proposes to think beyond or behind metaphysics, beyond or behind Hegel. Let's leave it for the moment.

3. Third indication, again recalled in the *Postface*: the beautiful is not relative to pleasure or the "pleasing" as one would, according to Heidegger, always have presupposed, notably with Kant. Let us not be too hasty about translating this as: the beautiful beyond the pleasure principle. Some mediations will be necessary, but they will not be lacking.

4. The beautiful beyond pleasure, certainly, but also art beyond the beautiful, beyond aesthetics as beyond callistics (Hegel says he prefers the "common word" aesthetics to this word). Like Hegel, who saw in it the destination of universal art, Heidegger places Western art at the center of his meditation. But he does so in order to repeat otherwise the history of its essence in relation to the transformation of an essence of truth: the history of the essence of Western art "is just as little to be conceived on the basis of beauty taken for itself as on the basis of lived experience." Even supposing, concludes Heidegger, that it could ever be a question of a "metaphysical concept" acceding to this essence.

Thus nothing rules out the possibility that this concept is even constructed so as not to accede to it, so as not to get around to what happens under the name of art. And which Heidegger already calls "truth," even if it means seeking that truth *beneath* or *behind* the metaphysical determination of truth. For the moment I leave this "beneath" or this "behind" hanging vertically.

Keeping to these preliminary indications, one receives Heidegger's text as the nonidentical, staggered, discrepant "repetition" of the Hegelian "repetition" in the *Lectures on Aesthetics*. It works to untie what still keeps Hegel's aesthetics on the unperceived ground of metaphysics. And yet, what if this "repetition" did no more than make explicit, by repeating it more profoundly, the Hegelian "repetition"? (I am merely defining a risk, I am not yet saying that Heidegger runs it, simply, nor above all that one must in no circumstances run it: in wanting to avoid it at all costs, one can also be rushing toward the false exit, empirical chit-chat, spring-green impulsive avantgardism.

And who said it was necessary to avoid all these risks? And risk in general?) And yet, what if Heidegger, too, once again under the lemmatic constraint, went no further than the "common representation" of art, accepting it as the guiding thread (saying for example also "works of art are before us," this one, that one, the well-known shoes of Van Gogh, etc.) of his powerful meditation ⎯⎯⎯

⎸

⎸

⎸⎯⎯⎯   deposits here the "famous painting by Van Gogh who often painted such shoes." I leave them. They are, moreover, abandoned, unlaced, take them or leave them. Much later, interlacing this discourse with another, I shall return to them, as to everything I leave here, in so apparently disconcerted a way. And I shall come back to what comes down to leaving, lacing, interlacing. For example more than one shoe. And further on still, much later, to what Heidegger says of the trait of the "interlacing", of the "tie which unties" (or frees, delivers) and of the "road" in *Der Weg zur Sprache.* Accept here, concerning the truth in painting or in *effigy,* that interlacing causes a lace to disappear periodically: over under, inside outside, left right, etc. Effigy and fiction ⎯⎯⎯

⎸

⎸

⎸⎯⎯⎯   and in this discrepant repetition, it is less astonishing to see this meditation, closed upon a reference to Hegel, open up by a *circular* revolution whose rhetoric, at least, greatly resembles that which we followed in the introduction to the *Lectures on Aesthetics.*

Why a circle? Here is the schema of the argument: to look for the origin of a thing is to look for that from which it starts out and whereby it is what it is, it is to look for its essential provenance, which is not its empirical origin. The work of art stems from the artist, so they say. But what is an artist? The one who produces works of art. The origin of the artist is the work of art, the origin of the work of art is the artist, "neither is without the other." Given this, "artist and work *are* in themselves and in their reciprocity by virtue of a third term which is indeed the first, namely that from which artist and work of art also get their name, art." What is art? As long as one refuses to give an answer in advance to this question, "art" is only a word. And if one wants to interrogate art, one is indeed obliged to give oneself the guiding thread of a representation.

And this thread is the work, the fact that *there are* works of art. Repetition of the Hegelian gesture in the necessity of its lemma: there are works which common opinion designates as works of art and they are what one must interrogate in order to decipher in them the essence of art. But by what does one recognize, commonly, that these are works of art if one does not have in advance a sort of precomprehension of the essence of art? This hermeneutic circle has only the (logical, formal, derived) appearance of a vicious circle. It is not a question of escaping from it but on the contrary of engaging in it and going all round it: "We must therefore complete the circle. It is neither a stopgap measure nor a lack. To engage upon such a road is the force of thought and to remain on it is the feast of thought, it being admitted that thinking is a craft." Engaging on the circular path appeals on the one hand to an artisanal, almost a manual, value of the thinker's trade, on the other hand to an experience of the feast as experience of the limit, of closure, of resistance, of humility. The "it is necessary" of this engagement is on its way toward what, in *Unterwegs zur Sprache*, gathers together, between propriation and dispropriation, the step, the road to be opened up, the trait which opens, and language, etc. That which, later in the text, joins the whole play of the trait (*Riss, Grundriss, Umriss, Aufriss, Gezüge*) to that of the stela, of stature or installation (*thesis, Setzen, Besetzen, Gesetz, Einrichten, Gestalt, Gestell*, so many words I will not attempt to translate here) belongs to that law of the *pas* [not/step] which urges the circle to the lemmatic opening of the *Origin:* "it being admitted that thinking is a craft. Not only the chief step of the work toward art, *qua* step of the work toward art, is a circle, but each of the steps we attempt to take here circles in that circle

Feast of the whole body, from top to toe, engaged in this circling step (*Hauptschritt, Handwerk, Denken*). What you want to do—going against the feast—is not to mix genres but to extend metaphors. You can always try: question of style.

not break the circle violently (it would avenge itself), assume it resolutely, authentically. The experience of the circular closure does not close anything, it suffers neither lack nor negativity. Affirmative experience without voluntarism, without a compulsion to transgression: not to transgress the law of circle and *pas de cercle* but *trust in them*. Of this trust would thought consist. The desire to accede, by this faithful repetition of the circle, to the not-yet-crossed, is not absent. The desire for a new step, albeit a backward one, *ties and unties* this procedure. Tie without tie, get across the circle without getting free of its law. *Pas sans pas* [step without step/step without not/ not without step/not without not, trans.]

so I break off here, provisionally, the reading of *The Origin.*

The encirclement of the circle was dragging us to the abyss. But like all *production,* that of the abyss came to saturate what it hollows out.

It's enough to say: abyss and satire of the abyss.

The feast, the "feast of thought" which engages upon the *Kreisgang*, in the *pas de cercle:* what does it feed on? Opening and simultaneously filling the abyss. Accomplishing: *den Kreisgang vollziehen* [to complete the circular path].

Interrogate the comic effect of this. One never misses it if the abyss is never sufficient, if it must remain—undecided—between the bottom-less and the bottom of the bottom. The *operation* of the *mise en abyme* always occupies itself (activity, busy positing, mastery of the subject) with somewhere filling up, full of abyss, filling up the abyss

25

ART AS FEMINISM: CAROLYN KORSMEYER

Feminism is the most significant social movement of the late 20th century. In changing the shape of society as a whole, it has profoundly affected not only the landscape of many intellectual disciplines, including the philosophy of art, but also the character of many artistic practices. In this selection from her book *Gender and Aesthetics,* Carolyn Korsmeyer discusses how the work of feminist artists has undermined many of the central dichotomies that lie at the heart of what she calls "the fine art tradition."

The reader of this volume is already well versed in the fine art tradition, and many of the dichotomies that underlie it. R. G. Collingwood (Chapter 11) traced the evolution of a concept of fine art—to which our own concept of art is heir—from a broader sense of art in which any skilled practice is called "an art," as in the title of Robert M. Pirsig's iconoclastic book *Zen and the Art of Motorcycle Maintenance.* Although tuning a motorcycle does not produce what most of us would recognize as a work of art, we all would acknowledge that there is an art involved in such activities.

The fine art tradition, realized in the writings of philosophers from Kant (Chapter 4) to Heidegger (Chapter 13), developed a notion of art that separated it from the normal affairs of life. As a result, not only was the experience of art held to be *sui generis,* but art objects themselves were taken to be of a radically different type from those everyday objects that populate our worlds—from sailing ships to sealing wax. In addition, aesthetic or artistic value was taken to be radically distinct from political significance, so that overt politics was seen as an intrusion into the more elevated sphere of art proper. The fine art tradition thought that art itself could only be validated by means of such a radical separation of art from the quotidian.

Korsmeyer is aware that a great deal of 20th-century art, such as Duchamp's infamous *Fountain,* attacked the pretensions of the fine art tradition. However, she believes that feminist artists have developed and refined this critique, bringing it to new heights. Citing the works of such artists as Jana Sterbak and Carolee Schneemann, she argues that contemporary feminist artists have forced a rethinking of the basic notion of an artistic tradition, the category of art itself, and the prevailing standards of taste.

Let's look at some of the dichotomies that Korsmeyer takes feminist art to have undermined. A first, and perhaps most significant from our point of view, is the distinction between art and craft. Although various attempts within the tradition to define art have not explicitly ruled out categorizing products of craft as art, there is no doubt that making such a distinction was of central importance to it. Craft products were denigrated for their utility, whereas works of art were elevated precisely in virtue of their uselessness.

Feminist artists have challenged this dichotomy by exhibiting products of crafts as art objects. Take Judy Chicago's famous work *The Dinner Party* (1974–1979). This mammoth work included products of weaving, embroidery, and ceramics, thereby challenging the notion that such crafts should be excluded from the domain of fine art.

But its radical critique of the traditional notion of art did not stop there. Although the work was conceived by Chicago, over a hundred other artists helped create it. The communal nature of this work's production undercut the idea that art is the product of a lone genius rather than a social group. Finally, the fact that the work depicted a dinner whose guests were feminists of all stripes gave the work a political content that was inseparable from its artistic merit, thereby challenging another dichotomy at the heart of the fine arts tradition: that the value of a work of art could not be related to its political significance.

Korsmeyer asks us to see the work of feminist artists as having profound impact on our concept of art. Although she declines speculation on the new concept of art that might emerge from these practices, she is convinced that feminists have assisted in the dismantling of a sexist (and racist) conception of art that once reigned supreme, thus giving a specific meaning to the core feminist assertion that "the personal is political."

STUDY QUESTIONS ON THE READING

1.   Korsmeyer claims that feminist art undermines some of the most basic assumptions of the fine arts tradition. What theorists whom you have read belong to this tradition, and what assumptions do they make that feminists have challenged?

2.   Feminist art is inherently political. Korsmeyer thinks this does not diminish its value as art. What examples does she give to support her contention? Do you agree? Explain.

3.   Jana Sterbak's work, *Vanitas: Flesh Dress for an Albino Anorectic*, features prominently in Korsmeyer's discussion. What features of this work mark it as a challenge to received notions about art? Does this make it good art? Explain.

4.   What are some of the strategies that the artists discussed by Korsmeyer use to challenge and overturn patriarchal traditions? Do you think these strategies succeed? Are they artistically valuable? Explain.

5. Korsmeyer claims that feminist artists produce works that explicitly register the specific situation from which they arose. What is unusual about this? How does it depart from traditional ideas?

6. Korsmeyer sees performance art as particularly significant. What ontological feature of performance art does she discuss? Why is this feature important? How does it challenge traditional assumptions about art?

❖

CAROLYN KORSMEYER: GENDER AND AESTHETICS

In 1997 the *New York Times* published a survey of opinions about the nature of art compiled from interviews with seventeen established experts: art historians, museum curators, critics, a philosopher, artists, a newsperson, and a Congressman involved with the National Endowment for the Arts. The questions they were asked included our title subject: what is art? One might expect well formulated definitions to emerge from such a group, but the opinions ranged from noncommittal to skeptical. Most expressed the view that it is pretty difficult to say what art is these days, partly because it is more or less impossible to rule out anything that it is not. "There is no single definition of art that's universally tenable," stated William Rubin, former director of painting and sculpture at the Museum of Modern Art. "There's no consensus about anything today," concurred Philippe de Montebello, Director of the Metropolitan Museum. "Even the notion of standards are in question." Art historian Thomas McEvilley was somewhat bolder: "It is art if it is called art, written about in an art magazine, exhibited in a museum or bought by a private collection." But artist Barbara Kruger was skeptical even about this open-ended statement: "I have trouble with categories," she stated. "I do know just the idea that because something's in a gallery, instantly it's art, whereas something somewhere else is not art, is silly and narrow. I'm not interested in narrowing definitions."

Theorists and practitioners have never been in complete agreement about the way to answer broad and value-laden questions, so a certain amount of disagreement is to be expected. Art has always been hard to define, since there are so many forms, genres, periods, styles, intents, and purposes that mingle together in its making and its reception. Nonetheless, the hesitation and discomfort this question prompted for many of these professionals, who would seem above all others to be in good positions to pronounce on the issue, signal a moment of theoretical crisis. To many, any kind of definition at all seemed ill-advised. "Now the idea of defining art is so remote I don't think anyone would dare to do it," said art historian and Guggenheim curator Robert Rosenblum. "If the Duchamp urinal is art, then anything is."

Why would these experts refrain from committing themselves more substantively about the nature of art? What sorts of things did they have in mind that prompted them either to draw back from a definition or to offer an apparently vacuous formulation: art is whatever is called "art"? To understand their caution let us consider several examples of art that challenge traditional artistic concepts. These cases will introduce both feminist art and the reasons for philosophers' persistent urge—despite the odds—to formulate a definition.

. . . In 1987 Czech-born Canadian artist Jana Sterbak exhibited a piece she entitled *Vanitas: Flesh Dress for an Albino Anorectic*. A garment stitched together from sixty pounds of raw flank steak was displayed on a model arranged in a seated pose. In the course of the exhibition, the meat slowly darkened and spoiled. While other art using more orthodox media may represent decay and mortality, this work literally rots before one's eyes.

Despite its discomforting features, Sterbak's works are far from the most confounding that audiences face today. There are many more notorious, including the daring work of a number of other feminists. Among the most disconcerting is a piece that Carolee Schneemann performed and documented in the 1970s titled *Interior Scroll*. During this presentation Schneemann removed her wrap and stood naked before an audience; she smeared her body with mud, reading from a text. And then she slowly extracted a long, rolled strip of paper from her vagina, reading aloud the message written thereon."

These two works—to which we shall return later—are entries in a feminist repertoire of art, and one agenda (among many) of some feminist artists has been to question the terms of classification and evaluation employed in art and to defy those standards in their own work—thereby resisting the gendered ideals that pervade art traditions. But the presentation of works that challenge tradition, categorization, and taste is hardly new. Probably the object most discussed in debates over the definition of art was produced in 1917, when Marcel Duchamp entered a urinal that he titled *Fountain* into the New York Armory show. While the jury for the show rejected his entry, it now stands as an icon of an important moment in twentieth-century art. But why?

To one who is not well-acquainted with the artworld over the last century, works such as these are likely to arouse consternation, bewilderment, offense, or discomfort. They appear to be not so much *difficult* art as *not art at all*. What qualifies beef as an art medium? What makes *Flesh Dress* a work of art? What qualifies Schneeman's performance as a [sic] exhibit of art rather than ordinary exhibitionism? What transforms a plumbing fixture made for entirely utilitarian purposes into a work of art? As Rosenblum noted, "If the Duchamp urinal is art, then anything is." But why should anyone accept this judgment? While they may be initially posed with outrage or naïvete, these are excellent questions. Critics, art theorists, and philosophers have grappled with them for decades, and not always with perfect confidence or success. It is art such as this that has brought the definitional question, what is art?, back into the center of aesthetic controversy. Feminist art, with its deliberate reversal of virtually all [traditional] aesthetic values has joined—and sometimes has led—movements within the artworld that perplex, astound, and exasperate, challenging the concept of art at its very core.

The role of feminism in these challenges dramatizes the fact that the historical situation of women artists . . . has radically altered. The sheer numbers of women who participate in the arts today is [sic] considerably greater than in the past for most art forms. This is the outcome not only of the reduction of overt sex discrimination, but also of considerable struggle on the part of feminist activists. Women did not just slide into the artworld because long-standing prejudice waned; they battled their way in. The subversive group of artists called the Guerilla [sic] Girls, based in New York, spent years picketing, harassing, and embarrassing the art establishment for the lack of representation of women artists in galleries and museums. Feminist artists in the US and Britain took on the art establishment with alternative exhibits and protests that garnered enough notice that they achieved a foothold in recognized art forums. The energy of the Women's Movement of the 1970s, itself arising in the tumultuous atmosphere of political activism in the US and Europe, brought public attention to the social situation of women through events that were art and politics in equal measure.

The influence of feminist movements has resulted not only in increased numbers of female artists, but also in many artists (women and men alike) who use art to investigate and explore gender itself. Other aspects of identity, including race, ethnicity, and sexual identification, are equally foregrounded by artists today. Art is a means to uncover aspects of social position that have been just as eclipsed and distorted as ideas about femaleness and maleness in cultural history. Music, literature, theater, dance—all have distinguished practitioners who express and explore race, sexual nonconformity, immigrant and diaspora status, social oppression, cultural identities, and cross-gender experiences. Sometimes in developing their own voices, these artists have been the avatars of new art forms, such as performance. Sometimes they defy traditional aesthetic norms, as does philosopher and artist Adrian Piper [see Chapter 23], who deliberately forecloses the pleasures afforded by aesthetic distance in her presentations exploring race and gender issues.

In addition to an influx of artists with complex political and theoretical perspectives, other changes have also radically affected concepts of the arts in comparison to the way they had developed from the eighteenth through the early twentieth centuries. The distinction between art and craft that played so prominent a role in the emergence of the idea of fine art is now often deliberately breached. As we shall see in more detail shortly, a number of artists have incorporated craft materials such as fabric and fiber into their gallery works. Indeed, one now occasionally finds traditional craft objects such as quilts hung on gallery walls. (While recognition of an expanded repertoire of artistic contribution is to be applauded, this elevation of traditional crafts is a mixed blessing. Part of the artistry of quilts is their fine stitchery, and their promotion to art status prevents the viewer from getting close enough to see tiny stitches; and of course one must not touch.)

What is more, the barriers between fine art and entertainment, between "high" and "popular" culture, are not as sturdy as they used to be. Jazz, blues, and rock music now receive almost as much theoretical attention as art music (and a good deal more of the market). Narrative arts are by no means limited to literature or theater but include popular and lucrative cinematic media, television, and video. There are entire art forms based on technology that was not available when the concept of fine art was refined: most notably photography (which faced an early struggle to be considered an art form), film, and digital arts. The makers, performers, and audiences for these genres do not as a rule subscribe to the same aesthetic values that reigned when the concept of fine art developed in modern history. Such departures from older art traditions are noticeable in every art form, though philosophical theory has probably been most affected by the revolutions that have taken place within visual art, which has witnessed such radical changes that the very concept of art has been brought into question.

This is by no means to declare the older tradition dead. As we shall see, it yet wields considerable authority over the art scene today. Nonetheless, there has been a loosening of categories within the arts, such that the confidence that theorists used to have about their ability to characterize the essential qualities of art has dwindled considerably. This loss of confidence and its effects on philosophy of art is one of the subjects of this chapter.

The impact of feminist art, both its continuity with other iconoclastic art movements and its distinctiveness, needs to be placed in relation to debates about art that permeate philosophy, criticism, and art itself. This discussion could take a number of different directions. Because feminism is first of all a political stance, many theorists have utilized Marxist approaches or the ideas of the Frankfurt school of critical theory to analyze the impact of culture in contemporary society. The influential work of British art historian Griselda Pollock is a case in point. Drawing on Marxist cultural theory, Pollock analyzes the patterns of exclusion that have erased women from the history of art and critiques the standards that underwrite the canons of "great art." The works of philosophers and social theorists of these movements offer potent perspectives on the culture of the twentieth century, damaged by two world wars, that have been fruitful in uncovering the political message latent in the high art tradition and providing critiques of cultural norms. Even more directly, European psychoanalytic and deconstructivist theories have been put to use by feminists probing the very construction of gender. . . . Here, however, I shall situate feminist art in relation to the largely analytic Anglo-American tradition, which has analyzed the concept of art in ways that indirectly illuminate feminist strategies in the artworld. . . .

FEMINIST WORK AND CHANGING CONCEPTS OF ART

Just as "feminism" does not describe a monolithic politics nor a single point of view about the role of women in society, so "feminist art" does not label one type of art, nor even a class of artworks that share similar themes or perspectives. Art critic Lucy Lippard observes:

> It is useless to try to pin down a specific formal contribution made by feminism because feminist and/or women's art is neither a style nor a movement,

much as this idea may distress those who would like to see it safely ensconced in the categories and chronology of the past. It consists of many styles and individual expressions and for the most part succeeds in bypassing the star system. At its most provocative and constructive, feminism questions all the precepts of art as we know it.

What feminist artists do share is a sense of the historic social subordination of women and an awareness of how art practices have perpetuated that subordination. That perpetuation has been accomplished by such things as ignoring women's work, objectifying women's bodies in painting and film, romanticizing the sexual exploitation of women in narrative, employing exclusionary criteria for women's creativity, or carrying on the symbolic systems that regard the feminine as a dark rival to the masculine.

With such issues in mind, not only do feminist and postfeminist artists participate in the complex self-reference that characterizes virtually all postmodern work, but they challenge and overturn patriarchal traditions, often with highly theoretical agendas aiding their creative production. Nancy Spero, for example, paints registers of delicately limned figures taken from ancient mythic traditions (Greek and Celtic) and installs them racing across gallery walls. Sometimes the images are juxtaposed to classic texts, presented as partially erased fragments; sometimes the texts allude to contemporary writings about women. This sort of play with tradition calls attention to the norms of the genre that are being queried or subverted, and hence a "knowledge of the history of art" is a special necessity. Sally Potter's film *Thriller* (1979) is a reprise and revision of the story of the popular Puccini opera *La Bohème*. Laura Mulvey and Peter Wollen's movie *Riddles of the Sphinx* (1976) recounts the Oedipus myth from the point of view of the Sphinx whose riddle launched Sophocles' drama, thus invoking not only Greek myth but also the psychoanalytic theory that Mulvey used to such influential effect in articulating her theory of the gaze.

In addition to questions and challenges raised within the genres of familiar art forms, there are two trends much employed by feminists that refuse the expectations of traditional arts: the use of nonstandard materials and the presentation of the body as a component of art.

The Medium and the Message: Fiber and Food

Since the fine-art tradition was fairly strict about excluding utilitarian craft objects, including things made for domestic use, many feminist artists have deliberately incorporated craft materials into their work. Moreover, since some craft traditions in which women participated were joint efforts and did not single out an individual creator, some feminist projects have been similarly collaborative, even though many of them are attributed to the artist who "directed" the whole show, as it were. Judy Chicago's large project *The Dinner Party* (1974–9). for example, is an enormous triangular table with place settings commemorating thirty-nine female figures from history and myth. It uses weaving, embroidery, and ceramics, and Chicago enlisted the skills of over a hundred other artists to put it together. Another collaborative installation on the part of twenty-four artists, *Womanhouse* (1972), set up an entire house with different rooms designed with feminist themes. Chicago's room in this project is called *Menstruation Bathroom,* a blood-splotched lavatory. We can regard it as a wry counterpoint of *Fountain,* for Duchamp's attention-getting urinal is, of course, a singularly male appliance.

Cloth and other fiber materials figure heavily in the work of Miriam Schapiro and Faith Ringgold. Ringgold employs quilts, a traditional women's craft form, in the fine art context of galleries, as vehicles for messages about politics and social issues, especially those involving race in America. This work uses the idiom of sewn fabric implicitly to criticize the exclusion of women's craft items from the art tradition by pointing back to objects commonly made for domestic use on the frontier, under slavery, in ordinary domestic necessity. Feminist uses of fiber, ceramics, and other craft materials may be seen as a challenge to the fine art–craft divide. The very materials employed *subvert* the fine-art tradition; but at the same time cloth and woven items refer to and revive women's artifacts *within* the fine-art tradition.

The use of craft materials associated with home and comfort to make painful and difficult social statements produces some interesting dissonance in the product. One thinks of quilts as benign items for warmth and decoration. But their designs are often more than decorative; they have long been used as family records or to depict historical events, many of them tragic or painful. The largest quilt on record is the AIDS quilt, a joint project that connected squares quilted by people all over the globe commemorating loved ones who died of AIDS. The incorporation of craft in fine art defies the distinction between the two and questions the denigration of domestic creativity. And as Ringgold's work makes evident, it also can be employed to confront another standard modernist aesthetic divide: the [sic] separation of aesthetic value from political significance.

The artistic employment of food is even more radically subversive of familiar concepts of art, for while craft materials represent artifacts that have been squeezed out of the fine-art tradition, foods represent substances that have been considered to have little or no artistic import at all. . . . [T]he low philosophical standing of taste, smell, and eating is powerfully embedded in cultural symbols, and it is these associations that contemporary "food artists" usually exploit. The use of foodstuffs as art media simultaneously explores aesthetic traditions and sabotages them. It probes at the concept of art and the values associated with high culture traditions, at the same time that it presents provocative reflections on gender, sexuality, and death.

Sterbak's *Vanitas: Flesh Dress for an Albino Anorectic,* to return to our initial example, is an interesting bridge between traditions of painting and the contemporary interrogation of those traditions. Its references are directed to the history of art itself, and it can be read as a manifesto against that history and its aesthetic values. Moreover, it reaches into political realms and embodies commentary on the worth attributed to the female body.

We can begin by placing *Flesh Dress* in a continuum of artistic production. Sterbak gives us some help with the title: *Vanitas.* This term alludes to a genre of European still-life painting popular in the sixteenth through eighteenth centuries. *Vanitas* motifs feature objects such as decaying foodstuffs, skulls, broken musical instruments, spilled coins, torn pages—any item that once was accorded value and is destroyed with the passage of time and therefore symbolizes the ultimate waste of worldly endeavors. (The label is taken from the first line of the book of Ecclesiastes: "*Vanitas vanitatis, et omnia vanitas* [Vanity of vanities, all is vanity].") *Vanitas* pictures are highly moralistic reminders of the fruitlessness of human effort and the error of placing value on things of this world that inevitably will be destroyed. The title places *Flesh Dress* in the same tradition as still-life painting, declaring its kinship with a long-recognized genre of art.

At the same time, its insistent literalness, for the dress is actually made of flesh, rejects the traditions of that medium, for Sterbak has chosen to work not with paint on canvas but with butchered meat. Her work will not survive to hang alongside its forebears in art museums; it decays rapidly and declares its decay in the very course of an exhibit. (It is preserved only through reports and photographic documentation.) In so doing, it mimics the aging of human flesh—in this case female flesh: a "flesh dress for an albino anorectic." Allusions multiply as we realize that the flesh is hanging outside the emaciated body of a very pale woman, her thinness indicating an extreme fashion that rejects too much female fleshiness. The meat is heavily salted, but all meat has an odor. Even looking at a picture of this piece arouses uncomfortable synaesthetic feelings: *What would it feel like against one's skin? Do age and rot smell the same? In the final analysis, is human flesh really just so much butchered meat?* Sterbak's work is not itself anti-art, but it partakes of the spirit of anti-art in its choice of medium.

The employment of meat and other foodstuffs is different from the incorporation of craft materials into venues of high culture, though it similarly questions fine-art traditions. But food and eating . . . are associated with femininity in a most extreme and disturbing way. The female body in many symbol systems is linked with both life and death. All bodies die, but the maternal body is also a source of life, and the decay of women's flesh is a kind of betrayal—beauty and sexual attraction are lost, the ability to produce life has withered, and the comfort and sustenance of a mother are no longer available. The flesh of *Flesh Dress* isn't even naked (we are used to that in art); it is *skinned*—disgusting, vulnerable, and impermanent. One difference between food in a traditional *vanitas* motif and in Sterbak's work is that the first is a theme explored *within art* and the second is a statement about the nature of *art itself*. What began as the object of an associative reference employed for moral and aesthetic purposes to convey messages about the transience of life, has been transmogrified into an actual art medium.

ARTISTS' BODIES

. . . [F]eminist theory participates in the critique of Enlightenment ideas, including skepticism about the universality of aesthetic values. This critical approach rejects the idea that the artist should create with an abstract, universal vision that eclipses his or her personal perspective, and replaces it with the insistence that all creativity has "position" inflected by history, gender, sexuality, social position or class, race, nationality, and so forth.

One means by which artists draw attention to specificity and positionality is by using their own bodies in their works. Ana Mendieta imprinted her body into the land art she created in the 1970s and 1980s as a means of expressing her views about the affinity between women's bodies and the earth. Virtually all of Cindy Sherman's works of the 1970s, 1980s, and into the 1990s include her own image, sometimes standing in for figures in compositions reminiscent of famous old master paintings, as with her series of *History Portraits*. Her *Untitled #224* (1990) is unsettling partly because of an implied gender crossover, for her face appears in the motif of the classical Bacchus or wine-god figure. Renée Cox's work *Yo Mamma* is a photograph of herself holding a child, an image that resonates with paintings and sculptures of the Virgin Mary and the Christ child, most especially Michelangelo's *Pieta*. In the act of substituting her own image for a familiar icon of a biblical narrative, Cox calls attention to the fact that she creates from a particular subject position identified in history by gender, race, culture, and sexuality.

It is evident even from just these three examples that this specificity of position means that the use of "the body" on the part of artists does not always signify the same thing. This fact is particularly dramatic when one considers the political impact of body images made by women artists from different nonwestern cultural traditions. Alongside the male-female dichotomy these works allude to additional oppositions between occident-orient, past-present, tradition-revolution. Just which cultural context is employed further diversifies the meanings of female flesh. The covered-over bodies hidden by the chador in Sherin Neshat's photographs of Iranian women holding guns, whose visible flesh is inscribed with Persian poetry, reference both Muslim tradition and revolution. The artificial, mechanized figures of Lee Bui evoke the highly technocratic society of contemporary urban Asia. Additional examples would further multiply the different types of eroticism, gender meanings, and social challenge that the presentation of bodies can signify Needless to say, these meanings are not limited to the use of female bodies. Male artists have also used their own flesh—depicted or presented—to heighten awareness of sex, gender, eroticism, and identity.

The literal use of flesh and the body of the artist has also become a major feature of performance art, a relatively new form in which feminist artists have been especially daring. Performance art affords an immediate means to engage with audiences and to explore and enact ideas about identity and the cultural construction of femininity. Since so much of the Euro-American visual-art tradition depicts female bodies (usually young and voluptuous), much performance art upsets that tradition by means of exaggeration, parody, violence, and reversal. Artists have used their own bodies as means to explore the pornography industry (risking confusion with pornography itself), violence against women, the sexual marketplace, race identification, aging, and mortality. Performance art employs the living flesh of the artist, and some have shed their own blood in their works, sometimes with irreversible effects. The French artist Orlan, for example, has undergone numerous plastic surgeries, broadcast on video links, that have permanently made her own body into an exemplar of a series of references to artistic renditions of idealized feminine appearance. Orlan's works refer to specific paintings and sculptures. But more generally, when women employ their bodies in performance, they can hardly avoid evoking echoes of the entire art tradition at the same time. Speaking of performance artist-musician Laurie Anderson, Susan McClary says:

> The fact that hers is a *female* body changes the dynamics of several of the oppositions she invokes in performance. For women's bodies in Western culture have almost always been viewed as objects of display. Women have rarely been permitted agency in art, but instead have been restricted to enacting—upon and through their bodies—the theatrical, musical, cinematic, and dance scenarios constructed by male artists. Centuries of this traditional sexual division of cultural labor bear down on Anderson (or any woman performer) when she performs.

Performance art has met with a high degree of controversy partly because of the directness of its presentations and the exposure of the bodies of the artists in ways that are unprecedented in the fine arts (though not in pornography). The work of Karen Finley, who calls attention to the sexual exploitation of women by smearing her body with foodstuffs resembling blood and excrement, gained special notoriety because of her participation in a lawsuit filed *against* the National Endowment for the Arts, some of whose members found her work too offensive to merit public expenditures. The performance of Carolee Schneemann mentioned earlier, *Interior Scroll*, shockingly made use of taboo interior space of the artist's body, from which she extracted a wound strip of paper—like both tampon and sacred scroll. The idea that there are secrets hidden within women's sex is an ancient conceit of myth, and the enactment of myth in and by a living woman both explodes and employs venerable symbols, collapsing the distinction between mythic body and real flesh, and also between representation and reality.

For some theorists, performance signifies the social and psychological production of gender itself. They adopt a strong version of social constructionism, which maintains that gender identity is not given by nature as a developmental feature of sexual dimorphism, but is imposed by social norms with which children are inculcated through education, manners, upbringing, and cultural discourse. The connections between gender identity and performance have entered feminist thinking from several philosophical entry points. Marilyn Frye, writing in the analytic tradition, has formulated an analysis of female and lesbian identity that employs the idea of performatives developed in speech-act theory. Judith Butler, more influenced by European philosophy, has developed an explicit theory of gender and sexuality as performance. In fact, related ideas can be traced back several generations, for (as Butler notes) in 1929 Joan Rivière, a Freudian psychoanalyst, wrote a suggestive essay on "Womanliness as Masquerade." Thus from multiple theoretical starting-points one can explore the idea that female identities are less given by nature than formed through patterns of culture.

The feminist uses of the real body in art are among the challenges directed to traditional distinction between art and reality. At first glance, it does indeed seem difficult to distinguish art from reality if the art object is not a representation but a real thing. Strictly speaking, however, the ontological distinction between artwork and real object, however one articulates it, still obtains with even the most radical of body arts. It is the artwork that is described by means of aesthetic predicates: daring, graceful, packed with meaning, etc. Schneemann's performing body may be co-extensive with her actual body, which is to say that physically they are one and the same (which is part of the impact of her performances). But it is the body-in-performance that is the referent for aesthetic judgments, not Schneemann herself. In this respect performance art, however radical in other respects, is comparable to dance, where the dancer's body creates the dance but is not identical to it. The ontological distinction between art and reality, strictly speaking, cannot be erased. One must grant, however, that it has been rendered nearly imperceptible; moreover, the idea that gender itself can be viewed as performance further blurs the borders between art, artifice, and "reality." Uses of the body in feminist performance art have the dramatic effect of obliterating the familiar distance between art and life, and in terms of the challenges posed to the concept of art, this apparent ontological shrinkage has had stunning impact.

SUMMARY

The last century has witnessed radical alterations to the [nature] of art and aesthetic opportunities. . . . To what extent do the philosophical, aesthetic, and artistic traditions that peaked in the eighteenth and nineteenth centuries still affect artists in the twenty-first century? This is a complicated question, and answering it is made more difficult by the fact that we are actually living in the time under assessment. We don't have the benefit of hindsight to judge the effects of the present art scene on developments yet to happen. Analyzing the artworld of today is necessarily tentative, for no one can foresee what the present will resemble from the perspective of the future.

We do not find with contemporary philosophical concepts of art and of the artist the same kind of exclusionary categories that prevailed as the fine-art tradition developed. (This is not to say that standards of evaluation and selection in the artworld today have erased all of the skewed value structures that excluded women's accomplishments of the past. That is a matter for a study of the critical reception of art, which I have not done here.) Women—of diverse ethnic and racial and national backgrounds—have been major presences in postmodern and feminist art and are among the pathbreaking innovators on the contemporary art scene. Their presence adds impact to the fact that the concept of art itself continues to be under scrutiny, and women artists embody in their very persons a challenge to the fine-art tradition. This we can see vividly in performance art as well as in the expansion of art to encompass non-traditional media.

Amid all these changes, have the concepts of artist and art also utterly changed, such that their implicit masculine gender has all but faded away? With due observance of the caveats expressed above, I suspect that this is not the case. The most noticeable reason for this judgment is that tradition remains the overarching point of reference for feminist and postmodern artists, who refer continually to the past, whether ironically, parodically, or confrontationally. Tradition unavoidably frames the work of even the most iconoclastic artists, for only God creates *ex nihilo*. The breakaway movements in art remain to that extent bound to rejected legacies, which therefore retain much of their power in these acts of confrontation. What will emerge from the collision of innovation and tradition that propels cultural history we have yet to see.

26

ART AS CULTURAL PRODUCTION: PIERRE BOURDIEU

Ever since Kant proclaimed the *disinterestedness* of aesthetic judgments (see Chapter 4), there has been an ongoing controversy among philosophers and art theorists about the relationship between works of art and the societies that spawned them. Although there have been spirited defenses of art's autonomy from its social context—such as that of Bell (Chapter 10)—there have been equally passionate attempts to show art's relationship to broader social tendencies—as in Benjamin's discussion of the changes wrought in art by advances in technology (Chapter 14). At the same time, contemporary discussions of art's nature have had to take account of artistic gestures that seem aimed at undermining the concept of art itself. By now, Duchamp's *Fountain* has made a number of appearances in this volume for its thumbing its nose at the pretensions of the art establishment as well as for its potentially revolutionary undermining of the idea of art itself. In his contribution to this volume, Pierre Bourdieu (1930–2002), the French sociologist and Marxist social critic, develops an account of art that not only treats art as a social phenomenon but also takes account of recent, apparently transgressive works of art. Bourdieu argues that these works amount to acts of "sacrilege" in that they aim to expose art to be more like normal industrial production than its adherents like to admit.

There is a well-known problem that art presents for Marxist theory. Marx had argued that the economic value of any object was equal to the value of the labor that went into producing it. But art objects, by this standard, are grossly overvalued, for no matter how long and hard an artist like Picasso may have worked on a painting, the value of his labor is radically overvalued when his work sells for millions of dollars. Bourdieu seeks to preserve Marx's theory by showing that the value of an artwork is, indeed, the value of the labor that went into producing it, only there is a vast social network whose value must also be calculated in estimating the value of a work of art. If we included the labor that goes into the production of *that*, he asserts, the value of a work of art would fit Marx's theory.

In this respect, Bourdieu's theory resembles that of Dickie's institutional theory of art. You will recall that Dickie argued in Chapter 19 that something was a work of art because the members of the artworld appraised it as such. One of the revolutionary aspects of this theory was its emphasis on the broad array of social actors who play a role in maintaining art as a social practice. Bourdieu also emphasizes these actors, but in a much more conflictual manner, for he asserts that art is also the product of a struggle. Young artists don't just placidly put their works forward for judgment by artistic elites, they are actively engaged in the attempt to supplant others and get their own works recognized.

So for Bourdieu, the idea of disinterestedness is simply a *misrecognition* or cover for the actual nature of art. In his contribution, he seeks to unveil the truth about art that is obscured by the artworld's claims about art as an autonomous realm that is not sullied by economic concerns. For this reason, he emphasizes the economic structure of the production of what he calls "cultural products" and that include works of art as their primary exemplars.

STUDY QUESTIONS ON THE READING

1.   Bourdieu speaks of the art business as predicated on a disavowal. What is being disavowed and why?

2.   Bourdieu calls the agent who produces a work of art its apparent producer. Why does he do this? Who does he think is the real producer of the work? How does this idea relate to Barthes's claim that the author is dead (Chapter 22)?

3.   Does Bourdieu think that artists like Duchamp are genuinely revolutionary? Why or why not? How does his view compare to that of Danto (Chapter 18)?

4.   Compare Bourdieu's view of the "artworld" with that of Dickie (Chapter 19)? What are the primary differences between them? Which view, if either, do you find more plausible, and why?

5.   There is an old saying that there is no accounting for taste. Why would Bourdieu disagree with this? What explains differences in taste, on his view?

6.   Creativity is often championed as a mark of artistic genius. Why would Bourdieu reject this idea as inadequate to the reality of artistic production?

❖

PIERRE BOURDIEU: THE PRODUCTION OF BELIEF

The art business, a trade in things that have no price, belongs to the class of practices in which the logic of the pre-capitalist economy lives on (as it does, in

From *Media, Culture and Society: A Critical Reader,* Richard Collins, et al., (Eds.), p. 131–163. © 1986 Sage Publications, Inc.

another sphere, in the economy of exchanges between the generations). These practices, functioning as practical *negations*, can only work by pretending not to be doing what they are doing. Defying ordinary logic, they lend themselves to two opposed readings, both equally false, which each undo their essential duality and duplicity by reducing them either to the disavowal or to what is disavowed—to disinterestedness or self-interest. The challenge which economies based on disavowal of the 'economic' present to all forms of economism lies precisely in the fact that they function, and can function, in practice—and not merely in the agents' representations—only by virtue of a constant, collective repression of narrowly 'economic' interest and of the real nature of the practices revealed by 'economic' analysis.

THE DISAVOWAL OF THE 'ECONOMY'

In this economic universe, whose very functioning is defined by a 'refusal' of the 'commercial' which is in fact a collective disavowal of commercial interests and profits, the most 'anti-economic' and most visibly 'disinterested' behaviours, which in an 'economic' universe would be those most ruthlessly condemned, contain a form of economic rationality (even in the restricted sense) and in no way exclude their authors from even the 'economic' profits awaiting those who conform to the law of this universe. In other words, alongside the pursuit of 'economic' profit, which treats the cultural goods business as a business like any other, and not the most profitable, 'economically' speaking (as the best-informed, i.e. the most 'disinterested,' art dealers point out) and merely adapts itself to the demand of an already converted clientele, there is also room for the *accumulation of symbolic capital*. 'Symbolic capital' is to be understood as economic or political capital that is disavowed, misrecognized and thereby recognized, hence legitimate, a 'credit' which, under certain conditions, and always in the long run, guarantees 'economic' profits. Producers and vendors of cultural goods who 'go commercial' condemn themselves, and not only from an ethical or aesthetic point of view, because they deprive themselves of the opportunities open to those who can *recognize* the specific demands of this universe and who, by concealing from themselves and others the interests at stake in their practice, obtain the means of deriving profits from disinterestedness. In short, when the only usable, effective capital is the (mis)recognized, legitimate capital called 'prestige' or 'authority,' the economic capital that cultural undertakings generally require cannot secure the specific profits produced by the field—not the 'economic' profits they always imply—unless it is reconverted into symbolic capital. For the author, the critic, the art dealer, the publisher or the theatre manager, the only legitimate accumulation consists in making a name for oneself, a known, recognized name, a capital of consecration implying a power to consecrate objects (with a trademark or signature) or persons (through publication, exhibition, etc.) and therefore to give value, and to appropriate the profits from this operation.

The disavowal is neither a real negation of the 'economic' interest which always haunts the most 'disinterested' practices, nor a simple 'dissimulation' of the mercenary aspects of the practice, as even the most attentive observers have supposed. The disavowed economic enterprise of art dealers or publishers, 'cultural bankers' in whom art and business meet in practice—which predisposes them for the role of scapegoat—cannot succeed, even in 'economic' terms, unless it is guided by a practical mastery of the laws of the functioning of the field in which cultural goods are produced and circulate, i.e. by an entirely improbable, and in any case rarely achieved, combination of the realism implying minor concessions to 'economic' necessities that are disavowed but not denied and the conviction which excludes them. The fact that the disavowal of the 'economy' is neither a simple ideological mask nor a complete repudiation of economic interest explains why, on the one hand, new producers whose only capital is their conviction can establish themselves in the market by appealing to the values whereby the dominant figures accumulated their symbolic capital, and why, on the other hand, only those who can come to terms with the 'economic' constraints inscribed in this bad-faith economy can reap the full 'economic' profits of their symbolic capital.

WHO CREATES THE 'CREATOR'?

The 'charismatic' ideology which is the ultimate basis of belief in the value of a work of art and which is therefore the basis of functioning of the field of production and circulation of cultural commodities, is undoubtedly the main obstacle to a rigorous science of the production of the value of cultural goods. It is this ideology which directs attention to the *apparent producer,* the painter, writer or composer, in short, the 'author,' suppressing the question of what authorizes the author, what creates the authority with which authors authorize. If it is all too obvious that the price of a picture is not determined by the sum of the production costs—the raw material and the painter's labour time—and if works of art provide a golden example for those who seek to refute Marx's labour theory of value (which anyway gives a special status to artistic production), this is perhaps because we wrongly define the unit of production or, which amounts to the same thing, the process of production.

The question can be asked in its most concrete form (which it sometimes assumes in the eyes of the agents): who is the true producer of the value of the work—the painter or the dealer, the writer or the publisher, the playwright or the theatre manager? The ideology of creation, which makes the author the first and last source of the value of his work, conceals the fact that the cultural businessman (art dealer, publisher, etc.) is at one and the same time the person who exploits the labour of the 'creator' by trading in the 'sacred' and the person who, by putting it on the market, by exhibiting, publishing or staging it, consecrates a product which he has 'discovered' and which would otherwise remain a mere natural resource; and the more consecrated he personally is, the more strongly he consecrates the work. The art trader is, not just the agent who gives the work a commercial value by bringing it into a market; he is not just the representative, the impresario, who 'defends the authors he loves.' He is the person who can proclaim the value of the author he defends (cf. the fiction of the catalogue or blurb) and above all 'invests his prestige' in the author's cause, acting as a 'symbolic banker' who offers as security all the symbolic capital he has accumulated (which he is liable to forfeit if he backs a 'loser'). This investment, of which the accompanying 'economic' investments are themselves only a guarantee, is what brings the producer into the cycle of consecration. Entering the field of literature is not so much like going into religion as getting into a select club; the publisher is one of those prestigious sponsors (together with preface-writers and critics) who effusively recommend their candidate. Even clearer is the role of the art dealer, who literally has to 'introduce' the artist and his work into ever more select company (group exhibitions, one-man shows, prestigious collections, museums) and ever more sought-after places. But the law of this universe, whereby the less visible the investment, the more productive it is symbolically, means that promotion exercises, which in the business world take the overt form of publicity, must here be euphemized. The art trader cannot serve his 'discovery' unless he applies all his conviction, which rules out 'sordidly commercial' manoeuvres, manipulation and the 'hard sell,' in favour of the softer, more discreet forms of 'public relations' (which are themselves a highly euphemized form of publicity)—receptions, society gatherings, and judiciously placed confidences.

THE CIRCLE OF BELIEF

But in moving back from the 'creator' to the 'discoverer' or 'creator of the creator,' we have only displaced the initial question and we still have to determine the source of the art-businessman's acknowledged power to consecrate. The charismatic ideology has a ready-made answer: the 'great' dealers, the 'great' publishers, are inspired talent-spotters who, guided by their disinterested, unreasoning passion for a work of art, have 'made' the painter or writer, or have helped him make himself, by encouraging him in difficult moments with the faith they had in him, guiding him with their advice and freeing him from material worries. To avoid an endless regress in the chain of causes, perhaps it is necessary to cease thinking in the logic, which a whole tradition encourages, of the 'first beginning,' which inevitably leads to faith in the 'creator.' It is not sufficient to indicate, as people often do, that the 'discoverer' never discovers anything that is not already discovered, at least by a few painters, already known to a small number of painters or connoisseurs, authors, 'introduced' by other authors (it is well known, for example, that the manuscripts that will be published hardly ever arrive directly, but almost always through recognized go-betweens). His 'authority' is itself a credit-based value, which only exists in the relationship with the field of production as a whole, i.e. with the artists or writers who belong to his 'stable'—'a publisher,' said one of them, 'is his catalogue'—and with those who do not and would or would not like to; in the relationship with the other dealers or publishers who do or do not envy him his painters or writers and are or are not capable of taking them from him; in the relationship with the critics, who do or do not believe in his judgement, and speak of his 'products' with varying degrees of respect; in the relationship with his clients and customers, who perceive his 'trademark' with greater or lesser clarity and do or do not place their trust in it. This 'authority' is nothing other than 'credit' with a set of agents who constitute 'connections' whose value is proportionate to the credit they themselves command. It is all too obvious that critics also collaborate with the art trader in the effort of consecration which makes the reputation and, at least in the long term, the monetary value of works. 'Discovering' the 'new talents,' they guide buyers' and sellers' choices by their writings or advice (they are often manuscript readers or series editors in publishing houses or accredited preface-writers for galleries) and by their verdicts, which, though offered as purely aesthetic, entail significant economic effects (juries for artistic prizes). Among the makers of the work of art, we must finally include the public, which helps to make its value by appropriating it materially (collectors) or symbolically (audiences, readers), and by objectively or subjectively identifying part of its own value with these appropriations. In short, what 'makes reputations' is not, as provincial Rastignacs [Eugene de Rastignac is a character in Balzac's novel, *Old Griot*—T.E.W.] naïvely think, this or that 'influential' person, this or that institution, review, magazine, academy, coterie, dealer or publisher; it is not even the whole set of what are sometimes called 'personalities of the world of arts and letters'; it is the field of production, understood as the system of objective relations between these agents or institutions and as the site of the struggles for the monopoly of the power to consecrate, in which the value of works of art and belief in that value are continuously generated.

FAITH AND BAD FAITH

The source of the efficacy of all acts of consecration is the field itself, the locus of the accumulated social energy which the agents and institutions help to reproduce through the struggles in which they try to appropriate it and into which they put what they have acquired from it in previous struggles. The value of works of art in general—the basis of the value of each particular work—and the belief which underlies it, are generated in the incessant, innumerable struggles to establish the value of this or that particular work, i.e. not only in the competition between agents (authors, actors, writers, critics, directors, publishers, dealers, etc.) whose interests (in the broadest sense) are linked to different cultural goods, 'middle-brow' theatre (*théâtre 'bourgeois'*) or 'high-brow' theatre (*théâtre 'intellectuel'*) 'established' painting or avant-garde painting, 'mainstream' literature or 'advanced' literature, but also in the conflicts between agents occupying different positions in the production of products of the same type: painters and dealers, authors and publishers, writers and critics, etc. Even if these struggles never clearly set the 'commercial' against the 'non-commercial,' 'disinterestedness' against 'cynicism,' they almost always involve recognition of the ultimate values of 'disinterestedness' through the denunciation of the mercenary compromises or calculating manoeuvres of the adversary, so that disavowal of the 'economy' is placed at the very heart of the field, as the principle governing its functioning and transformation.

This is why the dual reality of the ambivalent painter-dealer or writer-publisher relationship is most clearly revealed in moments of crisis, when the objective reality of each of the positions and their relationship is unveiled and the values which do the veiling are reaffirmed. No one is better placed than art dealers to know the interests of the makers of works and the strategies they use to defend their interests or to conceal their strategies. Although dealers form a protective screen between the artist and the market, they are also what link them to the market and so provoke, by their very existence, cruel unmaskings of the truth of artistic practice. To impose their own interests, they only have to take artists at their word when they profess 'disinterestedness.' One soon learns from conversations with these middle-men that, with a few illustrious exceptions, seemingly designed to recall the ideal, painters and writers are deeply self-interested, calculating, obsessed with money and ready to do anything to succeed. As for the artists, who cannot even denounce the exploitation they suffer without confessing their self-interested motives, they are the ones best placed to see the middle-men's strategies and their eye for an (economically) profitable investment which guides their actual aesthetic investments. The makers and marketers of works of art are adversaries in collusion, who each abide by the same law which demands the repression of direct manifestations of personal interest, at least in its overtly 'economic' form, and which has every appearance of transcendence although it is only the product of the cross-censorship weighing more or less equally on each of those who impose it on all the others.

A similar mechanism operates when an unknown artist, without credit or credibility, is turned into a known and recognized artist. The struggle to impose the dominant definition of art, i.e. to impose a style, embodied in a particular producer or group of producers, gives the work of art a value by putting it at stake, inside and outside the field of production. Everyone can challenge his or her adversaries' claim to distinguish art from non-art without ever calling into question this fundamental claim. Precisely because of the conviction that good and bad painting exist, competitors can exclude each other from the field of painting, thereby giving it the stakes and the motor without which it could not function. And nothing better conceals the objective collusion which is the matrix of specifically artistic value than the conflicts through which it operates.

RITUAL SACRILEGE

This argument might be encountered by pointing to the attempts made with increasing frequency in the 1960s, especially in the world of painting, to break the circle of belief. But it is all too obvious that these ritual acts of sacrilege, profanations which only ever scandalize the believers, are bound to become sacred in their turn and provide the basis for a new belief. One thinks of Manzoni [Piero Manzoni, a conceptual artist—T.E.W.], with his tins of 'artist's shit,' his magic pedestals which could turn any object placed on them into a work of art, or his signatures on living people which made them *objets d'art;* or Ben [Ben Vautier, a conceptual artist—T.E.W.], with his many 'gestures' of provocation or derision such as exhibiting a piece of cardboard labelled 'unique copy' or a canvas bearing the words 'canvas 45 cm long.' Paradoxically, nothing more clearly reveals the logic of the functioning of the artistic field than the fate of these apparently radical attempts at subversion. Because they expose the art of artistic creation to a mockery already annexed to the artistic tradition by Duchamp, they are immediately converted into artistic 'acts,' recorded as such and thus consecrated and celebrated by the makers of taste. Art cannot reveal the truth about art without snatching it away again by turning the revelation into an artistic event. And it is significant, *a contrario*, that all attempts to call into question the field of artistic production, the logic of its functioning and the functions it performs, through the highly sublimated and ambiguous means of discourse or artistic 'acts' (e.g. Maciunas or Flynt) are no less necessarily bound to be condemned even by the most heterodox guardians of artistic orthodoxy, because in refusing to play the game, to challenge in accordance with the rules, i.e. artistically, their authors call into question not a way of playing the game, but the game itself and the belief which supports it. This is the one unforgivable transgression.

COLLECTIVE MISRECOGNITION

The quasi-magical potency of the signature is nothing other than the power, bestowed on certain individuals, to mobilize the symbolic energy produced by the functioning of the whole field, i.e. the faith in the game and its stakes that is produced by the game itself. As Marcel Mauss observed, the problem with magic is not so much to know what are the specific properties of the magician, or even of the magical operations and representations, but rather to discover the bases of the collective belief or, more precisely, the *collective misrecognition*, collectively produced and maintained, which is the source of the power the magician appropriates. If it is 'impossible to understand magic without the magic group,' this is because the magician's power, of which the miracle of the signature or personal trademark is merely an outstanding example, is a *valid imposture*, a legitimate abuse of power, collectively misrecognized and so recognized. The artist who puts her name on a ready-made article and produces an object whose market price is incommensurate with its cost of production is collectively mandated to perform a magic act which would be nothing without the whole tradition leading up to her gesture, and without the universe of celebrants and believers who give it meaning and value in terms of that tradition. The source of 'creative' power, the ineffable *mana* or charisma celebrated by the tradition, need not be sought anywhere other than in the field, i.e. in the system of objective relations which constitute it, in the struggles of which it is the site and in the specific form of energy or capital which is generated there.

So it is both true and untrue to say that the commercial value of a work of art is incommensurate with its cost of production. It is true if one only takes account of the manufacture of the material object; it is not true if one is referring to the production of the work of art as a sacred, consecrated object, the product of a vast operation of *social alchemy* jointly conducted, with equal conviction and very unequal profits, by all the agents involved in the field of production, i.e. obscure artists and writers as well as 'consecrated' masters, critics and publishers as well as authors, enthusiastic clients as well as convinced vendors. These are contributions, including the most obscure, which the partial materialism of economism ignores, and which only have to be taken into account in order to see that the production of the work of art, i.e. of the artist, is no exception to the law of the conservation of social energy. . . .

ORTHODOXY AND HERESY

The eschatological vision structuring the opposition between avant-garde and 'bourgeois' art, between the material ascesis which guarantees spiritual consecration and wordly success (which is marked, *inter alia,* by institutional recognition—prizes, academies, etc.—and by financial rewards), helps to disguise the true relationship between the field of cultural production and the field of power, by reproducing the opposition (which does not rule out complementarity) between the dominated and dominant fractions of the dominant class, between cultural power (associated with less economic wealth) and economic and political power (associated with less cultural wealth), in the specific logic of the intellectual field, that is, in the transfigured form of the conflict between two aesthetics. Specifically aesthetic conflicts about the legitimate vision of the world—in the last resort, about what deserves to be represented and the right way to represent it—are political conflicts (appearing in their most euphemized form) for the power to impose the dominant definition of reality and social reality in particular. On the right, reproductive art constructed in accordance with the generative schemes of 'straight,' 'straightforward' representation of reality, and social reality in particular, i.e. orthodoxy (e.g., *par excellence,* 'bourgeois theatre') is likely to give those who perceive it in accordance with these schemes the reassuring experience of the immediate self-evidence of the representation, that is, of the necessity of the mode of representation and of the world represented. This orthodox art would be timeless if it were not continuously pushed into the past by the movement brought into the field of production by the dominated fractions' insistence on using the powers they are granted to change the world view and overturn the temporal and *temporary* hierarchies to which 'bourgeois' taste clings. As holders of an (always partial) delegated legitimacy in cultural matters, cultural producers—especially those who produce solely for other producers—always tend to divert their authority to their own advantage and therefore to impose their own variant of the dominant world view as the only legitimate one. But the challenging of the established artistic hierarchies and the heretical displacement of the socially accepted limit between what does and does not deserve to be preserved, admired and transmitted cannot achieve its specifically artistic effect of subversion unless it tacitly recognizes the fact and the legitimacy of such delimitation by making the shifting of that limit an artistic act and thereby claiming for the artist a monopoly in legitimate transgression of the boundary between the sacred and the profane, and therefore a monopoly in revolutions in artistic taxonomies.

The field of cultural production is the area *par excellence* of clashes between the dominant fractions of the dominant class, who fight there sometimes in person but more often through producers oriented towards defending their 'ideas' and satisfying their 'tastes,' and the dominated fractions who are totally involved in this struggle. This conflict brings about the integration in a single field of the various socially specialized sub-fields, particular markets which are completely separate in social and even geographical space, in which the different fractions of the dominant class can find products adjusted to their tastes, whether in the theatre, in painting, fashion or decoration. . . .

BEING DIFFERENT

It is not sufficient to say that the history of the field is the history of the struggle for the monopolistic power to impose the legitimate categories of perception and appreciation. The *struggle itself* creates the history of the field; through the struggle the field is given a temporal dimension. The ageing of authors, works or schools is something quite different from the product of a mechanical slippage into the past. It is the continuous creation of the battle between those who have made their names and are struggling to stay in view and those who cannot make their own names without relegating to the past the established figures, whose interest lies in freezing the movement of time, fixing the present state of the field for ever. On one side are the dominant figures, who want continuity, identity, reproduction; on the other, the newcomers, who seek discontinuity, rupture, difference, revolution. To 'make one's name' means making one's *mark*, achieving recognition (in both senses) of one's *difference* from other producers, especially the most consecrated of them; at the same time, it means *creating a new position* beyond the positions presently occupied, *ahead* of them, in the *avant-garde*. To introduce difference is to produce time. Hence the importance, in this struggle for life and survival, of the *distinctive marks* which, at best, aim to identify what are often the most superficial and most visible properties of a set of works or producers. Words—the names of schools or groups, proper names—are so important only because they make things. These distinctive signs produce existence in a world in which the only way to *be* is to be *different*, to 'make one's name,' either personally or as a group. The names of the schools or groups which have proliferated in recent painting (pop art, minimal art, process art, land art, body art, conceptive art, *arte povera,* Fluxus, new realism, *nouvelle figuration,* support-surface, *art pauvre,* op art, kinetic art, etc.) are pseudo-concepts, *practical* classifying tools which create resemblances and differences by naming them; they are produced in the *struggle for recognition* by the artists themselves or their accredited critics and function as *emblems* which distinguish galleries, groups and artists and therefore the products they make or sell. . . .

The consecrated authors who dominate the field of production also dominate the market; they are not only the most expensive or the most profitable but also the most readable and the most acceptable because they have become part of 'general culture' through a process of familiarization which may or may not have been accompanied by specific teaching. This means that through them, the strategies directed against their domination always additionally hit the distinguished consumers of their distinctive products. To bring a new producer, a new product and a new system of tastes on to the market at a given moment is to push the whole set of producers, products and systems of tastes into the past. The process whereby the field of production becomes a temporal structure also defines the temporal status of taste. Because the different positions in the hierarchical space of the field of production (which can be equally well identified by the names of institutions, galleries, publishers and theatres or by the names of artists or schools) are at the same time tastes in a social hierarchy, every transformation of the structure of the field leads to a displacement of the structure of tastes, i.e. of the system of symbolic distinctions between groups. Oppositions homologous with those existing today between the taste of avant-garde artists, the taste of 'intellectuals,' advanced 'bourgeois' taste and provincial 'bourgeois' taste, which find their means of expression on markets symbolized by the Sonnabend, Denise René and Durand-Ruel galleries, would have been able to express themselves equally effectively in 1945, when Denise René represented the avant-garde, or in 1875, when Durand-Ruel was in that position.

This model is particularly relevant nowadays, because owing to the near-perfect unification of the artistic field and its history, each artistic act which 'makes history' by introducing a new position into the field 'displaces' the whole series of previous artistic acts. Because the whole series of pertinent events is practically present in the latest, in the same way that the six digits already dialled on the telephone are contained in the seventh, an aesthetic act is irreducible to any other act in a different place in the series and the series itself tends towards uniqueness and irreversibility. As Marcel Duchamp points out, this explains why *returns* to past styles have never been more frequent than in these times of frenetic pursuit of originality: 'The characteristic of the century now coming to an end is that it is like a double-barrelled gun. Kandinsky and Kupka invented abstraction. Then abstraction died. No one was going to talk about it any more. It came back thirty-five years later with the American abstract expressionists. You could say that cubism reappeared in an impoverished form in the post-war Paris school. Dada came back in the same way. A second shot, second wind. It's a phenomenon typical of this century. You didn't find that in the eighteenth or nineteenth centuries. After the Romantics, came Courbet. And Romanticism never come back. Even the pre-Raphaelites aren't a rehash of the Romantics.'

In fact, these are always *apparent* returns, since they are separated from what they rediscover by a negative reference to something which was itself the negation (of the negation of the negation, etc) of what they rediscover (when, that is, the intention is not simply of pastiche, a parody which presupposes all the intervening history). In the present state of the artistic field, there is no room for naïveté, and every act, every gesture, every event, is, as a painter nicely put it, 'a sort of nudge or wink between accomplices.' In and through the games of distinction, these winks and nudges, silent, hidden references to other artists, past or present, confirm a complicity which excludes the layperson, who is always bound to miss what is essential, namely the interrelations and interactions of which the work is only the silent trace. Never has the very structure of the field been present so practically in every act of production.

Never too has the irreducibility of the work of cultural production to the artist's own labour appeared so clearly. The primary reason is that the new definition of the artist and of artistic work brings the artist's work closer to that of the 'intellectual' and makes it more dependent than ever on 'intellectual' commentaries. Whether as critics but also the leaders of a school (e.g. Restany and the new realists), or as fellow-travellers contributing their reflexive discourse to the production of a work which is always in part its own commentary or to reflection of an art which often itself incorporates a reflection on art, intellectuals have never before so directly participated, through their work on art and the artist, in an artistic work which always consists partly of *working on oneself* as an artist. Accompanied by historians writing the chronicles of their discoveries, by philosophers who comment on their 'acts' and who interpret and over-interpret their works, artists can constantly invent the distinguishing strategies on which their artistic survival depends, only by putting into their practice the practical mastery of the objective truth of their practice, thanks to the combination of knowingness and naïveté, calculation and innocence, faith and bad faith that is required by *mandarin games,* cultivated games with the inherited culture, whose common feature is that they identify 'creation' with the introduction of *deviations,* which only the initiated can perceive, with respect to forms and formulae that are known to all. The emergence of this new definition of the artist and his or her craft cannot be understood independently of the transformations of the artistic field. The constitution of an unprecedented array of institutions for recording, preserving and analysing works (reproductions, catalogues, art journals, museums acquiring the most modern works, etc.), the growth in the personnel employed, full-time or part-time, in the *celebration* of works of art, the increased circulation of works and artists, with great international exhibitions and the increasing number of chains of galleries with branches in many countries—all combine to favour the establishment of an unprecedented relationship between the body of interpreters and the work of art, analogous to that found in the great esoteric traditions; to such an extent that one has to be blind not to see that discourse about a work is not a mere accompaniment, intended to assist its perception and appreciation, but a stage in the production of the work, of its meaning and value. But once again it is sufficient to quote Marcel Duchamp:

> Q. But to come back to your ready-mades, I thought that R. Mutt, the signature on *The Fountain,* was the manufacturer's name. But in the article by Rosalind Krauss, I read: 'R. Mutt, a pun on the German, Armut, or poverty.' 'Poverty' would entirely change the meaning of *The Fountain.*
> M.D. Rosalind Krauss? The redhead? It isn't that at all. You can deny it. Mutt comes from Mott Works, the name of a big firm that makes sanitary equipment. But Mott was too close, so I made it Mutt, because there was a strip cartoon in the papers in those days, Mutt and Jeff, everybody knew it. So right from the start there was a resonance. Mutt was a fat little guy, and Jeff was tall and thin . . . I wanted a different name. And I added Richard . . . Richard is a good name for a loo! You see, it's the opposite of poverty . . . But not even that, just R.—R. Mutt.

Q. What possible interpretation is there of the *Bicycle Wheel*? Should one see it as the integration of movement into the work of art? Or as a fundamental point of departure, like the Chinese who invented the wheel?

M.D. That machine has no intention, except to get rid of the appearance of a work of art. It was a whim, I didn't call it a work of art. I wanted to throw off the desire to create works of art. Why do works have to be static? The thing—the bicycle wheel—came before the idea. Without any intention of making a song and dance about it, not at all so as to say '*I* did that, and nobody has ever done it before me.' Besides, the originals have never been sold.

Q. What about the geometry book left out in the weather? Can one say that it's the idea of integrating time and space? With a pun on 'geométrie dans l'espace' (solid geometry) and 'temps,' the rain and sun that transforms the book?

M.D. No, no more than the idea of integrating movement and sculpture. It was a joke. A pure joke. To denigrate the solemnity of a book of principles.

Here we see, directly exposed, the injection of meaning and value by commentary and commentary on commentary—to which the naïve but knowing exposure of the falsity of the commentary contributes in its turn. The ideology of the inexhaustible work of art, or of 'reading' as re-creation masks—through the quasi-exposure which is often seen in matters of faith—the fact that the work is indeed made not twice, but a hundred times, by all those who are interested in it, who find a material or symbolic profit in reading it, classifying it, deciphering it, commenting on it, combating it, knowing it, possessing it. Enrichment accompanies ageing when the work manages to enter the game, when it becomes a stake in the game and so incorporates some of the energy produced in the struggle of which it is the object. The struggle, which sends the work into the past, is also what ensures it a form of survival; lifting it from the state of a dead letter, a mere thing subject to the ordinary laws of ageing, the struggle at least ensures it has the sad eternity of academic debate.

27

ART AS CONTEXTUAL: DELE JEGEDE

The discovery of African art by early 20th-century Western artists and collectors played a crucial role in the development of abstract art. Picasso, most famously, was profoundly affected by his encounter with masks and other art objects from Africa. Despite these ostensibly positive reactions to African art, Western attitudes have been reproached for harboring within them a patronizing ethnocentrism. This reading is an instance of such criticism.

In his essay "Art for Life's Sake: African Art as a Reflection of an Afrocentric Cosmology," Dele Jegede (b. 1945), a Nigerian artist and scholar, attacks a variety of Western responses to African art for failing to understand the significance that art has within the cultures that produce it. Believing such failures promote demeaning attitudes, Jegede defends the dignity of Africa, Africans, and African art.

Jegede regards as a form of Eurocentric bias the use of the term *primitivism* to characterize African art. Although coined as an aesthetic category embracing not only African art, this label suggest that the works to which it is ascribed lack the refinement of Western art.

Not only must such usage be rejected if one is to appreciate African art, Jegede argues, but the typical manner of displaying African art objects in museums with no reference to their actual cultural roles within African societies must also be changed: Such decontextualized display is antithetical to the ways in which Africans themselves experience and appreciate their art. For, Jegede continues, art is not a cultural universal, but derives its particular meanings within specific cultures. To place an African art object in a museum case to be disinterestedly contemplated is, according to him, as Eurocentric a practice as labeling that object "primitive." This decontextualization robs the work of its most significant properties, those conferred by its role in specific cultural practices—for example, a mask is not simply an object whose form we might appreciate, but rather an effigy with specific ceremonial functions. Jegede's rich descriptions of African cultural practices are meant to demonstrate the limits of an appreciation of such art objects that isolates them from their place in the lives of African peoples. Here, the argument makes contact with those of Western philosophers, such as Adorno (Chapter 15) and Piper (Chapter 23), who also emphasize the importance of the role art objects play within social practices.

Jegede uses the term *Afrocentric* to characterize his approach to African works of art. "Afrocentrism," an intellectual stance that places Africa at the center of one's worldview, is, of course, a reaction to the Western tendency to view everything in relation to Europe, taken as the norm. Jegede and others think the appropriate way to counter this bias is to invert it.

Although Jegede is certainly right to decry some of the ways in which African art has been appropriated by Westerners, we need to ask whether his argument establishes as much as he desires. Has Jegede shown that the concept of art is as culturally specific as he claims? Has Jegede himself fallen prey to a Eurocentric tendency by uncritically applying the label "art" to African artifacts? Is his alternative to an art "for art's sake," an art "for life's sake," superior to views advanced in the West? These are some of the important and provocative questions that Jegede's essay raises.

STUDY QUESTIONS ON THE READING

1. Why does Jegede think terms such as "primitivism" and "tribalism" betray Eurocentric attitudes toward African art?

2. Consider some of the examples Jegede gives of how art objects function within African culture. Using these examples, explain the role that art has within Africa, according to Jegede. Does it make sense to call these objects "art"?

3. What is Jegede's conception of how, within African societies, objects become *art* objects? How does this conception of art differ from some of the Western conceptions you have studied?

4. Do you agree that displaying African art in a museum without any indication of its cultural role is Eurocentric? Explain.

❖

DELE JEGEDE, ART FOR LIFE'S SAKE: AFRICAN ART AS A REFLECTION OF AN AFROCENTRIC COSMOLOGY

African art has been maligned in the writings of Western scholars who have failed to understand its source and origin. This failure has led to misunderstanding and misinterpretation of the artistic production and expression of

African people. In this chapter I shall demonstrate the extent to which African art responds to an Afrocentric framework instead of to a European-centered notion of the artistic. Indeed I have appealed to both an experiential and a philosophical base for my arguments, particularly relying heavily on fundamental empiricism.

Some decades ago, growing up at home in Ikere-Ekit, a relatively large Yoruba town in Nigeria which was nevertheless omitted from the colonial map until recently, I remember paying intermittent Sunday visits to my grandmother. A wiry, smallish and alert woman, she was a priestess who had put behind her over seven decades. Seven decades according to the white man's calendar, a new system which grandmother never quite understood. She did not understand why the more convenient traditional calendar that relied on the physical appearance of the moon was discarded.

Visits to grandmother who lived in another quarter of the town arose, as time went by, less for the desire to check on her health than from the necessity to take care of my own welfare; she was the source of my pocket-money. For, not being exactly born with a silver spoon in my mouth—actually, the only available spoon to us children then, in a literal or metaphorical sense, was wooden—I needed the pennies which grandmother was ever so generous to part with. But I took care not to tax her generosity. My visits, cleverly spaced to produce maximum results, were always on Sundays. They were always after the Sunday service which you missed at the risk of invoking your school teacher's anger the following Monday. For one of the benefits of missionary education which many of us had was corporal punishment for frivolous absences from church and other God-related ceremonies.

As I have already mentioned, grandmother was a priestess. She was a devotee of Osanyin, the Yoruba god of medicine, symbolized by wrought iron staffs of varying heights, each with bird configurations on top. Grandmother had many of them arranged as if in a conference at one nook in her bedroom which admitted light through an only window of less than two feet high. The Osanyin staffs were often bedecked with an array of long, thickly strung cowries whose original color of white had turned into burnt umber at appointed curves and recessions—the result of frequent use and streaks of blood, now dry, from sacrificed pigeons. A small, raised platform of earth constituted the base into which the Osanyin staffs were set. It was from here that grandmother always picked those precious pennies which she often released to me at the end of my visit. Grandmother, her gentle gray hair often plaited in simple rows into which a parrot's red feather was occasionally inserted, would send through me to my father choicy lobes of kola nuts. That was a mark of affection.

Father, by virtue of being the oldest male, was an *olori ile,* that is, leader of our compound which comprised many households each of which was headed by a male adult, but all of whom traced descent to one common ancestor. At periodic intervals, father would lead all the other men to the family shrine located in a small shed built purposely for this, with us curious half-clad children in tow, to offer sacrifices to our ancestors. Such sacrifices were often made with healthy goats and strong, robust chickens. At the *ojubo,* "eye of the sacrifice," wrought iron staffs, now much bigger than grandmother's, and other pieces of artworks carved in wood or molded in clay, presided. Such occasions were often of particular interest to us children not because we, in our limited wisdom, cared that much about our ancestors who were at any rate invisible, but because we cherished the delicacies which goat meat and slaughtered chicken became once they found their way from the shrine to mother's pot of soup.

In those bygone days when hometown's peace had not been assaulted by incessant vehicular traffic, when the white man's tar had not silenced the gutsy dusts on the only main road, when the quiet town's skies had not been punctuated at calculated intervals by electric poles, I often stopped in wonderment at those carved posts, painted in an assortment of colors, which supported the low eaves of the sprawling, rectangular shrine located near the central market place. The only architectural spectacle that surpassed this was the palace of the *oba,* the divine ruler of the town. It had its antechambers and courtyards decorated with gorgeous murals and impressive doors and houseposts, many of which were carved by Olowe, acknowledged as perhaps the greatest Yoruba carver of the century. The artworks in the Ogoga of Ikere's palace inspired the *oba's* many wives to sing in their praise—songs that are still sung at annual ceremonies till this day, long after all the houseposts had disappeared.

Mother was a weaver. And I enjoyed helping her, as a child, at the dye pits, and on the loom in our corridor, where my task was to hold up the lamp, made in form of a small, earthenware with a wick soaked in palm oil. But mother was not in any way unusual or extraordinary. Like many others who were engaged in creative spheres like pottery, or mat weaving, she functioned within an expectancy pattern dictated by the culture. In her own right, she was a specialist.

Therefore, I have drawn copiously on my own firsthand experiences and observations by way of introducing this chapter. I have referred to these experiences also to underline the submission that a definition of African art cannot be meaningfully attempted within a Western framework. We may define art as being culture-specific. It may be customary in some circles to use as a point of departure the platform—by no means an infallible one—that art has a universal meaning. But we suffer from nothing by repeating the view which is shared by discerning minds that a people's perception of what qualifies to be art, in form, content, import and usage, varies from one culture to another. While in some cultures art may be perceived as belonging to the domain of the anointed—of a select and theatrical few known more commonly by the generic term artist—in other cultures, such as my examples above have shown, art is lived out; it is experienced intimately; it is expected and demanded. In such cultures as exist in traditional societies in Africa, art is integral to life and to man's well being. It is expressive of a people's world-view, and its absence creates an obvious but uncomfortable vacuum.

You may have suspected that the title of this presentation, "Art for Life's Sake," is suggestive of a complementary even if antipodal standpoint in relation to the more popular Western doctrine of art for art's sake. Let me confirm this suspicion. In doing so, however, let us pause to examine some of the distinct elements which characterize African art. Before this, a digression. A fairly long but appropriate digression. A Yoruba proverb says, "*A ko le fi ete sile ka maa pa lapa-lapa.*" Where a patient manifests both diseases, "We cannot devote all our responses to treating ringworm when leprosy has not even been touched." Let us then examine two leprous shibboleths in African art. I am referring to the terms "primitive" and "tribal."

Some Westerners have told us, over the years, that African art is primitive. These early students of African art, in assigning this label, functioned under a Eurocentric rationalization which reached its zenith in the evolutionist theory of Darwin—a nineteenth century theory which classified cultures on the assumption that only the white man had a monopoly on standards of development. Thus, on arrival in Africa, the white man proceeded to arrogate to himself the lordship and pre-eminence which, in his own country, he hardly merited. In the words of Sheldon Gellar "white settler farmers who came from lower middle-class backgrounds thus perceived themselves as 'gentleman farmers' and attempted to imitate the style of the upper class and aristocracy back home."[1]

The visage of this "new god" on African soil, easily distinguished as much by his skin color as by his tobacco pipe and pith helmet, became a conundrum which the African would attempt to unravel for the next century. Fueled by the cumulative effects of the doctrine of racial superiority, the white man on arrival in Africa expected to see a replication of Western culture, albeit with minor geographical modifications. He saw, instead, a remarkably different race and culture. Neither frescoes, nor etchings nor prints of the European sort were found. There were almost no equestrian, heroic or heraldic sculptures. In place of museums, he saw shrines. In place of the cross and the crucifix he saw masks, masquerades and an assortment of sacred objects in use. The European concluded the art was *fetish,* the religion *pagan,* and the people *primitive.* The general absence of written languages, as understood by Europe, was interpreted as absence of history. And the word "native," used in its most condescending and derogatory manifestations to refer to indigenous African peoples, was generously applied. All of this is symptomatic of ethnocentrism.

But all of this was not mere happenstance. As Michael McCarthy has demonstrated, much of Euro-American perception of Africa as subcultural and primitive is indebted to the gratuitous fabrications of early travellers, publishers and, in particular, of early geographers who substituted fancies for facts. McCarthy's own summary is relevant for our purposes here, and he deserves to be quoted at some length:

> Generally, the African narratives written, published and disseminated by travellers from the West indicated directly or implied obtusely that Africans lack civilization, or any redeeming type of social organization. As a race, they were promiscuous and cruel, and their behavior was more akin to beasts than to people, an idea advanced by portraying Africans as having less than human form. Africa, in addition, was seen as a mirror image of what Greece, Rome or Europe should never be: a land where nature had gone wild, where chaos and anarchy reigned, where people were deformed both in body and spirit, and where gross excesses of behavior were not the exception but the rule.[2]

---

[1] Sheldon Gellar, *Senegal: An African Nation Between Islam and the West* (Boulder, Colo.: Westview Press, 1982), 126.

[2] Michael McCarthy, *Dark Continent* (Westport, Conn: Greenwood Press, 1983), 14.

Today in the West, vestiges of this racial bent are very much apparent. Events in Africa are hardly reported by the mass media unless such confirm the stereotypical view of a dark continent. As a result of such constant reinforcement of negative views, many African Americans remain unconcerned about their roots. In fact, some are ashamed of Africa. Even in Africa itself, this negativism, although of slightly different manufacture, produced identical results. Educated Africans became disdainful of their cultures and embraced imported values. Some of them anglicized their names, while serious efforts were made to out-British the British, or out-French the French, in language, modes of dress and manner of perceiving. In Nigeria, some overly enthusiastic converts assisted the early missionaries in making bonfires of traditional carvings. For those who owed their education to missionary enterprise, religious indoctrination was inevitable.

In art-historical and anthropological circles, there has been a shift of attitude in recent years. As scholars in this book attest, African art is not primitive. But many non-Africans see Afrocentric insights as appeasement. Thus, in spite of the ritual acknowledgments scattered in many books to the effect that African art manifests admirable qualities all its own, many books still turn up with the title "Primitive Art." Some, in fact, would want us to believe that they have not found a suitable alternative to the term "primitive."[3]

The necessity for this explication is justified by the fact that the ghost of the term "primitive" has not been completely laid to rest. That this is so is confirmed by the recent College Arts Association conference which organized a panel on "Art Without History" which grouped graffiti, children's art and psychotic, naive, prehistoric and primitive art together.[4] And as recently as 1986, Roy Sieber, an eminent Africanist, considered this issue of primitivism strong enough to warrant an emphatic declaration: "African arts are not primitive, if by primitive is meant simple, crude, or original in the sense of being without a history."[5]

In recent years, attempts have been made to popularize the use of "tribal" as a substitute for "primitive." Yet, this attempt must fail. The reason why this term is being recommended by its apologists is because "it is possible to generalize about African art styles up to but not above the level of the tribe."[6]

The thrust of this argument is that the arts of African peoples do not share anything in common outside of their immediate areas of production. However as Asante and Asante demonstrate in their book *African Culture: The Rhythms of Unity,* there is much commonality in African culture.[7]

---

[3] Paul Wingert, *Primitive Art* (New York: Oxford University Press, 1962), 7.

[4] See footnotes to Barbara Frank's article, "Open Borders: Style and Ethnic Identity," *African Arts* 20. 4 (1987), 90.

[5] Roy Sieber, "Traditional Arts of Black Africa," in *Africa,* ed. Phyllis M. Martin and Patrick O'Meara (Bloomington: Indiana University Press, 1986), 212.

[6] William Fagg, "African Cultures," *Encyclopedia of World Art* (New York: McGraw-Hill Book Company, Inc., 1959), 1, 130.

[7] Molefi Asante and Kariamu Welsh Asante, eds., *African Culture: The Rhythms of Unity* (Westport, Conn.: Greenwood Press, 1985).

This recommendation must be stoutly rejected. Like the word "primitive," "tribal" offers an approach that attempts to put the "natives" in their place. It attempts to treat our art as discrete entities that cannot be meaningfully studied within the context of a system of relationships in which cultural and artistic intercourse is possible. It is, in a sense, a "divide and study" approach that negates, this time on a cultural plane, the preoccupation of modern day African nations with forging national unity and cultural identity. It is only Africa that appears qualified to be considered on the basis of tribe. The ludicrousness of this concept is underlined when we note that while small European ethnic groups are referred to as nations, nations in Africa are seen largely as agglomerations of tribes. In effect, proponents of tribality in African art are saying that because African countries are multi-lingual and multi-cultural, they do not necessarily intermarry or inter-trade, and are not necessarily influenced by each other's cultures. In other words, tribality as a replacement comes with the supposition that countries do not have any artistic legitimacy unless their artworks have a unifying national style. Tribality must be rejected because African art has a homogeneity that sets it apart from other world arts. At any rate, there are no compelling reasons why stylistic commonness should be a criterion for artistic analysis or historical studies.

Having rejected these two taxonomic approaches, what do we recommend? Simply that African art be seen, recognized, studied, analyzed or appreciated Afrocentrically. For particularistic studies, group identification is in order. And those interested enough will make the linkage. Thus, Nok, Benin, Ife and Igbo-Ukwu can be considered under the country, Nigeria; Dogon, Jenne and Bamana can be considered under Mali. These examples can be multiplied. Furthermore, comparisons can be made and conclusions drawn under various categories: *chronology, iconology,* and *stylistic.* And the arts can be categorized into appropriate rubrics: *ancient, traditional* or *modern.*

Having digressed to deal with these recurrent problems, let us now look at those elements which confirm our thesis that much of African art is tied to life, that it represents the physical translation of philosophical, religious and aesthetic tenets. The submission here is that African art addresses African cosmology. In many instances, it is a physical manifestation of abstract and subjective doctrines; it is a metaphor for socio-religious ethos.

There are two distinct and closely interdependent planes at which art functions. These are the *spiritual* and the *secular.* The spiritual domain involves religion, with the associational elements of ancestor worship and the various shrines—communal and personal—which are installed. Many African societies repose faith in their ancestors. Though dead, ancestors are believed to have the power to transform themselves into formidable spiritual entities who generally intercede in support of their offspring. It is this need to fulfill religious obligations, to appeal to, or venerate ancestors, or to appease malevolent powers, that has encouraged the production of artworks—in wood, metal, clay or composite materials—in considerable quantity.

Art, then, has an aesthetic constant that is determined primarily by performance. Frequently, it is the medium that becomes the issue, since unimprovement in human conditions is often blamed on the ineffectiveness of the particular artwork.

The concern for social security, group solidarity, personal and corporate welfare, procreation and survival is shared by many African societies. Survival in this context is not limited to human survival. It is recognized, for instance, that man cannot survive in the absence of reliable agricultural produce. Let us examine this a little further.

Most African communities attempt to be as self-sufficient as possible. Indeed, of all things agricultural self-sufficiency is an imperative. For this is one of the cardinal principles of survival. An African proverb says that a hungry stomach cannot accommodate or tackle other issues. Yet, farmers recognize that tilling the soil and planting the seeds may not be sufficient, on occasions, to ensure good harvest. They recognize their powerlessness in the face of inclement weather. Lack of rain, or an excess of it, may spell disaster for the crops, which would either dry up or remain bloated underground. It is this desire to appease the unseen forces responsible for such developments that has led man to resort to extraordinary means.

Enter the diviner. Through divination, he attempts to diagnose the cause and prescribe solutions. Probable questions the diviner might ask his oracle are: "Why are the gods angry with us?" "Have the ancestors forsaken us?" "What did we do wrong?" "How do we rectify this situation?" Responses from the oracle would vary from one situation to another. But it may result, as in the case of the Bamana of Mali whose *chi wara* headdresses are a specimen of creative elegance, in the people being advised to commission masks and dance with them.

In some cases, the oracle may reveal that the ancestors had been angered through a misdeed. There would be need for propitiation. Sacrifices may be ordered to be offered at the community shrine. This may involve the appearance of masquerades to cleanse the society of the desecration. Several carved figures, masks and masquerades in African art serve this purpose of atoning for a misdeed, cleansing any defilement, purifying the soil, supplicating for rain or asking for a successful harvest.

In this connection, art objects which are the usual physical elements of a shrine become the platform through which ancestral biddings are met. Sacrificial objects vary. In general, emphasis is placed upon edible things. Thus, animals such as pigeons, rats, chickens, snails, rams, goats and at times cows, may be sacrificed. What the ancestors need most is the blood of these animals, which is poured on the art objects in the shrine. Kola nuts, millet beer or palm wine, palm oil, corn and beans are some of the objects that may be used for sacrifice. Pieces of prepared dishes are also fed to the objects. It is the cumulative effect of this which produces the compulsive additiveness noted in some artworks, or the heavy encrustations on some of them. In many instances, encrustations are indicative of the degree of veneration which is attached to the spirit or medium personified by the art object.

Human survival is not tied up with agriculture-induced communal sacrifices alone. Survival could also have personalized dimensions. In patrilineal societies where emphasis is placed not just on children but on the gender, survival is considered threatened where a family fails to produce male children. Since inheritance is through the male line in patrilineal societies, concerned individuals often ask for spiritual or divine intervention. And where barrenness is suspected, the urge for spiritual ministration becomes more fervid.

Among the Yoruba of Nigeria, for example, numerous sculptures reveal this preoccupation with procreation; thousands of houseposts reinforce this love for children. The carver of almost every type of carving ranging from a Sango staff to Ifa divination bowls, from masks to *ibeji* (twins) figures, seizes on the least excuse to include a woman, sometimes with a baby on the back, in kneeling or standing position and surrounded at times by children.

Bare-breastedness in Yoruba sculpture does not have any indecent associations. It is regarded as complimentary since fullness of breasts is considered as a mark of ideal womanhood; breasts being a source of milk for babies and an aspect of aesthetic beauty. A Yoruba proverb confirms this: "*Funfun niyi eyin, gigun rege niyi orun omu sikisiki niyi obinrin.*" Literally, this means that "Whiteness is the glory of teeth, roundness is the glory of neck, full robust breasts glorify womanhood."

The Yoruba have perhaps the highest number of twins per capita in Africa and twins are treated with extraordinary affection. And if one of them should die, as often happens, a small carving is commissioned as a replacement. This figure is known as *ibeji*. It is treated in much the same way as the surviving one—clothed, bathed, rubbed and fed—in order to prevent the departed one from coming back to snatch away the surviving partner. Although children are profusely depicted in Yoruba sculpture, they are hardly portrayed with any youthful features. It is their relatively small size that becomes the criterion for identification.

But apart from these two instances of agricultural and human survival, art is also committed to prestige and class distinction. In other words, it is concerned with secular affairs. Rulers in several communities arrogate to themselves certain objects and materials, which can only be used by others with permission. Sometimes such objects are permanently exclusive to rulership. In such a case there will be no basis for any requests being made by others for permission. Blacksmiths, members of various regulatory societies, chiefs and paramount rulers all have their respective artistic forms which are emblematic of their status. For example, the beaded crown is the exclusive prerogative of the Yoruba ruler, known as *oba*. It is taboo for any non-*oba* to wear it. So also is the beaded staff which has the force of command. It is sent by the *oba* to summon any of his subjects, or appropriate any material that catches his fancy. Once a beaded staff is presented before you, immediate compliance is required.

In some instances, art objects perform motivating or mediatory functions. They are seen as personalized forces which are charged to ensure personal success and clear all obstacles in one's way. Such is the *Ikenga* figure, found among various peoples in Anambra, Imo, Benue and Bendel states of Nigeria. But it is among the Igbo peoples that Ikenga figures receive the most socio-cultural amplification.

The Ikenga sculpture, usually in wood, is thus a personal shrine which, once consecrated, is expected to ensure the owners' well being and prosperity. The Ikenga is a personal monument to the right hand which is regarded, symbolically as well as physically, as man's most trusted ally. A successful Ikenga is regarded as a personal spirit. As such, it is cared for, much in the same way as objects in shrines described above. Of course, an unsuccessful Ikenga suffers neglect; it could even be destroyed by its owner.

Finally, let us look at one spectacular feature of many African societies: the festival. It is a spectacle that serves as a theater where the secular and the spiritual interact. It is festivals which provide perhaps the single most important and widespread platform for appreciating not only masks and masquerades but also the arts in their totality. Masking traditions in many African societies have remained very popular, in spite of conversions to Islamic or Christian doctrines. One reason why this is so is that festivals, called by whatever name in various African societies, are usually moving spectacles, kaleidoscopes of colors in which the relationship between the secular and the spiritual is reinforced, and the complementarities between art and life are reinvigorated. Festivals—particularly those involving the appearance of masquerades—are total arts *par excellence.* For it is at a festival that the drummer talks in rhythms to the masquerader who in turn responds with the appropriate dance steps. Poetry finds resonance in the mouth of the singers while, in some situations, the theatrical and demonstrative musicality of masquerades explodes under colorful costumes.

Masqueraders move in pairs or, as is more common, in droves, amidst pomp and pageantry, with their acolytes drumming, chanting and, of course, dancing. Masks are hardly carved for mere aesthetic considerations; they are conceived of more in terms of their social functions. The purpose determines the birth of the mask. Their functions vary a great deal, ranging from entertainment to religion, from judicial to political administration. There are masqueraders who challenge man's physical and athletic fitness, just as there are those who test the efficacy of their medicine on others. Medicine as used in this context does not mean drugs, which are prescribed by medical personnel. It is made of powerful herbal concoctions, believed to be capable of exerting supernatural control over victims. There are masqueraders who police boys gathered for initiation at the camps, ensuring that they receive the usual traditional education.

In the majority of cases, masqueraders are regarded as ancestors reincarnated. Among the Dan of Cote d'Ivoire, masks are not mere carving. Once the carver has completed the carving, usually on commission, it becomes charged. It assumes a corporate, extraordinary existence. Among the Dan, as indeed among many other groups in Africa, a mask is not a mask. It is the material essence of a spirit. The spirit does not reside in the mask; it is the mask. Whether a mask is used or unused, it is not neglected or discarded. It is respected and consulted on important occasions, until it disintegrates or is invited to inhabit a replacement mask.

There are societies where masks cannot be conceived in isolation from costumes—where there is in fact no equivalent English word for masks, which are simply referred to as spiritual entities. Despite the spiritualness of masquerades, human beings as ordinary mortals continue to intercede to ensure smooth and successful proceedings as festivals, to prevent ugly accidents or forestall unpleasant developments. For this reason, emphasis is placed on the procurement of apotropaic medicines, some of which come in liquid, solid or powdery form, to be bathed with, consumed or rubbed into the skin, after appropriate incisions have been made. Some substances are sewn into small leather containers and worn on the body as charms and amulets, or built into the masks themselves.

Festivals could occur on a cyclical basis or on such rare occasions as obsequies for an important personage. They could occur in connection with traditional observances meant to cleanse the society, promote group solidarity, ensure security and maintain law and order. In most of these cases, masqueraders appear in their brilliant costumes. The costumes may be made from raffia, jute bag, nettings, brilliantly colored cloths which are made into dazzling applique works. They can also be made from other composite materials. Often, cowries, animal skulls, horns, and skins, small gourds containing medicine and birds' feathers add to the awesomeness of masquerades.

Drumming, dancing, chanting and compelling theatricality constitute a regular feature. Masqueraders dance according to designation and characterization. Ferocious and wild ones who are often temperamental and impatient usually task their drummers, as these have to walk, skip, or even run while maintaining appropriate rhythmic tempo. Audience participation is total, intensive and elastic. The audience moves with the colorful spectacle, and since only a few privileged and deserving members of the community have designated seats at the arena, the standing audience contracts and expands in response to the movements of the performing masqueraders.

It is impossible to exhaust the several overlapping levels at which art reinforces life in traditional Africa. We can only note, in conclusion, that a lot of African art pieces are, in some respect, emblematic of artistic decapitation. Taken out of context, masks stare at us coldly in museums, through bared teeth or hollowed eyes, from within beautifully crafted Japanese glass encasements.

In private collections, African artworks become transfixed on the mantle-piece or in wooden cubicles, bathed in a caressing interplay of lights, but with very little or no reference—suggested or amplified—to their contextual use or significance. Although we derive pleasure in appreciating these objects ex-situ, there is the danger of their being unduly romanticized.

It is a danger that can be avoided if we would allow the arts to lead us into renewing our contact with Africa, and into a greater and more intimate appreciation of the cultures and the peoples of the continent. It is within this context that collections of traditional African art in private, public or academic holdings derive stronger legitimacy. . . . The arts can be used to disprove racial innuendos and to re-direct the black man and woman towards the realization of positive self-affirmation. They can be used not only as indices of aesthetic cognition, but equally as important tools in stemming the marginalization of the blacks' contributions to world civilization.

28

ART AS POSTCOLONIAL:
KWAME ANTHONY APPIAH

Derrida (Chapter 24) chides the philosophy of art for, among other things, focusing primarily on Western traditions. What difference would it make if non-Western works were taken as seriously? We get some insight into this question from Kwame Anthony Appiah (b. 1950), a Ghanaian whose contribution to this volume is taken from his book *In My Father's House.*

Like Jegede, Appiah is concerned with the way in which the Western art world views African art. His examination of the process by which pieces were selected for the 1987 exhibit, *Perspectives: Angles on African Art,* shows that items were included in that show for economic as well as artistic reasons. This means that the artworld, far from operating solely on artistic or aesthetic principles, makes judgments based on art market considerations as well. Appiah is here attempting to expose the less exalted side of the art world—in this respect, at least, aligning himself with Piper (Chapter 23).

Appiah focuses on one work in the show, *Yoruba Man with a Bicycle,* which the African-American novelist and critic James Baldwin also noted precisely because it was *not* an example of primitivism, the sort of African art that has attracted most Western attention. In Appiah's terms, this piece is neotraditional, that is, it is produced for sale on the international art market.

In interpreting this work, Appiah discusses the importance of postmodernism, a perspective already invoked in earlier contributions to this volume. For Appiah, postmodernism rejects any claim to exclusivity and universality. In the case of art, modernists such as Bell (Chapter 10) argue for a set of universal criteria that can be used to judge whether something is a work of art. Objects that fail to meet these criteria are simply not art, no matter the culture in which they originate. African art was "discovered," in part, through the modernist assessment that it possesses the sort of "significant form" found in Western modernist works. But this strategy is precisely what the postmodernist rejects, just because it rests on the presumed existence of a set of universally valid criteria. Brandishing terms derived from deconstructionism (see Chapter 24) such as "Eurocentric," "phallocentric," "logocentric," etc., the postmodern theorist challenges the modernist to defend the claim to possess standards untainted by history and culture. Appiah clearly sides with the challengers.

An important characteristic of modernist thought is the opposition between self and other, an opposition whose validity is undermined, according to Appiah, by *Yoruba Man with a Bicycle*. We cannot see this work as simply the product of a radically different mentality: The presence of the bicycle in this work, a pastiche of African and Western elements, points to its essentially hybrid character. For the artist, both the traditional aspects of his culture and those appropriated from the West are simply vehicles for his creativity. According to Appiah, in this artist's imagination Africa and the West are not others to each other.

Appiah's reflections on this sculpture imply that, in our effort to understand what art is, we need to abandon the quest for a single standard that objects must meet to qualify as works of art. However, we must equally resist a full-scale relativism that would deny any commitment to transcendent values. In the end, he critiques the presumption that only the Western artist is a self-conscious creator while he also rejects the view that art gives us access to a genuine otherness.

STUDY QUESTIONS ON THE READING

1. What does Appiah find problematic in Susan Vogel's claim that only Africans will view art "in terms of their own traditional criteria"?

2. Appiah asserts that African art is a commodity. What does he mean by this? How does this affect our understanding of African art as art, according to Appiah?

3. What does Appiah mean by postmodernism? How is this relevant to understanding the nature of art?

4. What makes a work neotraditional, according to Appiah?

5. What does *Yoruba Man with a Bicycle* illustrate for Appiah? Why can't it be treated as simply an example of otherness?

6. Compare Appiah's assessment of African art with Jegede's. What are the important differences between them? With whom do you agree, and why?

KWAME ANTHONY APPIAH: IN MY FATHER'S HOUSE

You were called Bimbircokak
And all was well that way
You have become Victor-Emile-Louis-Henri-Joseph
Which
So far as I recall
Does not reflect your kinship with
Rockefeller.[1]

YAMBO OUOLOGUEM

In 1987 the Center for African Art in New York organized a show entitled *Perspectives: Angles on African Art.*[2] The curator, Susan Vogel, had worked with a number of "cocurators," whom I list in order of their appearance in the table of contents: Ekpo Eyo, quondam director of the Department of Antiquities of the National Museum of Nigeria; William Rubin, director of painting and sculpture at the Museum of Modern Art and organizer of its controversial Primitivism exhibit; Romare Bearden, African-American painter; Ivan Karp, curator of African ethnology at the Smithsonian; Nancy Graves, European-American painter, sculptor, and filmmaker; James Baldwin, who surely needs no qualifying glosses; David Rockefeller, art collector and friend of the mighty; Lela Kouakou, Baule artist and diviner, from Ivory Coast (this a delicious juxtaposition, richest and poorest, side by side); Iba N'Diaye, Senegalese sculptor; and Robert Farris Thompson, Yale professor and African and African-American art historian. Vogel describes the process of selection in her introductory essay.

The one woman and nine men were each offered a hundred-odd photographs of "African Art as varied in type and origin, and as high in quality, as we could manage" and asked to select ten for the show.[3] Or, I should say more exactly, that this is what was offered to eight of the men. For Vogel adds, "In the case of the Baule artist, a man familiar only with the art of his own people, only Baule objects were placed in the pool of photographs." At this point we are directed to a footnote to the essay, which reads:

> Showing him the same assortment of photos the others saw would have been interesting, but confusing in terms of the reactions we sought here. Field

[1] Yambo Ouologuem, "A Mon Mari." *Presence Africaine* 57 (1980), 65.

[2] Susan Vogel et al., *Perspectives: Angles on African Art.* New York: The Center for African Art, 1987; by James Baldwin, Romare Bearden, Ekpo Eyo, Nancy Graves, Ivan Karp, Lela Kouakou, Iba N'Diaye, David Rockefeller, William Rubin, and Robert Farris Thompson, interviewed by Michael John Weber, with an introduction by Susan Vogel.

[3] Ibid., 11.

aesthetic studies, my own and others, have shown that African informants will criticize sculptures from other ethnic groups in terms of their own traditional criteria, often assuming that such works are simply inept carvings of their own aesthetic tradition.

I shall return to this irresistible footnote in a moment. But let me pause to quote further, this time from the words of David Rockefeller, who would surely never "criticize sculptures from other ethnic groups in terms of [his] own traditional criteria," discussing what the catalog calls a "Fante female figure":[4]

> I own somewhat similar things to this and I have always liked them. This is a rather more sophisticated version than the ones that I've seen, and I thought it was quite beautiful . . . the total composition has a very contemporary, very Western look to it. It's the kind of thing that goes very well with contemporary Western things. It would look good in a modern apartment or house.

We may suppose that David Rockefeller was delighted to discover that his final judgment was consistent with the intentions of the sculpture's creators. For a footnote to the earlier "Checklist" reveals that the Baltimore Museum of Art desires to "make public the fact that the authenticity of the Fante figure in its collection has been challenged." Indeed, work by Doran Ross suggests this object is almost certainly a modern piece introduced in my hometown of Kumasi by the workshop of a certain Francis Akwasi, which "specializes in carvings for the international market in the style of traditional sculpture. Many of its works are now in museums throughout the West, and were published as authentic by Cole and Ross"[5] (yes, the same Doran Ross) in their classic catalog *The Arts of Ghana*.

But then it is hard to be *sure* what would please a man who gives as his reason for picking another piece (this time a Senufo helmet mask), "I have to say I picked this because I own it. It was given to me by President Houphouet Boigny of Ivory Coast."[6] Or one who remarks, "concerning the market in African art":

> The best pieces are going for very high prices. Generally speaking, the less good pieces in terms of quality are not going up in price. And that's a fine reason for picking the good ones rather than the bad. They have a way of becoming more valuable.
>
> I like African art as objects I find would be appealing to use in a home or an office. . . . I don't think it goes with everything, necessarily—although the very best perhaps does. But I think it goes well with contemporary architecture.[7]

There is something breathtakingly unpretentious in Mr. Rockefeller's easy movement between considerations of finance, of aesthetics, and of decor. In these responses we have surely a microcosm of the site of the African in contemporary—which is, then, surely to say, postmodern—America.

---

[4] Ibid., 138.

[5] Ibid., 29.

[6] Ibid., 143.

[7] Ibid., 131.

I have given so much of David Rockefeller not to emphasize the familiar fact that questions of what we call "aesthetic" value are crucially bound up with market value; not even to draw attention to the fact that this is known by those who play the art market. Rather, I want to keep clearly before us the fact that David Rockefeller is permitted to say *anything at all* about the arts of Africa because he is a *buyer* and because he is at the *center,* while Lela Kouakou, who merely makes art and who dwells at the margins, is a poor African whose words count only as parts of the commodification[8]—both for those of us who constitute the museum public and for collectors, like Rockefeller—of Baule art.[9] I want to remind you, in short, of how important it is that African art is a *commodity.*

But the cocurator whose choice will set us on our way is James Baldwin—the only cocurator who picked a piece that was not in the mold of the Africa of the exhibition Primitivism, a sculpture that will be my touchstone, a piece labeled by the museum *Yoruba Man with a Bicycle.* Here is some of what Baldwin said about it:

> This is something. This has got to be contemporary. He's really going to town. It's very jaunty, very authoritative. His errand might prove to be impossible. He is challenging something—or something has challenged him. He's grounded in immediate reality by the bicycle. . . . He's apparently a very proud and silent man. He's dressed sort of polyglot. Nothing looks like it fits him too well.

Baldwin's reading of this piece is, of course and inevitably, "in terms of [his] own . . . criteria," a reaction contextualized only by the knowledge that bicycles are new in Africa and that this piece, anyway, does not look anything like the works he recalls seeing from his earliest childhood at the Schomburg museum in Harlem. And his response torpedoes Vogel's argument for her notion that the only "authentically traditional" African—the only one whose responses, as she says, could have been found a century ago—must be refused a choice among Africa's art cultures because he, unlike the rest of the cocurators, who are Americans and the European-educated Africans, will use his "own . . . criteria." This Baule diviner, this authentically African villager, the message is, does not know what *we,* authentic postmodernists, now know: that the first and last mistake is to judge the Other on one's own terms. And so, in the name of this, the relativist insight, we impose our judgment that Lela

---

[8] I should insist this first time I use this word that I do not share the widespread negative evaluation of commodification: its merits, I believe, must be assessed case by case. Certainly critics such as Kobena Mercer (for example, in his "Black Hair/Style Politics") have persuasively criticized any reflexive rejection of the commodity form, which so often reinstates the hoary humanist opposition between "authentic" and "commercial." Mercer explores the avenues by which marginalized groups have manipulated commodified artifacts in culturally novel and expressive ways.

[9] Once Vogel has thus refused Kouakou a voice, it is less surprising that his comments turn out to be composite also. On closer inspection, it turns out that there is no single Lela Kouakou who was interviewed like the other cocurators, Kouakou is, in the end, quite exactly an invention: thus literalizing the sense in which "we" (and, more particularly, "our" artists) are individuals while "they" (and "theirs") are ethnic types.

Kouakou may not judge sculpture from beyond the Baule culture zone because he will—like all the other African "informants" we have met in the field—read them as if they were meant to meet those Baule standards. . . .

I do not—this will come as no surprise—have a definition of the postmodern to put in the place of Jameson's or Lyotard's. But there is now a rough consensus about the structure of the modern–postmodern dichotomy in the many domains—from architecture to poetry to philosophy to rock to the movies—in which it has been invoked. In each of these domains there is an antecedent practice that laid claim to a certain exclusivity of insight and in each of them postmodernism is a name for the rejection of that claim to exclusivity, a rejection that is almost always more playful—though not necessarily less serious—than the practice it aims to replace. That this will not do as a *definition* of postmodernism follows from the fact that in each domain this rejection of exclusivity takes up a certain specific shape, one that reflects the specificities of its setting.

To understand the various postmodernisms this way is to leave open the question how their theories of contemporary social, cultural, and economic life relate to the actual practices that constitute that life; to leave open, then, the relations between postmodern*ism* and postmoder*nity*. Where the practice is theory—literary or philosophical—postmodernism as a *theory* of postmodernity can be adequate only if it reflects to some extent the realities of that practice, because the practice is itself fully theoretical. But when a postmodernism addresses, say, advertising or poetry, it may be adequate as an account of them even if it conflicts with their own narratives, their theories of themselves. For, unlike philosophy and literary theory, advertising and poetry are not largely *constituted* by their articulated theories of themselves.

It is an important question *why* this distancing of the ancestors should have become so central a feature of our cultural lives. And the answer, surely, has to do with the sense in which art is increasingly commodified. To sell oneself and one's products as art in the marketplace, it is important, above all, to clear a space in which one is distinguished from other producers and products—and one does this by the construction and the marking of differences.

It is this that accounts for a certain intensification of the long-standing individualism of post-Renaissance art production: in the age of mechanical reproduction, aesthetic individualism—the characterization of the artwork as belonging to the oeuvre of an individual—and the absorption of the artist's life into the conception of the work can be seen precisely as modes of identifying objects for the market. The sculptor of the bicycle, by contrast, will not be known by those who buy this object; his individual life will make no difference to its future history. (Indeed, he surely knows this, in the sense in which one knows anything whose negation one has never even considered.) Nevertheless, there is *some*thing about the object that serves to establish it for the market: the availability of Yoruba culture and of stories about Yoruba culture to surround the object and distinguish it from "folk art" from elsewhere. . . .

I have been exploring how modernity looks from the perspective of the Euro-American intellectual. But how does it look from the postcolonial spaces inhabited by the *Yoruba Man with a Bicycle*? I shall speak about Africa, with confidence *both* that some of what I have to say will work elsewhere in the so-called Third World *and* that, in some places, it will certainly not. And I shall speak first about the producers of these so-called neotraditional artworks and then about the case of the African novel, because I believe that to focus exclusively on the novel (as theorists of contemporary African cultures have been inclined to do) is to distort the cultural situation and the significance within it of postcoloniality.

I do not know when the *Yoruba Man with a Bicycle* was made or by whom; African art has, until recently, been collected as the property of "ethnic" groups, not of individuals and workshops, so it is not unusual that not one of the pieces in the Perspectives show was identified in the "Checklist" by the name of an individual artist, even though many of them are twentieth-century; (and no one will have been surprised, by contrast, that most of them *are* kindly labeled with the name of the people who own the largely private collections where they now live). As a result I cannot say if the piece is literally postcolonial, produced after Nigerian independence in 1960. But the piece belongs to a genre that has certainly been produced since then: the genre that is here called *neotraditional*. And, simply put, what is distinctive about this genre is that it is produced for the West.

I should qualify. Of course, many of the buyers of first instance live in Africa, many of them are juridically citizens of African states. But African bourgeois consumers of neotraditional art are educated in the Western style, and, if they want African art, they would often rather have a "genuinely" traditional piece—by which I mean a piece that they believe to be made precolonially, or at least in a style and by methods that were already established precolonially. And these buyers are a minority. Most of this art, which is *traditional* because it uses actually or supposedly precolonial techniques, but is *neo*—this, for what it is worth, is the explanation I promised earlier—because it has elements that are recognizably from the colonial or postcolonial in reference, has been made for Western tourists and other collectors.

The incorporation of these works in the West's world of museum culture and its art market has almost nothing, of course, to do with postmodernism. By and large, the ideology through which they are incorporated is modernist: it is the ideology that brought something called "Bali" to Artaud, something called "Africa" to Picasso, and something called "Japan" to Barthes. (This incorporation as an official Other was criticized, of course, from its beginnings: Oscar Wilde once remarked that "the whole of Japan is a pure invention. There is no such country, no such people.")[10] What *is* postmodernist is Vogel's muddled conviction that African art should not be judged "in terms of [someone else's] traditional criteria." For modernism, primitive art was to be judged by putatively *universal* aesthetic criteria, and by these standards it was finally found possible to value it. The sculptors and painters who found it possible were largely seeking an Archimedean point outside their own cultures for

---

[10] Oscar Wilde, "The Decay of Lying: An Observation," in *Intentions*. London: Methuen, 1909, 45.

a critique of a Weberian modernity. For *post*moderns, by contrast, these works, however they are to be understood, cannot be seen as legitimated by culture- and history-transcending standards.

What is useful in the *neotraditional* object as a model—despite its marginality in most African lives—is that its incorporation in the museum world (while many objects made by the same hands—stools, for example—live peacefully in nonbourgeois homes) reminds one that in Africa, by contrast, the distinction between high culture and mass culture, insofar as it makes sense at all, corresponds by and large to the distinction between those with and those without Western-style formal education as cultural consumers.

The fact that the distinction is to be made this way—in most of sub-Saharan Africa excluding the Republic of South Africa—means that the opposition between high culture and mass culture is available only in domains where there is a significant body of Western formal training, and this excludes (in most places) the plastic arts and music. There are distinctions of genre and audience in African musics, and for various cultural purposes there is something that we call "traditional" music that we still practice and value. But village and urban dwellers alike, bourgeois and nonbourgeois, listen, through discs and, more importantly, on the radio, to reggae, to Michael Jackson, and to King Sonny Adé.

And this means that by and large the domain in which it makes most sense is the one domain where that distinction is powerful and pervasive—namely, in African writing in Western languages. So that it is here that we find, I think, a place for consideration of the question of the *post*colonality of contemporary African culture. . . .

For what I am calling humanism can be provisional, historically contingent, antiessentialist (in other words, postmodern), and still be demanding. We can surely maintain a powerful engagement with the concern to avoid cruelty and pain while nevertheless recognizing the contingency of that concern.[11] Maybe, then, we can recover within postmodernism the postcolonial writers' humanism—the concern for human suffering, for the victims of the postcolonial state (a concern we find everywhere: in Mudimbe, as we have seen; in Soyinka's *A Play of Giants*; in Achebe, Farrah, Gordimer, Labou Tansi—the list is difficult to complete)—while still rejecting the master narratives of modernism. This human impulse—an impulse that transcends obligations to churches and to nations—I propose we learn from Mudimbe's Landu.

But there is also something to reject in the postcolonial adherence to Africa of Nara, the earlier protagonist of Mudimbe's *L'Écart*: the sort of Manicheanism that makes Africa "*a body*" (nature) against Europe's juridical reality (culture) and then fails to acknowledge—even as he says it—the full significance of the fact that Africa is also "*a multiple existence.*" *Entre les eaux* provides a powerful postcolonial critique of this binarism: we can read it as arguing that if you postulate an either–or choice between Africa and the West,

---

[11] See Richard Rorty's *Contingency, Irony and Solidarity*. Cambridge: Cambridge University Press, 1988.

there is no place for you in the real world of politics, and your home must be the otherworldly, the monastic retreat.

If there is a lesson in the broad shape of this circulation of cultures, it is surely that we are all already contaminated by each other, that there is no longer a fully autochthonous *echt*-African culture awaiting salvage by our artists (just as there is, of course, no American culture without African roots). And there is a clear sense in some postcolonial writing that the postulation of a unitary Africa over against a monolithic West—the binarism of Self and Other—is the last of the shibboleths of the modernizers that we must learn to live without.

Already in *Le Devoir de violence,* in Ouologuem's withering critique of "Shrobéniusologie," there were the beginnings of this postcolonial critique of what we might call "alteritism," the construction and celebration of oneself as Other. Ouologuem writes, ". . . henceforth Negro art was baptized 'aesthetic' and hawked in the imaginary universe of 'vitalizing exchanges.'"[12] Then, after describing the phantasmic elaboration of some interpretative mumbo jumbo "invented by Saïf," he announces that ". . . Negro art found its patent of nobility in the folklore of mercantile intellectualism, oye, oye, oye. . . ."[13] Shrobenius, the anthropologist, as apologist for "his" people; a European audience that laps up this exoticized other; African traders and producers of African art, who understand the necessity to maintain the "mysteries" that construct their product as "exotic;" traditional and contemporary elites who require a sentimentalized past to authorize their present power: all are exposed in their complex and multiple mutual complicities.

> Witness the splendor of its art—the true face of Africa is the grandiose empires of the Middle Ages, a society marked by wisdom, beauty, prosperity, order, nonviolence, and humanism, and it is here that we must seek the true cradle of Egyptian civilisation.
>
> Thus drooling, Shrobenius derived a twofold benefit on his return home: on the one hand, he mystified the people of his own country who in their enthusiasm raised him to a lofty Sorbonnical chair, while on the other hand he exploited the sentimentality of the coons, only too pleased to hear from the mouth of a white man that Africa was 'the womb of the world and the cradle of civilization.'
>
> In consequence the niggertrash donated masks and art treasures by the ton to the acolytes of 'Shrobeniusology.'[14]

A little later, Ouologuem articulates more precisely the interconnections of Africanist mystifications with tourism, and the production, packaging, and marketing of African artworks.

> An Africanist school harnessed to the vapors of magico-religious, cosmological, and mythical symbolism had been born: with the result that for three years

---

[12] Ouologuem, *Le Devoir de Violence*. Paris: Editions du Seuil, 1968, 110.

[13] Ibid.

[14] Ibid., 111. Ouologuem, *Bound to Violence*. London: Heinemann, 1968, 94–95.

men flocked to Nakem—and what men!—middlemen, adventurers, apprentice bankers, politicians, salesmen, conspirators—supposedly 'scientists,' but in reality enslaved sentries mounting guard before the 'Shrobeniusological' monument of Negro pseudosymbolism.

Already it had become more than difficult to procure old masks, for Shrobenius and the missionaries had had the good fortune to snap them all up. And so Saif—and the practice is still current—had slapdash copies buried by the hundredweight, or sunk into ponds, lakes, marshes, and mud holes, to be exhumed later on and sold at exorbitant prices to unsuspecting curio hunters. These three-year-old masks were said to be charged with the weight of four centuries of civilization.[15]

Ouologuem here forcefully exposes the connections we saw earlier in some of David Rockefeller's insights into the international system of art exchange, the international art world: we see the way in which an ideology of disinterested aesthetic value—the "baptism" of "Negro art" as "aesthetic"—meshes with the international commodification of African expressive culture, a commodification that requires, by the logic of the space-clearing gesture, the manufacture of Otherness. (It is a significant bonus that it also harmonizes with the interior decor of modern apartments.) Shrobenius, "ce marchand-confectionneur d'idéologie," the ethnographer allied with Saif—image of the "traditional" African ruling caste—has invented an Africa that is a body over against Europe, the juridical institution, and Ouologuem is urging us vigorously to refuse to be thus Other.

Sara Suleri has written recently, in *Meatless Days*, of being treated as an "Otherness-machine"—and of being heartily sick of it.[16] If there is no way out for the postcolonial intellectual in Mudimbe's novels, it is, I suspect, because *as* intellectuals—a category instituted in black Africa by colonialism—we are always at risk of becoming Otherness-machines. It risks becoming our principal role. Our only distinction in the world of texts to which we are latecomers is that we can mediate it to our fellows. This is especially true when postcolonial meets postmodern, for what the postmodern reader seems to demand of its Africa is all too close to what modernism—as documented in William Rubin's Primitivism exhibit of 1985—demanded of it. The role that Africa, like the rest of the Third World, plays for Euro-American postmodernism—like its better-documented significance for modernist art—must be distinguished from the role postmodernism might play in the Third World. What that might be it is, I think, too early to tell. And what happens will happen not because we pronounce upon the matter in theory but out of the changing everyday practices of African cultural life.

For all the while, in Africa's cultures, there are those who will not see themselves as Other. Despite the overwhelming reality of economic decline; despite unimaginable poverty; despite wars, malnutrition, disease, and political

---

[15] Ouologuem, *Le Devoir de Violence*, 112. Ouologuem, *Bound to Violence*, 95–96.

[16] Sara Suleri, *Meatless Days*. Chicago: Chicago University Press, 1989, 105.

instability, African cultural productivity grows apace: popular literatures, oral narrative and poetry, dance, drama, music, and visual art all thrive. The contemporary cultural production of many African societies—and the many traditions whose evidences so vigorously remain—is an antidote to the dark vision of the postcolonial novelist.

And I am grateful to James Baldwin for his introduction to the *Yoruba Man with a Bicycle*—a figure who is, as Baldwin so rightly saw, polyglot, speaking Yoruba and English, probably some Hausa and a little French for his trips to Cotonou or Cameroon; someone whose "clothes do not fit him too well." He and the other men and women among whom he mostly lives suggest to me that the place to look for hope is not just to the postcolonial novel—which has struggled to achieve the insights of a Ouologuem or Mudimbe—but to the all-consuming vision of this less-anxious creativity. It matters little who it was made *for;* what we should learn from is the imagination that produced it. The *Man with a Bicycle* is produced by someone who does not care that the bicycle is the white man's invention—it is not there to be Other to the Yoruba Self; it is there because someone cared for its solidity; it is there because it will take us further than our feet will take us; it is there because machines are now as African as novelists—and as fabricated as the kingdom of Nakem.

29

ART AS VIRTUAL: DOUGLAS DAVIS

Douglas Davis (b. 1933) is a conceptual artist and educator. In his essay "The Work of Art in the Age of Digital Reproduction (An Evolving Thesis: 1991–1995)," Davis takes off from Walter Benjamin's classic discussion (see Chapter 14). As you recall, Benjamin was concerned that technological processes that allow art objects to be reproduced mechanically would undermine art's auratic nature. Davis attempts not only to bring Benjamin's analysis into the digital present but also to criticize him for his failure to acknowledge the liberatory potential of modern technology.

Davis's basic thesis is that virtual reality enhances rather than threatens the possibility of aura. This is because the dichotomy between an original and its mechanical copy has been replaced by a new relationship. Agreeing with Benjamin that the aura of the *original* decays through the possibility of reproduction, Davis argues that rapidly evolving digital techniques endow *every copy* with its own unique aura. Rather than destroying aura, digital technology infinitely replicates it. This is because it allows each of us not simply to reproduce the original exactly but also to enhance it in accord with our individual preferences. Instead of one *Mona Lisa* and its millions of identical reproductions, each of us can alter it on screen as we see fit. The resulting products are not mere mechanical reproductions, but have the vitality of original works.

Davis is also critical of the pessimistic assessments of technological development that lie behind the claims of theorists such as Benjamin. Where the latter saw only the possibility of increasing social control, Davis speculates that educated elites may one day contest such control, wresting away and using the new technology for liberatory ends. Although he refrains from predicting the precise course such a process might take, he insists that other theorists have underestimated the potential of these oppositional elites.

As we find ourselves "plugged in" in more and more aspects of our lives, these reflections on the significance of the digital future for our conception of art are a good place to end our exploration of art's nature. As Davis sees it, rather than denying us the potential for creativity, the Internet and its related technological innovations inaugurate the era of the postoriginal original. When each of us is free to bestow aura, the correlative concepts of the *original* and its *mechanical reproduction* will have to be consigned to the dustbin of history.

STUDY QUESTIONS ON THE READING

1. Why does Davis think that Benjamin's claim that technological reproduction marks the end of aura is mistaken? Do you agree? Why or why not?

2. Why does Davis think that the Internet opens up the possibility of deconstructing the original–copy distinction? Do you think this is a positive development? Why or why not?

3. Davis is critical of those who see Internet technology only as a vehicle for social control. Why? Do you agree? Why or why not?

4. How can the Internet enhance individuality, according to Davis?

5. How does the existence of virtual art change our understanding of art's nature?

6. What does Davis mean by a "postoriginal original"?

7. Does the existence of digital art invalidate all previous theories of art? Why or why not?

DOUGLAS DAVIS: THE WORK OF ART IN THE AGE OF DIGITAL REPRODUCTION (AN EVOLVING THESIS: 1991–1995)

I am adding my finger to your sentence.
You can feel it as you type now, on your hand, can't you?
—THE QUEEN OF TOUCH[1]

There is a police that is brutally and rather "physically" repressive
(but the police are never purely physical) and there are more
sophisticated police that are more "cultural" or "spiritual," more
noble. But every institution destined to enforce the law is a police.
—JACQUES DERRIDA[2]

---

[1] Queen of Touch, online message, America OnLine, Dec. 15, 1994.

[2] Jacques Derrida, "AfterWord," in *Limited, Inc.* Evanston, IL: Northwestern University Press, 1988.

The work of art in the age of digital reproduction is physically and formally chameleon. There is no clear conceptual distinction now between original and reproduction in virtually any medium based in film, electronics, or telecommunications. As for the fine arts, the distinction is eroding, if not finally collapsed.

The fictions of "master" and "copy" are now so entwined with each other that it is impossible to say where one begins and the other ends. In one sense, Walter Benjamin's proclamation of doom for the aura of originality, authored early in this century, is finally confirmed by these events.[3] In another sense, the aura, supple and elastic, has stretched far beyond the boundaries of Benjamin's prophecy into the rich realm of reproduction itself. Here in this realm, often mislabeled "virtual" (it is actually a *realer* reality, or RR), both originality and traditional truth (symbolized by the unadorned photographic "fact") are being enhanced, not betrayed.

But the work of art is not only changing its form and means of delivery. By far its most provocative extension is into the intimate bowels of our body, mind, and spirit. Beside this, all changes, even the Internet, even our recent evolution into the World Wide Web, pale. No single element of the messaging now going on disturbs the guardians of traditional modernity more than this single fact. A few years ago, Frederick Jameson, the senior and singular Marxist art theorist of our day, finally accepted video as the real heart of contemporary art. But he complained, rightly, about its inability to foster communication of any kind.

Yet now we see communicative networks ribbing the globe. You and I, online, are strapped down—maybe—like Prometheus by a web of incisive personal signals. I have no doubt that Jameson and his colleagues will shortly proclaim that this new and highly intensive method of linking is improper material for high art. He won't be moved by "The Queen of Touch" (whose real name I don't know and don't need), who reached out to me one night when I was thinking about this piece. Art, in the traditional realm, is a commodity that must pretend to universality. It must reach out to touch many fingers, not just yours or mine.

Let us try to turn this objection back, and not only here, in this essay, which I invite you to amend, refute, or enhance, on paper or online. Let us act as well. When *InterActions*, a recent exhibition of mine, opened at the Lehman College Art Gallery in New York's embattled Bronx, I knew the WWW only from hearsay. As the weeks went on, I embraced it. I went to Geneva, where the Galerie St. Gervais allowed me to communicate with New Yorkers live over the Internet in a performance. Later, Lehman College Art Gallery imported the means not only to create a WWW home page but also to prompt direct responses from around the world. We hung both *InterActions* and a new Web-style exhibition out on the digital nerve system on December 8, 1994—they're

---

[3] Walter Benjamin, "The Work of Art in the Age of Mechanical Reproduction," in *Illuminations* (New York: Harcourt, Brace & World, 1968). [See Chapter 14—T.E.W.]

still there.[4] And we decided to invite the world to compose its own sentence, perhaps the longest ever written (as well as the first that is truly multiple in authorship): thus its title, *The World's First Collaborative Sentence*. We opened the "sentence" to words, photographs, video, graphics, WWW links, and sound sent via the Internet, the World Wide Web, email, regular mail, and personal visits (children visiting the gallery in the Bronx, for example, are handed paper, pencils, video cameras).

As I write now, more than half a year later, the "sentence without a period" stretches at least a city block, if not more. At first we announced that when the sentence reached 3 miles in length—or February 15, 1995 (whichever came first)—we would stop it, temporarily, by typing in a period. When I followed through on our pledge in Warsaw, however, I knew it was wrong to stop the world—only God might take so final a step. On the next day, we unlocked the overnight conceptual gate. Now the "life sentence" will go on as long as the world continues to write and think.

You'll have to look hard in this collage of images, sounds, and words at any time, now or in the next century, to find a single *universality*. Each fragment, each image, each sound is unique, personal, quivering with the sense of self. My Queen of Touch—that is, the idea she represents—is taking over the world mind and splitting it apart. This is precisely what the work of art in the age of digital reproduction is trying to tell us. Can we understand and follow?

INFINITE FORMS

A word about the difference between analog signals and what might be called digital messages. Analog signals may be compared to a wave breaking on a beach, breaking over and over but never precisely in the same form. That is why copying an audio signal or video signal in the past always involved a loss in clarity. But digital bits, compatible with the new generation of tools that see, hear, speak, and compute, march in precise, soldierly fashion, one figure after another. This means that any video, audio, or photographic work of art can be endlessly reproduced without degradation, always the same, always perfect. The same is true for handmade images or words that can be scanned—that is, converted to digital bits.

But more to the point, each of these bits can be endlessly varied. My photographic self-portrait can be turned upside down, my ear can be chopped off, the background can be changed from black to gold—and this manipulation, like Ted Turner's colorized black-and-white film classics, will reproduce in this manner forever, millions and millions of times. My virtual self (that is, a three-dimensional working model of the author) can be transmitted even now from New York to Lodz, Poland.

---

[4] Both *InterActions* and *The World's First Collaborative Sentence* can be found at the World Wide Web address http://math240.lehman.cuny.edu/art.

Needless to say, these modes of address and interaction are charged with powerful social and psychological implications. In the end, they will touch each of us, as artists, photographers, film-makers, video-makers, writers, readers, viewers, voters, consumers, managers. In a valuable early essay based upon research and interviews with humanists and social scientists at Stanford in 1984, Peter Lyman concluded that the cybernetic premise upon which computer programs were based led inevitably to the centralization of control:

> A computer is both an object, a machine, and a series of "congealed" social relations which have been embedded within the object: it is a tool which makes the work of writing more efficient; its software contains a cybernetic model of knowledge derived from technical culture which does not address the ethical and social issues which have been part of the project of qualitative social research; it is embedded within an everyday male culture of aggressive images of control which constitute a cultural barrier for some users.[5]

As prescient as Lyman was about one direction that digitalism or politics might still take—in league with Derrida—he overlooked an equally powerful reverse direction. So did Benjamin and George Orwell. It seems clear as the century unwinds that the prophets of technocratic control, frightened by Hitler, by Stalin, by *1984*, overlooked the capacity of an educated elite (infused with the anarchic vitality of contemporary fine and popular cultures) to resist control naturally, without conscious intent. Our prophets further overlooked the sheer profit awaiting those inventors and entrepreneurs able to create sensitive, intuitive computer programs, among them HyperCard and QuickTime; videoconferencing software (just hitting the market as I write this) like Sun's ShowMe and the primitive but freewheeling CUSeeMe developed by Cornell University; and the complex of browsers able to instantly access the World Wide Web (such as Mosaic and Netscape). Each of these programs in one way or another unlocks for the individual user a pluralist world of visual imagery, transmitted on demand and by personal choice.

These events empower imagination rather than reason, as new tools placed in the hands of people with open minds always have. No hard-headed determinist would have predicted, in the fifteenth century, the evolution of the printed word into concrete poetry or James Joyce's *Ulysses*. Marshall McLuhan himself did not detect the coming of CNN, C-Span, Ernie Kovacs, David Letterman, what we now call interactive video, or indeed the World Wide Web itself. But I do not doubt the potential for a ferocious backlash, already in evidence at this writing as the U.S. Congress considers whether and how to purge the Internet of "indecent" messages. Derrida's warning must be heeded: the cultural police are with us again, refined down to subtle harmonies. Our task is to protect above all the higher, more complex realms of speech and action.

In this quest we ought to be aided by certain natural tendencies overlooked by Lyman and his colleagues. The instant access enjoyed by the Stanford

---

[5] Peter Lyman. "Reading, Writing and Word Processing: Toward a Phenomenology of the Computer Age," *Qualitative Sociology* (Spring–Summer, 1984): 75–89.

researchers decades ago can be seen as a decentralizing movement, too. It leads some of us to argue that all information is potentially and morally free, that is, beyond government control or individual copyright. More than a decade after Lyman, libraries increasingly offer not stolid, imperious texts but fields of knowledge on a terminal with which the user can interact, revising and extending the central text. Potentially, the reader is now, as Lyman said in another context, the author.[6]

The handmade arts of writing, drawing, and painting, normally presumed to be beyond digitization, are also affected, though in different ways. Now small personal computers able to respond to handwriting on a screen are available, at once reclaiming the hand and subjecting it to infinite replication. The moment a painting can be scanned, the original landscape, portrait, or color field can be altered or cloned in the manner of a vintage film. Already Ethan Allen, the furniture chain, markets paintings reproduced on canvas by laser transfer technology acting on dutifully scanned bits.

Only the unwary mind would deny the further inevitability that a "neurasthenic" computer, programmed by humanoid codes (a fuzzy logic program, for example, such as those already used by the Japanese to run washing machines and park cars) will shortly *create* paintings from first stroke to last. Or that the rapid introduction of voice commands to a host of computerized functions, in cameras as well as word processors, will open up an incalculable range of sound structures, beginning with simple spoken commands. Urszula Dudziak's wonderful layered singing, using a digital tape recorder that allows every line of a song to invade the next line, pointed in this direction years ago. Virtual art is as certain a fixture of the Digital Age as the kind of virtual reality created by microprocessed programs that insert the user in a totally artificial universe through the medium of stereoscopic glasses and sensate digital gloves. Thus clad, we can walk, think, and feel the manmade world in virtually the same way we experience the "real" world.

VISION AND REVISION

Yet more is at issue here than simply reproducing or mimicking the art of the hand. The mind is at issue, too, most of all in the perceptions it will now inexorably bring to both art and life, to that sacred line between "original" and "fake." Often the forger—of Rembrandt, of Vermeer, of classical Greek and Roman art—argues that his work brings pleasure in the same measure as the copied master. A stylish gallery in New York called True Fakes, Ltd., openly indulges this thesis. On another level, all post-Dada vanguard art has seemed to defy the sanctity of the original. A truly provocative artist like Elaine Sturtevant, whose Warhols and Rauschenbergs often improve on the "originals," represents the other end of this pole, as does all critical theory that emphasizes mind rather than matter (or product).

---

[6] Conversation with the author, May 1992.

The very act of deconstruction implies that the breaking apart and re-arranging of the primal elements of art, or of the sentence, has its own singular value. Derrida's refiguring of the text is simply one obvious example. Another, the dominant mode in architecture of the past decade, is the collaging together of disparate orders taken from discordant centuries, as in Michael Graves's proposal to revise and enlarge the Whitney Museum. A third example is the digital rearrangement of photographic reality using a simple software program like Adobe Photoshop, now common coin for virtually every art student under 25. As William Mitchell points out in his recent book, *The Reconfigured Eye: Digital Images and Photographic Truth,* the early years of this decade marked the moment when the apparently truthful silver-based photographic emulsion gave way to the apparently deceptive computer-processed image.[7] Larry Friedman's Shakespeare Project at Stanford, which revises filmed or taped scenes, moving sounds and lines (as digital soldiers) from one pair of lips to another, is a consequence of this moment, as is the compact disc recently issued of Handel's *Messiah,* providing no less than *nine* "original" versions of the work, each track instantly available to the ear while a second track is playing.

By finding the means to transfer my early video works from analog to digital media, I can contemplate revisions on my computer that will allow me to change my mind, two decades later, about points where I erred long ago. This allows me to produce a "post-original original." Not long ago, using VideoFusion software, I revised the last few seconds of *The Last Nine Minutes,* the conclusion to the first artist's satellite broadcast, which I co-produced and performed with Joseph Beuys and Nam June Paik for the opening of documenta 6 in 1977. In the revision, I crash through the TV screen and land in your hands in a multiplicity of colors.

Digital video, the equivalent of digital audiotape or DAT, blurs the line between live and taped imagery. With a Sony 8-mm camera, it is impossible to *see* the difference between the live close-up of a face and a taped close-up, even after it has been transferred several times between camera and VCR. In New York, the Blue Man Group, an ensemble that has turned performance art into highly accessible theater, plays constantly on the ambiguity between "live" and "taped" through its use of a portable camera and a large, mural-sized screen poised on the lip of the stage. When members of the group disappear off-stage, the audience is never sure whether their antics behind the curtain, labeled "live" on the screen, are actually live or taped.

In QuickTime movies sent over computer networks and the phenomenon of video conferencing, we see yet further squeezing of now and then, here and there, real and artificial, original and manipulated. For example, the act of digitizing live long-distance video signals sent from Peking to Los Angeles allows us the luxury (or deceit) of distorting, toning, and stretching verbal and visual

---

[7] William Mitchell, *The Reconfigured Eye: Digital Images and Photographic Truth* (Cambridge, MA: MIT Press, 1992), 18.

messages as they are filed and stored on the computer terminal.[8] The work of a primal filmmaker like Dziga Vertov could be received, deconstructed or rearranged, then archived; later, if we wished, the original signal could be re-presented in the state first intended.

Compressing the video signal before transmission currently allows an even purer and cleaner signal to be sent over a dedicated phone line than can be sent via satellite or analog relay. This digitized signal can be stored or directly viewed on large, high-definition video screens by entire classrooms or auditoriums, providing visual access far beyond the scale of the computer terminal itself. Not far from my studio in New York's Soho, at the Here Arts Center, I can "dial" my colleagues in Moscow via the PictureTel teleconferencing system; the signal passes through a studio at Brown University in Providence, Rhode Island, that is linked to a Sputnik satellite and is received in Moscow, at the Institute of Space Research. When my Moscow friends respond, the signal reverses course, landing at Here for a minimal sum. Here, as in many other cases, There is Here.

William Mitchell's description of the implications of digital photography apply to all media transformed in this way:

> The distinction between the causal processes of the camera and the intentional process of the artist can no longer be drawn so confidently and categorically.... The traditional origin narrative by which automatically captured . . . images are made to seem casual things of nature . . . recited . . . by Bazin, Barthes and Berger, Sontag and Scruton—no longer has the power to convince us. The referent has come unstuck.[9]

PERSISTENCE OF AURA

I am not predicting that our culture will entirely embrace the purely technocratic meaning of the digital world. The great mistake of theoreticians in the past, as we have seen, was to ignore resistance, contradiction, inspired madness, and primal human cussedness. Walter Benjamin saw accurately the logical implications of mechanical reproduction. He ignored antilogic. He erred in assuming that the world would bow to logic, that the endless reproduction of a painting or a photograph would diminish what he called the "aura" of the original. As Sidney Tillim once pointed out in *Artforum*, nothing like this has

---

[8] "Three Cultures at Issue," a teleconference or global classroom planned for 1996, will employ these methods. Managed by the Center for Long-Distance Art and Culture at the Lehman College Art Gallery, it will also involve the Guggenheim Museum, New York; the Tretyakov Gallery, Moscow; the Russian State University of the Humanities; the Center for Contemporary Art and Warsaw University, Warsaw; Lodz University and the Museum Sztuki, Lodz, Poland; and selected universities in Scandinavia and the Baltic countries. Its vital supporters and advisers include Takeshi Utsumi, Gary Welz, Peter Knight, Sun Microsystems, Apple Computer, and the U.S. Information Agency.

[9] Mitchell, 30.

happened.[10] We still bid wildly at auctions and employ armies of scholars to find the "original," the "authentic" masterpiece. Each fall, legions of artists, critics, and collectors flood hungrily into galleries and museums in pursuit of the new, or at least the illusion that something *different* is about to happen. As these legions increase, spawned by universal education, and as they turn to the computer terminal, where networked information allows contact with exhibitions and voices thousands of miles away, the search turns universal, eroding all lines between east and west, north and south.

In his quiet, quite incredible book *The Cultural Politics of Everyday Life: Social Constructionism, Rhetoric, and Knowing of the Third Kind,* John Shotter argues that identity, "a unique first-person 'I'," can only be defined in terms of social interaction.[11] At a moment when long-distance discourse, friendship, love, and lust are simpler than placing a telephone call was in my youth (I refer of course to the Internet "chat lines," public and private), the status of the first person rises in potential. My Queen of Touch could have reached me from New Zealand or New Guinea as easily as from Brooklyn. On the surface, Shotter seems to align himself with the Social Constructionists, engaged in framing an ideological position as rigid as Marxist determinism used to be or as supply-side economics was in the early 1980s. But the fact is that he sees this situation—of global discourse—as open-ended, verging on the third realm of knowing. None of us can say where these unprecedented links will end, or take us.

As I have worked to create a global classroom devoted to long-distance art, theater, and other media simultaneously connecting students in Poland, Russia, and the United States, all of those involved have tried to frame flexible goals. It is simply impossible to conceive of the papers, dialogues, and joint performances that will result from the bonding of these disparate societies, particularly now, when the swift ease of email seems certain soon to include the capacity to deliver both hypertext and exact renditions of vintage manuscriptions.[12] Certainly we will end with metaphors of unprecedented richness, asymmetry, and contradiction. Yet it is only through such figures that we will begin to refute the entrenched conviction that the world mind is one mind.

Twenty-five years ago, in a prescient essay, A. Michael Noll, an engineer then conducting theoretical research for Bell Telephone Laboratories, sensed the contradictory implications of the digital computer: its very dexterity, he predicted, would free many of us to indulge in spiraling, multifaceted, even chaotic patterns, not simple order or reproduction.[13] Now there is clear evidence of this reversal, following hard upon the world's refutation of Benjamin.

---

[10] Sidney Tillim, "Benjamin Rediscovered: The Work of Art After the Age of Mechanical Reproduction," *Artforum* 21, No. 5 (May 1983): 65–73 .

[11] John Shotter, *The Cultural Politics of Everyday Life: Social Constructionism, Rhetoric, and Knowing of the Third Kind* (Toronto, Canada: University of Toronto Press, 1993), 260.

[12] See Julie Chao, "New Adobe Software Conveys Documents in Cyberspace," *Wall Street Journal,* May 5, 1995.

[13] A. Michael Noll, "The Digital Computer as a Creative Medium," *IEEE Spectrum* 4, No. 10 (October, 1967): 89–95.

Perhaps every dominant mode, or style, is rejected in the end. Even now, in an age when copying is high art, when the simple physical availability of vintage masterpieces is dwindling, when postmodern theories of assemblage and collage inform our sensibility, the concept of aura (if not of its material realization) persists.[14] Surely it must now be further transformed, simply to survive the technical assault brought on by the digital age. But transformed into what? Dematerialized idea? Symbol? Presence?

Of course these questions are impossible to answer definitively at a moment when the digital era is dawning. They are nonetheless pressing enough to warrant the hazard of a guess, informed at once by the elite culture, by vulgar analogies in the popular culture, and by the demographics of the century now coming to a close. If the clutch of tendencies variously described as "poststructuralism," "postmodernism," "post-avant-garde," and "appropriation" (together with a wide variety of post-painterly tendencies prefixed by "neo") have any single, unifying thread it is the discordant power of unique interpretation, or reinterpretation. When I deconstruct meaning, I recreate it within a subjective context that is inevitably unique, no matter how ordered or predestined. One night at the Astor Place Theater in New York, chancing upon the Blue Man Group's *Tubes* show for the third time, I found myself saluted by name on the electronic message screen flashing in the middle of the proscenium stage shortly after I sat down. Later I learned that I had been detected by a computer program through the use of my credit card.

Granted, this is individuation employed either as wit or whimsy. But surely at Astor Place we can detect a stubborn resistance to technology's supposedly fatal inhumanity. Not long afterwards, I participated in a virtual reality panel at the Jack Tilton Gallery in New York. At no point did I detect from any of the artists present or—more significantly—from the audience a single gram of insensitivity to the phenomenological danger posed by immersion in a created world. When I predicted in the question-and-answer session that we would shortly see a call in the art colleges for courses in "real reality" to counterbalance the dictates imposed by "virtual reality," the audience agreed vociferously, surprising me.

But I shouldn't have been surprised, nor should you. My wish, everyone's wish is to find ways to increase the power of our subjective presence in the other reality, precisely as the painter orders his or her field. Jenny Holzer speaks directly for this contrarian impulse: "I haven't quite figured out how my worlds will look," she writes about the potential of virtual reality. "One thing I do want to explore is what happens when you fly through a floor."[15]

It is not so much the signifiers in each of these cases that matters as it is the signified, or the punch line to the joke, which is widely shared by our new

---

[14] Douglas Davis, *The Museum Transformed: Design and Culture in the Post-Pompidou Era* (New York: Abbeville Press, 1990), 175–179.

[15] Jenny Holzer, "Activity Can Be Overrated," in *Through the Looking Glass: Artists' First Encounters with Virtual Reality*, ed. J. Cirincione and B. D'Amato (New York: Softworlds, 1992), 25–29.

audience. This educated (yet democratized) elite, mixing all classes, creeds, and colors, is now immense in both East and West. Gorbachev's *perestroika* revolution rode on its back, an overwhelming social fact ignored by our media and political strategists. Without hesitation, artist, audience, and publisher in each of the incidents described above embraced the individuating mark, not the erasure of presence that accompanies replication (the "copy"). It seems to me a reversal of Benjamin and Orwell to find digital technology so accomplished at providing that individuating mark. VideoFusion software allows me exquisite variations in video copying: now each issue of *The Last Nine Minutes* can subtly reorder pace, pitch, even the shades of red, blue, green, and white. And it is not only the reader-user envisioned by Peter Lyman who can alter books printed out on library computers. The proprietors of hand-held Newtons and Sharp Wizards will soon be able to call up entire videos and films as well as books on their hand-held screens. They will edit this information as they walk along and transmit the results, probably via a wireless Net, to friends and colleagues across the city, the nation, the world.

What begins to emerge in the first digital decade is a fine-grained sensitivity to the unique qualities of every copy, including the digitally processed photograph. Four years ago in Russia I found an old book in which the one-time owner had glued six copies of a photograph of a woman. Not one copy resembled the others, save in its sharing of a single, forgotten source. His work inspired me to continue copying in his book, in a myriad ways, images of Russian, Polish, and American women who had moved me, utilizing faxes, laser-jet printers, and Stylewriter II printers as copying modes. Similarly, for the past few years Lucio Pozzi has been reperforming his original performances in New York with the aid of the Dia Foundation, among other sources, never conceding the slightest indication to the audience that they are old or revised versions of an allegedly superior original. Each time he performs, the work is immanent for those in position to see it. The Roman numerals beside so many of our popular films (*Back to the Future II*) are vulgar signifiers of what I am trying to say: it is the repetitive copy that is dead, not the original. The one and the other are not separate.

My last example is harder to explain but central to my thesis. In 1971, not knowing entirely what I meant, I proclaimed in a manifesto for an early interactive television performance (in which viewers sang and shouted over telephone lines, creating participative "music" for our actions): Open a Channel to Every Mind . . . Let Every Mind Communicate with Every Other Mind.[16] In the few years that have passed since I first published the ideas in this essay you are now reading, we have witnessed a meteoric rise in the use of both Internet and World Wide Web. Though originally developed in the United States and Europe for scientific-military purposes, the Web has been joined by artists,

---

[16] *The Electronic Hokkadim*, jointly sponsored by the Corcoran Gallery and WTOP-TV in Washington, D.C., funded by a small grant from the National Endowment for the Arts. The word "Hokkadim" is derived from the ancient African word "Hochet," which describes a ritual form of participative music.

writers, philosophers, inventors, salesmen, and lovers all over the world. What is already increasingly apparent—though totally unforeseen as recently as 1992—is that the moment when finally "everyone talks to everyone" is the moment when the inner self is liberated rather than chained.

Liberated for what purpose? Again I argue that we cannot predict this. In a 1994 opinion piece published in the *Rocky Mountain News,* I pleaded with the U.S. Congress, in considering legislation to advance the building of the Internet, *to leave us alone.*[17] Let anarchy thrive. Let our voices be freed from control, so that in interaction with each other, new modes of thinking, art-making, and deep personal touching can occur. I cited another element of the message I received from the Queen of Touch on a chatline in the middle of the night: "You may be the King of Words, but I am the Queen of Touch. Here is my hand . . . tighten your fingers."[18]

No one could have imagined this fanciful personal exchange occurring over the authoritarian computer as recently as 1984, when I recall countless voices warning against the consolidation of police-state power in technocratic hands. Nor could they have predicted any lines as moving as those described by Jon Katz, media critic of *Rolling Stone,* in the *New York Times.* Katz and many others have found a deepening of personal exchanges on the Internet. Separated from each other by space and time, people find themselves able to say what often cannot be said face to face. Death is surely among these hitherto unspeakable subjects, as Katz discovered one night in early 1994 when he and others on a chat line received the following message:

> My daughter has cancer. As some of you know, she is 8. In all the world I never conceived of all the sorrow I would feel at learning this, all the horror at watching her suffer so stoically through test after test. There is not a lot of hope just a lot of medicine. We are preparing ourselves for the worst. . . . I have decided to journal every day, those of you who can bear to read it. Feel free to answer, to offer sympathy, encouragement or whatever else you are feeling. Please feel free to check me if I am too sorry for myself or for her.[19]

For these and various other reasons, the supposedly indomitable powers of mindless collectivization and reproduction, threatened throughout this century, do not seem at its end to be in the ascendant. Rather we respond to the reverse, which poses its own dilemmas. We reach through the electronic field of ease that cushions us, like amniotic fluid, through the field that allows us to order, reform, and transmit almost any sound, idea, or word, toward what lies beyond, toward the transient and ineffable—a breath, for example, a pause in conversation, even the twisted grain of a xeroxed photograph or videotape. Here is where the aura resides—not in the thing itself but in the originality of the moment when we see, hear, read, repeat, revise.

---

[17] Douglas Davis, "The Net Works," *Rocky Mountain News* (May 8, 1994).

[18] Queen of Touch.

[19] Jon Katz, "The Tales They Tell in Cyberspace Are a Whole Other Story," *New York Times* (January 23, 1994).

ABOUT THE AUTHORS

Theodor Adorno (1903–1969) was one of the founders of the Frankfurt School, a group of Marxist theorists interested in updating Marx's theories to the reality of the 20th century. Adorno was particularly interested in art and culture, trying to understand whether it could provide human beings with a hint of freedom in a world that he saw as increasingly administered and, hence, unfree.

Kwame Anthony Appiah (b. 1950) is Laurance S. Rockefeller University Professor of Philosophy at the University Center for Human Values at Princeton University. He has written on a range of very diverse topics in philosophy, including conditionals, semantics, and the philosophy of culture.

Aristotle (384–322 B.C.) was a systematic philosopher of the first order. He developed an account of the nature of existence that exerted tremendous influence on philosophers in the Western tradition. The basic concepts he put forward—such as those of substance and accident—still remain part of the philosopher's lexicon.

Roland Barthes (1915–1980) was one of the most important literary and cultural critics of his time. He was a founder of the mode of analysis known as structuralism, in which the object of criticism was the deeper structure exhibited by a work. He wrote many influential books. His attack on the notion of authorship has been very influential.

Monroe C. Beardsley was professor of philosophy at Temple University. His work in aesthetics and the philosophy of literature has had great and wide impact. He was a member of the group known as the New Critics, who attacked previous literary critics' practice of going beyond the meaning of the text. Together with William Wimsatt, he formulated "the intentional fallacy," criticizing theorists who thought that the intentions of the author determined the meaning of a work.

Clive Bell (1881–1964) was an art critic and poet who was very interested in postimpressionist art, which he helped to introduce to Great Britain. He was a member of the Bloomsbury Group, a circle of artists and intellectuals living in London. He was married to Virginia Woolf's sister, Vanessa Stephen, herself a significant artist.

Walter Benjamin (1892–1940) was a German Marxist philosopher and literary critic associated with the Frankfurt School, although he was not a member of it. He was influenced as much by Jewish mysticism as he was by Marxism, giving his work a unique slant. He committed suicide on the Franco-Spanish border while attempting to escape from the Nazis when it appeared that he and his party would not be permitted to cross.

Pierre Bourdieu (1930–2002) held the Chair of Sociology at the Collége de France. His work was wide-ranging, always including a great deal of empirical evidence. His book, *Distinction: A Social Critique of the Judgment of Taste* (1984), argued against the idea that there is a single standard of taste, claiming instead that tastes are a mode of social classification and hierarchialization.

R. G. Collingwood (1889–1943), the Waynflete Professor of Metaphysical Philosophy at Oxford University, was both an archaeologist and a philosopher. In addition to his influential *The Principles of Art* (1938), he is known for his work in the philosophy of history and metaphysics.

Arthur Danto (b. 1924) is the retired Johnsonian Professor of Philosophy at Columbia University and remains the art critic for *Nation* magazine. Danto has published in a great number of different fields of philosophy, and his work in the philosophy of art has made him something of a celebrity. He has published many volumes of his writings on art, including the pathbreaking *Transfiguration of the Commonplace* (1981).

Douglas Davis (b. 1933) is a pioneering artist in the field of new media. He is also a prolific writer, having published four books of art theory. He is a performance artist who has collaborated with, among others, Joseph Beuys—the German conceptual artist—and Nam June Paik—the Korean-born American video artist.

Jacques Derrida (1930–2004) was one of the most significant French philosophers of the 20th century. He taught philosophy at various schools in Paris and, later, in the United States as well. He was the originator of deconstruction, a method for the interpretation of philosophical texts that attempts to show how texts undermine their own most basic assumptions. He was a prolific writer, addressing a wide range of issues in almost every field of philosophy.

John Dewey (1859–1952) was important as both a philosopher and a social activist. His ideas, particularly on education, greatly influenced social policy in the United States. As a philosopher, he was a pragmatist, opposed to the reification of dualisms that structured previous philosophical theories. He wrote on a wide range of topics, from aesthetics to metaphysics and educational philosophy.

George Dickie (b. 1926) is emeritus professor of philosophy at the University of Illinois at Chicago. He has published many important books and essays in the philosophy of art. His "institutional theory of art" has been very influential among contemporary analytic aestheticians.

Sigmund Freud (1856–1939) was the founder of psychoanalysis. Although he initially developed psychoanalysis as a way of treating sick individuals, Freud came to see it as providing a general theory of human behavior and cultural history. The latter trend was realized in works such as *Civilization and Its Discontents* (1930), in which Freud used his theory of human psychology to interpret broad cultural developments.

Nelson Goodman (1906–1998), professor of philosophy at Harvard University, was a wide-ranging and influential philosopher. His writings included books on aesthetics, epistemology, philosophy of science, and philosophy of language. He was a pragmatist and a nominalist, eschewing abstraction and cant. His *Languages of Art* (1968) remains an important study of art as a form of symbolic communication.

G. W. F. Hegel (1770–1831) was, despite the density of his prose, the most influential philosopher of the 19th century. In a series of lengthy and difficult books, Hegel put forward his philosophy of absolute idealism that countered the Kantian claim that knowledge was limited to appearances. His *Phenomenology of Spirit* (1807) traces the development of consciousness from a naïve faith in immediate knowledge to the philosopher's understanding of existence. Along the way, virtually all human history and a variety of social developments are given their place in the rational progress of humankind.

Martin Heidegger (1889–1976) was the most influential Continental philosopher in the first half of the 20th century. His magnum opus, *Being and Time* (1928), began what he termed the "destruction of Western onto-theology." Although the work was never finished—the published part represents only its first third—it had tremendous influence on later philosophers. A member of the Nazi party, Heidegger sought to clear his name after World War II, but questions remain about his sympathy with National Socialism.

David Hume (1711–1776) is one of the classic figures in the empiricist tradition. His main publications are *A Treatise on Human Nature* (1739–1740), *An Enquiry Concerning Human Understanding* (1748), and *An Enquiry Concerning the Principles of Morals* (1751). In addition, he wrote many essays and a history of Britain.

Dele Jegede (b. 1945) is Chair of the Art Department at Indiana State University at Terre Haute. He has written extensively on questions of African art.

Immanuel Kant (1724–1804) is best known for his attempt to reconcile the competing schools of philosophy known as rationalism and empiricism in a series of three "critiques": *The Critique of Pure Reason* (1781, revised 1787), *The Critique of Practical Reason* (1788), and the *Critique of Judgment* (1790). Foremost among his teachings is the claim that all our knowledge is of appearances rather than things as they really are, a thesis grounding his "transcendental idealism."

Carolyn Korsmeyer is professor of philosophy at the State University of New York at Buffalo. She has written on issues in aesthetics and the philosophy of the emotions, having published a book on food as an aesthetic phenomenon. She is currently president of the American Society for Aesthetics.

Friedrich Nietzsche (1844–1900) began his professional life as a philologist. Unable to accept the limitations of academic life, Nietzsche left his job and produced a series of incisive works that attempted to counter what he saw as the deficiencies of modern European culture. *The Birth of Tragedy* (1872) was his first book and is marked by an adherence to academic philosophy that is shed in such later works as *Thus Spoke Zarathustra* (1883–1885).

Adrian Piper (b. 1948) is unusual in being both an important contemporary artist and a philosopher. She is professor of philosophy at Wellesley College. She is also an important postmodern artist who, working in a variety of media, has focused on racism, racial stereotyping, and xenophobia. As a philosopher, she is interested in questions of rationality and the self.

Plato (428–347 B.C.) is one of the first as well as one of the greatest philosophers in the Western tradition. His dialogues initially recorded events in the life of his great teacher, Socrates, but went on to propound Plato's own systematic philosophy. The central idea of Plato's metaphysics is that the things we take to be real are merely appearances of a more fundamental reality, to which he gave the name "Forms."

Arthur Schopenhauer (1788–1860) was a renegade follower of Kant. His magnum opus, *The World as Will and Representation* (1819 and 1844), accepts Kant's division between a world of appearances and reality itself, except that Schopenhauer argues that the will can penetrate appearances ("the veil of Maya") and see reality as it is. The result is a pessimistic philosophy that sees life as full of pain and suffering.

Leo Tolstoy (1828–1910), the great Russian novelist, had a deep fascination with philosophy, as any reader of *War and Peace* (1865–69) knows, for that novel contains elements of a philosophy of history dispersed within its narrative. As a writer, he had a deep concern about social issues that motivated his interest in the philosophy of art.

Kendall Walton (b. 1939) is Charles L. Stevenson Collegiate Professor of Philosophy at the University of Michigan. In addition to his book, *Mimesis as Make-Believe* (1990), he has published many influential essays on a variety of different issues in the philosophy of art.

Morris Weitz (1916–1981) taught philosophy at Swarthmore College as well as at Ohio State and Brandeis Universities. He was deeply influenced by the later writings of Ludwig Wittgenstein. He published articles in the philosophy of art and of literature and edited important anthologies on aesthetics and 20th-century philosophy.

CREDITS LIST